UNDERSTANDING DESKTOP COLOR

2ND EDITION

MICHAEL KIERAN

PEACHPIT PRESS

Understanding Desktop Color, 2nd Edition

Copyright © 1994 by Michael Kieran

Peachpit Press, Inc.
2414 Sixth Street
Berkeley, CA 94710
510/548-4393
510/548-5991 (fax)

Cover design: **TMA** Ted Mader Associates

ISBN 1-56609-164-0

9 8 7 6 5 4 3 2 1

Printed in the United States of America

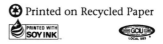 Printed on Recycled Paper

Dedicated to Jane

for you are the mountain,
the sky that breathes,
the ocean that receives,
the spark that ignites.

"We would that words become shooting stars, like gods, that they would rise up from the dead page into living forms of light and dark, into fountains of color."

William Shakespeare

ACKNOWLEDGMENTS

*"Writing? Writing's easy. All you have to do
is put down whatever occurs to you.
But the occurring, now that's hard."*

Stephen Leacock

Desktop color is one of my consuming passions in life. The other is my family. I thank my wife, Jane, and children, Christopher and Andrew, for their understanding and encouragement. (A special thank you to Chris, who suggested this book be called *The Shocking True Story of Desktop Color*.)

My editorial team included three exceptional authors. Copy editor Sheila Kieran (my mom) is the author of two books and thousands of magazine and newspaper articles. Editor Chris Dickman is the author of the best-selling *Mastering CorelDRAW*, and publisher of the *Mastering CorelDRAW* journal. Technical reviewer Bruce Fraser is a contributing editor to *MacWEEK*, and co-author of the definitive study on color management systems.

The network of supporting people without whom this book would have been possible includes my partner, Jane England, and my other friends and colleagues at Desktop Publishing Associates in Toronto, including Janet Ferguson, Sherwood Fleming, Judy Horn, and Mary Ann Yung. My brothers and sisters, Susan, Patricia, Mark, Jon, Frances, and Andrew also contributed immeasurably.

Layout artist Peter Dako spent many hours ensuring that every page looks as perfect as possible. For their assistance with the cover design, I thank Veronica Langridge and John Negru.

A number of other people were kind enough to provide information, illustrations, and feedback:

Steve Abramson, George Adam, Wayne Arvidson, Larry Baca, Ernie Bardocz, Rudolph Burger, Katie Biehrle, Peter Broderick, Dodie Bump, Ted Cheney, Cliff Chirls, David Ciuba, Anastasia Dellas, Deborah Doyle, Allen J. Dunn, Caren Eliezer, Peter Engeldrum, Patti Fortuna, Sandra Fuhs, Chuck Glassier, Kathleen Goodhue, Kim Haas, Melody Haller, Jim Hamilton, Glenn Hayworth, Lisa Herbert, Chuck Humble, Jennifer Jones, Myron Kassaraba, Craig Kevghas, Kristin Keyes, Todd Kirkpatrick, Ted Knight, MaryBeth Leone Getten, Jeff MacInnis, Paul Marshall, Amy Matchen-Hadad, Thad McIlroy, Laurie McLean, David Methven, Nicky Milner, Ranjit Mulgaonkar, Gerald Murch, Kimberley Myers, Joe Niehueser, Jack Nixon, John O'Halloran, Robin O'Leary, Connie Ohlsten, Michele Palmer, James P.W. Parsons, Michael Paterson, LaVon Peck, Rosa Radicchi, A.J. Rogers, Michael Roney, Heide Rowan, Harvey Schafer, Rochelle Schiffman, Courtland Shakespeare, Jim Sharp, Peter Shaw, Kevin Sims, Joanne Sperans, Shane Steinman, Brad Stevens, Roy Stewart, Chris Straghalis, Michael Thorne, Jean Vosler, Peter Warren, and John Willis.

Naturally, responsibility for any mistakes rests with me. Please feel free to let me know about them, and I'll make corrections in the next edition of this book. Desktop color is changing rapidly, and I'm having a great time keeping up with it.

Michael Kieran
Toronto, August 1994

C O N T E N T S

Chapter 4 # Color Management 141

Chapter 12   # Output Service Providers   471

Introduction

"All that is visible is color."
Aristotle

Since its inception in 1985, desktop publishing has rapidly overtaken traditional publishing methods. Within five years of the release of the first page layout programs for Apple Macintosh and IBM-compatible computers, new technology had totally supplanted the old way of setting type and laying out a page.

Desktop publishing, initially dismissed by some in the prepress industry as a "fad," has today blossomed into a multi-billion dollar industry that produces everything from daily newspapers to annual reports.

Although many publishers continue to work primarily in black-and-white, an increasing number are using color, some for the occasional highlight to brighten up documents, others as an essential ingredient that inspires radical new designs.

Indeed, color is rapidly becoming an essential aspect of publishing, not just in the graphic arts but for many kinds of routine business documents. It took less than a decade for black-and-white desktop tools to make traditional typesetting obsolete, and desktop color is taking off even more rapidly.

Why are people so eager to publish in color? The principle reason is that color *communicates*. The emergence of powerful, inexpensive computers was supposed to lead to an era of paperless communication, but one look at most peoples' offices convinces you that quite the opposite has occurred. Paper is proliferating faster than ever. Thanks to desktop publishing, many documents contain dozens of fonts, sometimes to the point of obscuring the underlying message.

In order to make their communications stand out—to ensure that their message is read and understood—an increasing number of publishers are relying on color. Color informs, provokes, entices, and persuades. Many research studies have confirmed the obvious—adding color to documents lengthens a person's attention span, enhances recognition, increases the amount of information retained and remembered.

Powerful new tools for desktop color production are driving the growth of a huge new market in short-run color publishing. An entirely new group of users—many with a background in black-and-white desktop publishing—now have the freedom to create color documents that are completely produced *and reproduced* in-house. Others generate colorful documents that are designed, enhanced, color-corrected, and separated on the desktop, then reproduced by offset lithography or other commercial printing methods.

There are two main aspects to the desktop color revolution:

- In the prepress industry, traditional craft-based tools and techniques are being supplanted by electronic production methods. Although this transition is radically altering the graphic arts business, it is largely invisible to the general public, other than in the increasingly widespread use of color for all types of publications and products.

- In offices everywhere, corporate publishers are starting to create short-run, on-demand color documents. This new domain—office color—is about to have a massive effect on everyday business communications.

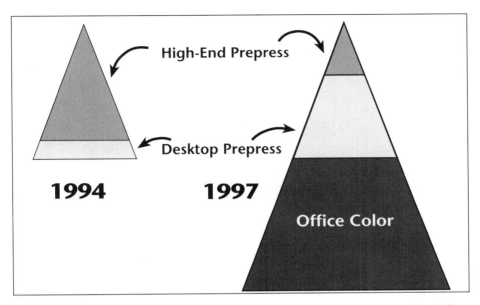

Fig. I-1

In 1994 (left), desktop tools accounted for only a small percentage of color prepress volume in North America. By 1997 (right), this will increase to more than 80%. Meanwhile, a massive new market, desktop office color, will emerge.

Adding color to your publications is now relatively easy, but using color effectively still requires specialized skills. Publishing in color is at least ten times more complex than in black-and-white, and offers endless opportunities for technical glitches that can be embarrassing, time-consuming, and very costly. Until recently, color publishing required the services of highly trained people working in commercial printing or color trade shop environments. The proliferation of desktop tools has made color publishing accessible to just about anyone, but there's a big difference between knowing the features of a software program and knowing how to use them effectively.

Learning to produce good color documents takes time, and can easily become very expensive if you do a lot of *on-the-job training* (better known as making mistakes). But it involves skills that can be learned and applied.

Where can you acquire the key distinctions, discover the important trends, learn the essential skills in color publishing? If you have a few years to spare, you might consider an apprenticeship program at a local print shop or color trade shop. Failing that, read this book.

Who should read this book?

This book is for you if:

- you know how to use one or more popular desktop programs such as PageMaker, QuarkXPress, Ventura, Illustrator, FreeHand, CorelDRAW, Photoshop, and PhotoStyler, but don't have a lot of experience working with color; or
- you're well versed in traditional color prepress, but don't have much experience with desktop software and hardware.

If you don't fit into one of those categories, put this book down and look for something else, perhaps on Italian furniture design.

If you're looking for a book that takes the place of your software's documentation, this is not it. It certainly includes a few tips and tricks that you might not find even by digging through the manuals, but I'm assuming you already know the rudiments of your programs and how to use the manuals and on-line help. My purpose is more comprehensive and more real world.

This book is designed to address the needs of both the graphic arts professionals who use desktop publishing tools for design-intensive creative layouts, and those working in corporate publishing environments where the emphasis is on producing large volumes of long, complex, structured documents.

It is, first, for people who will actually be using desktop color. It is also for those who, while not working with these tools hands-on, are responsible for managing or supervising the use of color publishing systems. Many readers will have previous hands-on experience with black-and-white desktop publishing, and be eager to understand and use the new color tools. Others will come from the color prepress and publishing business, trying to adapt to the new technologies transforming their industry.

Desktop color isn't necessarily a difficult field, but it *is* complex—there are many key distinctions, technologies, and products you must understand. If you're interested in more than the fundamentals of the software itself, and if you, and the people you work with, are using a variety of color hardware and software, this is for you.

To that end, this book is structured so that you'll learn about all the key issues and technologies in color publishing and how they relate, to each other and to the work you do every day.

Color, Color, Color

Chapter 1 explores the concept of color models, and how they can be used to exchange consistent color information between people, applications programs, computers, and peripheral devices.

Chapter 2 examines traditional color production methods in order to help you understand how desktop color tools both integrate with and replace them. It also describes the five major printing technologies, as well as the newest color reproduction method—high-speed color copiers.

Chapter 3 offers a detailed explanation of the crucial concept of halftoning, both traditional photographic halftones and the newer digital halftone technology. Halftones are essential for color reproduction, as well as for reproducing black-and-white photographs.

Chapter 4 is devoted to color management and color calibration, with specific procedures you can use to ensure consistent color from scanner to computer to proofer to the final printed piece.

Chapter 5 provides a detailed look at the hardware necessary for desktop color, including processors, memory, hard disk storage, and display. Desktop scanning is explained in Chapter 6, with examples of different kinds of scanners and their relative advantages and disadvantages.

Chapters 7, 8 and 9 cover the central domains of color publishing—imaging, drawing, and page layout respectively. This is where much of the knowledge you've gained in the first half of the book can be applied. Most desktop publishers spend a lot of time in two or three key applications programs, typically for imaging, drawing, and page layout.

Chapter 10 discusses conventional high-end prepress systems and their relationship to desktop tools. The final two chapters are devoted to output issues, with color printers explored in Chapter 11, and high-resolution imagesetter output (plus such related issues as trapping and imposition) covered in Chapter 12.

Because the desktop color field is so new, all key terms and distinctions are defined, both in the text and in a detailed glossary at the back of the book. As well, tips are scattered throughout the text to assist you in getting the best possible quality from these new tools and techniques.

Macintosh and Windows

The word "desktop" throughout this book refers to Apple Macintosh and Windows-based computers, and the book is designed to be relevant for people working on both hardware platforms.

The desktop publishing era began with PageMaker 1.0 running on the Macintosh. The program was an immediate hit with publishers, typesetters, graphics professionals, and the countless anonymous volunteers responsible for church newsletters everywhere. In 1987, Aldus introduced a version running in the Microsoft Windows environment, which quickly came to dominate the market for high-quality corporate publishing.

Although there were initially some different features between the Mac and Windows versions of PageMaker, these were gradually eliminated so that, starting with version 5.0, the two are identical— so much so that they share the same documentation. A similar story has unfolded with virtually all the major desktop publishing applications, including QuarkXPress, Illustrator, FreeHand, and Photoshop —all are now available on both platforms.

In fact, these are the very applications programs discussed in this book:

- drawing programs—Adobe Illustrator, FreeHand, and CorelDRAW;
- imaging programs—Adobe Photoshop and PhotoStyler;
- page layout programs—PageMaker, QuarkXPress, and Corel Ventura.

In addition to exploring the color features of each program, the emphasis is on how they work together. The suggestions contained here are distilled from the expertise of many experienced designers, publishers, and color trade shop operators.

Desktop color is here—today. True, there are some issues that haven't been completely resolved, including color management and workflow issues. But software designers are hard at work, right now, creating solutions for these and other problems, leaving you free to concentrate on creating beautiful, spectacular, color publications.

And that's really the ultimate purpose of this book—to provide you with the distinctions you need to make color publishing more understandable, more productive, and more fun.

A crucial moment in color publishing

We are at a crucial moment in color publishing: new technologies have challenged traditional methods of color production, and are beginning to supplant them. The emergence of desktop color is altering the fortunes of many companies, those with significant investments in the traditional methods of color production as well as those developing innovative products and processes.

Only time will tell which of these products, companies, and industries will survive and even thrive. As history shows repeatedly, business opportunities open and close rapidly in any moment of dramatic technological change.

For desktop publishing in color, that moment is now.

Color Models

"Color expresses something by itself."
Vincent van Gogh

I t was a dark and stormy night. Yes, it was dark, but how dark? Was the sky a dark bluish-gray, or was it perhaps a darkish gray-blue? The problem is that what appears as one thing to you looks distinctly different to me. In order to solve the communication problem, we must have *color models*.

A color model is a way of expressing color as numbers, as data that can be manipulated with computers. Like human languages, color interchange models are consistent communication symbols designed to simplify the transfer of information. They are essential, not only for enabling people to communicate with one another about colors, but for exchanging color information and maintaining color consistency between computers, peripherals, and applications programs. Therefore, this exploration of color models is a foundation for the later discussion of calibration and color management systems.

Before we can build a framework for describing colors, however, we need to agree on what different colors "mean".

Color and human perception

Human color vision is a remarkable thing. It helps humans distinguish a familiar face in a crowd, appreciate the beauty of a sunset, or paint a masterpiece of light and shadow.

Color is inspirational, evocative, and emotional. It is a subtle, sophisticated phenomenon, with a strong emotional pull that makes the proper use of color essential in art, design, and commerce. According to its hue, a color can be classified as warm or cool, light or dark, vivid or dull, tranquil or exciting, artificial or natural.

But what is color, *really*?

- To the Impressionist painters, color was a window on the soul, a bridge to a world of indescribable human experience.
- To a physicist, color is a phenomenon of waves and particles, with one aspect or other emphasized, depending on the properties being observed.
- To a chemist, color is a characteristic of molecules and the way their electrons interact.
- To a marketing executive, color is a tool for evoking emotional responses that trigger people to buy things.

Color is not an objective property of nature, but rather a perception that occurs in living beings. There are no absolutely "correct" colors, just our shared cultural interpretations about what is meant by such words as "red" and "green".

Color changes according to the perceptions of the observer. Although a scientific instrument can be used to objectively define the color "fire-engine red", there is no getting around the fact that individuals see something slightly different, even if they are looking at exactly the same color. In fact, many external factors affect our perceptions of color, including culture, mood, and phases of the moon.

The nature of color

For thousands of years, color has been interpreted as an integral part of any object. The development of civilization brought with it the urge and the ability to represent, not only the objects of the natural world, but those of imagination, dreams, and religious aspirations.

Fig. 1-1
Leonardo thought carefully about how pigments could be designed to capture the colors within them for centuries.

By the end of the Renaissance, the sophisticated use of color was well established, especially in painting. Such artists as Leonardo da Vinci experimented with new pigments and special materials in an attempt to produce, not just more pleasing colors, but colors that might resist fading and maintain their brilliance over the years. A visit to the Mona Lisa at the Louvre will prove the success of his endeavors. Color was the norm until the invention of the printing press and, for centuries, all printed representations were in "black and white".

In order to use color publishing tools effectively, it's useful to understand the basics of both color and human physiology related to color. Those basics did not become evident until the late 1660s, when Sir Isaac Newton performed many of his original experiments with color and discovered what made things colorful.

Fig. 1-2
Newton's experiments with optics formed the basis for our modern understanding of light, the color spectrum, and the concept of additive colors.

Newton focused his attention on the nature of the spectrum—the colors seen in a rainbow, or in light that has been passed through a prism. When white light shines through a prism, it explodes into a panoply of colors, arranged in the sequence red, orange, yellow, green, blue, indigo, violet, as shown in the color illustration on page 76.

Some of the subtlety inherent in color can be understood from Newton's simple experiments, in which two prisms were arranged to project different colors onto the same spot on a white background. Combining two such colors will produce a third color that usually lies between the two source colors in the spectral sequence. Certain pairs of colors—called complementary colors—can be combined to create white.

The 19th century physicist James Clerk Maxwell added to our understanding of color models by demonstrating that a very broad range of colors could be produced by combining just three light sources—red, green and blue. These three are the *light* primaries used in reproducing color on a computer monitor or television set. But they aren't the only primary colors. In working with color models, there are often references to psychological primaries, complementary primaries, and pigment primaries.

The *psychological* primaries are black, white, red, green, blue, and yellow—colors that evoke strong human emotions. Secondary or *complementary* colors are created from a balanced mixture of two light primaries—magenta, for instance, is a mixture of red and violet-blue. Althoughs you probably learned in kindergarden that the *pigment* primaries are red, yellow, and blue, they are actually cyan, magenta, and yellow.

Light	red	green	blue			
Pigment	cyan	magenta	yellow			
Psychological	black	white	red	green	blue	yellow
Complementary	cyan	magenta	yellow			
Print	cyan	magenta	yellow	black		

Fig. 1-3
Two people talking to one another about "primary colors" might be talking about two very different things. There are many kinds of primary colors.

Newton also explained *metamerism,* a common "illusion" in which a pair of colors look identical when viewed under some light sources but markedly different from each other under certain other light sources.

Metamerism is seen as a problem in the paint, plastic, and textile industries, but it is essential for color printing with just three colorants (CMY). If the printing industry had to make spectral "matches" to colors (using only three inks), there would be no color reproduction industry.

A common example of metamerism can occur if you take a fabric sample with you to the hardware store when you want to select a complementary paint color for your living-room wall. The fabric and paint chip might match perfectly under the store's fluorescent lighting, but look quite different from each other in your home's blend of incandescent and natural light. When shopping for clothing, consider the lights under which they'll be worn.

Physiology of color vision

The visible spectrum, which extends from infrared to ultraviolet, is only a tiny slice of the overall electromagnetic spectrum that encompasses everything from ultra-low frequency to cosmic radiation. It is this band of energy that is absorbed in the eye and interpreted as color.

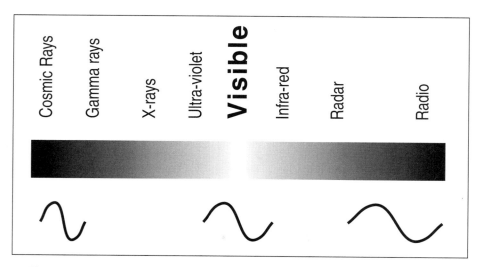

Fig. 1-4
The electromagnetic spectrum stretches from cosmic rays and gamma rays through the band of visible light to radar and radio waves.

Our perception of color is determined by the anatomy and physiology of the human visual system, consisting of the eyes, the brain, and the optic nerves that join them. The iris diaphragm regulates the amount of light that passes through the lens to strike the retina, a network of cells and neurons that covers the entire back half of the eye—except the point at which the optic nerve joins the eye (quite literally, the *blind spot*).

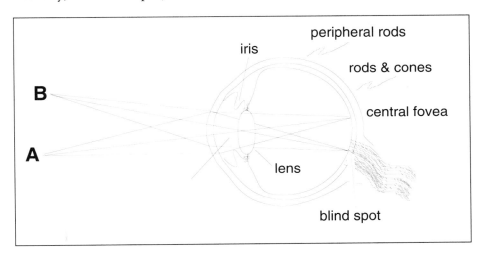

Fig. 1-5
The human eye focuses light from point A onto the central fovea of the retina, which is dense with light-receptive rods and cones, except at the blind spot, where it connects with the optic nerve. Light from point B is not detected.

About 130 million light-sensitive cells—some rod shaped, some cone shaped—are densely packed into the retina and respond to light by sending electrical signals to the brain. The rod-shaped cells, which are concentrated on the periphery of the retina, transmit black and white information only, but are more sensitive to dim light. You can't detect color very well after dusk because you're "seeing with your rods".

Similarly, astronomers trying to see detail in a faint object will center it in the eyepiece of the telescope, then look away to the edge of the field, in order to point the cones of their eyes at empty space, so the rods can pick out especially dim points of light.

Fortunately, we are not obliged to live in a world devoid of color. There are three kinds of cone cells, each with a peak sensitivity to one of the light primaries (red, green, and blue). All the color we see is the product of the mix of signals coming from those three types of cones. The human eye works according to the same red, green, blue color model that is also central to those other staples of modern life, the color television set and the computer monitor.

The RGB color model

Color monitors work by combining percentages of red, green, and blue to create the appearance of millions of other colors. In the RGB system, the red, green, and blue components of each picture element, or *pixel*, in the image are assigned a number, usually an integer between 0 and 255. Adding equal amounts of these three primaries produces pure white light—which is why RGB is known as an *additive* color model.

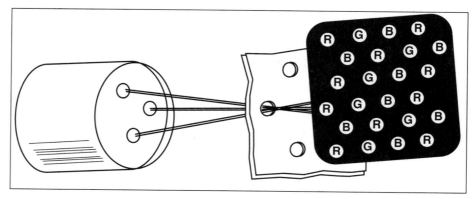

Fig. 1-6
A color monitor uses an electron gun to energize red, green, and blue phosphors on the inside of the tube.

Although it is widely utilized, the RGB model is limited because it is *device-dependent.* This means that there are color variations, not only between monitors from different manufacturers, but even between "identical" monitors from any given manufacturer. All monitors differ in their response to specific voltages, and will drift: colors will vary according to the specific monitor on which they are displayed.

All color models can be represented with a three-dimensional geometric shape, or *color space.* The RGB color space is shaped like a cube, with red, green, and blue at opposing corners.

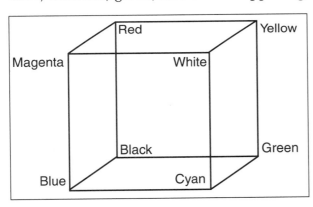

Fig. 1-7
The RGB color space can be represented by a cube, with red, green, and blue at opposing corners.

In addition to its use in color monitors, the RGB model is at the heart of all color scanners, even those that ultimately record color information in some other format. Color scanners work by recording, at each pixel, the intensity of the light that has reflected from the original (when scanning a photographic print) or transmitted through the original (when scanning a slide or transparency).

The original light source provides a full-spectrum white light, and the scanner's detectors are mounted behind a set of red, green, and blue filters. The scanner analyzes the color detected at each pixel in the image, and converts it into its red, green, and blue components.

Color photographic film works the same way—with three layers sensitive to red, green, and blue light. Upon processing, the exposure in the red-sensitive layer controls the amount of cyan dye formed in the image, the green light magenta dye, and the blue yellow.

Color images, in photographic transparency films, are formed in the same manner, conceptually, as printing—the subtractive process.

Although the RGB system is great for color scanners, monitors, and film, it simply doesn't work well for putting colored inks on a page. Unfortunately, combining red, green, and blue inks on paper produces a very limited range, or *gamut,* of colors (a few thousand, compared to the millions of colors that can be displayed on a monitor). The solution when printing is to replace the RGB model by using the colors complementary, or opposite, to red, green, and blue.

The CMY color model

The cyan, magenta, yellow (CMY) model is the perfect complement to the RGB model: it is a *subtractive* color model, based on the opposite of the additive principle behind the RGB model.

The printing process relies on light reflected from the image on the page to the eye, as determined by the light-absorbing properties of the inks. The color of any part of an image, therefore, results from the frequencies of light it reflects. In a subtractive color model, a white surface can be thought of as reflecting all the wavelengths of visible light; a black surface absorbs all of them; and a green surface absorbs (subtracts) all but the green wavelengths.

If you start with pure white light and remove all the red light, what's left is a greenish-blue color, *cyan.* Similarly, removing the green component from white light leaves a reddish purple color, *magenta.* And removing blue from white light leaves its exact complement, *yellow.*

In theory, combining equal percentages of cyan, magenta, and yellow produces pure black, the exact opposite of white. In practice, things don't work out quite that way. The problem is that inks (and toners, dyes, waxes, and other colorants) are *non-ideal pigments*— they are always contaminated with other colors. It's practically impossible to create a cyan ink, for instance, that does not contain a tiny bit of magenta.

A graph from a scientific instrument called a *spectrophotometer* shows that a theoretical "pure" yellow ink reflects all of the yellow component of any incident light that shines on it, and reflects all other color components. In reality, even the most expensive commercially available yellow ink is not a perfect reflector of yellow light, and is contaminated with colors in the red-blue part of the spectrum.

In practice, combining equal amounts of cyan, magenta, and yellow produces a dark, muddy brown. To create a solid black (and to enhance contrast and detail, especially in the darker parts of images), it is necessary to also use black ink.

The CMYK color model

In a perfect world, the CMY model would generate deep, solid black tones, and it wouldn't be necessary to add black ink to the color separations. But, given that it's not a perfect world, black is added to cyan, magenta, and yellow, resulting in the CMYK color model. Black is represented by the letter K, not B, to avoid confusion with blue, and because the black component is always the *key* to a set of color separations.

CMYK is among the most important color models, because it is the basis for almost all color reproduction processes. Combining percentages of the four process color inks on a press produces the appearance of tens of thousands of colors, enough to reproduce color photographs. Note that although a computer monitor can display millions of colors, a printing press can reproduce only thousands. All the other colors seen on the printed page are being created in the eye (or perhaps the mind) of the beholder.

Another major advantage to using four rather than three process colors is evident when printing black type, whether on a printing press or a desktop printer. Instead of having to create black type by combining cyan, magenta, and yellow (which would result in fuzzy text whenever the registration was less than perfect), the type can be created with black ink alone. Other advantages include better overall contrast within photographic images, better detail in the shadow tones (the darker parts of an image), and the ability to replace expensive colored inks with black when printing.

However, there are some major problems associated with using the CMYK model, rather than CMY. First, of course, is that image files are one-third larger, because there are four channels or plates instead of three. A more serious problem is that of converting RGB data into CMYK form, a procedure known as *color separation.*

Because cyan is the complement of red, magenta the complement of green, and yellow the complement of blue, there is one—and only one—unique set of CMY values for any given set of RGB values. Therefore, converting a color from the RGB to the CMY model is a fairly simple calculation.

However, things get much more complicated when black ink is added. A specific shade of purple, for instance, might contain anywhere from 10% to 40% black, with the other three process colors adjusted accordingly. Thus, for a given set of RGB values, there are an *infinite* number of possible CMYK values, resulting in a very complex calculation. In color separating any image, the actual CMYK values will be derived by separation formulas, or *algorithms*, using such techniques as undercolor removal (UCR) and gray component replacement (GCR), which are explored in detail in Chapter 4.

Despite its limitations, the CMYK model is the best tool currently available for reproducing full-color photographs. This may change in the future, as a result of research currently underway to expand the gamut of the color printing process by working with more than four process colors. For a closer look at this technology, called *high-fidelity* color, see Chapter 10.

The HSB color model

Of all the color models, the one that most closely resembles our everyday experience of color is the hue, saturation, brightness (HSB) model and its variants.

Hue refers to the name of a color—green is one hue, orange is another. Saturation describes how deep or vibrant a color is—primary colors are fully saturated while pastels are unsaturated, and grays are totally desaturated. Brightness refers to adding or removing white from a color.

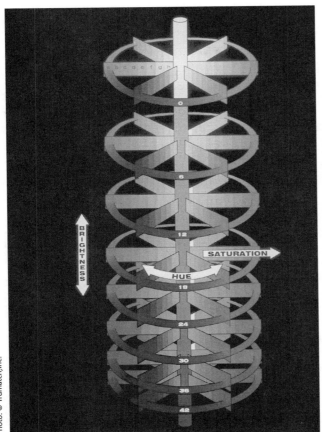

Fig. 1-9
In the HSB model, neutral tones make up the central axis of a cylinder, with saturation increasing toward the periphery and brightness increasing toward the top.

Photo: © Trumatch, Inc.

The hue, lightness, saturation (HLS) model is a variation on HSB in which the luminance component is based on linear changes in how light or dark a color is, whereas the brightness component in the HSB model uses a non-linear approach that more closely approximates how humans actually perceive color. Virtually all color publishing and graphics programs support the HSB model or one of its variants, because working in HSB closely corresponds to the way people instinctively describe colors.

Imagine, for example, that you've just bought a new car, and a friend has asked you what color it is. You would probably begin by describing its *hue*, or basic color, green for example. Then you could elaborate by describing its *saturation*, calling it a vivid, primary green. Finally, you could specify its *brightness*, adding or removing whiteness to make the color brighter or darker.

Most color computer applications use the HSB model as the basis for a *color picker*, such as the Photoshop color picker shown in the color illustration on page 77. The brightness and saturation of the selected color can be adjusted by moving the cursor through the large square (up or down for brightness, left or right for saturation), while, on the right side, the hue wheel has been stretched out into a bar.

Fig. 1-10
The rectangle at the top of the PhotoStyler color picker is a linear representation of the hue wheel. You modify saturation by dragging the cursor from left to right in the large square, and brightness by dragging up or down.

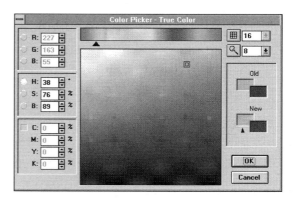

In the same way that the RGB model could be represented as a three-dimensional color space by a cube, the HSB color space can be represented by a cylinder, as shown in color on page 75. Taking any horizontal slice through this shape produces a hue wheel, following the established progression from red, orange, yellow, and green to blue, indigo, and violet, then back to red.

All "colors" falling along the central axis in the HSB model are neutrals—no color *cast* whatever and therefore pure shades of gray. Regardless of where they started on the periphery of the model, the colors have become less saturated as they get closer to the core, so that when they reach the central axis they are completely desaturated.

The CIE color model

As previously mentioned, a major problem with the color models discussed so far is their device dependence—the same data sent to different devices results in different colors being output. A given set of RGB values, for instance, will produce noticeably different colors when displayed on monitors from different vendors (or even the same monitor at two different times).

Research has focused on measuring how the human eye perceives color, rather than the way color is interpreted by an input scanner or rendered by a particular output device.

In fact, this problem has been closely studied since the 1920s by a group of color scientists, the International Committee on Illumination, better known by its French name, la Commission Internationale de l'Eclairage, or CIE. In 1931, the CIE defined a color model, CIE XYZ, in which three numbers (X, Y, and Z) are used to represent colors according to where they fall on three different axes: a luminance axis, a line connecting blue and yellow, and a line connecting green and red. The CIE model is based on color information gathered using a spectrophotometer, which precisely measures color values with reference to a standard object, standard illuminant, and standard observer.

Strictly speaking, CIE is not a color model, it is a "color stimulus specification system". Although only recently applied to color imaging and reproduction, the CIE system has proven invaluable in such industries as paint, plastics, textiles, not to mention the basis for the world's TV systems.

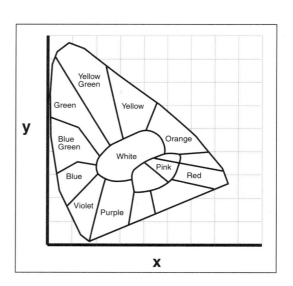

Fig. 1-11
In the CIE XYZ model, white is in the middle, green is at the top, red is in the lower right corner and blue is in the lower left corner.

Without the recent explosion in color publishing, the various CIE models would be obscure technicalities of interest only to color scientists. However, because the CIE system can be used to store color information in a device-independent manner, it has become a crucial part of "open" desktop color solutions that incorporate products from many vendors. Chapter 4 examines how the CIE model serves as the foundation for a new generation of color management systems from Apple, Kodak, EFI, Agfa, and others.

In the years since 1931, two main variants of the original CIE XYZ system have been proposed, CIEL*u*v and CIEL*a*b, and many color scientists today favor the CIEL*a*b system.

The key concept behind all these color spaces is whether or not they can be transformed into CIE XYZ. If the *chromaticities,* or XYZ values, of the RGB primaries ("lights") and the white point (reference illuminant) are known, then the following color models can be mathematically transformed into CIE XYZ: RGB, HSB, HSL, and YCC. In general, CMY and CMYK cannot be accurately transformed into XYZ (because we lack accurate physical models of colorants on paper).

In practical terms, the transform is built empirically by measuring the CIE color coordinates of an array of color patches with known amounts of colorant, such as the dot areas found in test targets.

The YCC color model

There's another color model that has become increasingly common lately: the YCC model developed by Eastman Kodak as the foundation for its Photo CD product. Photo CD is Kodak's attempt to build a bridge between its traditional photographic film business and the world of electronic imaging. (There is a complete discussion of Photo CD in Chapter 6, on scanning.)

In order to make a single Photo CD capable of holding more than 100 high-resolution photographs, Kodak developed a very powerful compression technology, that reduces an 18Mb image file to less than 5Mb.

The YCC color model is at the heart of this compression strategy: it works by first separating luminance information (grayscale) from chrominance information (hue). This is similar to the way color television signals are encoded, so that the luminance information produces a complete picture on black-and-white sets, while the addition of chrominance data converts the picture to full color.

The main advantage of PhotoYCC is its speed, especially in comparison to CIE-based color management systems, in converting from one model into another. The importance of YCC as a color model is indicated by Adobe Systems' decision to add it as an internally supported model in PostScript Level 2.

Spot and process color

There are two ways of printing in color: spot and process. Spot color printing is used whenever a precise color is required, such as for a corporate logo, and is based on pre-mixing ink of the desired color *prior to printing*. Spot colors are also known as custom colors, special colors, match colors, or as PANTONE MATCHING SYSTEM colors.

Process color printing is based on the fact that it is possible to create the *appearance* of a multitude of colors by combining—on the page—percentages of cyan, magenta, yellow, and black inks. Process color is most cost-effective when there are more than three colors on the page, and is essential for reproduction of full-color photographic images.

Spot color printing is the more cost-effective method when only one or two colors are required on the page. Moreover, spot color inks include colors that are impossible to attain with process inks, including silver, copper, and vibrant forest green.

PageMaker, QuarkXPress, and other page layout and drawing applications allow you to work with both spot and process colors in the same document. Most such programs offer a choice between printing the spot colors on separate pieces of film or having them converted to the closest equivalent process colors. For instance, if your design includes two spot colors in addition to four-color photographs, you can instruct your page layout program to output either six pieces of film (two spot and four process) or to print only four pieces of film (with the spot colors converted to their closest approximate process equivalents).

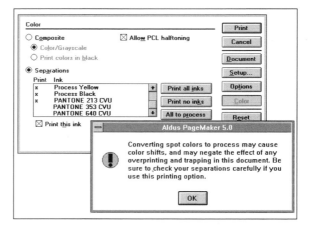

Fig. 1-12
When printing a document containing both spot and process colors, PageMaker allows you to decide whether or not to convert the spot colors to the nearest process color, and warns about potential color shifts.

Most jobs printed with spot color inks are one-, two- or, occasionally, three-color jobs, to provide some color when the budget cannot cover full four-color treatment. Some really expensive print jobs run with five, six, seven, or eight colors—the four process inks plus one or more spot color inks.

Why would you want to include both process and spot colors in the same publication? The most common reason is to include photographs while still achieving an exact match with special corporate colors, such as those used for a logotype or product packaging. A corporate identity is a valuable asset, one in which a company may have made a considerable investment, and which could be severely damaged by printed materials that show the wrong colors.

Process and spot colors are also combined in fancy brochures and promotional pieces. Take a close look at a brochure for an expensive automobile, for instance, or the annual report of a large corporation, and you'll often find process colors (for the pictures) combined with spot colors (both for highlight color and for *spot varnishes* that cover only selected parts of each page).

PANTONE MATCHING SYSTEM

In North America, the most commonly used spot color specification method is the PANTONE MATCHING SYSTEM from Pantone, Inc., whose colors are often referred to as PMS colors. It's important to distinguish PMS (the system) from Pantone (the company), because Pantone makes other color specification tools, including some for working with process colors.

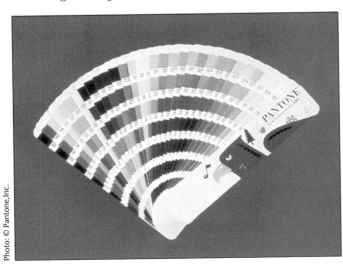

Photo: © Pantone, Inc.

Fig 1-13
The PANTONE MATCHING SYSTEM relies on swatch charts showing sample colors on coated and uncoated stocks.

The PANTONE MATCHING SYSTEM is an attempt at maintaining fidelity between original art and the finished printed piece. It is based on a series of books of color swatches, available for both coated and uncoated paper stocks, and a set of ink formulations for creating such colors on a printing press. There are 1,012 PMS colors, mixed from combinations of 12 base inks.

Using the PMS method, a graphic designer can specify that the logotype on a client's letterhead be printed as Pantone 350, and be reasonably sure that the resulting color will be the same deep forest green shown in the PANTONE MATCHING SYSTEM swatch book—whether it's printed in Minnesota or Montreal.

Just as with process colors, you can overlay percentages of spot inks to produce totally different colors—a great way to add variety to a two-color job. However, unlike process inks, which are transparent, spot inks are "solid" and can produce hideous colors when combined, so it is best to try those only after you have had some experience and know exactly what you're doing.

A great many ink manufacturers and software developers advertise their products as complying with the standard Pantone colors, thereby providing publishers with some measure of certainty that color type and graphics will print in the desired shades. In practical terms, it means that the artist or designer can specify a colored graphic within a desktop program, secure in the knowledge that, while the on-screen representation may not match the sample in the swatch book precisely, the printed piece will come reasonably close to the intended color.

Note, however, that desktop color printers advertised as "Pantone certified" can only approximate PMS spot colors, because they are limited to four colorants (CMYK), rather than containing pre-mixed samples of the more than 1,000 colors in the PANTONE MATCHING SYSTEM. They will almost certainly come closer to matching PMS colors than printers that have not been Pantone certified, but there are many PMS colors they will not be able to exactly match.

Strictly speaking, the PANTONE MATCHING SYSTEM and other spot color specification methods are not color models, in that they do not directly express colors as numerical data. However, they are important tools for people working with the design and production of color documents.

The major limitation of the original PANTONE MATCHING SYSTEM was that it is based on specially mixed inks, rather than on the four process inks. Until the recent release of new CMYK matching systems from Pantone, Trumatch, and Focoltone, this made it difficult to specify colors being reproduced with process color. The advantage of all three CMYK systems is that they enable designers to select colors efficiently, without *ever* choosing a color that falls outside the range of four-color process reproduction.

Pantone Process Color System

In addition to its well-known spot color system, Pantone also makes a CMYK-based color specification system, designed for those working with process rather than spot colors. The Pantone Process Color System specifies more than 3,000 colors in CMYK percentages. The first 2,000 are two-color combinations and their shades, and the remainder are three- and four-color combinations based on printability and the input of designers.

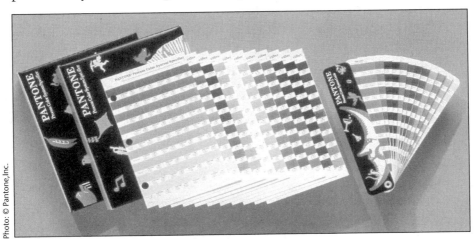

Photo: © Pantone, Inc.

Fig. 1-14
The Pantone Process Color System Specifier is a two-book set that presents the same process color values in a tear-out chip format. Each chip is identified with its corresponding CMYK percentages.

One limitation of the Pantone Process Color System is that it specifies colors in 3% and 5% increments, as opposed to the 1% increments used by Trumatch. According to Pantone, all screen values have been specifically chosen to perform within the quality control tolerances and capabilities of today's printing presses.

The new system is also available in Pantone-licensed software applications, and has been formulated in versions for SWOP inks (Specifications for Web Offset Publications) and Euroscale. This helps you ensure that your commercial printer can closely match on press the colors you have specified on the computer.

Matching spot and process colors

While some Pantone spot color inks can be matched almost identically with process inks, others will vary radically. Any designer determined to get precise colors will need a copy of the Pantone Process Color Imaging Guide. Like most Pantone guides, this one contains small swatches of the approximately 1,000 spot colors in the Pantone Matching System.

What makes the Process Color Imaging Guide distinctive is its inclusion, next to each spot color swatch, of a sample of the closest possible color that can be created in the four-color process system. (While it would be useful to include a sample, the color pages in this book are printed with only the four process inks, making it impossible to accurately show the spot colors.)

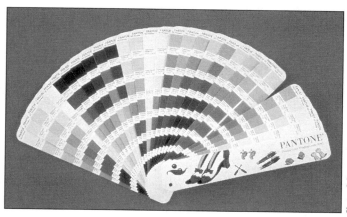

Fig. 1-15
The Pantone Process Color Imaging Guide shows spot and process colors side by side.

Photo: © Pantone, Inc.

The Process Color Imaging Guide is important to designers because it graphically conveys the fact that many spot colors are difficult or impossible to produce with *any* combination of cyan, magenta, yellow, and black. Imagine, for example, a designer who is creating a corporate identity program for a business, with a company logotype that can be created only as a spot color. While there will be no problem printing the business cards or letterhead, if the company wants to run an advertisement in a full-color magazine, it will either have to pay a horrendous price for having the magazine print its ad with a fifth (spot) color, or settle for a process color approximation that might seriously damage the company identity program.

The opposite problem can also occur: some colors can be created only by combining the four process colors, and cannot be closely approximated with a single spot color. In helping designers to avoid these problems, the Pantone Process Color Imaging Guide becomes an essential color tool.

Trumatch

For many years, commercial printers were limited to producing colors that could be created with halftone screens specified to the nearest 5%—they could specify a tint containing 35% magenta, but not one containing 37% magenta. This limitation precluded the use of some colors, and resulted from the fact that they were working with mechanical (photographic) halftone screens, which are only available in 5% increments.

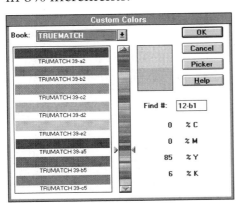

Fig. 1-16
The Trumatch process color specification system is supported within all major desktop color programs, and also comes as a swatch set, chip book, and disk.

By contrast, digital prepress technology allows the user to specify the exact screen values needed to produce any color, in increments of 1%. This freedom has greatly expanded the possibilities for designers and illustrators, who can now create artwork using a much greater gamut of possible colors. Working with computers gives you more color choices than using traditional tools.

The Trumatch Swatching System is designed specifically to improve the accuracy of color specifications for process color. It offers more than 2,000 computer-generated colors that specify exact percentages of cyan, magenta, yellow, and black for process inks. The Trumatch system is supported by PageMaker, QuarkXPress, FreeHand, Illustrator, CorelDRAW, Photoshop, PhotoStyler, and many other leading color publishing programs.

One of the most innovative aspects of the Trumatch system is the way its colors are organized: first by hue (along the color spectrum starting with red); second by saturation (from deep, vivid tones to pastels); and third by brightness (by adding or removing black). There are 50 hues in the Trumatch system, with 50 *tints* or shades of each hue. The intuitive logic of the HSB system makes it easy for designers to get just the right color. To get a greener color, for example, the hue value is changed toward Trumatch color 17 (green). By increasing the saturation value, it is possible to get a more vivid color while to get a darker color results from decreasing the brightness value.

Focoltone

The Focoltone Color System is an innovative way of selecting and matching process colors. Focoltone is designed to help everybody involved in *process* color reproduction—print buyers, designers, prepress houses, and printers. The Focoltone colors are printed on swatches, specifier sheets, and charts, and are supported by QuarkXPress, Adobe Photoshop and Illustrator, FreeHand, PageMaker, and other leading desktop color applications.

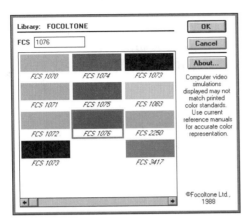

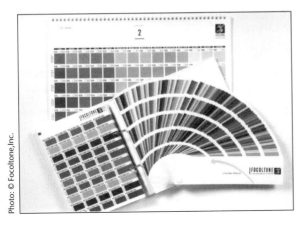

Fig. 1-17
The Focoltone color picker (shown here in PageMaker) organizes colors according to their CMYK components.

The Focoltone color range consists of 763 four-color combinations that contain single tints of all four process inks from five to 85%. By selecting colors from this palette, the designer can be confident that the specified colors will be closely approximated on press.

The charts in the Focoltone systems show not only the specified color, but all the other colors which make it up. Each line on the chart starts with a four-color process color and continues by showing the 14 combinations that can be created from it. There are four single colors, six combinations of two colors, and four combinations of three colors. This simple but unambiguous methods guarantees the designer and the press operator that the specified color can actually be printed, and that they're talking about the same color. A special set of charts is available for color reproduction on newsprint.

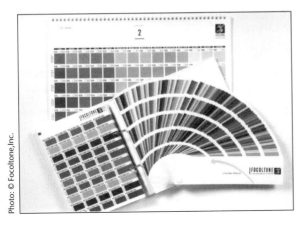

Fig. 1-18
The Focoltone chart shows, for each four-color process color, the 14 possible combinations of its CMYK components.

Putting color models to work

Obviously, the seemingly simple task of describing a color in an unambiguous way can be quite daunting. Communicating descriptions of color between people, programs, and peripherals requires a thorough understanding of color models.

Because of the differences between the various color models, it is important to work in the model that will provide the best color fidelity. For example, when the project being created in a publishing or graphics program is going to be reproduced using process colors, be sure to specify the colors in the software according to their CMYK values. (These are the values that will be used to create a prepress proof, as well as the film and printing plates.)

On the other hand, when designing a brochure that will be printed as black plus one spot color, you usually specify that color according to its PANTONE MATCHING SYSTEM number (or some other spot color system), which the printing company needs in order to mix the correct ink for your print run. Always keep in mind that the colors displayed on screen, whether spot or process, will often not match those printed on paper.

Choosing the right colors

One of the most difficult aspects of working in color is choosing the right colors. While seemingly so simple as to be unworthy of mention, the importance of color to readability is vital—as you know if you've ever been to a seminar where the presenter's slides featured green type against an orange background, rendering them barely legible. When creating a drawing, technical illustration, page layout or presentation in color, readability is crucial. After all, the whole point of publishing is *communication*, and if people can't read what's in front of them, there is, obviously, no communicating taking place.

This problem may seem trivial to experienced designers, but is real concern for many people in corporate publishing environments. Fortunately, the color experts at Pantone have developed an inexpensive utility program designed to help you pick the right colors. Called ColorUP, it consists of two modules. The first, ColorUP

Palette Chooser, is a library of more than 700 professionally-created color palettes, each optimized for output to 35mm slides, on-screen presentations, overhead transparencies or color printers.

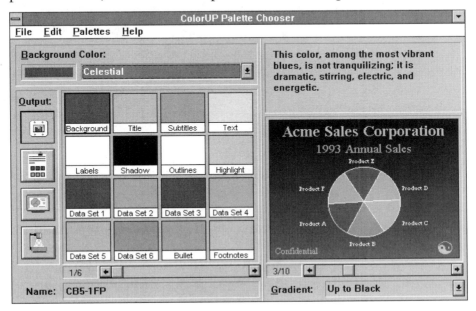

Fig. 1-19

The ColorUP Palette Chooser makes it easy to select groups of colors that work well together. Palettes can be customized, and can be exported to many popular drawing and presentation programs.

The purpose of the program is not to calibrate screen colors to output device colors, but to provide complementary sets of colors that work well together. In the program's documentation, Pantone warns that colors output to a slide film recorder are often darker than those displayed on a color monitor, particularly blues, greens, purples, and reds.

ColorUP Palette Chooser is available for both Macintosh and Windows-based computers, and can export palettes to a wide variety of applications.

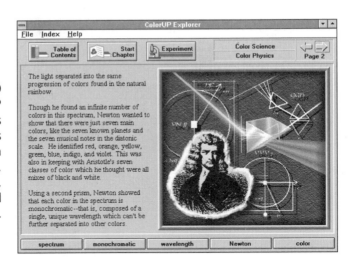

Fig. 1-20
The ColorUP
Explorer provides
fascinating tidbits
of information on
color science,
psychology,
harmony and
reproduction.

The second module is called ColorUP Explorer, and it's a kind of electronic encyclopedia of color science, full of ideas and information on using color in business documents and presentations. ColorUP Explorer includes a variety of interactive experiments that make it easy for novice color publishers to understand concepts such as dithering, color models, and separation.

From models to the real world

Having basic information on how color characteristics can be represented in a variety of different models, and how, with the exception of CIE, all these models are dependent on the color rendering abilities of specific devices, we turn to the next problem—and it's a big one.

How can you ensure consistent color matching, not only between application programs, but also between different input and output devices, and ultimately across different hardware platforms? Before tackling these and other questions of color management in Chapter 4, let's look closely at how color documents are reproduced, both with conventional printing presses and with the new digital color devices.

Color Reproduction

*"Color, once reduced to certain definite rules,
can be taught like music."*
Impressionist painter Georges Seurat

During the past hundred years, the ability to print full-color documents has transformed the human ability to communicate. Virtually all media we experience daily have shifted from black-and-white to color, and the arrival of powerful desktop color production tools has only accelerated this trend.

In the 1950s, many magazines used color photographs sparingly, if at all, because color separations and printing were so expensive. Today, even the smallest special-interest magazines are bursting with color.

Photography itself has undergone a similar transformation. A few decades ago, it cost a lot more to buy a roll of color film (and get it developed and printed), than it did to shoot in black-and-white. Today, just the opposite is true: inquire at any camera store about taking pictures in black-and-white, and you'll discover that it's now much less expensive to use color.

The same thing has happened with daily newspapers. Until recently, most newspapers looked like the Wall Street Journal—plenty of black type, but no color illustrations or photographs. Now, most look like USA Today—heavy on colorful infographics but almost devoid of long, analytical news stories and detailed feature articles.

Yet the color revolution has only begun. The proliferation of low-cost high-quality color publishing has already started to alter our everyday common-sense interpretation of what constitutes a good-looking document. This transition is affecting both the commercial graphic arts industry and the everyday business world.

This chapter focuses on **two different aspects** of desktop color publishing. The first is the use of desktop tools for *color prepress—* the scanning, image enhancement and color separation tasks essential to the production of color publications, which until now have required conventional prepress methods. The second is the explosion in *short-run* color production that is beginning to make color cost-effective for in-house newsletters, brochures, training materials, and other publications produced in quantities of a few hundred copies or fewer.

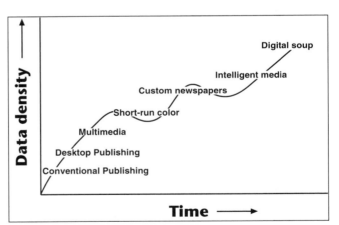

Fig. 2-1
Historically speaking, we are today somewhere between conventional publishing and the omni-present polymorphic digital soup.

There is actually a third aspect to color publishing—*multimedia—* but it is beyond the scope of this book. It can be defined as any publishing activity in which the final output medium is something other than paper, and includes everything from CD-ROM-based games to interactive television. Multimedia is so powerful because it takes our current understanding of a page, and adds the element of time, creating an interactive page that changes 30 times each second.

Multimedia today is a nascent industry, but the hardware and software required for integrating sound, video, and animation on the desktop are rapidly increasing in quality while decreasing in price. The outcome of this trend is an increasingly media-rich environment for business and entertainment in which sounds and images combine to create an overwhelming rush of information.

Until recently, publishers assumed that their words and pictures would be delivered to customers (readers) on sheets of paper. Increasingly, as digital information becomes the currency of the 1990s, the assumption is no longer valid. When publishers hire a designer to create a new publication, they're paying for more than ink on a page. Designers are rewarded for interpreting the client's intended message into some kind of coherent, graphical communication, some *visual intent.*

The key to successful publishing in the future will be to develop ways of creating visual intent that can be expressed consistently across many different output media. A company's logo, for instance, will need to look great whether output to interactive television, CD-ROM, PCT (personal communications thing), or even print. The requirement is not just for multimedia, but for *media agility.*

While we're not setting out on a detailed exploration of the way prepress tools will be used in non-print publishing, the inevitable evolution away from print and toward time-based media should be

Fig. 2-2
Multimedia is already here, if you're satisfied with a relatively low level of interactivity, like watching TV on your computer.

in the back of your mind throughout what follows. Indeed, much of what we describe here as prepress should actually be thought of as *pre-publishing.*

The traditional prepress process

To put into perspective the rapid transition to desktop color publishing, consider how color prepress tasks were performed in the past. Until the middle of the nineteenth century, color printing was a complex, time-consuming process, practiced by skilled craftsmen. Publications that contained color photographs were created by hand, with artists painting the colors on top of drawings that had already been rendered in black-and-white.

Until the early twentieth century, color printing was originally limited to discrete ink colors (what we now call spot colors); the development of different photographic methods, including the Dufay process and the Warner-Powrie process, gave the word "process" the meaning of any printing method that could reproduce a wide range of colors. When full-color printing was in its infancy, the three primary colors were referred to as yellow, red (which we now call magenta), and blue (cyan). Even today, older people in the business may refer to magenta as "process red" and cyan as "process blue."

The theory of full-color reproduction with cyan, magenta, and yellow was established in the 1880s and widely commercialized in the 1890s, replacing the older technology of multi-color printing known as *chromolithography.* A few years later, black was added, both for improved reproduction of type and enhanced tonal range in photographs. By the early 1900s, color printing had become so inexpensive it could be used for publishing books, magazines, and other documents.

For most of the twentieth century, color separations, and color correction were performed mechanically. To separate an original color photograph into its cyan, magenta, yellow, and black components, the original was photographed through a set of colored filters in a graphic arts camera. The resulting films often had to be color corrected by *dot etching*, in which a skilled technician manually applied the appropriate chemicals in the right place for precisely the correct amount of time. Dot etching has been rendered obsolete, first by high-end electronic prepress systems and now by desktop tools, but for many years it was a crucial aspect of color reproduction.

Fig. 2-3 The graphic arts camera in the background was used to create the separation films being inspected by this prepress technician.

Photo: © 3M

For decades, complete pages were assembled by combining columns of type that had been created with proprietary phototypesetting equipment. These pages, called *galleys*, would be waxed and affixed to artboards, which would then be shot in a graphic arts camera to make film negatives. Meanwhile, the photographs would also be captured and color separated in the camera, then taped with great precision to the film of the type, a process that was known as *film stripping*.

The big shift in prepress production took place in the late 1970s and early 1980s with the arrival of color electronic prepress systems (CEPS) from Scitex and its competitors. Within a few years, mechanical color production techniques quickly declined in popularity, to the point where they are now virtually obsolete.

The age of electronic prepress

Scitex started out as a small company specializing in creating color separations for the textile industry, but soon branched out, making equipment for creating the separations used in fabricating electronic circuit boards, and then into color prepress.

As the electronic prepress market expanded quickly, Scitex found itself competing with Crosfield, Hell Graphics Systems (now Linotype-Hell), Dainippon Screen, and others.

All these high-end vendors have one thing in common: they have made hundreds of millions of dollars in the past fifteen years by selling prepress systems based on proprietary hardware and software. Despite what they may be saying today about their enthusiasm for embracing desktop-based "open systems", each of them is being dragged, kicking and screaming, into the world of PostScript (desktop) color publishing.

Until now, high-end prepress vendors have priced their products according to the productivity value of their software, which just happens to run only on their proprietary hardware. This has enabled many of them to maintain excellent profit margins. As desktop color takes over, the high-end vendors are starting to realize that software is their biggest asset, but they must move quickly before off-the-shelf "shrink-wrapped" software packages match their products in functionality.

Film stripping

For decades, one of the most labor-intensive aspects of prepress has been film stripping, in which individual pages are assembled into *flats* (complete sheets, ready for plate making). In fact, there are three different tasks that film strippers perform: page assembly, imposition, and trapping—all of which are being taken over by desktop tools.

Until the emergence of desktop technology, many film strippers were kept busy assembling individual elements (type, illustrations, and photographs) into complete pages, but this part of the job has been largely taken over by such page layout programs as PageMaker and QuarkXPress.

Photo: © Scitex

Fig. 2-4
A film stripper manually assembles pages, builds color traps, and creates impositions before the job goes on press.

Another important task for strippers involved assembling completed pages into flats (usually two, four or eight pages per flat), a process known as *imposition*. Imposition is a crucial part of the prepress process, but in the past three years a number of very powerful desktop imposition programs have become available, reducing the dependence on skilled technicians who perform this function. Chapter 12 examines the way imposition is being transformed from a complex manual procedure into a semi-automatic desktop routine.

No Trap

Trap

No Trap

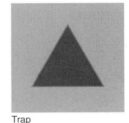

Trap

Fig. 2-5
Color traps are little overlaps where colors abut, to compensate for misregistration on press (top). If properly constructed, traps are almost invisible, even with good registration (bottom).

Manual film stripping is also used in *color trapping,* a procedure in which the size of individual type and graphic elements is slightly increased or decreased in order to compensate for slight misregistrations on press. Trapping, which is also undergoing a transition from complex craft to routine desktop procedure, is described in greater detail in Chapter 12.

Almost all trade shops today have the ability to produce pages both electronically and through the older manual methods. Indeed, despite the desktop revolution, most will continue to require the services of at least a few film strippers. For the foreseeable future, there will always be some imposition and trapping jobs that can be completed more quickly and less expensively on the light table than on the computer.

Workflow

One of the major limitations in color publishing today is the lack of flexible, effective tools for managing the interaction between multiple users on any publishing project. By its very nature, publishing is a collaborative activity, but neither the traditional proprietary publishing systems nor desktop systems provide the tools necessary for multiple users to share the work.

However, there has been some progress in this area recently, with desktop vendors gradually developing the computer networks and software packages required for collaborative publishing. The on-going transition from stand-alone workstations to local area networks is making it increasingly easy to share graphics, documents and other files, but this helps more at the logistical, rather than management, level.

One of the first software products to assist in managing publishing workflow is the Quark Publishing System (QPS), developed by the people who make the QuarkXPress page layout program. QPS is oriented specifically toward the requirements of the newspaper market and, to a lesser extent, magazines, but is not well suited to other kinds of collaborative publishing.

Other vendors are busy designing workflow products that will manage job ticketing, tracking, and revision control, but these areas are not well served at present by either proprietary or desktop software. Adobe is currently developing a workflow product, code-named Metro, that provides a client-server framework around which systems integrators can build complete project management systems for publishers. Initially, Metro is being customized for magazine and catalog publishing, but the program can also be adapted to many other kinds of publishing environments.

Digital distribution of advertising

According to many people in the publishing, prepress, and printing industries, the world revolves around advertising. Without ads, none of today's glossy magazines could survive. But the distribution of advertising has been one of the last bastions of conventional analog technology.

Virtually all ads now are created on the desktop, often in conjunction with high-end prepress systems. Once an ad has been finished and approved, however, it is usually output as films and proofs, often in quantities of 100 or more, for delivery to every magazine or other publication running it. Not only is this wasteful and environmentally harmful, it means that the advertiser will find it very difficult to incorporate last-minute changes or to customize an ad for different regions or countries.

To solve this problem, people throughout the publishing and prepress industries have recently come together to define a standard for the digital distribution of advertising for publications. The proposed standard is being called, sensibly enough, Digital Distribution of Advertising for Publications (DDAP). The DDAP proposal builds on standards already accredited by ANSI (the American National Standards Institute) and ISO (the International Standards Organization).

In the mid-1980s, ANSI and ISO adopted five standards (collectively known as IT8), which cover the transfer of data for color photographs, line art, geometric art and black-and-white images, as well as the transfer of color proofs from electronic prepress systems to digital color proofers. Subsequent IT8 standards govern color targets for scanner calibration, the characterization of four-color process printing, and a definition of RGB color data for use in the graphic arts industry.

The DDAP specification adds standards for digital proofing, repeatability, data transmission, image compression, and procedural guidelines to ensure that the right ad is sent and received. When implemented, DDAP will also make it easier for publishers to take advantage of long-run direct-to-plate technology, thereby providing better quality, faster turn-around, lower production costs, and better consistency.

To date, an impressive number of companies in the publishing and prepress industries have thrown their support behind the DDAP initiative, including most of the world's largest ad agencies and magazine publishers. However, several issues have yet to be resolved, such as the question of whether the data for an ad should be in an editable format. It seems likely such problems will be resolved quickly, given the considerable benefits to both advertisers and publishers in making the move to digital distribution.

Proofing

The color printing process is rife with opportunities for error, and when something goes wrong, everyone starts looking for someone to shoulder the blame, and the expense. Disputes about color quality are legendary in the printing industry, and every commercial printer has had to eat at least one big print job that didn't meet the client's standards, even if it wasn't actually the printer's fault.

There are many factors that can sabotage the quality of a color printing job. Here are some recent printing disasters:

- the brochure printed with Pantone 375 spot color (lime green), when the client thought it was ordering Pantone 357 (forest green);
- the catalog containing process colored type that was completely unreadable, because of misregistration;

+ the corporate newsletter filled with fuzzy low-resolution photos, each overprinted with neat handwriting that read: "position-only, replace with final art".

As more and more color production shifts from professional systems to the desktop, it becomes increasingly important to have a way of confirming—*proofing*—color accuracy. Some disasters can be avoided by producing an appropriate color proof and interpreting it properly. The whole issue of quality is especially important for desktop color, not only because less expensive equipment is being used, but also because many of the new users have little experience in color production.

Photo: © 3M

Fig. 2-6
For decades the publishing industry has relied on off-press proofing methods, such as laminated film proofs, to ensure color accuracy.

Proofing can be divided into two categories: on-press and off-press. On-press proofs are produced on an actual printing press, preferably the same one that will ultimately be used to print the final job. Typically, such proofs are produced by using the job's final film to make plates, which are used to print a few proof sheets with the paper stock and ink intended for the actual job. Because of the time and expense involved, on-press proofing is usually reserved only for the most complex or critical jobs, although it continues to be widely used in the Far East where labor costs are substantially lower than in North America.

A much more common method is off-press proofing, in which the job's final film is exposed onto various materials to create a proof that, with reasonable accuracy, reflects the ultimate appearance of the printed sheet. There are many different kinds of off-press proofs, varying in cost, quality, and suitability for specific print jobs. The most common are *film proofs*, made from the same film that will ultimately be used to make the printing plates that will go on press.

Film proofs

There are two major kinds of film proofs: those in which the four layers of colored material are fused together, and those in which the layers are stacked on top of one another. For quality commercial printing, the most commonly used film proofs are DuPont Cromalin, 3M Matchprint, and Fuji ColorArt, all of which are created by exposing four separate pieces of plastic, then fusing or laminating them together.

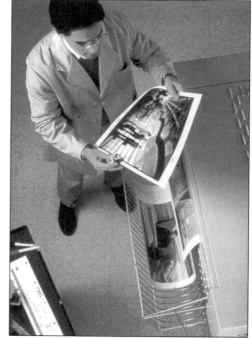

Fig. 2-7
Matchprint III is a film proofing system from 3M that provides a very close match to the actual printed sheet.

Photo: © 3M

Overlay proofs, such as ColorKey, NAPS, and Chromacheck, consist of four layers of plastic, and can therefore diffuse light between the layers, resulting in some image softness and color cast. If you're concerned about critical color matching, a laminated proof, such as a Cromalin, Matchprint or ColorArt, is a better choice than an overlay proof. However, overlay proofs have the advantage of being somewhat less expensive than laminated proofs, and also enable the press operator to see how each process color is supposed to print.

Digital proofs

The introduction of electronic prepress systems led to the proliferation of another kind of proof: the direct digital color proof, or DDCP. (Many commercial printers believe that digital proofs should be called *pre-proofs,* because a real proof can be made only from the job's final film. However, direct-to-plate and direct-to-press printing, which do not require film, will soon be commonplace.)

Most of the high-end prepress vendors sell digital proofers as part of their "complete solution". The continuous-tone color prints from these devices are widely used during the design and approval stages, and some clients even use them as final proofs (without going to the additional expense of having a film proof made).

Photo: © 3M

Fig. 2-8
Dye sublimation printers such as this 3M Rainbow can be used to create digital proofs that can shorten the design and approval cycle and reduce costs.

Recently, another kind of digital color proofer has become increasingly popular: the dye sublimation printer. These printers produce continuous tone output that closely resembles a conventional photograph, except that they are unable to render fine lines (such as the serifs in small type) accurately. They are relatively inexpensive (from about $5,000 to $30,000), but print only on special photographic media, which typically cost $4 to $10 per page. Dye sublimation printers are described in more detail in Chapter 11, which covers all kinds of color printers.

Although most veteran press operators and color separators would cringe at the thought, an increasing number of publishers are using color copiers, such as those from Xerox, Canon, and Kodak, to produce low-cost color "proofs". Obviously, the output from these machines is far from the quality of conventional film proofs, but improvements in calibration technology have made digital copiers useful as pre-proof devices.

No proofing system is perfect—none can invariably guarantee the "best match" to the printed sheet. There are too many variables in the printing process itself, such as ink hues, uncontrolled densities on press, and human unpredictability and error, not to mention that prepress proofing materials are *not* ink on paper. If you've got to have a proof that will *exactly* match the final printed sheet, the only way to get one is with a press proof, made with the same paper, inks, and printing press being used for the actual job.

Interpreting color proofs

Nothing could be simpler then approving a color proof. You look it over and if everything seems okay and the colors look pretty good you sign off and that's that, right? Wrong!

A color proof is a legal document in a high-stakes game. In the printing industry, where million-dollar print runs proceed on the basis of the client's signed approval of a Cromalin or other prepress proof, there's an old saying: "the chrome is the contract." If the printed piece looks pretty much like the proof you approved, you have very few grounds for complaint.

Actually, the standard printing trade customs that govern most commercial printing in North America do not even require that the printed piece exactly match the original or the proof. According to the Graphic Arts Council, "Because of differences in equipment, processing, proofing substrates, paper, inks, pigments, and other conditions between color proofing and production pressroom operations, a reasonable variation in color between color proofs and the completed job shall constitute acceptable delivery." We'll leave it up to the lawyers to decide what a "reasonable" variation might be.

Once you've reached the proof stage, how can you be sure that everything is correct? There are a number of factors to look for when viewing final proofs for a four-color process printing job. The first essential in proofing is to standardize the lighting conditions.

For optimal color correspondence between the original, the proof, and the printed piece, the major variable is illumination of the viewing area, which by convention is set to a color temperature of 5,000 Kelvin (5,000K). Even within this standard, there is plenty of room for variation. The correct color temperature must prevail throughout the viewing area, which is why many printing companies will have viewing booths scattered throughout various parts of the

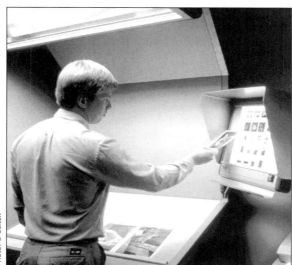

Photo: © Scitex

Fig. 2-9
Color trade shops and commercial printers use 5,000K viewing booths to match colors between the original image and the proof or press sheet.

plant. In fact, some film houses are lit throughout by 5,000K fluorescent tubes.

Once you've stabilized the viewing conditions, there are two different checklists you should follow, at least in your mind, as you assess each proof. The first set is by eye (without the use of a magnifier). Check carefully to ensure that:

- all pages are present and in the correct sequence, with all color elements in perfect register;
- all photos are correctly placed, properly scaled and cropped, and not flopped;
- no images have been inadvertently masked over or trimmed off;
- all type, linework, and other elements are the correct color;
- borders and rules that read across spreads align perfectly;
- trim size and folding are correct;
- color illustrations are vivid and rich, and all critical color areas have been accurately matched;
- there are no blemishes, spots, or broken letters.

The second set of observations requires a magnifier, also called a *loupe, glass,* or *linen tester*. To evaluate a color proof, you must look at it closely. Start by purchasing a good magnifying glass with a minimum eight-power magnification, and preferably 12-power or higher. Most professionals prefer a swivel-arm design, because it can be rotated to any position and is relatively free of distortion.

Use the magnifier to assess:

- sharpness: ensure that detail areas are crisp and clean;
- color accuracy: compare the proof to the original under a color-correct light source;
- neutral areas: make sure they are completely free from green or blue casts, all the way from white to gray to black;
- registration: all elements must be properly registered to eliminate fuzziness, shadows, and color changes;
- size: all photos, art, type, and pages must be precisely the correct size;
- borders: they should be correct size, color, position;
- captions: they must be correct in content, size, position;

- pagination: all pages and folios must be placed correctly, with crop marks and scores indicated where necessary;
- spots and scratches: along with pinholes and dust, must be removed from film and plates;
- broken type: there should be no white specks on type, no sections partially or completely covered.

To complete your interpretation of a proof, you must assess the tonal quality of photographs. Here are some important factors to look for:

- do the images match the original?
- do food, fabric, metallics, and, most especially, flesh tones, look natural?
- are images clean, sharp, and bright?
- are there details in the highlights or are they blown out?
- are the neutral tones neutral?
- are there undesirable color casts?
- are there moiré patterns, streaking, or banding?

To identify potential press problems, many printers use color control bars, such as those sold by the Graphic Arts Technical Foundation. The entire control bar series is usually printed on the proofs, with various specific elements included on the production run, depending on available trim space.

There's one more thing to check for, which sometimes requires special attention: make sure all corrections from any previous proofs have been made accurately. For further suggestions on checking and correcting color proofs, I recommend the book *How to Check and Correct Color Proofs* (listed in the bibliography).

You don't have to work with color for long before you're able to recognize that the brilliant colors displayed in a proof can be difficult or impossible to replicate on press. Many factors can contribute to unsatisfactory results, from subjective color perception to paper and ink densities. Color proofs can help you avoid unpleasant surprises before they occur, but only if you know what to look for. Here, too, some factors apply to synthetic color graphics, while others are relevant only to natural photographic images. Once the final proof has been approved, it's time to go on press.

The commercial printing industry

Let's look for a moment at how the printing industry has evolved so far, in order to get an idea of where it's going as we head into the twenty-first century. The commercial printing industry started in the middle of the fifteenth century with Gutenberg, although even by then wood-block printing had been in use for more than a thousand years. Gutenberg's system of moveable type is an example of a printing technique called *letterpress*, in which the image areas on a printing plate are raised above the non-image areas.

In the decades following Gutenberg's innovations, the availability of low-cost printing engendered a rapid increase in literacy that significantly altered education, science, government, and almost all other domains of human activity. A further increase in the cost-effectiveness of commercial printing occurred in the late seventeenth century as part of the industrial revolution, when printing presses came to be powered by machines rather than by human muscle.

But the greatest increase in printing has occurred during the twentieth century, as the quality and speed of offset litho printing increased while the cost continued to decline. Despite the influence of radio, television, movies, and other electronic media, the printing industry continues to flourish, in part thanks to the ease with which electronic tools (such as desktop publishing) enable anyone to become a publisher. This will change, of course, with the transition to electronic distribution of information, although it is too early to say how quickly the change-over will occur.

The companies making up the printing industry today can be categorized any number of different ways:

- according to how the paper is fed into the press: either sheet-fed or web-fed;
- according to the length of the press run: anything less than 5,000 impressions is a short run, while anything more than 100,000 is a long run;
- according to the type of material being printed: some companies are general commercial printers, while others

specialize in forms, labels, packaging, fine art, catalogs, and so on;

◆ according to the printing technology in use: letterpress, flexography, lithography, screen printing, or gravure.

Printing technologies

When most people today talk about "printing", they are referring to *offset lithography*, or *litho*, the method used to print most books (including this one), magazines, brochures, and other commercial publications. But there are other printing methods that are, in some cases, far more cost-effective. Let's explore each of the five main printing methods in order to understand how they differ, and to help you decide which to use for a given printing application.

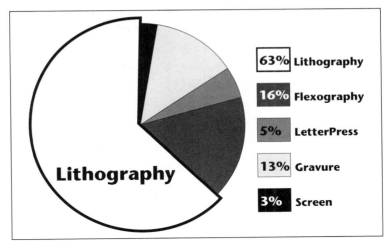

Fig. 2-10
Offset lithography makes up by far the largest percentage of the print market, followed, in order, by flexography, gravure, letterpress, and screen printing.

First, it is necessary to distinguish between the two different ways in which paper is fed into a press: sheet-fed and web. In the first, paper is cut into individual sheets prior to printing. Most sheet-fed presses can print on only one side of the sheet at a time, although perfecting presses, or *perfectors*, can print on both sides simultaneously.

The most popular kind of sheet-fed presses today have five or six inking stations, or *towers*, which means they can print jobs that combine four-color process with one or two spot colors (or varnishes), or jobs that require four-color on one side of the sheet plus one or two spot colors on the other. Sheet-fed printing is used for everything from one-color business cards to glossy annual reports, and everything in between.

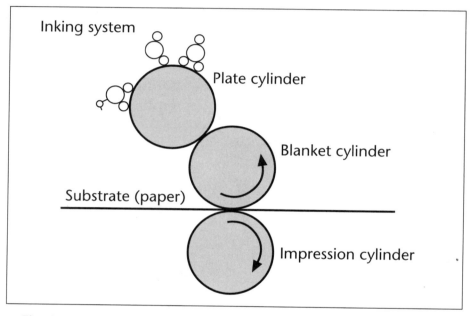

Fig. 2-11
A sheet-fed press prints on one or both sides of cut sheets. A sheet-fed press that can print on both sides at once is known as a perfector.

In web printing, paper is supplied to the press in large reels, and both sides are usually printed at the same time. Web printing takes longer for make-ready (press preparation) and is typically used only for longer jobs (50,000 impressions or more), such as newspapers, magazines, catalogs, and direct-mail pieces. However, during the late 1980s a variety of smaller half-web presses made this method more economical for shorter runs as well.

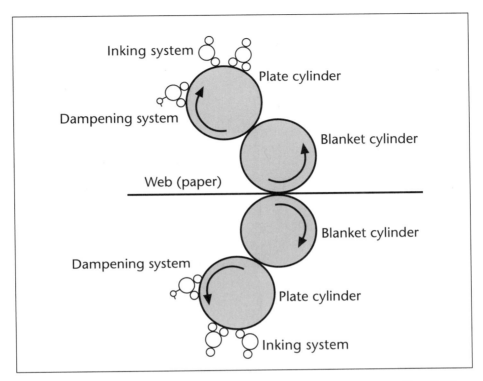

Fig. 2-12
A web press uses paper in large reels, and often includes binding functions at its back end.

On some huge web presses, such as those used for producing daily newspapers, the machine automatically splices the reels of paper to maintain a nonstop flow of printed newspapers at speeds of more than 100 feet per second. Many large web presses have sophisticated binding and trimming modules at the back end, capable of taking 12 or more 32-page *signatures* and folding, trimming, and gluing or stapling them into finished magazines.

Letterpress

Letterpress is the oldest method of printing, based on cast metal type or plates on which the image or printing areas are raised above the non-printing areas. Ink rollers contact only the top surface of the raised areas, and the inked image is transferred directly to paper.

Fig 2-13
Early printing made use of the
letterpress process to create both text
and graphics, such as this woodblock
style capital.

When viewed under a magnifier, letterpress can be distinguished by the slightly heavier edge of ink around each letter. This is the result of the ink spreading slightly as the result of the pressure of the plate on the printed surface. Despite this effect, the letterpress image is usually sharp and crisp.

Letterpress dominated the printing business for more than 300 years, though today it is virtually obsolete, except for short-run poetry, hand-crafted artistic books, and printing numbered tickets. Because of its relatively high cost, slow speed, and the gradual decline in the ranks of skilled craftspeople, letterpress seems to be on the way out. There will probably always be a small market—people who want the best possible printed diplomas, certificates, and invitations—but the days of letterpress as a significant part of printing are over.

Flexography

Flexography is a form of letterpress based on flexible rubber plates and is used for printing in color on just about anything that will go through a press: cellophane, polyethylene, gift wrap, foil, shopping bags, toilet paper, milk

Flexography produces brilliant colors, making it ideal for packaging and novelty printing. Although, initially, the quality of flexo printing didn't match that of other processes, especially for halftones, it has improved substantially, to the point where it is capturing market segments, such as newspapers and magazines, long held by gravure.

Gravure

Gravure printing is based on the *intaglio* principle—the image areas consist of cells or wells etched into a metal cylinder or plate, and the cylinder or plate surface is the non-printing areas. The plate surface rotates through a vat of ink, then a blade scrapes off the excess ink. The depth of the recess controls the amount of ink retained and hence the density of any particular cell. The ink remaining in the countless recessed cells forms the image by direct transfer to the paper as it passes between the plate cylinder and the impression cylinder.

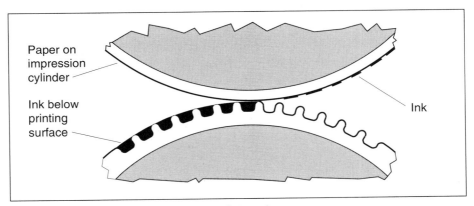

Paper on impression cylinder

Ink below printing surface

Ink

Fig 2-14
The gravure process is the opposite of letterpress, in that the image areas are recessed below the surface of the printing plate, rather than raised above it.

Gravure plates are more expensive than those needed for most other printing systems, and gravure is therefore usually limited to jobs with large print runs, often a million impressions or more. The advantages include excellent consistency and reproduction of photographs, plus the fact that gravure plates last much longer than conventional ones.

Increasingly, over the past five years, the market for gravure printing has been threatened, especially in the newspaper and magazine industries, by improvements in the quality and cost-effectiveness of flexography. At the same time, many large newspaper markets have been broken into smaller, more tightly focused segments, further decreasing the competitive position of the gravure process.

Screen printing

Screen printing is a specialized technique that uses a fine silk, nylon, or steel screen mounted on a frame. The screen contains a stencil of the image, created either manually or photomechanically, so that non-printing areas are protected by the stencil. Ink with a paint-like consistency is pushed through the screen with a rubber squeegee, forcing it onto the paper below.

Although screen printing is not appropriate for many commercial applications, it is often the most cost-effective method for printing on mugs, key chains, and, of course, T-shirts. Screen printing can sometimes be distinguished by the thick layer of ink, and sometimes by the texture of the screen on the printed surface. It is used primarily in the textile and packaging industries.

Although desktop publishing tools are not widely used for the production phase of screen printing, they are, as with all other parts of the contemporary graphic arts industry, an essential aspect of the design of original artwork that will ultimately be reproduced with screen printing.

Offset lithography

Lithography is the most widely used printing method, because it provides the most acceptable compromises between cost and quality for the bulk of printed matter: books, magazines, newsletters, price lists, catalogs, directories, annual reports, and the like. The process takes its name from the Greek word *lithos*, meaning stone, because flat stones were originally used in the process (and still are for some kinds of fine-art prints).

Lithography is described as a *planographic* printing method, because the image and non-image areas are essentially on the same plane of a thin metal plate, with the distinction between them maintained chemically.

Photo: © Heidelberg

Fig 2-15
In a lithographic press the image is offset from the printing plate to an impression cylinder before being transferred to the sheet.

The most common version is called *offset* lithography because the ink is offset from the plate to a rubber blanket, and then from the blanket to the paper. This is necessary because even the smoothest papers can quickly abrade the surface of a metal plate, requiring a new plate every few thousand impressions. Offsetting the image onto a rubber *impression cylinder* makes it possible to print 100,000 copies or more from a single plate.

Although most litho plates are made from aluminum or other metals, an increasing percentage are made from synthetic materials or, for very short runs, from paper.

A litho plate is designed so that the image areas attract grease and repel water, while the non-image areas attract water and repel grease. When the plate is mounted on the press, it comes in contact with rollers wet by a dampening solution, then by rollers wet by ink.

The non-image areas pick up the dampening solution and repel ink. The image areas are coated with ink, which is offset onto the rubber impression blanket cylinder. The ink is transferred to the paper as it passes between the blanket cylinder and the impression cylinder. The result—a major advantage of the offset method—is that the soft rubber surface of the blanket creates a crisp impression on a variety of papers and other surfaces, both rough and smooth.

Litho presses, especially high-speed presses with multiple towers, are well suited to color production. A six-color offset press, for example, can print a job with the four process colors plus two additional spot color inks or varnishes—with only one pass through the press.

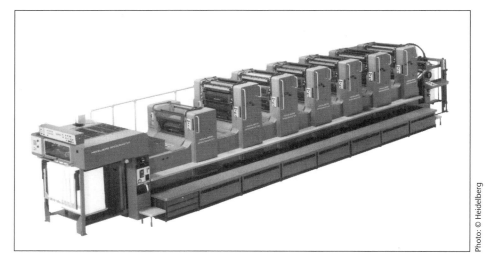

Photo: © Heidelberg

Fig 2-16
This Heidelberg six-color press can print on both sides of the sheet in a single pass, and contains a seventh unit for adding a varnish or other coating.   .

Many small printers have only a single one-color or two-color press, with which they crank out a variety of printed products, often containing black only or black plus one spot color. In some cases they use a two-color press to print full-color (CMYK) jobs, by feeding the same sheet of paper through the press a second time.

Although printing presses have become faster and more sophisticated in recent years, they are still complex, mechanical devices that require highly skilled operators. For example, to obtain maximum quality, the press operator will often adjust the amount of ink flowing through each of the *keys* (the valves that feed ink into the press).

The major press manufacturers, such as Heidelberg and Komori, now sell computer-controlled presses that constantly measure the ink density throughout the printed sheet, and automatically adjust the ink keys accordingly. Despite these advances, printing remains as much a craft as a science.

Waterless printing

One of the most exciting areas of innovation in the printing industry is *waterless* printing—eliminating the water-based *fountain* or *dampening solution* that is used in conventional lithography to isolate the non-image areas from the image areas. As noted earlier, the image and non-image areas on a lithographic plate are on the same plane (unlike a gravure or letterpress plate).

The litho process works because oil and water don't mix—the inks are essentially oily and the fountain solution is mostly water. Using water, however, creates all kinds of problems: paper stretch, the need for extensive drying time, and paper waste during make-ready, not to mention the resultant impact on the environment.

There are three main advantages to waterless printing: quality, productivity, and waste reduction. Although screen rulings of as many as 800 lines per inch are possible, most waterless printing takes place at 300 lpi, compared to the 133 to 175 lpi of conventional offset litho. This can make a substantial difference in the quality of the finished printed piece. Waterless printing also results in minimal dot gain, increased dot sharpness, and higher ink densities, all of which contribute to enhanced print contrast and quality.

Increased productivity comes from faster make-ready, higher running speeds, and less downtime for dampener maintenance. Reduced waste results from the fact that there is much less spoilage during the make-ready process.

The key to waterless printing is the plate material, and the largest supplier of waterless plates is Toray Industries of Japan. The Toray method uses differential adhesion to keep image and non-image areas separate during printing. After a plate has been exposed and developed, the non-image area is composed of a very thin (two-micron) coating of ink-repellent silicone, while the image area, slightly recessed, consists of an ink-receptive photopolymer material.

Waterless printing also requires changes in inks and press configurations. The waterless plate is designed to resist viscosity, so high-viscosity inks must be used. Also, in conventional lithography the water has a cooling effect on the surface of the printing plate. To compensate, the printing units in a waterless press must be fitted with a temperature control mechanism to maintain the ink temperature level—and, thus, the viscosity—precisely.

The only major disadvantage of waterless printing (other than the rather substantial cost of buying a waterless press or converting a conventional press to waterless operation) is that the plates tend to scratch more easily than conventional litho plates, and must therefore be handled with extra care. Another constraint is that waterless printing uses special inks that are not yet widely available.

Paper and ink

One of the most important factors in print quality and cost is paper, which accounts for between a third and a half of the cost of most printing jobs, but is often given insufficient attention. Other than the cost, the paper's physical characteristics will determine both its overall appearance and the ability of the printer to print on it.

Among the factors important to paper quality are:

- whiteness: the absence of any color cast;
- brightness: which must be very high for reproducing images with good contrast and sharpness;
- gloss: for optimal reproduction of photographs and tints;
- opacity: the more opaque the paper, the less visible the images on the other side and on subsequent pages;
- smoothness: smoother papers increase the line frequency at which halftones can be reproduced;
- absorbency: low absorbency is necessary for good color quality, while higher absorbency improves ink transfer and reduces drying time.

Recycled paper

These days, people and companies are increasingly sensitive to the environmental implications of printing, including the question of whether a given piece was printed on recycled paper and whether it is, in turn, recyclable.

What actually constitutes "recycled paper"? Most grades contain a mix of virgin fiber, post-commercial fiber, and post-consumer fiber. Post-commercial fiber comes from scraps produced by printing companies, binderies, and envelope makers. Post-consumer fiber is collected from offices, stores, and homes for reuse.

Most recycled coated papers contain one-half virgin fiber and one-half post-commercial fiber, with little or no post-consumer fiber. Uncoated stocks may come entirely from post-commercial fiber, or may contain as much as 20% post-consumer fiber. Describing these papers as "recycled" is a bit misleading, because post-commercial paper has been recovered for decades. Truly recycled paper made completely from post-consumer fiber is new, and not yet widely used.

Fig. 2-17
The recycled logo (left) identifies paper containing recycled content, but not necessarily from post-consumer waste. The recyclable logo (right) means that a paper can be recycled, not that it necessarily contains any recycled content.

Recycled paper stocks are still somewhat more expensive than paper created with virgin pulp, but the price gap has narrowed in recent years and, with continued public support for the recycling concept, there may soon be little or no price difference.

Ink

Finally, there is ink. Often taken for granted, ink usually consumes less than three per cent of a printing budget, but has a significant effect on the overall quality of the final piece.

Theoretically, the most important characteristic of ink is its color strength or range—the objective being to use inks that give the widest possible color gamut, to allow more accurate reproduction of original colors. In practice, other concerns must be considered as well: the pigment's resistance to light, moisture, and chemicals; fineness of pigment particles; ability to flow well; toxicity and environmental effects.

There are specialty inks, formulated for a variety of purposes, that can be called for by the designer with stringent production requirements or a generous budget. They include fluorescent, metallic, matte or dull inks, fade resistant or ultra-violet (UV) resistant, scuff resistant, moisture resistant, scented, magnetic, heat-transfer, invisible, and luminescent inks, and inks that change color when water, heat or chemicals are applied to them.

Direct to plate

Many jobs involve printing tens or hundreds of thousands of copies, quantities far too large for even the fastest color copiers. But jobs that will be printed with offset litho no longer necessarily require film. A small but increasing number of publishers are now going *direct to plate*.

Direct to plate technology is quite simple: the digital output from a computer is sent to an imagesetter loaded with paper or metal plate material, rather than with film. (These paper plates aren't the kind you might take on a picnic—they're printing plates made of paper, suitable for print runs of as many as 10,000 or so impressions.)

The major advantages of direct to plate technology are the cost savings and the environmental benefit that results from not wasting the film and chemicals normally required prior to plate-making. The major disadvantage is the difficulty in proofing: obviously there is

Fig. 2-18
Many imagesetters now output directly to plate material, thereby eliminating the time, cost, and environmental effects of film.

Photo: © Gerber Scientific

no way to make a film proof, and if something goes wrong, it is seldom discovered until the job is on press, at which point corrections can be extremely costly and time-consuming.

The plating material used in direct-to-plate imagesetters is also best suited to relatively short press runs, typically fewer than 25,000 impressions. Despite these potential problems, the use of direct to plate is growing, especially for one-color (black only) or two color (black plus one spot color) jobs.

Direct to press

Another emerging technology for color reproduction is the *direct to press* method, in which computers are connected directly to a printing press, so that pages can be printed without an intermediate film stage. The leading contender in this field is the GTO-DI press, a partnership between Heidelberg (one of the world's largest manufacturers of printing presses) and a small start-up company called Presstek. The Heidelberg GTO-DI combines a conventional GTO press (capable of printing on paper up to 14-by-20 inches), with Presstek's direct imaging (DI) technology.

Photo: © Presstek

Fig. 2-19
The Heidelberg GTO-DI adds direct imaging technology to a
conventional offset litho press, so you can
go directly from desktop to press.

In the GTO-DI system, PostScript output from a Mac or PC is sent
directly to the press, on which blank plates have been mounted.
The original version of the GTO-DI used a tiny spark to "burn" or
image the plate. This method had significant quality problems, and
has been superseded by Presstek's new Pearl technology in which a
laser is used to vaporize the image areas.

The printing plates are a key component of the DI technology.
They are made from a three-layer sandwich, with a polyester or metal
base on the bottom, an infrared absorbent material in the middle,
and a silicon coating on top. The middle layer is tuned to the output
wavelength of the laser, and vaporizes when exposed to the laser
beam. Unlike the old spark-erosion method, which was limited to a
resolution of 1,016 dpi, the Pearl technology supports resolutions
up to 2,540 dpi.

One unusual aspect of the GTO-DI method is that it is waterless.
As previously mentioned, virtually all offset litho printing presses

use a water-based solution to keep the ink away from the non-image areas of the page. Because of the silicon coating on its plates, however, the GTO-DI does not need to use water or any other liquid as a dampening agent. This accounts for one of its advantages: make-ready times are somewhat less than those of a conventional offset press.

Photo: © Presstek

Fig. 2-20
The Presstek Pearl direct imaging technology mounts on a Heidelberg GTO-DI press where the dampening system would be on a conventional press.

The major advantage of the GTO-DI system is the reduced cost of printing short runs (under 5,000 impressions), as compared with a conventional litho press. Another advantage is that the system eliminates most registration problems because the plates are mounted on the press before being imaged. One problem inherent in direct-to-press technology is that it is impossible to accurately proof the pages before they're printed. Traditional film proofs are not possible, because no film is made prior to burning plates.

Although the GTO-DI was originally targeted at print runs from 500 to 5,000 impressions, the arrival of metal plates has stretched this to 20,000 or more. However, the GTO-DI is most cost-effective on shorter runs, particularly those in the 2,000 to 5,000 range, because of its reduced prepress costs. Once the press run gets over 10,000 copies, a conventional press will probably prove more economical.

It remains to be seen whether the GTO-DI approach will prove successful. Initial versions produced pages with a print quality that would be suitable for some low-end applications but not good enough to replace conventional high-quality commercial printing. However, quality improved substantially with the introduction of the Pearl technology. In fact, the quality of output from the GTO-DI is now good enough to compete head-to-head against conventional offset printing.

Direct-to-press has the potential to become an important printing method, though in the next few years it will certainly face stiff competition from short-run digital color presses and high-speed color copiers.

Printing without a press

There's another way of reproducing documents, both in black-and-white and color, that's distinctly different from the five printing methods described above: *xerography*, also known as photocopying. One might hesitate to call this printing, because it does not involve a printing press, but copiers are about to become one of the most important ways of reproducing color pages.

Like most reproduction technologies, xerography began as a strictly black-and-white process but has been enhanced with the ability to create full color documents. The first color copiers were introduced by Canon in the 1970s, and quickly found acceptance in such specialized market segments as design and advertising.

Photo: © Xerox

Fig. 2-21
High-speed copiers, such as this Xerox DocuTech, can print 135 pages per minute in black-and-white, and similar full-color copiers are on the horizon.

In 1987, Canon introduced the first color copiers that could also connect to a computer and act as color printers. Since then, the company has captured the largest portion of the worldwide color copier market, although it now faces competition from Xerox, Agfa, Kodak (which sells a modified version of Canon's copiers), Minolta, and others. These and other color output devices are described in detail in Chapter 11.

Color publishers can use copiers in two ways. Publishers who will eventually print thousands or millions of copies of their publications on a conventional printing press find that color copiers provide a quick, inexpensive way of creating "pre-proof" composites, or *comps*. These are extremely helpful during the design and approval stages of most kinds of publication, and are especially useful for catalog and magazine work in which there are often thousands of pages in production at any one time, each of which may go through a dozen or more sets of changes.

The second role for color copiers is as digital printing presses: a quick and easy way to produce a "short run" of a few hundred or a thousand copies of a full-color document.

Short-run color

The Printing Industries of America trade association (PIA) has a formal definition of short-run color: any printing job of fewer than 5,000 impressions! This makes sense, given the cost and time consumed in the make-ready process if a conventional printing press is used. The printer will often waste a few hundred sheets of paper just getting the inks up to the correct density levels and fine-tuning the balance between the inks and the water solution. To reduce the per-copy printing cost to a reasonable level, the make-ready costs must be spread over the largest possible number of copies.

However, this does little to help the business person who is attending a meeting or conference and wants to leave behind a colorful document for each of the five or 50 or 500 participants. Until now, there has been no cost-effective way to do this. Color copiers now are making it both possible and cost-effective.

Color copiers don't just copy. By adding an interface unit, you can connect a color copier directly to your Macintosh or PC, or even make it a shared resource on a local area network. This enables you to print directly to the copier, with each page a digital original of the highest possible quality.

In the next few years we will see rapid growth in truly short-run color printing, where only a few copies, a few hundred or few thousand copies are required. Today, most color copiers can produce no more than ten pages per minute, and can print on only one side of the page. You can reasonably expect that, by 1996, you will see color copiers printing on both sides of the page at speeds in excess of 40 pages per minute. Suddenly, it will become very easy to produce short-run color documents cheaply.

After the press—binding

After printing, many documents are not yet finished; they must be bound into their final form as books, magazines, brochures, or whatever. Papers for sheet-fed printing come in standard sizes, such as 25-by-38-inches for text basis (normal weight) papers. Typically, these sheets have four to eight pages per side, to form an eight-page or 16-page *signature*.

Smaller magazines and newsletters are often bound by *saddle-stitching*, in which small wire staples hold the pages together. Saddle-stitching is commonly used for publications of as many as 100 pages. When a publication is too large to be held together with staples, the individual signatures are stitched, then glued together, in a process known as *perfect binding*. (This is a major misnomer: in time, as the glue dries and the book's spine cracks, pages may fall like autumn leaves, in a decidedly imperfect way.)

If your job is printed on a sheet-fed press, there are many different ways it can be bound. Web presses usually incorporate in-line binding, with folding and trimming taking place automatically at the back end of the press.

A typical eight-page newsletter, for example, being printed in a press run of a few thousand copies, will have been imposed eight-up (so that each signature contains two complete newsletters). Each finished sheet will then be cut, folded, stitched (stapled), and trimmed to final size, then boxed or packaged for delivery to the customer or mailing house.

Market evolution

Many commercial printers do not have the machinery necessary for any type of binding operation more complex than a simple saddle stitch, which is why there is a different set of companies known as trade binderies. A modern trade bindery can provide numerous services other than saddle stitching and perfect binding, including scoring and folding, die-cuts (cutting shapes from the printed sheet) and embossing. Indeed, many publishers routinely send jobs to be printed without being conscious of the fact that their commercial printer will be sub-contracting part of the job to a trade bindery.

This relationship between commercial printers and trade binderies can be seen as a model for the evolution of the prepress industry during the next few years, as more and more printers bring color scanning, separation, and output operations under their control, either by building in-house prepress capability or by forming partnerships with existing trade shops and service bureaus.

With all the emphasis on prepress, and the rapid growth of desktop color publishing, what's going to happen to the commercial printing industry? Certainly, printers will go through a period of upheaval as multimedia, electronic distribution, and other technologies kick in, but it seems likely there will continue to be a need for printing for the foreseeable future. Despite the rapid pace of technological change, the printed page has many attributes that are difficult or impossible to attain with electronic media, including portability, ease of browsing, and cost.

There is still the question of how individual printing companies will survive in the new order. The driving factors in the printing business are now convenience, speed, reliability, and single-point accountability. As desktop color production takes over in the next few years, an increasing number of print buyers are going to want to give their commercial printer a cartridge or tape containing the finished page layout files and have the printer accept responsibility for shepherding the job through the prepress process and into print. Much as trade binderies are an essential—though largely invisible— part of many print jobs, prepress itself may soon disappear as a major concern for many color publishers.

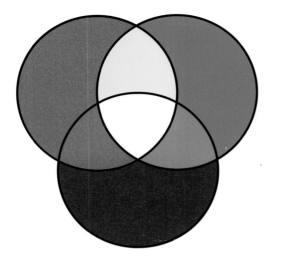

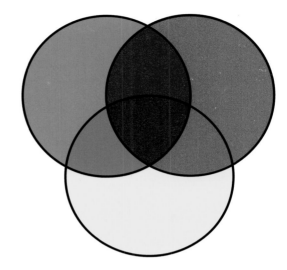

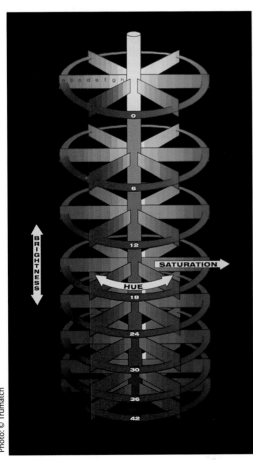

Photo: © Trumatch

Color Models:

RGB is an *additive* color model in which equal proportions of red, green, and blue (above left) can be combined to create white.

CMYK is a *subtractive* color model used for full-color printing. Combining equal proportions of cyan, magenta, and yellow (above right) should, in theory, produce solid black. In practice, it produces a dark muddy gray (below left), so black ink must be added to make solid black (below right).

The hue, lightness, saturation (HLS) color model (left) is an intuitive way of selecting colors, and forms the basis of the Trumatch color picker. Colors are represented as a cylinder, with the hues arranged around its circumference, saturation increasing toward the central axis and brightness increasing from bottom to top.

The Color Spectrum

All visible light exists within one narrow band of the electromagnetic spectrum, extending from infra-red to ultra-violet through the familiar rainbow pattern of red, orange, yellow, green, blue, indigo, and violet.

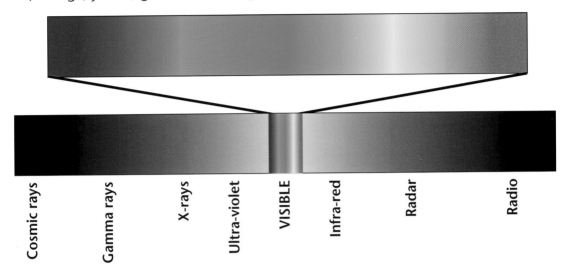

Cosmic rays   Gamma rays   X-rays   Ultra-violet   VISIBLE   Infra-red   Radar   Radio

The CIE Model

Unlike other color models, whose interpretation of color is based on a specific input or output device, the CIE model is device-independent, which makes it ideal as a reference color space for color management systems. Because of limitations in the CMYK printing process, the chart shown here is only an approximation of the range of colors in the CIE color space.

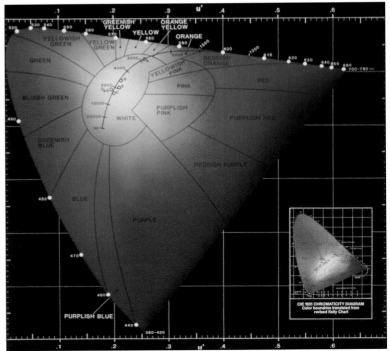

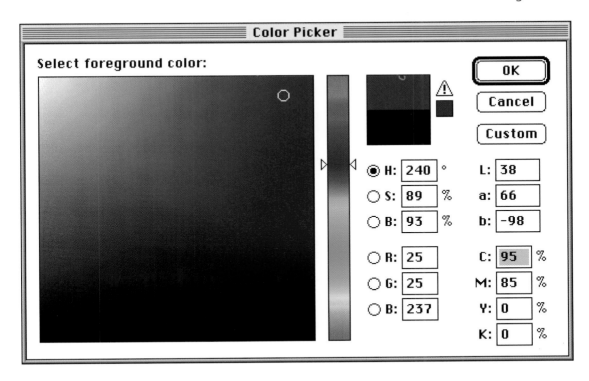

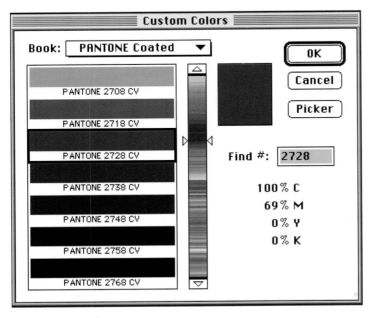

Color Pickers:

The color picker in Adobe Photoshop (above) shows the RGB, HSB, CMYK, and CIELAB values for the selected color, plus a gamut alarm warning that this color cannot be printed with CMYK inks under the defined printing conditions.

Clicking on the Custom option shows Photoshop's support for the Trumatch, Focoltone and PANTONE MATCHING SYSTEM color matching methods.

Pantone Color Guides

Although best known for its PANTONE MATCHING SYSTEM spot color guide (right), Pantone also makes process color matching tools.

The Pantone Process Color System (below) contains more than 3,000 CMYK colors.

The Pantone Process Color Imaging Guide (bottom) is an important tool for designers, because it shows, side by side, each of the spot colors in the PANTONE MATCHING SYSTEM with its closest equivalent process color.

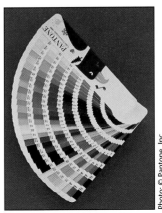

Photo: © Pantone, Inc.

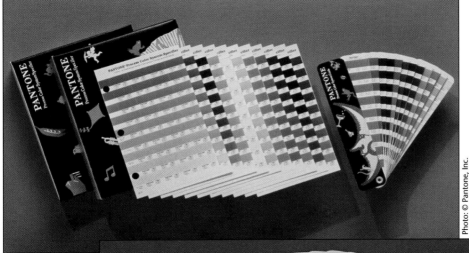

Photo: © Pantone, Inc.

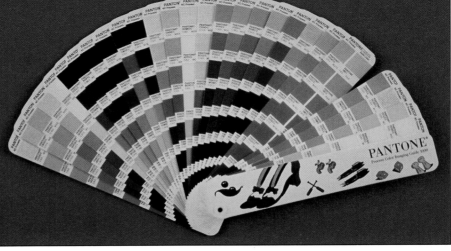

Photo: © Pantone, Inc.

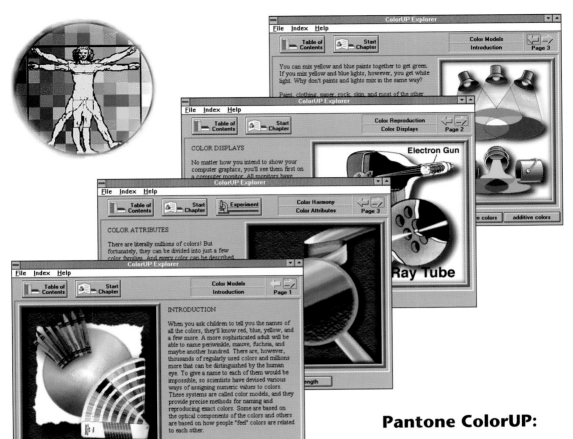

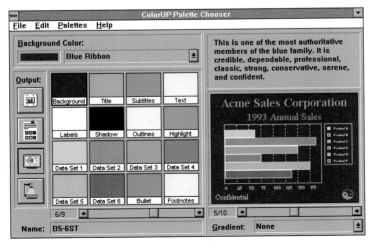

Pantone ColorUP:

The Pantone ColorUP Explorer (above) is an interactive encyclopaedia of color science, with experiments that help you understand concepts such as color models, color mixing and separation.

The ColorUP Palette Chooser (left) helps you choose color combinations that complement rather than conflict with one another. After choosing a palette, you can export it to any major publishing or presentation package.

The Color Imaging Process

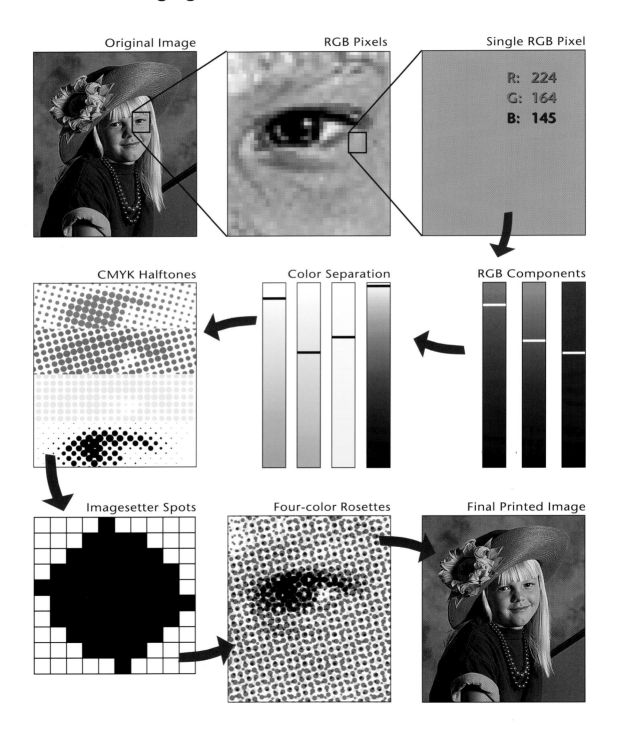

Original Image

RGB Pixels

Single RGB Pixel

R: 224
G: 164
B: 145

CMYK Halftones

Color Separation

RGB Components

Imagesetter Spots

Four-color Rosettes

Final Printed Image

Color Separation

Color separation is the process of converting an image from the RGB (red, green, blue) model into its CMYK (cyan, magenta, yellow, and black) components.

Separating a color photograph (above) produces four pieces of film, each of which is actually a grayscale image (below). People in the color prepress and printing industries are able to work with these black-and-white films, knowing in their mind's eye how the final image will ultimately appear in full color. For those just learning how color prepress works, it sometimes helps to view each film according to the process ink it will print (bottom).

Moiré Patterns

An image output with supercell screening (top) shows virtually no moiré, while the same image output with the black screen rotated ten degrees (bottom) is riddled with objectionable moiré patterns.

Dithered and Continuous-tone Output

An image printed with an eight-bit printer (below left) can contain up to 256 distinct colors, so the printer must therefore use dithering, or dot patterns, to create the appearance of more colors.

A 24-bit printer (below right) can create 256 shades of cyan, 256 shades of magenta, and so on, at each pixel, and can therefore create continuous-tone output.

Color Conversions

Specifying process colors in popular applications programs as RGB or HSB values can create problems when they are converted to CMYK.

For example, an RGB color of 40% red and 20% green is converted differently in PageMaker and QuarkXPress. Similarly, an RGB color of 46R 98G 32B is converted by FreeHand into a pale lime green, and by Photoshop into a deep forest green.

PageMaker
0C 50M 100Y 60K

QuarkXPress
60C 80M 100Y 0K

FreeHand
54C 2M 68Y 0K

Photoshop
84C 29M 98Y 25K

Gray Component Replacement

Photoshop, PhotoStyler, and other imaging programs allow you to specify the amount of black ink used in a set of color separations. A bright, high-key image (this page) shows a marked variation in the density of the black channel when Photoshop's Gray Component Replacement parameter is set to Heavy (top) and Light (bottom). A dark, low-key image (opposite) shows less difference in the black plates when black generation is set to Heavy (top) and Light (bottom).

Photoshop's Separation Setup dialog box (right) shows how increasing black generation proportionally reduces the other process colors.

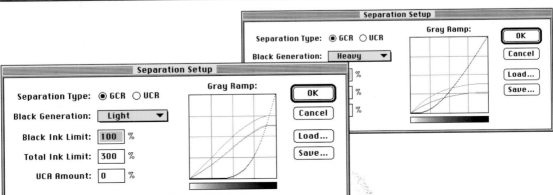

Scanner Calibration

The Kodak Q60 target is used to calibrate desktop and high-end scanners.

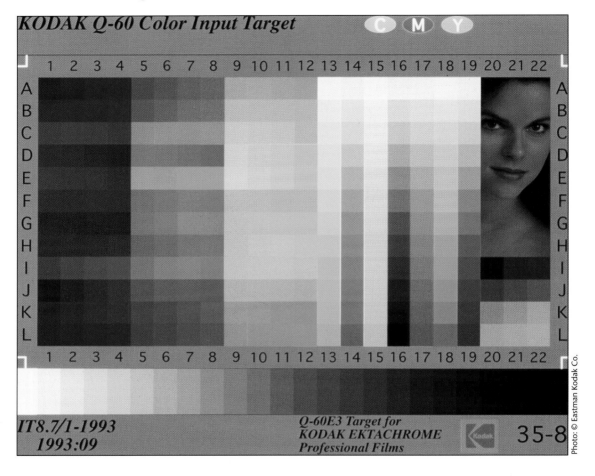

Digital Photography

As digital cameras increase in quality and drop in price, many color publishers will be able to capture images without scanning. This photograph was captured with a Kodak DCS-200 digital camera as an RGB file, then converted to CMYK format in Photoshop prior to being output.

Frequency Modulated Screening

Conventional halftones consist of variable-sized dots with constant spacing. Frequency modulated (FM) halftones are made of tiny microdots, whose size is constant but spacing appears random. With a magnifier, compare the FM halftone below with the conventional halftone of the same image on the next page.

Photo: © Michael Kieran

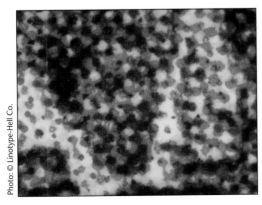

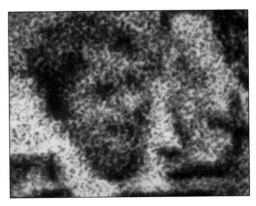

Photo: © Linotype-Hell Co.

Conventional Dot Structure   FM Dot Structure

Scanning: High-End, Desktop Drum, Photo CD

To compare the quality of different types of scanners, we've scanned the same image three times: the picture below was scanned on a high-end Dainippon Screen SG-747 drum scanner, the version at the bottom of this page with Kodak Photo CD, and the image at the top of the opposite page with a Screen 1030AI desktop drum scanner.

JPEG Compression

Starting with the original high-end scan, the images below have been compressed using the JPEG (Joint Photographic Experts Group) method at compression ratios of (left to right) 18:1, 12:1, and 3:1. Even with compression of 12:1, the image shows very little degradation in quality after being decompressed and printed.

Duotones, Tritones, Quadtones

Photoshop provides a flexible set of tools for creating duotones, tritones, and quadtones, which are grayscale images printed with two, three, and four inks respectively. This page features three duotones of the same original grayscale image (top left), printed with (clockwise) cyan, magenta with a black boost, and magenta with a heavy shot of black in the quarter-tones.

Opposite, you can mix CMYK inks to create quadtones that are cool (top) or warm (middle) according to the proportions of the inks, as shown in the Duotone Options dialog box. Magenta, yellow, and black can be mixed to create a tritone with a sepia flavor (bottom). The original full-color image of Hadrian's wall is at bottom right.

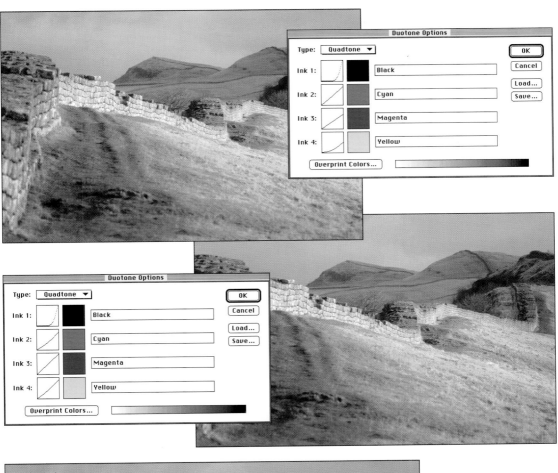

MonacoCOLOR

MonacoCOLOR is a Photoshop plug-in that enables non-professional users to obtain professional quality scans. The program is based on the idea of intelligent tonal mapping—it analyzes the histogram of the raw scanned RGB data, optimizes the tonal values to create better output, then uses custom color separation tables to convert the scan into CMYK format. MonacoCOLOR was applied to the original scan (left) to produce a version with the correct tonal mapping and color separation values (right).

Photo: © Monaco Systems

Photoshop Filters

Photoshop, PhotoStyler and other imaging programs let you quickly apply a variety of filters to an original image (top left), both to enhance the image (blur or sharpen), and to create special effects such as (clockwise) Find Edges, Pointillize, Wave and Ripple.

Photo: © Michael Kieran

Aldus Gallery Effects

These images were created in Aldus PhotoStyler using the Gallery Effects plug-in modules to transform an original image (top left) with effects such as (clockwise) Dry Brush, Film Grain, Spatter, Smudge Stick, and Graphic Pen.

Digital Stock Shots

A single PhotoDisc CD-ROM contains hundreds of high-resolution, full-color stock shot photographs, suitable for use in brochures, newsletters and other publications.

Drawing on the Desktop

Designer John Hersey used Aldus FreeHand 4.0 to create this cover for the 8th edition of the Graphic Artists Guild's Handbook on Pricing & Ethical Guidelines.

Color Trapping

The blue star on the red background is difficult to print in perfect register (left), resulting in light leaks (center). One solution is to spread (expand) the stroke around the object (right). Solutions to other common trapping problems are shown below.

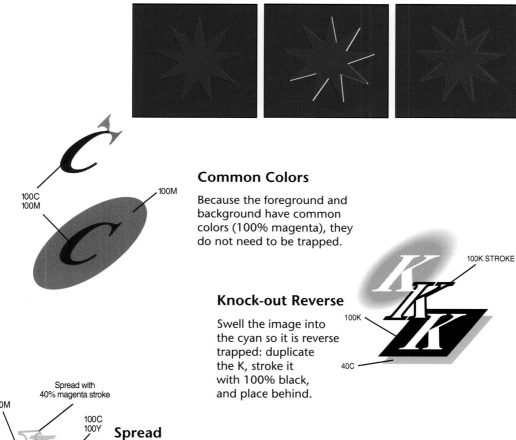

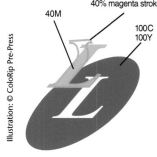

100C
100M

100M

Common Colors

Because the foreground and background have common colors (100% magenta), they do not need to be trapped.

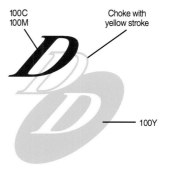

100K STROKE

Knock-out Reverse

Swell the image into the cyan so it is reverse trapped: duplicate the K, stroke it with 100% black, and place behind.

100K

40C

Spread with
40% magenta stroke

40M

100C
100Y

Spread

The 40% magenta is the least dominant color, so spread it: stroke with 40% magenta, and overprint.

100C
100M

Choke with
yellow stroke

Choke

Yellow is least dominant color, so choke it: overprint the D, duplicate it, then paste behind, fill with white (no overprint, stroke with yellow).

100Y

Illustration: © ColoRip Pre-Press

Illustration: © Courtland Shakespeare

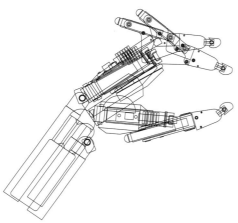

Integrating Vector and Bitmap Art

This remarkable illustration, by master computer artist Courtland Shakespeare, combines vector art created in CorelDRAW on a PC (the robot hand) and Adobe Illustrator on the Macintosh (Ms. Cyborgette), with a city background image from a Corel stock shot CD-ROM.

Digital Halftones

"By convention there is color,
by convention sweetness, by convention bitterness,
but in reality there are only atoms and space."

Democritus, circa 400 B.C.

Look closely at any black-and-white photograph in a book, magazine, or newspaper. From a distance, it appears to contain many shades of gray. Now, look more closely. As you can see in the picture on the next page, the image is actually composed of many tiny black dots, some smaller, some larger, arranged in a regular grid pattern. This optical illusion—which fools the eye into seeing shades of gray where there are actually only black dots—is called *halftoning*. Until recently halftones were created photographically with an etched glass screen, which is why halftoning is also known as *screening*; today, many are created digitally.

Unlike type or pen-and-ink drawings, which can be reproduced as solid areas of black ink on white paper, photographs (whether black-and-white or color) contain many different shades, or tones—they are *continuous-tone* images. A printing press, however, is a binary device—at every tiny spot on the paper, there is either ink or no ink. On a one-color press, for instance, there is no way to create gray tones in certain parts of a photograph by laying down a thinner or thicker layer of black ink.

This is where halftoning fits in. In order to reproduce on a printing press the many shades of gray or color in a photograph, the continuous-tone image must first be converted into dots by the halftoning process. Color tints, whether created with spot or process inks, must also first be screened.

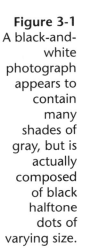

Figure 3-1
A black-and-white photograph appears to contain many shades of gray, but is actually composed of black halftone dots of varying size.

Photo: © PhotoDisc, Inc.

This chapter explains the key concepts in halftoning, beginning with conventional photographic halftones and extending the ideas into the world of digital computers. As explained in the previous chapter, the final product of the prepress process is film: four halftone film separations in the case of process color printing. The essential concept in this chapter is that each of those separation films is actually a halftone.

The halftone illusion

In viewing a halftone, the eye converts the precise grid of dots into the appearance of objects. Some of the greatest of the Impressionist painters—including Georges Seurat and the other Pointillists—relied on the same visual response to create their pictures.

If you look at any screened image under a magnifier, you can see how the image is made up of countless tiny dots:

- the bright areas (*highlights*) consist of a few small black dots totally surrounded by white space;
- the middle gray areas (*midtones*) consist of medium-sized dots;

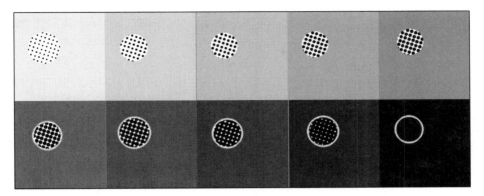

Figure 3-2
The halftone illusion is that different densities of dots are seen as
varying intensities of gray. Here, the density increases in 10%
increments from 10% gray at top left to 100% black at bottom-right.

♦   the darkest areas (*shadows*) consist of dots that are so large
    they overlap, with very small white areas between them.

Why not ignore the halftone process and print the photograph
directly on the page? Because, quite simply, you can't. Printing is an
all-or-nothing process: either the press puts down ink at a given
place on the paper, or it doesn't.

Using the halftone principle, we can create a gray tint by
controlling the pattern of black and white areas so they look gray.
The same principle applies to photographs: by controlling the size
of the dots, it's possible to achieve a full tonal range from white
through various shades of gray to solid black. This overcomes the
inherent limitation of the press in reproducing a range of tonal values.

Resolution and gray scale

In order to understand why halftones are so important, let's look at
the human visual system, which comprises the eyes, optic nerve,
and brain. There are two aspects of human perception that are
especially important in understanding color printing: resolving detail
and perceiving shades of gray.

The ability to resolve visual detail varies from person to person,
and with factors such as age, fatigue, and emotional state. *Resolution*

is a measure of how close two lines must be before they blend into a single shape and it becomes impossible to distinguish them as separate. In general, most people can resolve about 1/800th of an inch, which is why typesetting has traditionally started at about 1,000 dots per inch. At this resolution, the tiny spots making up each character disappear, and only the character itself is discernible.

People perceive type and linework quite differently than they perceive photographic images. In order to remain crisp and sharp, type and linework should be scanned and printed at the highest available resolution. Photographs and other halftoned materials, however, do not need to be scanned at very high resolution, although they must be output at high resolution to maintain detail and to avoid sharp bands of gray or colors.

One of the challenges of electronic imaging is that if there aren't enough shades of gray in a graphic or photograph, distinct bands of lighter and darker shades will be seen, which distract the eye. This phenomenon, known as *banding* or shade-stepping, can be reduced or eliminated by ensuring that there is enough gray information in the original scanned image, and that the output device has sufficiently high resolution.

Most people can distinguish about 100 shades of gray: when shown a sample made of 100 small squares, ranging from pure white to pure black in one percent increments, each square will look slightly darker or lighter than the adjacent squares. Visual acuity decreases with age, however, and after the age of 40 most people can detect fewer than 100 distinct shades of gray.

One might therefore conclude that only 100 shades of gray are needed in a screened photograph in order to avoid banding, but it's not quite that simple. In most photos, the area of interest is in the middle tones, rather than in the highlights or shadows. As well, the eye perceives 100 shades in the specific area on which you focus. Therefore, to eliminate the banding problem, a photograph must contain at least 200 distinct gray steps between white and black.

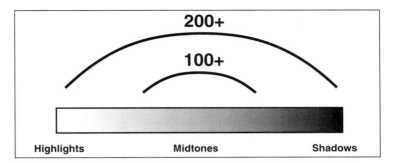

Figure 3-3
To avoid banding, we must capture at least 100 shades of gray in just the midtone area, and, therefore, need at least 200 shades between pure white and solid black.

To summarize: when creating halftones, whether through traditional photographic means or with computers, it is essential there be sufficient grays in the printed image to avoid banding. It is equally important to maintain detail in the image.

Scanning—creating pixels

Although halftoning is used only for output, digital halftoning is based on the zeros and ones inside a computer; it makes sense to begin with scanning, which determines how they get inside the computer in the first place.

In the desktop world, scanned images are usually stored as Encapsulated PostScript (EPS) files, or in the tag image file format (TIFF) invented by Aldus in collaboration with the major scanner manufacturers. To understand scanning, and its role in digital halftoning, let's build a TIFF file from scratch. This will not only help explain the origin of the zeros and ones, but will also help us understand why image files are so large, especially for color photos.

There are many different kinds of scanners, including flatbed, drum, and slide scanners, but for this exercise the scanner type doesn't really matter. To calculate the size of any scanned file, the first thing is to find the number of pixels in the image, which is determined by the image size and the scanning resolution.

Determining scanning resolution

It's essential to decide on the optimal scanning resolution *before* going anywhere near the scanner. Therefore, you need to know the final output size before you scan. If the scan resolution is too low, there will be too few pixels in the image and it will appear coarse and splotchy when printed. If the resolution is too high, the image file will be unnecessarily large, which can be a major obstacle to productivity.

Some color publishing novices scan all their images at the highest resolution available on their scanner, in the mistaken belief that the more data stored in the file, the better the image quality. The result is huge files that take forever to save, load, separate, and print.

The rule of thumb is that, for an image being reproduced size-as, the scan resolution (in *pixels per inch*, or ppi) should be twice the line screen (in *lines per inch*, or lpi) required for final output. Thus, if your commercial printer tells you that a 150-line screen will be used on press, the scan resolution for a photo being reproduced size-as should be approximately 300 ppi.

Photo: © PhotoDisc, Inc.

Figure 3-4
At a scan resolution of 72 ppi (left) individual pixels are obvious in this 32Kb image. At 300 ppi (center) the image is 224Kb and looks fine. Increasing the scan resolution to 600 ppi produces a 672Kb file but has a negligible effect on image quality.

So far, we haven't taken into account any difference between the size of the original and that of the final printed image. If the original is a 4-by-5-inch transparency that will be blown up to 8-by-10 inches on the page (a 2:1 scale factor), the scan resolution will also need to be doubled, in this case to 600 pixels per inch. This explains why the high-end drum scanners found in a professional color trade shop support scan resolutions in excess of 3,000 pixels per inch. For example, a 35mm slide that will be output as a 20-by-24-inch poster is being scaled up by a factor of 20:1 and thus needs to be scanned at 3,000 ppi.

The two-times rule is not carved in stone: many color publishers have found they can reduce this factor to 1.8, or even 1.6, without a noticeable degradation in the quality of output. If large files are slowing your system to a crawl, consider using a factor of less than 2.0 when calculating scan resolution.

To test this, simply scan the same image at a number of different resolutions, then append the test files to the back end of the next job you have printed. Keep detailed notes on all the variables used, and in a short time you'll develop a good sense of how low you can set the scan resolution before noticeably degrading image quality. Even a slight reduction in scan resolution can produce a significant increase in processing speeds. Decreasing the factor from 2.0 to 1.6, for example, results in a 36% reduction in file size and a corresponding increase in processing speed.

Calculating the image file size

In order to get a handle on the problem of color image file size, imagine that you have a full-page original photograph (8.5-by-11 inches), which must be scanned to be printed at actual size with a 150 line screen. From the formula above, it is clear that the scanning resolution will be 300 ppi, which is typical of many desktop scanning situations (where no enlargement is required).

In this example, each square inch of the original contains 90,000 pixels (300 times 300), and the original has an area of about 90 square inches (8.5 times 11), which means that the scanned file contains about 8 million pixels.

Now we're ready to calculate the file size. Rather than starting directly with color images, let's begin with a black-and-white logo, then move to a grayscale picture, and from there to a full-color image.

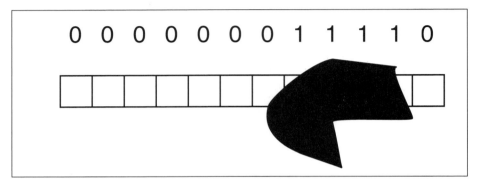

Figure 3-5
When scanning line art, each pixel captures a single bit of information and is represented as being black or white, even if it actually contains some shade of gray.

In the case of a black-and-white logo (or of any black artwork against a white background), each pixel is either black or white and can therefore be represented by a single *bit* (binary digit), a zero or one. There are eight bits in a *byte*, meaning that the 8 million pixels in the photo would require 8 million bits, which equals 1 million bytes, or 1 megabyte (Mb).

In the case of a black-or-white *bi-level* (black or white) scan, each pixel is represented by a single bit, either a zero or one, depending on whether the incident light striking that pixel had sufficient energy to go over the detector's threshold level. Bi-level scan files are very small, and therefore ideal for capturing type or logos consisting entirely of black and white (with no intermediate shades of gray). The problem with bi-level scanning is that it provides no way of representing shades of gray, and, thus, no way of creating color.

Pixel depth

With a grayscale photograph, using a single black or white bit for each pixel does not allow us to represent the many different shades of gray in the original. As shown above, the scanned image must contain more than 200 shades of gray in order to be perceived as having continuous tones.

Consider a scanner in which each pixel has "depth"—instead of generating a single bit, it can work with two or more bits per pixel.

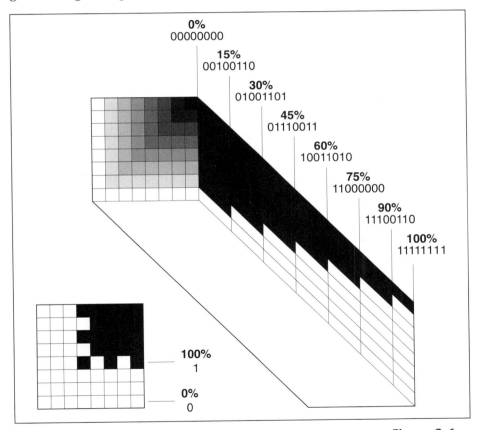

Figure 3-6
A grayscale photograph (containing 256 levels of gray) requires eight bits (one byte) for each pixel.

A scanner that can sense and transmit multiple bits per pixel can be used to capture grayscale information: increasing the number of bits greatly increases the number of shades of gray.

In any computer system, a single bit of data can represent only one of two possible states: on or off, zero or one, and so on. With two bits of data, four possible states can be represented: 00, 01, 10, and 11. Three bits of data can represent eight different states (000, 001, 010, 011, 100, 101, 110, and 111. With eight bits, we can represent 256 discrete states (in this case, 256 shades of gray).

Fig. 3-7	
Bits per pixel	Shades of gray
1	2
2	4
3	8
4	16
5	32
6	64
7	128
8	256

This concept, known as *pixel depth*, explains why we need one byte (eight bits) of data for each pixel, in order to capture 256 shades of gray. Now we're ready to calculate the file sizes for scanned grayscale photographs. A full-page photo contains 8 million pixels, and when scanned as a grayscale image will require 8 million bytes (one byte per pixel), or 8Mb.

To extend this concept from grayscale to color requires understanding of a crucial concept: a color photograph is simply a composite of three grayscale channels (red, green, and blue), or four grayscale channels (cyan, magenta, yellow, and black).

To confirm this, just look at a set of film separations—each of the cyan, magenta, yellow, and black films is actually a grayscale image. Another way of observing this is with a desktop imaging program such as Adobe Photoshop or Aldus PhotoStyler, which can display a color photograph as individual RGB or CMYK channels.

Figure 3-8
An RGB image file (shown in color on page 80) can be broken down into three grayscale channels: red, green, and blue (top, left to right). After being separated into a CMYK file, it consists of four grayscale channels: cyan, magenta, yellow, and black (bottom).

This leads to an inescapable conclusion: a full-page photograph containing 8 million pixels will require 24Mb when scanned as an RGB image (8Mb times three), and 32Mb when scanned in CMYK format (8Mb times four).

The example shows that even a relatively small photograph can fill a multi-megabyte file. Because most scanning software now shows the size of the proposed image file, you can change settings such as cropping, scaling, and resolution to modify the file size until it comes within acceptable limits. It also emphasizes why you need heavy-duty computing hardware for maximum productivity when working with color images, a topic we explore in detail in Chapter 5.

Figure 3-9
Each square inch of a
300 ppi image
contains more than
10Kb of data for a
bi-level black-or-white
scan; 90Kb for a
256-grayscale scan;
and 270Kb for a 24-bit
color scan.

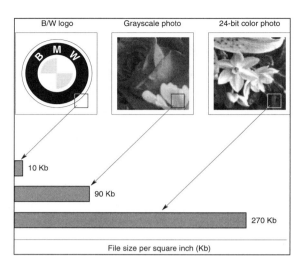

We can summarize the above results in table form. Using a 300 ppi image saved as an uncompressed TIFF file, the size of the file varies with the pixel depth of the image.

Bits per pixel	Image type	Shades of gray or colors	4-by-5" image (Mb)	8.5-by-11" image (Mb)
1	line art	1	0.2	1.0
4	grayscale	16	0.9	4.1
8	grayscale or color	256	1.8	8.2
24	color	16,777,216	5.3	24.7

That is also the reason color publishing with desktop computers can be so time-consuming. Traditional high-end prepress systems allow the operator to work with a low-resolution screen image in real-time, then apply any retouching or color correction commands to the high-resolution image in the background, while the operator goes on to the next task. By contrast, desktop color programs currently force you to work with huge image files all at once, which has a negative impact on productivity. However, some of the software innovations discussed in Chapter 7 will soon help address this problem.

Photographic halftones

The discovery of halftoning has greatly enriched human culture by enabling people, who would otherwise never have had the opportunity, to experience drawings, photographs, and paintings. Following the invention of photography in the 19th century, printers needed a simple way to mass produce photographic images. Prior to that time, books and newspapers contained illustrations in which shades of gray were represented by lines and cross-hatch patterns, which were engraved into the printing plates to create the illusion of shading.

Figure 3-11
A pen-and-ink sketch of typographic pioneer Frederick Goudy shows how cross-hatch patterns can be used to create simple gray shading without halftones.

In the 1860s and 1870s, many researchers worked on the concept of halftoning, which would enable the realistic reproduction of photographs in black-and-white and, much later, in color. Once the technical problems in halftoning began to be resolved, the technology took off. One of the earliest halftones was printed in the New York Daily Graphic in 1890, and within ten years halftones were commonplace in weekly newspapers.

Until very recently, halftones were created photographically with a specialized device called a graphic arts or *stat* camera. Light is projected through a sandwich consisting of a negative (of the original image) and a ruling screen (which converts the image into dots), and then exposes the high-contrast blank film underneath. The size of each dot on the film reflects the darkness or density of the image at that point in the original photograph.

Figure 3-12
A photographic halftone is created by placing a glass screen between the original negative and a piece of copy film (which will become the halftone), then shining light through them.

There are four properties of a halftone screen that are essential to quality color reproduction: *dot density*, *dot shape*, *screen angle*, and *screen frequency* (also known as *line screen*). By adjusting those variables, it is possible to create a variety of screen effects, from a coarse stubble for special effects to a fine gray fill that approximates the continuous tones of an original photographic print. As we shall see, these parameters govern both the conventional halftones created photographically and the newer digital halftones created with desktop computers and other electronic systems.

Dot density

The most fundamental characteristic of any halftone is its density—whether a specific area is dark or light. This is better understood by using the proper term, *dot area density*, which emphasizes the fact that in any given area, the density is that proportion covered by halftone dots. A midtone area, for example, has a density of about 50%, whereas a highlight area has a density of 10% or less, and the density of a shadow area is 90% or more.

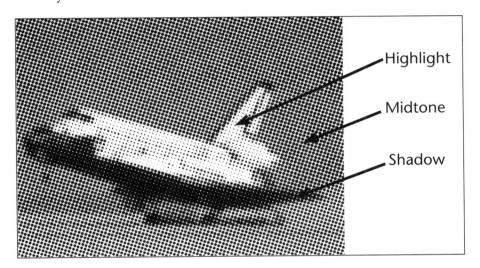

Figure 3-13
This close-up view of a halftone shows the difference between dots in the highlight, midtone, and shadow areas.

Densities are measured with a *densitometer*, a crucial instrument for process control in the prepress and printing industries. By measuring densities throughout the print production process, prepress and printing specialists can ensure that dot densities remain consistent from design to film to plate to final printed sheet.

Dot shape

The dots that make up a halftone can be any shape but, typically, they are elliptical or diamond. Why not use round halftone dots? The problem is apparent in any shadow area where round dots get bigger and bigger until they reach solid black. The result is that once the edges of the circles meet, they produce open spaces that look like little four-pointed stars. Under normal printing press conditions, these little stars tend to *fill in* with ink, creating shadow tones that are darker than they should be.

Figure 3-14
Round halftone dots tend to create shadow areas that are too dark, due to the filling in that occurs as the edges of the dots connect.

One solution is to create halftone dots that start out (in the highlight areas) as a circle, change to a square around 50% (in the midtones), and then become an open white circle on a black background (in the shadows). This modified dot shape is less likely to plug up in the shadows.

However, this improved dot shape still shares one problem with round halftone dots: as the square-shaped dot approaches the 50% point, all four corners connect with the corners of adjacent dots, creating a visual impression of a sudden increase in darkness, a phenomenon known as *optical jump*.

For many kinds of photographs, a better solution is to use elliptical dots, because as the ellipse increases in size the ends on the long side meet before the ends on the short side. This divides the optical jump into two parts, resulting in a smoother rendition of the gray scale. For this reason, images with important information in the midtones, such as photographs of peoples' faces, are often output with elliptical dots.

There's another reason for using other than round shaped dots: to create special effects, such as those made with line-shaped or cross-shaped dots. Custom dot shapes can be created with both traditional and electronic halftoning.

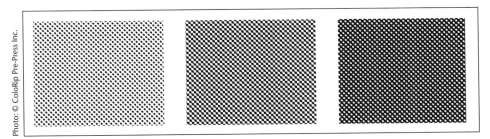

Figure 3-15
Elliptical halftone dots (shown here at 30%, 50% and 70%) are widely used because they tend to minimize midtone jump.

In the old days, creating custom dot shapes was simply a matter of using a special screen in the stat camera. Today, high-end prepress systems allow you to program the output device (film recorder) for different dot shapes, and virtually all desktop graphics and page layout programs let you specify the dot shape to be used on output.

Screen frequency

As you can see by examining any screened image through a magnifier, the halftone dots line up in rows, with a specific number of lines per inch (lpi). This number is the *screen frequency*, or *line screen*.

Screen frequency must be selected in accordance with the paper and printing conditions to be used for a given job. For example, most black-and-white newspapers are printed with a 75-line screen (75 lpi), with color newspapers printed at 90- to 100-line screens. Typically, color flyers and brochures are printed with 100- to 133-line screens, and most magazines and books with 125- to 150-line

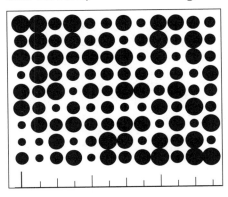

Figure 3-16
The screen frequency is the number of rows of halftone dots in each inch.

screens. Some high-quality magazine and book printing is done at screen frequencies of 200 lpi or higher, but 150 lines is about the maximum for most commercial printing.

Photo: © Michael Kieran

Figure 3-17
The quality of an image depends on the line screen at which it is printed, as shown by this photograph, reproduced at 75 lpi (left), 100 lpi (center), and 150 lpi (right).

The important thing to know about screen frequency is that it's up to your commercial printer to identify the optimal line screen for each print job. As a customer, all you need to do is follow their recommendation, and ensure your service bureau or other output service provides film with the correct screen values.

Don't be tempted to output your pages at a higher screen frequency, based on the idea that higher line screens mean better quality. The reason high-quality jobs can be run at higher screen frequencies is that they are printed on coated (glossy) paper stocks, which do not allow the inks to spread as much as uncoated stocks. Printing on newsprint with a 150-line screen is like writing on a paper towel with a fountain pen, and will simply cause the halftone dots to enlarge significantly (excessive *dot gain*), resulting in a noticeable loss of detail, especially in the darker parts of each image.

One problem with photographic halftones is that they can't be changed: a halftone produced as a 133-line screen for a magazine can't be converted easily to an 85-line newspaper screen. Attempting to photographically enlarge or reduce the image causes changes to the screen frequency and the halftone pattern breaks down. Enlarging it makes the dot pattern become apparent; reducing it makes the dark areas fill in and go black. The only option is to re-screen the image to the desired size and frequency.

Screen angles

The concept of screen angles is most easily understood by looking at any of the black-and-white photographs printed in this book. If all the halftone dots were lined up along the horizontal or vertical axis, the dots themselves would be immediately apparent, and would distract the eye from the content of the image. Therefore, for printing in black-and-white, the halftone screen is almost always rotated 45° from the horizontal, because this helps fool the eye into seeing the image itself, rather than the dots that make up the image.

Figure 3-18
Black-and-white halftones are usually printed at a 45° screen angle (left). If printed at 0° (right), the halftone dots would distract from the content of the image.

Although this works for black-and-white printing, early experiments with color printing showed that unsightly blotches, called *moiré patterns*, would occur whenever two halftones were printed on top of one another.

Moiré patterns are unsightly dark areas appearing in a regular grid in all or part of an image, especially in darker areas or in those, such as images of fabrics, already filled with patterns. They are caused by interference between the screens used in color printing, and can be minimized by carefully choosing and maintaining certain screen angles.

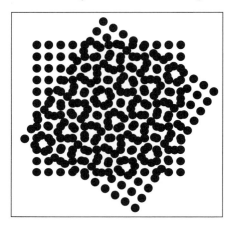

Figure 3-19
Moiré effects are coarse patterns caused by interference between halftone screens.

Early printers worked with three colors, and found the best results came from using screens that were offset from one another by 45°: yellow at 0° (along the horizontal), cyan at 45° to the right of the vertical, and magenta at 45° to the left of the vertical.

With four-color printing, however, the situation became somewhat more complicated. Extensive research has shown that when two or more screens overlap, the moiré effect is kept to an absolute minimum when the screens are precisely 30° apart from one another. But the screens can be rotated only through 90° (a 0° screen is the same as a 90° screen, at least for a round dot), which means that screens can be exactly 30° apart when printing only two or three colors, but not four.

If all four screens can't be 30° from one another, the next best thing is to have three offset from one another by 30° and the other offset by 15°. This results in the traditional color separation angles of 75°, 15°, 0°, and 45°, for cyan, magenta, yellow, and black respectively. Black, which is usually the most obvious color, remains concealed by being furthest from the horizontal and vertical axes.

Yellow, the lightest color, is printed precisely along these axes. To identify the orientation of elliptical or other non-round dot shapes, the 15° screen is sometimes expressed as 105°.

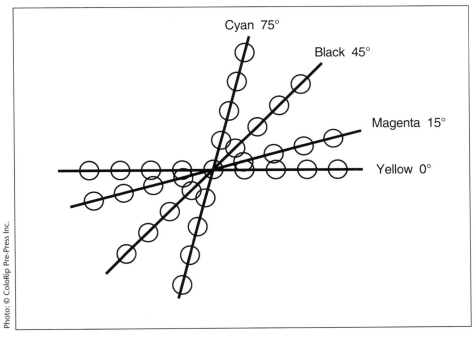

Figure 3-20
The conventional screen angles for process color separations are 75°, 15°, 0°, and 45°, for cyan, magenta, yellow, and black respectively.

A skilled color separator may change these default screen angles according to the content of a particular image. For example, in a fashion catalog consisting primarily of photographs of people, the accuracy of flesh tones is crucial. Because flesh tones often contain a large percentage of magenta, a savvy color separator may set the screen angles for the magenta film at 45° and the black film at 75°, reversing their normal values. However, unless you understand exactly what you're doing, don't mess with the default screen angles in your applications program or imagesetter.

Whenever the four process color halftones are laid on top of one another at different screen angles, they produce a pattern known as a *rosette*. There are two main kinds of rosettes: open-centered, in which the halftone dots form the perimeter of an empty circle, and dot-centered, in which the circle has a halftone dot at its center.

Digital halftones

Halftones are crucial to the world of electronic publishing because laser printers and imagesetters, like printing presses, are unable to reproduce shades of gray. But computers can't work with photographic dots; therefore we need to create an electronic equivalent of the photographic halftone: we need *digital halftones*.

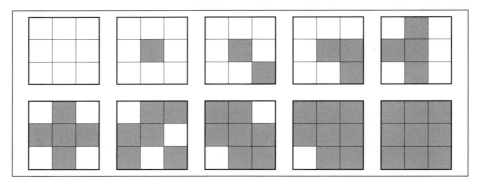

Figure 3-21
Digital output devices can't vary the size of a printer spot, so they group them together to create dots of various shapes and densities. The smallest addressable unit on a laser printer or imagesetter is a *printer spot*, and these spots must be combined to form digital halftone dots.

As we have seen, the four parameters that define a conventional photographic halftone are dot shape, screen frequency, and screen angle. The PostScript page description language provides operators that let you (or any PostScript application program) specify these same parameters when creating digital halftones. By turning on and off specific printer spots, the PostScript *spot function* tells the imagesetter how to create areas of varying density.

In most respects, PostScript is an excellent environment for working with halftone information, which is one reason for its success in the publishing industry. An important characteristic of PostScript is that its halftoning machinery operates independently of its scaling and rotating commands, so that gray-filled objects and halftoned images can be scaled and rotated without affecting their screen angle, frequency, or cell shape.

Throughout this book, we use the term *pixels per inch* (ppi) to describe the resolution of an input device, such as a scanner. However, when discussing monitors and output devices (printers and imagesetters), we use the more common *dots per inch* (dpi). As we explore digital halftoning, it's important to distinguish between the smallest addressable unit of an output device (a *printer spot*) and the larger entity (the *halftone dot*) formed by grouping together many printer spots. When an imagesetter is described as having a resolution of 2,540 dpi, we mean that it can create 2,540 printer spots per linear inch, and these spots can be grouped together to form halftone dots.

Dot density

Digital devices create halftones by grouping many printer pixels together to form a *digital halftone cell*. Switching on and off individual

 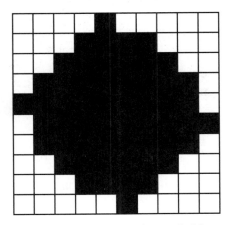

Figure 3-22
A halftone cell made of 25 printer spots can represent only 26 levels of gray (left), while a cell made of 100 spots can produce 101 levels of gray (right).

pixels within the halftone cell effectively changes the size of the dot, and hence the density of the halftone cell.

The more spots in the halftone cell, the more shades of gray can be attained. A group of 25 laser spots in a five-by-five matrix produces 25 different shades of gray, plus white (all pixels off). Turning on all the spots produces solid black; if one spot is off (white), the result is 96% black, and so on. Using a larger matrix of spots for the halftone cell makes it possible to create more shades of gray—a 16-by-16 matrix contains 256 spots and can represent 256 levels, plus white.

Dot shape

The fact that PostScript (and other electronic systems) generate halftone dots by grouping printer spots together means they can be used to create dots of virtually any shape. At the time the PostScript language was being created, developers at Adobe Systems thought that a halftone dot should be perfectly round, so that's the way they programmed it—as round dots that get bigger and bigger until they reach solid black. But they ran into the same problem with optical jump that had long plagued conventional halftones, so they went back to the drawing board and took another look at traditional photographic halftone dots.

Photo: © ColoRip Pre-Press Inc.

Figure 3-23
The PostScript spot function for 30%, 50% and 70% densities shows that the dots are round in the highlights and shadows, but square in the midtones.

The result was a modification to the PostScript spot function to create halftone dots that start out and end up round (in the highlights and shadows), but are square at 50%. As we have seen, this modified dot

Figure 3-24
PostScript lets you create halftone dots of virtually any shape, such as (clockwise from top left) elliptical, square, diamond or line. You will need a magnifier to see these shapes.

shape is less likely to plug up in the shadows, while continuing to provide smooth gradations of gray in the mid-tone regions.

By varying the spot function, you can create different shapes of halftone dots for special effects. With a little programming, even dots in the shape of tiny bow ties or windmills are possible.

Screen frequency

The inevitable trade-off in digital halftoning is that there are a limited number of gray tones that can be created for any combination of output resolution and screen frequency. A five-by-five halftone cell matrix output on a 300 dpi laser printer produces 60 cells per inch (300 divided by five) or a 60-line screen. But it results in only 26 gray levels (five times five, plus white), while the eye can detect more than 100 levels.

You have to print on an output device with higher resolution to get all the gray levels needed while maintaining a sufficiently high screen frequency. An imagesetter at 2,400 dpi, for example, can create a halftone dot with a 16-by-16 matrix to produce 256 shades of gray, with a screen frequency of 150 lines per inch (2,400 divided by 16).

To summarize, a high-resolution output device (such as an imagesetter) allows you to create digital halftones suitable for reproduction, while a low-resolution device (such as a desktop laser printer) requires trade-offs between screen frequency and the number of gray levels.

Screen angles

In most respects, creating digital halftones with PostScript (or any other electronic technology) is just as good as creating conventional halftones photographically—except, that is, for the screen angle problem. Screen angles may sound esoteric, but you don't need a graduate degree in mathematics to understand the difference between "rational" and "irrational" screen angles, let alone their significance.

We have already seen how all electronic devices, such as laser printers and imagesetters, create halftone dots by grouping together many individual printer spots. We've also seen that, unless the output device produces film separations with halftone dots at precisely correct screen angles, many images will be ruined by ugly moiré patterns. Fortunately, under the control of a clever screening program, an imagesetter can activate the appropriate spots to create almost any screen angle imaginable, thereby virtually eliminating the moiré problem.

The number of halftone cells per inch determines the frequency of a screen, while the rotation of the cell determines its angle. The calculations of a screen's angle and frequency take place in *device space*, which means that the halftone screen characteristics are dependent on the device resolution.

One of PostScript's strengths is its ability to produce seamless gray screens, in which each halftone cell is a matrix exactly the same size as its neighbor—each adjacent cell must tile *seamlessly* with its neighbors. However, at any given angle or frequency, especially at low resolutions, there are only a limited number of matrix patterns that will repeat seamlessly.

The halftoning mechanism allows a fixed set of screen frequencies and angles for a given device resolution; it is not always possible to reproduce a requested angle or frequency on the output device. The actual values used may be shifted in frequency or angle from those requested. Because the screen values used in color separation are sensitive to any slight deviation in angle, shifting often leads to moiré patterns. In fact, a variation of as little as 1/100th of a degree can produce visible moiré.

Selecting a particular screen angle affects the way the halftone cell interacts with the recorder grid. At some angles, such as 0° and 45°, the corners of each halftone cell intersect the grid at the corners of a spot. Each halftone cell, therefore, has the same shape and contains the same number of spots. These are the *rational* angles, so called because their tangent can be expressed as the ratio of two whole numbers—that is, as the ratio between the number of spots horizontally and the number of spots vertically.

The tangent of an angle is the ratio between the length of the opposite and adjacent sides. A rational number is one that can be expressed as the ratio of two whole numbers, or integers. An *irrational* number is a number such as π(pi), which starts with 3.14159 and continues for millions of decimal places without a repeating pattern. At irrational tangent angles, such as 15° and 75°, the corners of each halftone cell do not precisely fit on the recorder grid, resulting in halftone dots with variable shapes and number of spots.

These irrational tangent angles pose a serious problem. If we select a screen based on an irrational tangent angle, each dot description must be calculated individually, which requires a substantial amount of computing power. For the past 15 years, vendors of high-end color systems have taken this brute-force approach through specialized screening hardware that individually calculates the shape of each halftone dot.

This technology was invented at Hell Graphic Systems (now part of Linotype-Hell), and was licensed by most of the other major high-end prepress system vendors, including Scitex, Crosfield, and Dainippon Screen.

Desktop systems lack the horsepower to calculate different shapes for each halftone dot, so they make each dot the same shape (for a given set of film separations), although naturally the sizes of the dots vary. Unfortunately, this makes it impossible to ensure that the dots will align with the grid at all screen angles—in particular at such irrational tangent angles as 15° and 75°.

The original PostScript halftones—Adobe rational tangent or RT Screening—sought to minimize moiré by using screen angles and frequencies that approximate the conventional angles. Instead of generating the precise screen angle desired, RT Screening rounds the irrational tangent angle up or down to the nearest rational tangent angle. This ensures that all dot shapes are identical, and need only be calculated once.

Although RT screening is relatively fast, rounding to the nearest rational angle also forces you to modify the screen frequency, which can result in moiré and other quality problems. Indeed, unsightly moiré patterns caused by interference between overlapping screens are visible in many color separations produced with early PostScript-based systems, especially in the shadow tones or darker areas.

In 1989, after analyzing the mathematics of these interference patterns, Adobe was able to devise new halftone screen frequency and angle values that reduced moiré when printed. These new values, which were known as the Adobe *recommended RT* angles, use an unusual set of angles: the black and yellow screens stay at 45° and 0°, but the cyan and magenta move to approximately 71.5° and 18.5° respectively.

These new screening parameters were incorporated into existing PostScript Printer Description (PPD) files, which are used by applications and printer drivers to access specific features of a device, and to provide such printer-specific information as lists of built-in fonts. Many PostScript printers and all imagesetters have a PPD.

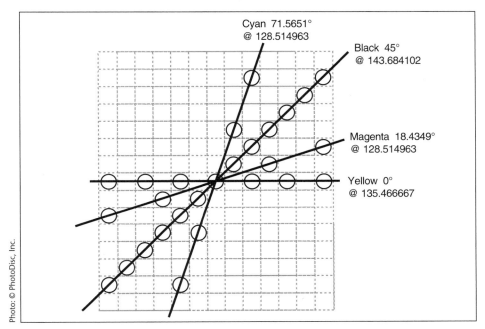

Cyan 71.5651°
@ 128.514963

Black 45°
@ 143.684102

Magenta 18.4349°
@ 128.514963

Yellow 0°
@ 135.466667

Photo: © PhotoDisc, Inc.

Figure 3-25
The Adobe Recommended RT angles force the screen frequencies of a
nominal 133-line screen to vary from 128 lpi to 143 lpi.

Although the Adobe-recommended RT angles reduced moiré, they
didn't come close to eliminating it.

Supercell screening

A much better solution to the screen angle problem was unveiled in
1992, when Adobe, Agfa, and Linotype-Hell, working independently,
arrived at the same conclusion: the best way to approximate irrational
tangent screen angles is to work with *supercells* consisting of hundreds
or thousands of individual digital halftone cells.

The new screening tools—HQS Screening (Linotype-Hell), Accurate
Screens (Adobe), and Balanced Screening (Agfa)—produce desktop
color separations of outstanding quality. In fact, they look great even
when compared side-by-side with output from high-end color
systems. During the past few years, each of the major imagesetter
vendors has released raster image processors (RIPs) that make use of
one or more of these supercell screening methods.

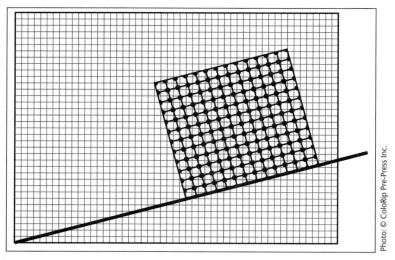

Figure 3-26
By creating a sufficiently large supercell, the Adobe accurate screen
algorithm can create a digital halftone screen of any frequency, precise
to a thousandth of a degree.

Supercell screening does not enable an imagesetter (or more precisely,
its RIP) to create the exact irrational 15° and 75° angles, but it allows
them to get much closer than was possible with previous kinds of
rational screening. With RT Screening, for example, the 75° angle is
typically rounded to 74.9°; with Accurate Screens it is rounded to
74.9998°. The screen angles created through the supercell method
are still rational, but they are much closer to the desired irrational
angles, which is why moiré is almost but not totally eliminated.

The degree of accuracy to which the requested values are achieved
is dependent mainly on the amount of memory available for their
use, although resolution is also an important factor. In PostScript
Level 2, the memory is managed dynamically, so that when memory
is not being used for halftoning, other parts of the system can use it.

Within a supercell, some individual halftone cells no longer fit
the grid precisely, resulting in dots with a variety of different shapes.
However—and this is the big however—every supercell begins with

a spot that is precisely on the grid, which means you can rotate the supercell into virtually any angle you want, simply by making the supercell sufficiently large.

This makes it possible to specify—and get—screen angles that almost perfectly match the traditional angles. Naturally, you pay a price in performance for the greater angular accuracy of a supercell—describing a supercell containing many halftone cells requires more calculations than describing a single halftone cell.

Performance issues

An interesting phenomenon occurred in conjunction with the introduction of supercell screening. The hardware in which screening takes place (the RIP) also improved, in particular through the use of integrated RISC (reduced instruction set computing) chips that significantly speed the rasterizing process.

The first PostScript RIPs from Adobe Systems were actually specialized computers—hardware RIPs. By contrast, virtually all of Adobe's competitors decided to create RIPs with software, which has now become the standard approach—so much so that Adobe itself now sells a software RIP, the Adobe Configurable PostScript Interpreter, or CPSI.

CPSI is a PostScript interpreter that original equipment manufacturers (OEMs) can incorporate into printers, imagesetters, color proofers, slide film recorders and other peripherals. It is available for a variety of hardware platforms, including Macintosh, Sun SPARC workstations, Windows-based PCs, and others. CPSI has been licensed by numerous peripheral vendors, including Agfa, DuPont, 3M, and Scitex.

The shift away from hardware RIPs has made it easier for RIP manufacturers to achieve performance increases simply by taking advantage of the ever-increasing speed of Macs, PCs, and UNIX-based machines, without needing to continuously rewrite their software. In fact, the increased speed of the new RIPs more than compensates for any additional calculation required to handle the supercells.

Hardware screening

To further increase the output speed of PostScript-based systems, Adobe has developed a coprocessor chip called PixelBurst that significantly accelerates the rendering of screened images for high-resolution imagesetters and printers. The rated engine speeds of network printers and imagesetters have increased dramatically in recent years, but often these devices can't run at their rated speeds because they cannot render images fast enough. A hardware-based screening accelerator such as PixelBurst can eliminate image rendering as a bottleneck in the printing process.

PixelBurst speeds things up by implementing in silicon all the functions required to render a display list (a list of PostScript commands from a PostScript interpreter) into a bitmap, ready to be sent to a marking engine. It can render screened images at up to 100 million pixels per second, with the result that a typical color image (such as the Musicians photograph used as a screening test in the Seybold reports) that normally takes more than 10 minutes to RIP can be processed in 62 seconds.

The problem with PixelBurst (at least in the minds of Adobe's competitors) is that it works only with RIPs based on Adobe's CPSI. To protect their markets, a number of RIP vendors are now developing various kinds of hardware accelerators. Following the introduction of Adobe's PixelBurst, a number of RIP vendors have shipped screening accelerators, including Harlequin, whose Harpoon product set new records for speed. Many other vendors, however, have continued to rely on the main processor for their screening calculations.

Halftone quality

Despite the fact that supercell screening has raised the bar defining a new standard of quality for desktop color output, designers and production people now argue about which new supercell method is the best.

In terms of quality, all the new supercell screening techniques eliminate most of the moiré problem, and all produce output that is markedly better than the familiar RT Screening. Beyond that, the "best" output must be a subjective assessment. I've looked closely at images output with many supercell screening systems at screens from 133 to 300 lines, and, in most cases, the quality is every bit as good as the best of the high-end systems.

The major difference between the three major supercell methods is that only Agfa's Balanced Screening uses pre-calculated screen descriptions to take some of the burden off the RIP. The other two major methods (Accurate Screens and HQS) require the RIP to calculate the description of each screen for each combination of imagesetter resolution and screen frequency.

With Agfa's system, once the matched screen sets are installed on your RIP (one for each combination of imagesetter resolution and halftone screen frequency), they can be applied at high speed during the screening process. Agfa Balanced Screening comes with a customizable software filter that intercepts screening setups from your applications programs, and automatically substitutes the appropriate sets of matched screen values.

Adobe and Linotype-Hell claim quality advantages for their systems, claims you'll need to assess yourself. Regardless of which method you choose, supercell technology is a significant step forward for color publishers working with PostScript-based systems, because it virtually eliminates the moiré problem. This removes one of the last few quality and productivity barriers between desktop and high-end prepress systems, forcing ever onward the rush to total desktop color.

Banding

There are other halftone quality issues that must always be monitored during the design and production process, including banding, dot gain, and dot distortion. One important quality issue concerns the problem of *banding* in graduated fills, a distracting effect in which distinct steps, rather than a smooth progression of shades, are visible.

Figure 3-27
The top rectangle contains a 4" blend from 20% black to 80% black in 39 steps, and shows obvious banding. The middle rectangle is the same blend with 124 steps (the optimal number). The bottom rectangle is the same blend with the maximum number of steps (256), which doesn't increase quality but can significantly increase the time it takes to output.

We have already seen the relationship between *dpi* (the spots per inch, or number of distinct spots that can be created on each linear inch of output), and *lpi* (the lines per inch, a measure of screen frequency). And we know that PostScript can produce only 256 shades of each of the process colors, but that there may be many fewer shades produced in a specific image, depending on the dpi of the output device and the lpi of the halftone screen.

For example, a 300 dpi laser printer generating a 75 lpi screen will produce 16 shades of gray (four times four), while a 2,400 ppi imagesetter generating a 150 lpi screen will produce 256 shades (16 times 16).

There are a variety of adjustments that can be made to minimize banding, including decreasing the distance or increasing the percentage of gradation, raising the output resolution, or lowering

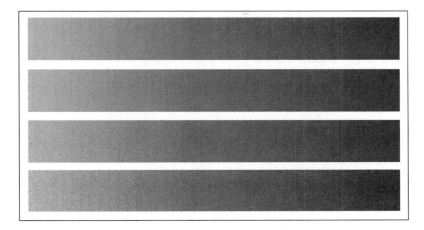

Figure 3-28
A 4" blend from 20% black to 80% black in 49 steps contains apparent banding (top). To eliminate banding, it has been imported into Photoshop, where the Noise filter has been applied with Gaussian distribution and a factor of 3, 6, and 9 (top to bottom).

the screen frequency. Alternately, you can use an imaging program to blend in a small amount of background noise, thus minimizing the banding effect.

To maximize quality and reduce banding in blends and fills, there are a number of factors that can be adjusted. For the best possible results, especially when blends and fills are an important part of an illustration:

- use a high-resolution output device (2,000 dpi or better), and use the highest available resolution when printing your files to take advantage of the maximum number of shades permitted by the available screen ruling;

- reduce the screen ruling to produce 256 shades of gray;

- increase the change in tint values between the beginning and ending tints in a fill, or reduce the distance over which the blend extends.

With blend functions that allow you to control the number of steps, there are two equations for finding the optimal number for producing smooth gradations. The number of tints available for a 0-100% color change equals the printer resolution (in dpi) divided by the screen frequency (in lpi). Multiplying this number by the desired percentage change in color identifies the optimal number of steps in the blend.

From these equations, you can conclude that:

- to take maximum advantage of the number of tints available, you must use a step for each tint;
- using more steps than there are tints available doesn't improve the look of the blend, but does increase the file size and, therefore, the print time;
- using an output device with higher resolution increases the number of tints available and, therefore, increases the potential smoothness of the blend;
- if you have control of screen frequency, increasing the frequency always decreases the number of tints available, thereby decreasing the potential smoothness of the blend;
- while decreasing the screen frequency increases the number of tints available, it also increases the coarseness of the printed artwork.

To sum up: at 2,400 dpi, you have access to 256 shades with a 150 lpi screen, which should be sufficient for most color work.

Dot gain

In any print production method, the size of the halftone dot is a decisive factor in determining the printing quality. As we have seen, the dot size is influenced by the halftone values for each specific area of the image, with highlight image areas being broken down into smaller dots, and dark image areas consisting of larger dots. When a dot is transferred first from the film to the printing plate, and then to the blanket, and finally to the printing stock, the dot size, and thus the halftone value, can be altered by a variety of factors.

These variations must always be anticipated and compensated for during the prepress process, or they will cause problems later for the press operator. *Dot gain* occurs when dots spread out as they are placed on paper, and always makes the printed piece appear darker than the film, usually by ten to 20%. (For example, a 50% dot will appear as a 60% or 65% dot.)

Dot gain varies from press to press, from web to sheet-fed, and with different kinds of paper and ink. It affects the midtones much more than the highlight or shadows—the tiny dots in the highlights are too small to show much increase in size, while the dots in the shadow areas already overlap. The solution is to deliberately make the negative films slightly lighter (less dense) than desired, especially in the midtones, knowing that dot gain will darken the printed piece.

Another kind of dot gain takes place as the film is exposed in the film recorder, because reflections within the film itself create a small halo around each dot. Many kinds of film now contain a thin *anti-halation* backing that minimizes this effect. Dot gain can also occur between the film and the plate, but trade shop technicians are responsible for detecting and minimizing such errors.

Dot gain is inevitable; the goal is not to eliminate it but to ensure that it is compensated for consistently. Color trade shops and commercial printers have traditionally allowed for dot gain by factoring it into the film proof, based on their knowledge of the particular press, paper, and other conditions for each printing job. In making the proof, they deliberately increase the size of the halftone dots to approximate the dot gain on press.

You can measure the effects of dot gain for any given combination of press, paper, and ink: commercial printers have books of charts and graphs on predicting dot gain. Some application programs, such as Photoshop, allow you to pre-compensate for dot gain by building a *transfer curve*. Be sure to check with your printer before pre-compensating for dot gain; otherwise their production people will have a difficult time printing your excessively light negatives.

Also, despite the fact that a number of graphics and imaging programs allow you to customize the transfer function, you're best off not tinkering with it in an application unless you have a clear understanding of the density effects on your output.

Dot distortion

Unlike a conventional photographic halftone, the appearance of PostScript halftone dots depends on the quality of the printer spots of which they are made—on whether the edges of each dot are hard or soft. A hard dot provides a more precisely defined area—a sharper image—than a soft one, at least in theory.

The concept of a hard versus soft dot was intensely debated 20 years ago, when many people proposed a hard dot because they felt it was essential to any attempt to calibrate different devices. However, the soft dot proponents won the battle because of technical limitations in the imaging hardware, and because the soft dot acts to soften the edge of lines and curves found in type, and can be more easily adjusted through dot etching.

But the technology has advanced significantly in 20 years. With continuing innovations in the PostScript language and in imagesetter film and laser technologies, the quality of PostScript spots—and, therefore, PostScript halftones—continues to improve. For example, early PostScript imagesetters created a spot about 20 microns in diameter, while the newer imagesetters create one less than eight microns across. The result is that PostScript halftones typically have a harder dot than conventional photographic halftones.

In addition to dot gain and hardness, there are many other dot variations on press that can affect printing quality, including:

- *filling in*, the reduction of non-printing areas in the shadows until they disappear completely;
- *sharpening*, a decrease in the size of halftone dots;
- *slurring*, a distortion in the shape of halftone dots from circles into ovals, caused by relative motions between the printing plate and rubber blanket, or between the blanket and the press sheet;
- *doubling*, the appearance of a shadow halftone dot, adjacent to the regular printed dot, resulting from the ink on the dot being transferred by the rubber blanket.

Such variability can be controlled only by checking the press during the make-ready process, and taking densitometry readings for each process color. As the run continues, the press operators are responsible for ensuring there are no dot gain, slur, doubling, or other distortions.

Many of these problems can be minimized or eliminated by a skilled press operator, though there are some quality problems that can't be solved, even after many adjustments and proofs. Given exactly the same CMYK data, for example, every printing company will produce slightly different results because of variations in paper, inks, temperature, and humidity, among other factors. The best way to minimize these variations is by constant reference to an approved proof.

Stochastic screening

Just as the brouhaha about rational and irrational screening seems to be fading to a dull roar, along comes something completely different to once again alter the screening landscape—*stochastic* screening.

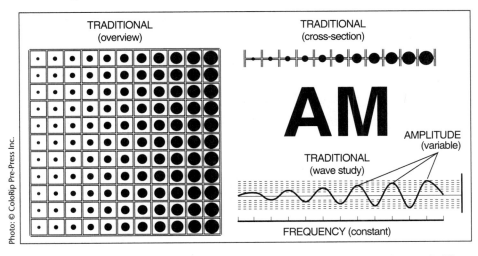

Figure 3-29
Conventional halftone screens are "amplitude modulated": their frequency remains constant while the amplitude (size) of each dot varies.

The word "stochastic" is from the Greek and means "to aim", and is meant to convey the sense of screening in which the halftone dots appear to be randomly placed, rather than forming regular rosettes.

As we have already discussed, conventional halftone screening uses variable-size dots arranged in rosette patterns at precise screen frequencies, with dot sizes changing in proportion to the tone value of the original image. By contrast, stochastic screening uses very, very small *microdots* of uniform size (typically 15 to 20 microns in diameter) varied in number per surface area, or frequency, according to the tone value to be reproduced. These microdots are thus *frequency modulated*, which is why this technology is commonly called *FM screening*.

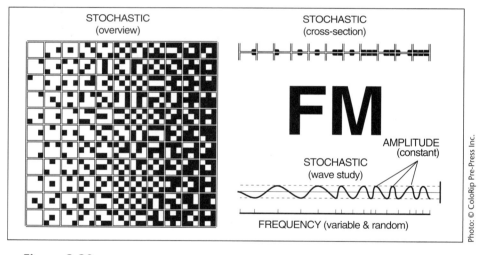

Figure 3-30
Stochastic halftone screens are "frequency modulated": their amplitude (size) remains constant while the spacing (frequency) of dots varies.

The pseudo-random arrangement of the microdots totally eliminates moiré patterns—and screen angles. You can get a better idea of the qualitative differences between conventional and FM screening by closely examining the color photographs reproduced on page 87.

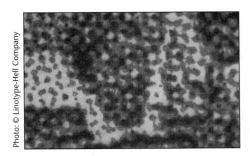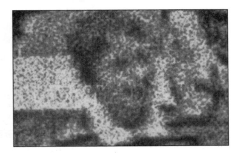

Figure 3-31
Unlike the dots of varying size found in a conventional halftone (left), a stochastic halftone (right) is made of many small dots, all the same size, which appear to be randomly distributed.

Both Linotype-Hell and Agfa have developed products based on FM screening. According to Linotype-Hell, their stochastic Diamond Screening "produces quality virtually equal to that of continuous-tone photographic prints." It is available as an option on their RIP 50 and RIP 60 products. Agfa makes similar claims for its product, which is called CristalRaster screening.

FM screening has the potential to reduce file sizes by one-third to one-half, with correspondingly shorter RIP times, which would prove to be a significant boon for designers, service bureaus, color trade shops, and commercial printers.

Commercial printers like FM screening because the apparently random placement of microdots provides greater contrast without loss of shadow detail. Also, tonal range is improved, and higher ink densities make for better detail rendition and color saturation. The press operator has more tolerance in setting plate registration, because there are no screens to align. This allows more time to be spent on printing and less on shifting line screens, adjusting ink levels, and cleaning blankets.

Another advantage of FM screening is a reduction in dot gain, especially in the midtones, because the small microdots spread out less than conventional halftone dots. The problem of optical jump in the midtones also disappears. Moreover, an image printed with FM screening can be rescanned without a degradation of quality, which is impossible with conventional halftones. The major problems in printing with frequency modulated screens are in proofing and platemaking, both of which can be challenging because of the tiny spots. However, many printers are solving these problems and taking advantage of the benefits of FM screening.

There are two main application areas for FM screening. The first is in the reproduction of high-quality images of problematic fabrics (such as silks and herringbone tweeds), detailed textures, regularly repeating backgrounds, and geometric designs that may cause interference patterns.

The other potentially important application for FM screening is in the emerging technology of *high-fidelity* color publishing (printing with more than four process inks), discussed in detail in Chapter 10. Because FM screening does not involve screen angles, it eliminates the moiré problems that would occur when printing five or more process colors on top of one another.

Indeed, over the next few years, FM screening could become an essential technology for color publishing. Although still in its infancy, it holds the potential to reduce the size of color image files while increasing their quality.

Color Management

"Colors seen by candlelight
Will not look the same by day."
Elizabeth Barrett Browning

 o other aspect of publishing is as simple, but as complex, as *color management*—matching colors between an original image, scanner, monitor, color printer, and final press sheet.
In theory, color management is simple: the colors in the final printed piece either match those in the original image, or they don't. In practice, however, it's quite complex, because of differences in the color models, colorants, and devices employed at every stage of the print production process. The problem is especially acute with color photographs, because the human eye is intolerant of colors that are off, especially the *memory colors* of food, trees, water, and above all, flesh tones.

Prior to the emergence of desktop publishing, color management wasn't much of a problem, because vendors of high-end systems calibrated their hardware and software at the factory through *color look-up tables* that compensated for the characteristics of each input, display, and output device. These tables are sufficiently accurate that, with practice, people in the prepress industry can get a rough idea of what the final printed sheet will look like, based on the colors displayed on a monitor. But high-end prepress vendors are able to use look-up tables only because they build or integrate all the components in the system.

Today, most publishers work with "open systems" containing components from a variety of vendors, and color management requires much more attention and coordination. In this chapter, we look at the hardware and software tools available for desktop color management, and how to use them to achieve consistent, predictable color throughout the design and production process. We also focus on the crucial issue of how RGB images get color separated into their CMYK components.

WYSINAWYG

In theory, desktop publishing is based on a concept called WYSIWYG: What You See Is What You Get. What you see on screen is supposed to be what you'll get on the printed page. In practice, especially when working in color, desktop publishing is full of surprises: What You See Is Not Always What You Get (WYSINAWYG). In fact, in some cases, what you see is not even close to what you get.

How you solve this problem depends, in part, on whether you're working with spot or process color, and whether your documents contain only colored type and synthetic art (from such programs as Adobe Illustrator and FreeHand), or full-color photographs.

Matching spot colors

When working with spot colors only (rather than process-color photographic images), your best bet is to completely ignore the colors on the monitor or desktop color printer. Instead, simply specify all colors from a swatch book, such the PANTONE MATCHING SYSTEM.

Your commercial printer will refer to a similar swatch book when pre-mixing the specified spot colors, so you can be assured of a pretty close match: the printed colors are automatically "calibrated" to your design without regard to the RGB values used by the display monitor. Note, however, that the swatch colors will change considerably as they age, particularly with exposure to bright light, making it prudent to purchase a new swatch book every few years.

Better still, create your own swatch book, using the same combination of display, output device, and printing press as for your final output. Tape it next to the monitor for comparison, so that the screen rendition gives a general impression of how the colors look on the two devices.

Remember, the PANTONE MATCHING SYSTEM and similar color matching systems are based on unique ink colors and, therefore, are limited to use in spot-color printing. In spot-color printing, a specific ink is formulated to create each color, rather than the full-color printing done with the cyan, magenta, yellow, and black process inks. Spot colors are not used for reproducing full-color photographs, except for the "touch plate" high-fidelity technique discussed in Chapter 10.

Matching process colors

One of the major challenges in color publishing is ensuring that the colors in an original photograph can be rendered accurately on a computer monitor, then output with equal fidelity to a desktop color printer and (in most cases) ultimately to a printing press.

In many design studios, the people creating drawings and page layouts spend most of the day staring at a computer monitor, so everything else must be made to match the monitor. The situation is somewhat different when color photographs are involved, because the key concern becomes matching the monitor, proof, and final output to the original picture.

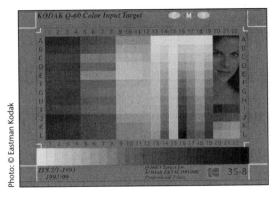

Photo: © Eastman Kodak

Fig. 4-1
Color calibration tools, such as an ANSI IT8 target or this Kodak Q-60 target, can improve your chances of getting the colors you want on press.

When working with synthetic art (drawings created in such programs as FreeHand, Adobe Illustrator, and CorelDRAW), process color swatch books can be a useful tool for attaining the correct colors in the final offset printed piece. Agfa, for instance, sells a $25 process color swatch book that shows thousands of four-color combinations.

As with spot color swatch books, the key is to completely ignore the colors displayed on the monitor. If you're drawing a landscape with a blue sky in the background, simply choose the desired shade of blue from a swatch book, being sure to use a book printed with the same kind of paper (coated or uncoated) planned for your publication. The swatch book will list the CMYK components for each color: a dark sky blue, for instance, might consist of 80% cyan, 20% magenta, and 10% black (with no yellow). In the drawing program, create a custom color with these CMYK percentages and apply it to the sky. Regardless of what the color looks like on the monitor, the color on the final printed sheet should closely match that in the swatch book.

Color matching becomes much more problematic when you're reproducing full-color photographs. There are three main reasons why it can be difficult—and in some cases impossible—to match colors on the printed page with those on the monitor:

- First, there is the variation between the colorants used in the monitor and those used for printing. A monitor creates colors with red, green, and blue *phosphors*. A printed page, by contrast, creates colors with *inks*, *dyes*, *toners* or *waxes*. Different colorants have different spectral properties, and will not look the same, especially under a variety of lighting conditions.

- Second, computer monitors create radiant light: colors are created when electrons from an electron gun strike colored phosphors on the inside of the cathode ray tube, causing them to emit red, green, and blue light. By contrast, printed colors are perceived by reflected light, as photons from the illuminating source (such as a lamp or the sun) are selectively absorbed by the colorants on the page, with the remainder reflected back to the observer. The human eye interprets radiant and reflected light differently, so colors on the monitor will not precisely match those on the page.

◆   Third, computer monitors operate according to the RGB color model, but printers use either the CMY or CMYK model (sometimes both, as in the case of thermal wax printers that can be used with either three-color or four-color ribbons), and printing presses are CMYK devices. These different color models have vastly different *gamuts*: there are many RGB colors that cannot be accurately recreated in the CMYK model, and vice versa.

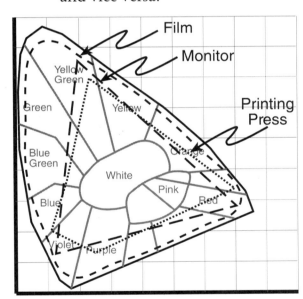

Fig. 4-2
The eye perceives much more tonal information than can be captured on film. A printing press can reproduce tones impossible on a monitor, and vice versa.

In fact, reproducing color photographs is always an exercise in tonal range compression, or *gamut mapping*. The original scene contains colors not captured on film, the film contains colors not captured by the scanner, and the scanned image contains colors that can neither be displayed on screen nor printed on paper.

Because of these factors, there are two distinct parts to the color-matching problem. First, some colors can be created on one device but not the other. Second, when the monitor colors can't be matched exactly, there must be some way for the printer to produce the closest possible color.

A great deal of research has gone into developing *color management systems*—software that mediates between the representation of color on different devices.

Calibration and characterization

Color management tools help you match colors between different devices (where exact matching is possible), map out-of-gamut colors into those that can be produced on a specific device, and provide previews of out-of-gamut colors so you can take corrective action.

There is a key distinction at the heart of the color management process—the difference between *calibration* and *characterization*. Every input and output device is unique, and even two devices made by the same manufacturer will have slightly different responses to the same signal. Two monitors, for instance, when provided with the same set of RGB values, will interpret those signals differently to produce slightly different colors on screen.

To calibrate a device, therefore, means to *normalize* its responses so that it produces a predictable color from a specific set of input values. This means that devices have to be recalibrated whenever operating parameters change or to compensate for internal changes, such as a monitor's "drift" as its phosphors fade over time.

When "calibrate" is used in this way, it makes no sense to talk about calibrating a monitor to a printer. A monitor can be calibrated only to itself.

To correlate colors across multiple devices, we need a new concept—*characterization*. To characterize a device is to build a mathematical model that represents the entire color gamut and distortion of that device (or type of device), relative to a defined reference. A device characterization, or *device profile*, can then be combined with color conversion and gamut tools to form a comprehensive color management system.

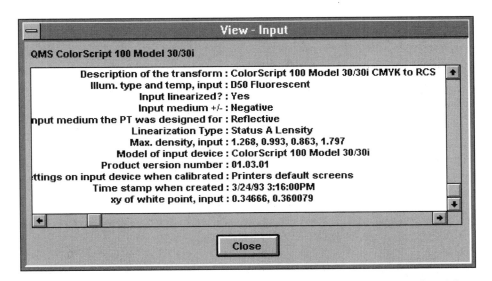

Fig. 4-3
A device profile contains data on the color rendering properties of a particular kind of input or output device, such as this profile for a QMS ColorScript 100 printer.

Calibration *normalizes,* or makes a device linear, and generally refers to the color response of a specific device, whereas characterization usually refers to a class of devices. Thus you would calibrate your specific GonzoPrint color printer to ensure it produces the appropriate colors for any input signal, but you would require a device characterization (which is identical for all GonzoPrint printers of the same model) in order to achieve color correspondence between your scanner, monitor, and printer. Calibration, therefore, takes place *before* color management.

Until recently, characterizing a device required expensive scientific equipment, which meant that desktop publishers could calibrate their equipment but not create custom device profiles. This is beginning to change, with some color management systems now including tools that allow end users to create their own custom profiles. In fact, it is now possible to create a device profile for a specific device, rather than for a class of devices.

Monitor calibration

Because the monitor is the peripheral through which most publishers make decisions about color accuracy, it should be the first component calibrated. The keys to calibrating a monitor are to set the *gamma* and *white point.*

A monitor's gamma is a measure of the response curve of each of the red, green, and blue channels, from black to full intensity. Typical gamma values for color monitors are in the range from 1.8 to 2.2. Actually, each of the RGB channels has a separate gamma response, but most systems use a single averaged value.

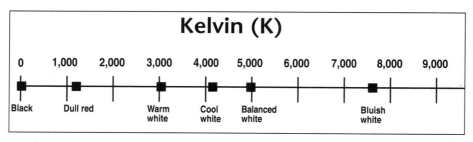

Fig. 4-4
As color temperature increases along the Kelvin scale, colors change from black through red to various shades of white.

The white point of a monitor is the color of white produced when all three color channels (red, green, and blue) are at full intensity. It's specified as a *color temperature*, measured on the Kelvin scale, with images getting bluer as their temperatures rise. The North American prepress industry has agreed on standard viewing conditions of 5,000K (approximately the color temperature of daylight at noon), while color television sets (and the European prepress industry) work on 6,500K, and many computer monitors have relatively high (bluish) white points between 8,000K and 9,500K.

To improve color correspondence between the screen and printed artwork or proofs, set the white point of your monitor to match the color temperature of the ambient light in which you view the artwork. When working with multiple monitors, be sure that all are set to the same white point, otherwise some will look distinctly more blue or orange than others.

If the monitor is being adjusted to match printed output, its white point will often be reduced to approximately 5,000K to match paper white. However, this reduces the intensity of the signal sent to the electron guns, and therefore can reduce the monitor's dynamic range. Some vendors, such as SuperMac and Barco, make monitors with a 5,000K white point.

Photo: © Radius

Fig. 4-5
A photometer connects to your monitor and computer to ensure that a specific set of RGB values produces the correct color.

For precise monitor calibration, you'll need a display calibrator, such as those made by Radius, RasterOps, and SuperMac. These devices contain a light detector, or *photometer*, which attaches to the monitor with a little suction cup and measures the intensity of the light emitted by the monitor. More expensive calibrators contain a *colorimeter* and can measure the *chroma* of each channel, in addition to the luminance.

The photometer and its accompanying software are used to measure the light output from the display so you can adjust the color temperature and gamma settings to achieve specific design objectives, or to calibrate with monitors in another location. The color temperature controls allow you to compensate for lighting conditions, while gamma control permits improvements in the display of scanned images so that shadows and details appear more accurately on screen.

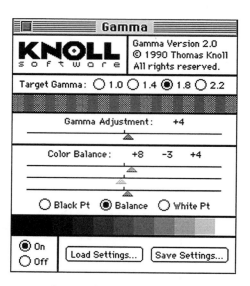

Fig. 4-6
The Gamma control panel that comes with Adobe Photoshop lets you set the gamma, color balance, white point, and black point for your monitor.

Some applications programs provide rudimentary monitor calibration tools that do not require the use of a photometer. The Macintosh version of Adobe Photoshop, for instance, comes with software for setting the gamma, color balance, and white and black points of your monitor. If you have a third-party monitor calibration utility installed, you should use either that utility or the Photoshop software, but not both. Your calibration utility will update Photoshop's color space descriptor file, although you will still need to enter the gamma, white point, and phosphor type in the Gamma text box within Photoshop's Monitor Setup dialog box.

One other important point regarding monitor calibration: the appearance of any image on screen will be strongly influenced by the ambient lighting in the room. In general, as the ambient lighting gets brighter, the effective gamut of the monitor decreases. For consistent color matching, viewing conditions must be standardized prior to calibrating the monitor. (If you want to get really picky, you could worry about differences in color perception caused by the color of clothing worn by different observers. To minimize these effects, I recommend doing color publishing in a dark room while wearing no clothes.)

Photo: © Barco Graphics

Fig. 4-7
Proper color management requires both a calibrated monitor (such as the Barco Reference Calibrator display at left), and a 5,000K light source (right).

Once you have calibrated your monitor, it should need to be recalibrated only when conditions change (such as the room lighting or the monitor's brightness and contrast settings), or every month or so as its phosphors drift. It's a good idea to tape down your monitor's brightness and contrast controls after calibration, and maintain consistent lighting conditions. The latest generation of monitors incorporate a microprocessor, which can facilitate easier and more accurate calibration.

Scanner calibration

Calibrating a scanner is somewhat different from calibrating a monitor or printer, because there is little, if anything, that can be done to adjust the scanner's color response. The separation filters inside a scanner tend to be rather stable over time, so the chromatic component of a scanner's color characteristics do not change much. Scanner calibration therefore usually consists of scanning a gray wedge (a neutral density step target) and then updating the scanner's linearity correction lookup tables.

Among the most popular scanner calibration programs is Savitar ScanMatch. It consists of a target (available for both flatbed and slide scanners), plus software that creates a scanner profile precisely tuned to your specific scanner's color characteristics. The profile can then be used to optimize future scans so that the image displayed on the monitor automatically matches, as closely as possible, the original artwork.

Fig. 4-8
The Savitar ScanMatch scanner calibration package is based on a Pantone color target.

ScanMatch comes with a Pantone scanner calibration target that is optimized for calibrating scans of four-color artwork, and there are a variety of optional enhancements available, including calibration kits for photographic prints, transparency scanners, Photo CD images, and desktop printers. ScanMatch runs on any Macintosh computer, and is compatible with Photoshop and with Apple ColorSync (discussed in detail below). It has also been licensed to Electronics for Imaging as part of the EfiColor Works package.

The other popular approach to scanner calibration is the *adaptive calibration* method developed by Light Source as part of its OFOTO product. Adaptive calibration eschews the use of factory default device profiles, and works instead by having you calibrate your scanner to your printer through a closed-loop "scan-back" process. Be aware, however, that such "point to point" calibration is not the same as a complete color management system.

The first step in adaptive calibration is to print on your desktop color printer a digitally generated image file containing an array of color patches. If the final output device is a printing press, a color proof must be made from the digital target. The printed target is then scanned back into OFOTO using a flatbed color scanner. OFOTO then compares the pixel values in the original target with those in the scanned image in order to create a correction transform, or pair-wise calibration, between the scanner and printer combination. OFOTO is explored in further detail in Chapter 6.

Imagesetter calibration

The final component to be calibrated is the imagesetter, a task that, for many desktop publishers, remains the responsibility of people working in a service bureau, color trade shop or commercial printing environment. (An imagesetter is a high-resolution laser printer that creates output on photographic media such as film, resin-coated paper or plate material.)

As discussed in the previous chapter, the output from an imagesetter consists of pixels grouped together into *halftone dots*. The key concept is that the overall size of these dots on film (the dot area density) must closely match the density specified within an applications program.

To calibrate an imagesetter is to *linearize* it—that is, to adjust it so that it produces an absolutely straight line of gray values from the brightest highlight to the darkest shadow tone. A tint area specified as a 39% gray in an application program, for example, must produce a halftone dot area density of 39% on film.

Fig. 4-9
The diagonal line represents an ideal imagesetter with a linear response. The curve below it is from an uncalibrated imagesetter, and the bottom curve shows the correction that must be added in order to produce a linear response.

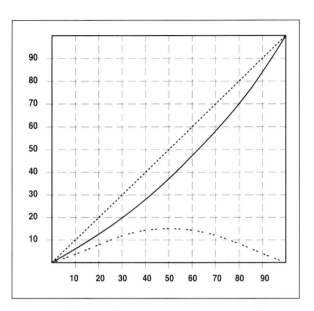

To interpret film output, you will need a densitometer capable of working in both transmission mode (with transparencies and output films) and reflection mode (for hard-copy originals and press sheets). To begin, you must find the optimal exposure setting that will give the necessary densities without creating severe halftone errors.

Most imagesetters have an exposure test, which creates a page composed of lines generated with different intensity settings. The service bureau technicians will run this page through the processor, and measure the results with a densitometer in order to decide on the optimal exposure for a given type of emulsion. Every time a test page is run, it is annotated as required and filed. You should run a test page every time you change a significant variable, such as media, chemistry or prep files.

Calibration will be effective only after the other parts of the system, such as the photo processor, have been stabilized. If dot densities are more than 5% off the required values, it makes no sense to begin the calibration process, because you are locking on to an unstable target. Once an imagesetter has been calibrated, it should not have to be reset until there is a change in some other part of the system. Calibration, when done properly, is a "set it and forget it" process, except when any technical parameter changes.

Please note that linearization is usually achieved through a set of PostScript commands called a *transfer function*. Therefore, even though some desktop color applications programs allow you to directly alter the transfer function, you are best off leaving it alone.

Many service bureaus and color houses use full-function imagesetter calibration programs, such as the Precision imagesetter calibration program sold by Kodak, or Color Calibration Software for PostScript Imagesetters, developed by Michael Thorne of Technical Publishing Services (TPS).

Kodak Precision generates mathematically correct calibration tables for permanent storage on the RIP, which allows the user to define the uncalibrated screen percentages and enter them into the Precision table. Using the data, Precision builds and stores the calibration tables specific to each line screen, resolution, and media type. Because the tables are stored on the RIP, it automatically selects the correct table based on the specific job being processed. Another significant advantage of RIP resident calibration is a linearization utility that corrects compatible software applications without intervention, optimizing the output device for any data sent to it by the application.

The other main competitor in this category is the TPS Color Calibration Software for PostScript Imagesetters (CCSPI), which is based on a test page that you print on an imagesetter, then measure with a densitometer. The software computes the required correction curve and installs the appropriate transfer table in the imagesetter, thereby ensuring that output from all your applications will be correct. It can hold all halftone screens to within 1% of the value requested by your applications programs, thus ensuring optimal results on press.

The test page lets you measure your imagesetter's performance against a wide range of variables. You might find, for instance, that you get a completely different densitometer response on paper than on film. Or you might find that the response varies according to the imagesetter's resolution, the halftone dot shape or the screening method used. The CCSPI package allows you to adjust the system's response to changes in any of these variables.

In order to maximize performance, CCSPI pre-computes the transfer table, and directly supports a variety of densitometers through the imagesetter's serial port. It also provides independent control of page geometry (essential for flexographic printing) and dot gain (for accurate color reproduction under different printing conditions).

Innovation in Colorimetry

One of the most challenging aspects of color management is that, until recently, it has been very difficult to measure colors precisely. Precise color measurements can be made with a spectrometer, but these instruments typically cost $10,000 or more and require a trained professional to produce good results.

Light Source Computer Images, a small California company that makes the OFOTO scan control program, has introduced a revolutionary new device, Colortron, that provides fast, inexpensive color measurement. Colortron is a hand-held device that can be used as a spectrometer, film densitometer, monitor calibration device, and light meter. About twice the size of a mouse, Colortron attaches to the ADB port of a Mac or serial port of a Windows-based PC, and captures 32 bands of spectral data (each slice only 10 nanometers wide), which it displays on screen as a unique curve for each color.

Colortron has a 3mm aperture through which the color target is illuminated by an internal light source and measured. The Colortron device itself is pretty cool, but the software that comes with it is really amazing. These tools allow the graphic artist, color production worker or prepress operator to view a captured color or its spectal signature on screen, view a readout of the color measurement as described in various color models (such as RGB and CIE), view the color as it would appear under a wide variety of lighting conditions or against different colored backgrounds, search through Pantone libraries to display the nearest Pantone spot or process color, or instantly create a custom Pantone ink or textile formula to match.

A variety of interchangeable attachment heads allow reading of self-luminous targets, such as light from a monitor, density of film emulsion or ambient light in any environment. By using spectral information to describe color and communicate it throughout the design and production process, Colorton helps you focus on your intent, and leaves the technical details of color matching to the computer. Colortron cost less than $1,000.

Device-independent color

Once every peripheral device has been calibrated, you're ready to build relationships between them that will help ensure the best possible color correspondence. That's the job a color management system is designed to perform: to ensure that colors match as closely as possible between different devices such as scanners, display monitors, color printers, and printing presses. Therefore, a color management system must be built around a color model that is device independent.

To be useful as a standard, a color model must also be convertible to other standard color systems, translate easily to and from the device-dependent color models used by peripherals, and provide an intuitive user interface so that both color novices and professional graphic artists can select colors with ease.

All input and output devices are based on device-dependent color models, such as the RGB or CMYK models. This means that a given set of CMYK values sent to two different printers (even two from the same vendor) will produce different colors on the printed page. In order to translate between these different models, virtually all modern color management systems are based on the CIE series of device-independent models devised by the Commission Internationale de l'Eclairage.

The CIEXYZ version of the CIE model and its derivatives (CIELAB and CIELUV) are device-independent because they're defined without reference to a particular display or output technology. Until recently, there was a great deal of controversy within the desktop color industry about which color models are most important for color matching, but the dust is beginning to settle, and the consensus seems to be that both CIE and RGB models will remain important for the foreseeable future.

Most computer users want to work with the colors displayed on the monitor, and have the software take care of problems in printing those colors. Therefore, RGB will continue to be important as a device-dependent way of dealing with different display monitors. At the same time, the systems software and applications programs will exchange color information using the CIE color model. Rather

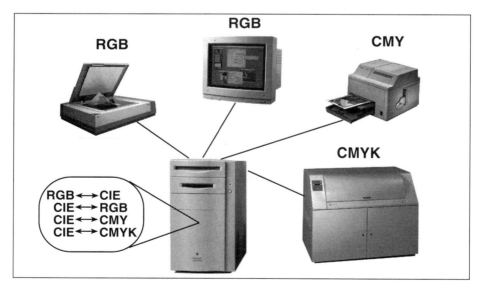

Fig. 4-10
Although CIE is the standard model for exchanging color information between peripherals, the devices themselves continue to rely on RGB or other device-dependent models.

than converting RGB data into CIE format, then converting the CIE data to CMYK, most color management systems use CIE as a *reference color space*, and convert directly from RGB to CMYK.

Although there are some limitations to the CIE model, virtually all the major players in the desktop color industry now agree that it is the best choice as the standard color model for device-independent color management. In fact, the CIE model (or one of its variants) forms the basis for the color management solutions proposed by Adobe, Agfa, Apple, EFI, Kodak, Microsoft, and others.

Color management systems

Color management systems adjust the color relationships between scanners, monitors, printers, imagesetters, and printing presses to ensure consistent color throughout the print production process.

The key question in color management is whether you can trust that the colors you see on the monitor or in the output from a desktop printer faithfully represent the colors that will appear in the final printed piece.

There are three main parts to a color management system:
  - a set of device profiles that represent (as CIE values) the gamut, or range, of colors that can be scanned, displayed or printed by any device;
  - a method of converting between the device-dependent color model used by a scanner, monitor or printer (usually RGB, CMY, or CMYK) and the device-independent CIE color model;
  - software tools for providing the user with on-screen previews of how colors will appear when printed on a particular device.

There are four full-function color management systems now available, each with all the features described above—EFI EfiColor, Agfa FotoFlow, the Kodak Precision CMS from Eastman Kodak and the Pantone Open Color Environment.

Kodak CMS

Kodak brings decades of experience in color science to the color management field, and it shows. Kodak's KCMS group provides a number of color management solutions, both for end users and integrated into products from other vendors. For instance, Kodak supplies the default color matching modules that will be used in future versions of the Microsoft Windows and Sun Solaris operating systems.

The Kodak Precision CMS was developed over the past decade by Kodak Electronic Printing Systems (KEPS), and is at the heart of their mid-range Prophecy prepress system and Macintosh-based PCS100 system. The Precision CMS is also featured in such products as Photoshop (version 2.5.1 for the Mac), PhotoStyler, DayStar Digital ColorMatch, RasterOps CorrectColor, and SuperMac SuperMatch.

Kodak has created an extensive library of device profiles for use with these systems and applications, as well as software that lets you create your own profiles. The Precision Input Color Characterization package, for example, makes it possible to create profiles for your particular scanner or Photo CD system. There is also the Precision Imagesetter Linearization Software for PostScript imagesetters, and the Precision Color Printer Calibration Software for desktop color printers.

Kodak Precision is based on the CIELUV color model, and uses proprietary transforms and device profiles to attain a very high level of color matching. It supports both gamut mapping and gamut compression, enabling the best possible match regardless of gamut differences between input, display, proofing, and final output devices.

In addition to the full-function Precision CMS, Kodak originally sold a second color management system, ColorSense, which was based on the RGB model and came with a monitor calibrator (photometer). One of its main selling points was an intuitive user interface, which made it easy for non-professional users to view and modify multiple images, save a color correction in a file or adjust the color, brightness or contrast of the display. However, ColorSense lacked CMYK support and other features essential to the prepress market, and it has since been bundled into the Precision CMS, providing users with the best of both packages.

Kodak is working closely with Adobe, Apple, Microsoft, and Sun Microsystems to bring cross-platform standardization to color management, based on a standard device profile format.

EfiColor

The EfiColor color management system from Electronics for Imaging (EFI) is based on operating system-level software that compensates for the distortions associated with various input devices, monitors, printers, papers, and inks. The EfiColor system uses device profiles to translate colors into the appropriate device's color space, allowing users to manually or automatically adjust colors that cannot be accurately reproduced. EFI initially incorporated EfiColor into specific applications, such as Cachet, QuarkXPress, and Photoshop, but now sells an all-in-one solution called EfiColor Works, which includes a variety of components for complete scan-to-print color management.

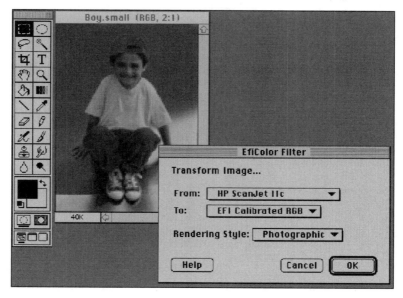

Fig. 4-11
EfiColor Works comes with a Photoshop filter that lets you adjust the color relationship between any two supported devices.

EfiColor Works includes:

- the second-generation EfiColor processor, which provides more accurate color conversions, faster performance, and compatibility with Apple's ColorSync architecture;
- EPS XTension, which allows QuarkXPress users to manage placed encapsulated PostScript (EPS) and Desktop Color Separation (DCS) files, spot colors (from Pantone and Trumatch), and Adobe Illustrator and FreeHand graphics;
- EfiColor for Scanners, which lets you calibrate and characterize any RGB scanner (reflective or transmissive), based on target images.
- EfiColor for Adobe Photoshop, which provides color separation tables that replace those built into Photoshop.

The system includes EFI's complete library of more than 100 device profiles, plus tools for creating scanner profiles and custom device profiles.

Fig. 4-12

EfiColor Works
includes a profile
editor that lets you
customize the transfer
function for your
particular input and
output devices.

A key part of EfiColor

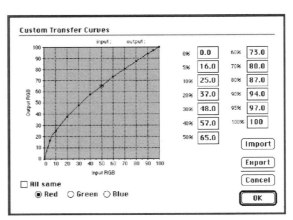

Works is the Profile Editor, which allows you to manually customize any scanner, monitor, printer or press profile according to specifications such as gamma, dot gain, screen frequency, screen angle, dot shape, maximum ink coverage, calibration curves, and default gray component replacement. For example, if a particular monitor displays too much red, you can use the Profile Editor to alter the transfer curves to pull back on the red content of the display.

Agfa FotoFlow

Agfa FotoFlow is a family of products that, together, provide a complete color management solution. The core product in the FotoFlow line is FotoTune, a standalone application that works with CIE-based device profiles, which Agfa calls ColorTags. FotoFlow comes with a variety of ColorTags for popular scanners, monitors and printers, especially those made by Agfa.

Fig. 4-13

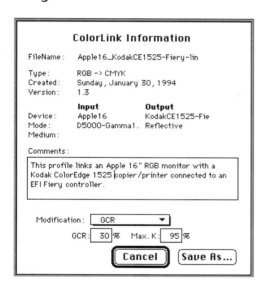

FotoFlow lets you create unique ColorLinks that connect the profiles of two different devices, such as a monitor and printer.

One of the unique aspects of FotoTune is that it enables you to merge two ColorTags to create a unique ColorLink, which can transform color data directly from the color space of one device (such as a scanner) to that of a second device (a monitor or printer). This can increase the speed and accuracy of converting colors from one device to another.

FotoFlow comes with a color reference target that you can scan to create a unique device profile for your scanner. This target, which Agfa sells separately as FotoReference, meets the IT8 standard of the American National Standards Institute (ANSI). It is available in both transmission format (as a 35mm slide or 4-by-5-inch transparency) and reflection format (as a 5-by-7-inch print). Data files are provided on a Macintosh or PC floppy disk as CIELAB values corresponding to the 288 color samples on the target.

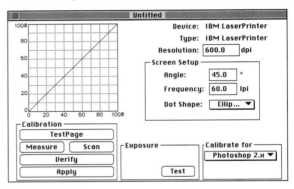

Fig. 4-14
The MC Calibrator module in FotoFlow lets you customize the calibration parameters for your particular devices.

FotoFlow also includes a calibration module, MC Calibrator, which works with popular scanners, monitors, printers, and imagesetters.

Pantone Open Color Environment

Although most of the desktop color industry has settled on color management tools based on the CIE model, Pantone has teamed up with Light Source (maker of the OFOTO scan control program) to create an alternative color management system based on a theory called Appearance Equivalency (AeQ). The Pantone Open Color Environment (POCE) consists of two components: a color matching technology for continuous tone (photographic) images and system-level Color Selectors for solid and process color selection.

POCE is different from most other color management systems in a number of ways:

♦ it supports both spot and photographic color matching in a single Color Matching Method (CMM);

♦ through its many licensees, Pantone has made the CMM and device profiles available to end users at *no charge*;

♦ it uses the Adaptive Calibration technology developed by Light Source to enable users to create and modify their own custom device profiles;

◆ it is designed specifically to operate at the operating system level, and supports cross-platform color matching between Macintosh, Windows and UNIX-based machines.

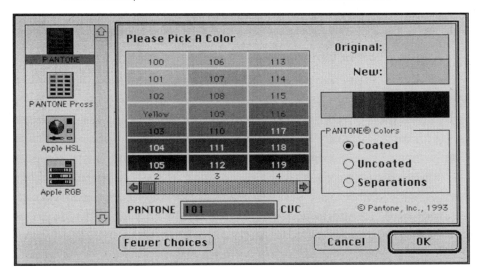

Fig. 4-15
A color picker for the Pantone Open Color Environment shows its support for PANTONE MATCHING SYSTEM, Pantone Process colors, and the HSL and RGB color models.

POCE is compatible with Apple ColorSync and has been endorsed by a number of leading hardware and software companies, including Adobe, Aldus, Corel, Fractal Design, GCC, Iris, Lexmark, QMS, Sharp, Tektronix, and Xerox.

Color management where?

The color management products described above are valuable tools that can help color publishers attain more consistent results, but, with the exception of the Pantone Open Color Environment, they are limited by the fact that they work within individual applications programs, rather than in the operating system.

Until recently, the only way to take advantage of CMS technology was to use one of the few applications programs with built-in CMS support.

These include:

+ QuarkXPress 3.2 and 3.3, which come with an XTension that provides EfiColor support;

+ PhotoStyler 2.0, which comes with Kodak's Precision color management system;

+ Photoshop, when used with the optional EfiColor plug-in;

+ EFI Cachet, a color correction application that incorporates EfiColor;

+ Kodak PCS100, a Macintosh-based version of Kodak's mid-range Prophecy color prepress system.

A number of other vendors have indicated they will build support for color management into the next major release of their products. Aldus, for instance, has announced that Kodak's Precision CMS will be built into the next versions of PageMaker and FreeHand.

Although the fact that an increasing number of desktop color applications provide color management support is, in general, a good thing, it misses an essential point: to be truly useful, color management must be supported, not only in individual applications programs, but throughout the entire computer system, from scanner to monitor to printer to imagesetter. Ideally, color management systems must be supported at the *operating system* level, not just at the *applications program* level.

Building CMS support into specific applications goes a little way toward solving the color matching problem, but leaves unanswered how it will be achieved across multiple programs, let alone different hardware platforms. To date, the best attempt at a solution has come from Apple Computer's ColorSync.

Apple ColorSync

In early 1993, Apple shipped the ColorSync color management system, which is an extension to its System 7 operating system. As an extension, ColorSync consists of a single file you simply drag into your system folder: the next time you turn on your Mac, ColorSync takes effect.

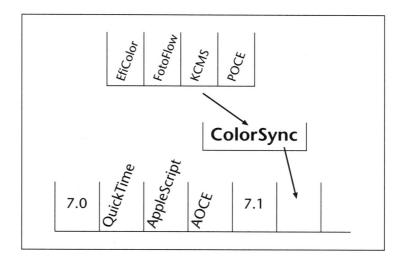

Fig. 4-16
ColorSync plugs into System 7, along with extensions such as
QuickTime (for multimedia), AppleScript, and the QuickDraw GX
graphics engine.

ColorSync is not designed to be a full-function CMS that competes with third-party color management systems: it is meant to complement EfiColor, FotoFlow, Precision, and POCE, not replace them. ColorSync is a base architecture that provides rudimentary CMS functions at the operating system level, so that third-party vendors can add value by building full-function CMS software on top of ColorSync. Most major CMS vendors have announced that their products will plug directly into ColorSync. The first version of ColorSync had some severe limitations, particularly its lack of high-quality color space conversions and of support for CMYK.

ColorSync 2.0, which was announced by Apple in late 1993, solves most of these problems, and has transformed the color management industry. The key enhancement in ColorSync 2.0 is a standard format for device profiles, developed by the leading CMS vendors as a result of meetings organized by FOGRA, the research institute for the German printing and publishing industry. It will take a year or so for all the major software and peripheral vendors to support the new format but, once they do, a single device profile will work with any color-managed application, any system-level color management tool, any PostScript printer driver.

The ColorSync 2.0 device profile format is based on a rather clever structure that will continue to allow color management vendors to offer varying levels of color matching according to each customer's requirements and budget. First, it supports color metric tagging, which lets any file identify what color space it is using. A small descriptor in a TIFF file (as a tag in the file header) or an EPS file (in a document structuring comment) will inform any applications program about the source of the color data the file is carrying.

Second, the format greatly enhances a structure introduced in ColorSync 1.0, which provides for public data fields (whose contents are prescribed) and private fields (that can contain anything the profile creator wants). In ColorSync 1.0 the public portion was too small to be really useful, forcing vendors of full-function CMS products to use lots of private data in their device profiles. The result was low-quality color output, unless you were using profiles and a color matching method from a single vendor.

ColorSync 2.0 solves this problem by expanding the size of the public fields so they produce a quality of color matching that should satisfy the vast majority of users. Adding additional data to the private field would raise the quality of color matching to the level required by the professional prepress industry. Such data would be accessible only to customers using a particular vendor's CMS, and would have no effect when used with a competitor's CMS.

ColorSync 2.0 also features EPS and TIFF file tagging, support for PostScript Level 2, and an improved color matching method. It provides support for 3-D lookup tables, high-fidelity color, and color spaces other than CIEXYZ. Among the companies that have announced plans to support the ColorSync 2.0 device profile format are Adobe, Agfa, EFI, Kodak, and Pantone.

Whither Microsoft?

Where do the recent developments in color management systems, leave Microsoft (and by extension, all Windows color publishers)? Until now, technically speaking, up the creek without a paddle.

Microsoft has stated publicly that it will add CIE-based CMS technology to the Windows graphic device interface (GDI) as part of Windows 4.0 (code-named Chicago), which is expected in early 1995. In its view, Windows' current color matching capabilities are sufficient for the majority of users, a claim most color publishers would dispute.

In any case, this once again leaves Windows color publishers at least a year behind their Macintosh colleagues, with no useful way of solving the color management problem. A glimmer of hope appeared in late 1993, however, when Microsoft announced it had licensed Kodak's color matching method to use as the default color management engine in Windows 4.0. Like Apple ColorSync, this framework will allow color transform engines from other vendors to be plugged in as well.

When this occurs, it will represent a major victory, not just for Windows-based publishers but for anyone who needs to exchange color documents between the Macintosh and Windows worlds. Kodak is one of the key members of the group that standardized the ColorSync 2.0 profile format, and has already announced it will convert its substantial library of device profiles to make them compatible with the new standard. This will ensure a useful level of cross-platform compatibility between ColorSync and Windows. Any device profile compatible with ColorSync 2.0 will work with any color-managed application, any system-level CMS, and any PostScript Level 2 printer driver.

The PostScript language

The PostScript language, developed by Adobe Systems, was an enabling technology in the birth of desktop publishing, and is now firmly entrenched as the standard page description language for all kinds of publishing applications. Therefore, recent enhancements to PostScript that address its limitations in color management and a number of other areas are especially important for color publishers.

PostScript provided early desktop publishers with three significant advantages: typographic flexibility, typographic quality, and device independence:

- PostScript's typographic flexibility derives from the fact that it represents characters (and all other vector graphics) as *outline* shapes that can be described according to mathematical formulas, rather than as bitmaps. The problem with bitmap fonts is that you need a different bitmap pattern for every typeface, size, weight, and attribute, which quickly clogs up your hard disk and limits your design freedom. PostScript devices store fonts as tiny (one point) outlines, then scales them to any required size. Another aspect of PostScript's typographic prowess is the availability of tons of fonts: there are more than 10,000 PostScript typefaces on the market, with more arriving every day.

- In the old days of metal type, character shapes were hand-crafted to vary slightly from small to large point sizes to maximize printability and readability. A similar capability is built into PostScript Type 1 fonts (the vast majority of PostScript fonts). By embedding in each character "hints" on how its shape should change at various point sizes, especially at low resolutions, type designers can ensure that PostScript fonts match or exceed the quality of metal type.

- PostScript's device independence was a crucial ingredient in its becoming the standard page description language for electronic publishing. By converting type outlines (and graphics) into bitmaps in the output device (rather than in the host computer), PostScript makes it possible for desktop publishers to proof pages on a low-cost desktop laser printer, then send them for output to a high-resolution imagesetter, knowing the pages will look identical (except for resolution). This capability helped spur the growth of both desktop publishing itself (most designers can afford a $2,000 laser printer but not a $200,000 imagesetter), and the service bureau industry.

PostScript isn't the only outline-based font format and page description language on the market. Microsoft and Apple now aggressively promote the TrueType font format. Although these have achieved significant success in the office publishing market, to date they have not become a serious force in the professional publishing industry.

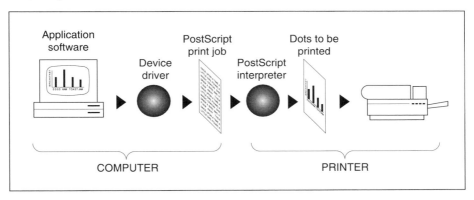

Fig. 4-17
PostScript achieves device independence by rasterizing graphics in an interpreter inside the output device, not the host computer.

A key concept in PostScript is the *interpreter*, or *raster image processor* (RIP) that is an essential part of every PostScript output device. In general, we speak about a desktop laser printer containing an interpreter, while high-resolution PostScript imagesetters have a RIP, but strictly speaking they are the same thing.

A RIP converts the lines, curves, and images that make up any graphic or page layout created in a PostScript applications program and converts them into bitmaps at the resolution appropriate to a specific marking engine. In a 300 dpi laser printer, for instance, a one-inch line segment will be made of 300 printer spots, while a 2,540 dpi imagesetter will put 2,540 tiny spots along the same inch.

Despite PostScript's central role in the emergence of electronic publishing, it has always had some limitations: for instance, originally it was very slow. Since shortly after its inception, many publishers have wanted to extend PostScript's capabilities in numerous ways.

Between 1985 and 1990, Adobe Systems provided its original equipment manufacturers (OEMs) with extensions to PostScript that enabled them to add numerous enhancements, including support for Japanese and other ideographic languages, as well as Display PostScript, which makes it possible to have true What You See Is What You Get (WYSIWYG) screen display.

Then, in late 1990, Adobe released a new definition for PostScript, called PostScript Level 2, which incorporates all the existing extensions plus many new features, some of great significance to color publishers.

PostScript Level 2

All programs that print to conventional PostScript printers (we can now think of them as Level 1 printers), will print to Level 2 printers. In other words, PostScript Level 2 is upwardly compatible with existing PostScript language programs and print drivers. One of the major features in PostScript Level 2 is that it is built around the CIE color model.

Among the enhancements in PostScript Level 2 are:

♦   greater speed—always important in computer systems but especially so with PostScript, which has been described as everything from sluggish to glacial;

♦   dynamic memory allocation, which further improves performance and reduces the occurrence of RIP crashes by redistributing memory as it is needed during the process of PostScript interpretation;

♦   RIP-based separations, making it possible to send composite color files to a RIP as a single "logical file", which can be transmitted and interpreted much faster than four individual separation files;

- support for a variety of other color models, including the Photo YCC model used in Kodak's Photo CD products;
- support for JPEG compression (which lets you reduce an image file to one-tenth its original size, then later decompress it with virtually no loss of quality) in the printer, rather than in the application, thus enabling you to send compressed files directly to the printer;
- downloadable resources (fonts, forms, and patterns), which means that elements that appear on more than one page need only be downloaded to the printer once, and be ripped once;
- support for supercell screening algorithms, such as Adobe Accurate Screens, which enable PostScript-based systems to produce color separations every bit as good as those produced on conventional high-end prepress systems.

One very important aspect of PostScript Level 2 is the way it handles color management. PostScript Level 2 can work with color images and graphics in a number of device-independent color spaces, including CIEXYZ and CIELAB. The PostScript Level 2 interpreter converts the device-independent color data into the CMYK color space of a particular color printer by interpolation through a *color rendering dictionary* (CRD). Adobe Systems provides a default CRD for each color printer for which they license PostScript Level 2, although additional dictionaries can be provided by the printer manufacturer or third parties, such as CMS vendors.

The fact that PostScript Level 2 supports downloadable CRDs means that users can choose where they want color transformations to be calculated: in the printer or in the host computer. In some systems, the most productive workflow is to perform color management in the workstation, then send the corrected color data to the printer. However, color transformations are extremely processor-intensive, and could therefore slow down the workstation.

Adobe Systems has announced that future Macintosh and Windows PostScript drivers will be able to extract data from the device profiles stored on the workstation's hard disk, repackage it as a CRD, then download it to the PostScript printer. Pages containing raw color data could thus be sent directly to the printer, which would perform the necessary computations. That would slow the printing process (at least until most printers contain high-speed RISC chips), but would reduce the overhead on the workstation. ColorSync device profiles are not in the same format as PostScript CRDs, but their information content is the same, so PostScript drivers will be able to transform one into the other.

Color separation

Printing full-color photographs and drawings is based on the illusion that four colors can be combined to create the appearance of thousands of colors. Color separation is the opposite of color printing—it involves breaking the thousands of colors in an original photograph into their cyan, magenta, yellow, and black components. These will later be recombined on a printing press to recreate the original colors in the eye of the viewer.

There are three ways of creating color separations:

- *photographically*, with a camera and colored filters, as they have been since the 1890s;
- *electronically*, inside a scanner, as they have been since the inception of digital prepress systems in the late 1970s;
- *in software* running on a Macintosh or Windows-based computer, as they have been since the emergence of desktop prepress tools in the late 1980s.

Photographic color separations

To understand color separation, let's start with the old-fashioned photographic method, in which a graphic arts camera is used to photograph the original through three filters, corresponding in color to the additive primaries (red, green, and blue).

Placing a red filter over the lens produces a negative recording of all the red light reflected or transmitted from the subject: a red separation negative. When a positive is made from this negative, the silver in the film will correspond to the blue and green areas that absorbed red. This negative has *subtracted* the red light from the original subject, and thus the positive is a recording of the blue and green in the scene, the color cyan. The corresponding positive is the *cyan printer*.

Similarly, shooting the original through the green filter creates a negative recording of the green component in the original scene. The corresponding positive is a recording of the other additive primaries (red and blue), and is therefore the *magenta printer*. Likewise, the blue filter produces a negative recording of all the blue in the subject. Its corresponding positive records the red and green, which combine to produce the *yellow printer*.

As we saw in the chapter on color models, there is a big difference between the theory and practice of color separation. In theory, it should be possible, by combining varying percentages of cyan, magenta, and yellow inks to create any color. In practice, the color gamut from combining these three process colors is finite: there are some colors outside the gamut of CMY printing that simply cannot be printed with just these three inks.

Furthermore, when the three subtractive primaries are printed together, most of the colors other than yellow and red are slightly dirty and muddy. For instance, there is often too much magenta in the greens, blues, and cyans because of unavoidable limitations in the pigments used in the inks.

Even with compensations made in the color separation negatives and positives to overcome limitations in ink colors, the final result usually lacks full contrast. A fourth *black printer* is added to increase the contrast of the grays and deep shadows, with other colors reduced proportionately so that inks transfer properly on the press.

In traditional color production, many pieces of intermediate or *working film* are typically used during color correction and image sharpening, prior to making final film. For example, a two-page spread in a magazine may require 50 or more pieces of working film to isolate specific areas for tints, gradients, reversed type, photographs and special graphic effects. One reason desktop color separations are catching on so quickly is that they allow color trade shops and commercial printers to save a great deal of time and money by going directly from layout to final film, without all the intervening pieces of working film.

To maintain control over the tonal structure of the image, it is essential that film negatives be properly exposed and developed. A balanced set of separations produces neutral grays without any color cast. In practice, however, equal combinations of cyan, magenta, and yellow will reproduce as a brownish gray color, forcing you to deliberately make the separations out of balance, with slightly stronger cyan to compensate.

Even after color correction, sometimes there will be specific areas of the image that lack the proper balance or correct tonal detail. In such cases, a technician known as a *dot etcher* will make the appropriate corrections, either with a custom mask or by applying a density-reducing chemical solution by hand.

The photographic separation method dominated color production for many years, but in the past two decades, it has largely been replaced by electronic scanning, which itself is now being supplanted by desktop color separations. All three methods can produce high quality, when they are used by a knowledgeable operator, and it's impossible to say unequivocally that one is better than another. The factors that make color separation by electronic and desktop tools dominant have much more to do with economics, speed and user control than with quality.

Electronic color separations

The 1970s and 1980s saw the emergence of high-end electronic prepress systems from such companies as Scitex, Crosfield, Hell Graphics Systems (now Linotype-Hell), and Dainippon Screen, based on a new halftoning technology known as electronic dot generation (EDG). As discussed in the previous chapter, these high-end systems still create halftone dots, but do so electronically, rather than photographically. Each digital halftone dot is constructed from many individual printer spots, and by turning on and off specific spots you can create halftones with just about any dot density, dot shape, screen frequency, and screen angle.

The main similarity between electronic scanning and the photographic method is that, ultimately, both depend on the subjective skill of the person adjusting the controls. The main difference is that, in electronic scanning, virtually all steps take place inside a computer rather than in a camera.

In the photographic method, light from every point of the color original passes simultaneously through the lens of a camera onto a sheet of film. In the electronic method, each tiny segment of the original is pinpointed by a light source and recorded instantly, after which the scanning laser moves to the next segment.

Until very recently, almost all high-quality scanning was performed with huge drum scanners, expensive devices used mostly by professional color trade shops and commercial printers. However, desktop drum scanners costing less than $40,000 are now widely available, and they will continue to drop in price until, in the not-so-distant future, they become routine peripherals.

At the input end of the scanner, the color original is wrapped around a transparent drum, which revolves around the light source. The light source can also be located outside the drum for reflective art. To color separate the original, a light beam is split into three beams after passing through, or being reflected from, the original. The intensity of each beam is measured by a photocell covered with a filter that corresponds to one of the red, green, and blue additive primaries, thus separating each area of the image into its three RGB color components.

Because the scanner input is RGB and its output signal is CMYK, conversion from one to the other is a central issue in color scanning. Different scanner vendors have their own proprietary algorithms for effecting these separation conversions, and it seems unlikely at this late date that the high-end color industry will make any serious progress toward widespread technical standards. Some serious work has already been done in the area of establishing file format "standards" in the color prepress industry, but these do not address differences in color separation algorithms.

The scanner's output can be directed three different ways. In the old days, virtually all high-end scanners had two drums, one for scanning (the "acquire" module) and the other for film output (the "record" module). Film separations were usually created "on the fly" during scanning, so that the exposed film was ready to be processed when the scan was finished. This method is still used for separations that will be manually stripped into complete pages (rather than being assembled on a desktop or high-end system).

A second option is to send the scanner's output to the prepress system's central computer for storage, after which it can be directed to a film recorder (sometimes the record unit on the same scanner, but more often a separate high-speed film recorder). The third option is to direct the output to a retouching or page assembly station where it can be retouched or combined with text and linework into complete pages prior to being sent to a film recorder.

Desktop color separations

In the late 1980s, just as the color trade shops were beginning to get a handle on their expensive proprietary prepress systems, the entire color prepress world was shaken by the emergence of desktop color tools. Programs such as PageMaker and QuarkXPress suddenly made it possible to create complete pages (even very long documents) on inexpensive microcomputers, while imaging packages such as Photoshop enabled relatively unskilled end users to enhance and manipulate scanned images.

Meanwhile, the arrival of PostScript-based film recorders (imagesetters) from Linotype-Hell, Agfa, Scitex, Optronics, Scantext, and others made it possible to output film separations of the highest possible quality. The first generation of imagesetters were based on a flatbed mechanical design that was sufficiently precise for spot color but not for high-quality process color separations. Flatbed imagesetters were soon superseded by drum-based imagesetters, which are just as precise as conventional drum-based film recorders.

Meanwhile, on the software side, the quality of the first desktop separation algorithms couldn't match that of conventional high-end systems. But during the early 1990s the color separation algorithms used in desktop applications programs improved substantially, to the point where in many cases they now match the quality of conventional methods. In fact, as the quality of desktop software has improved during the past few years, an increasing number of color publishers have started creating color separations directly on the desktop, rather than through photographic or high-end electronic systems.

The advantages of creating separations on the desktop include:
- reduced file size during image editing, because there are only three channels of data to work with (RGB) rather than four (CMYK);
- lower cost, because you can create separations yourself, rather than paying a professional to do it for you;
- greater flexibility, because you have complete autonomy and can decide at which stage of the production process images are to be separated;
- greater control over the separation process, because you can edit the color look-up tables that convert RGB information into CMYK format.

The major disadvantage is productivity—high-end scanners perform separation in specialized hardware in real time (as the image is being scanned), while desktop systems must perform color separation as an extra step. This can be quite time-consuming, especially with large image files or on a computer with less than state-of-the-art processing power.

Full-function desktop imaging programs such as PhotoStyler and Adobe Photoshop let you fine-tune the formulas used to convert the image's RGB data into CMYK format, a topic we explored in detail in Chapter 7.

Controlling ink coverage

One of the physical constraints of the printing process is that it is difficult to stack four wet layers of ink, one on top of the other. Although you might be able to specify nice bright colors in an applications program by heavily saturating all four process colors, the resulting film could not be printed.

In theory, printing 100% of each of cyan, magenta, yellow, and black would result in 400% coverage. In practice, it is difficult to print any job that has more than 300% total ink coverage, and most printers feel more comfortable with a maximum of 260% coverage. The SWOP (Specifications for Web Offset Publications) standard, for instance, which is used by many magazine and catalog publishers, dictates a maximum 300% coverage, which most printers adjust downward to 280%.

Maximum allowable ink coverage is a function of the speed of the printing press, which, in recent years, has increased to a point where the paper is in contact with each impression cylinder for less than 1/500th of a second. Because of the natural *tack*, or stickiness, of inks, and the fact they are being laid down wet on one another, it's important to keep ink coverage to a minimum to prevent an ink from pulling the previously applied one off the sheet.

The best way to minimize ink coverage is to remove approximately equal amounts of cyan, magenta, and yellow from the separations and replace them with the appropriate amount of black. Reducing ink coverage improves *ink trapping* (the ability of paper to firmly hold each layer of wet ink), which should not be confused with the color trapping described in Chapter 2.

As discussed earlier, the original RGB data from the scanner can be converted to CMY data with a simple mathematical formula, but the tricky part is adding the appropriate amount of black. Until recently, this wasn't something color publishers really needed to worry about, because the files produced by high-end scanners had already been separated into their CMYK components. But as high-quality desktop scanners (and Photo CD) proliferate, an increasing number of desktop color publishers are starting with RGB images that must be separated prior to being printed. And to separate these images properly, one has to understand *undercolor removal* (UCR) and *gray component replacement* (GCR).

Undercolor removal

The traditional solution to the problem of excess ink coverage is to incorporate undercolor removal into the color separations, by reducing the yellow, magenta, and cyan dot values wherever black is going to print—in effect removing color from the neutral scale—and increasing the amount of black ink to compensate.

The major advantage of UCR is that it reduces the overall ink coverage on the sheet, thereby improving the ability of the sheet to hold onto the ink without smearing. Separations produced with UCR result in more detail and better color saturation, especially in shadow areas. Applying UCR also tends to control dot gain and minimize registration problems.

Note that black ink is being used, not only to create solid black, but also to add detail and deepen shadow areas. Also, the process color inks are more expensive than black; UCR saves the printer money by reducing the amount of process ink required and substituting an appropriate amount of black.

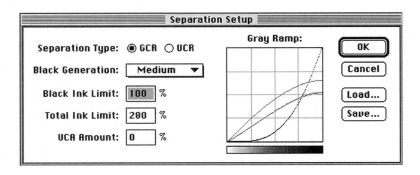

Fig. 4-18
Adobe Photoshop provides control over both UCR and GCR, with a graphical representation of how much cyan, magenta, and yellow ink is being replaced by black.

The major drawback of UCR is that, as it's increased, the maximum density of the printed sheet decreases, resulting in reduced contrast and quality. Critics of UCR suggest that when good-quality paper and ink are available, and the press has been set to minimize dot gain and maximize ink trapping, UCR should not be needed.

Gray component replacement

Gray component replacement is a variation on undercolor removal that has become more popular recently and is built into most color scanners. The theory behind GCR is that whenever dots of cyan, magenta, and yellow are present in the same color, that color also has a gray component. Some or all of this gray component can be printed with black ink, thereby reducing the amounts of colored inks required. Taken to the extreme, it is possible to print almost any color by using two of the three colored inks plus black.

GCR separations are sometimes called *achromatic* (without color), because a color photograph scanned with GCR has the gray component of each color removed and replaced with the appropriate amount of black. Using GCR increases the amount of black ink used, with a proportionate reduction in cyan, magenta, and yellow inks. Other benefits of GCR include reduced consumption of expensive colored inks, and less paper wastage at the make-ready stage, because of the thinner ink film. Finally, lighter paper can sometimes be used. These benefits may be insignificant to some color publishers, but they are a major factor for magazine and catalog publishers, who can pocket the savings associated with reduced ink and paper costs.

GCR also helps solve a major problem in process color printing: producing consistently neutral grays. In traditional process color reproduction, the neutral gray tones are created by delicately balancing the three process inks. A slight variation in the amount of any of them can result in significant color shifts. But GCR removes this problem: neutral grays stay neutral because grays are made primarily with black ink. Another advantage of GCR is that it reduces the effects of variations on press, so that when ink coverage varies, the colors becomes slightly lighter or darker, rather than changing hue.

The major problem with GCR, as with UCR, is the reduced density of darker colors, which will be more of a concern in some jobs than in others. For example, the amount of GCR and UCR should be limited whenever large areas of strong, dense blacks are required. High GCR levels also limit the press operator's ability to adjust the inks to attain a particular color balance. To help correct for excessive color reduction, many scanners and desktop imaging programs include a feature for *undercolor addition*, adding color selectively to dark tonal areas.

Unless you know exactly what you're doing (and have discussed it with your commercial printer), leave it to your color house to decide whether to use GCR or UCR on a given separation. Although the technical controls for these are appearing in an increasing number of desktop color programs, they still require the judgment of an experienced color professional.

If you've accepted responsibility for creating color separations in Adobe Photoshop, set the black generation in the Separations Setup dialog box to "Light", unless there are compelling reasons to do otherwise. This will produce film with minimum GCR, which commercial printers will find virtually identical to conventionally separated separations. The "None" setting for GCR has no practical value, and the "Maximum" setting can be dangerous, because any neutral color will appear grainier than the rest of the picture, because of the total absence of three of the four inks.

A few rules worth following when setting GCR:

- when the most important part of an image is relatively dark, use little or no GCR (because excess black in the shadows will ruin the image);
- when the most important part of an image is a light neutral (less than 50% black), use GCR to guard against disasters caused by over-inking of cyan, magenta or yellow;
- when creating a tritone or quadtone with process inks, use heavy GCR (to minimize the possibility of color shifts caused by over-inking one of the process colors);

+ if the same image appears on more than one page, use GCR to minimize the potential for hue variation;
+ where misregistration is likely on press, use a heavier black to control it.

Color separation quality

When desktop color began in the late 1980s, the quality of desktop color separations did not come close to those produced on conventional high-end systems. With the emergence of extremely precise desktop drum imagesetters, improved separation algorithms and accurate screening technology, desktop systems now produce separations that are every bit as good as those from proprietary high-end equipment.

In scanning color photographs, the problem of non-ideal pigments is solved by having the scanner operator key in adjustments to the relative strengths of the different inks. Similar compensations have to be made in desktop color separation programs. For instance, to compensate for the fact that cyan often appears more blue than it should, the operator may want to decrease slightly the magenta content of any area containing cyan, and increase cyan approximately 10% in any neutral areas.

The crucial ingredient in creating any set of separations is the skill of the operator. Whether the tools are inside a camera, a high-end prepress system or a desktop microcomputer, it is the person controlling them who determines the accuracy of the separations and, thus, the quality of the final printed piece.

Hardware Essentials

"All vision is color vision, for it is only by observing differences of color that we distinguish the forms of objects."
Nineteenth-century physicist James Clerk Maxwell

n a perfect world, there would be no computer hardware. There would be software, of course, but you wouldn't need to hassle with hard drives and RAM chips in order to use it. The software would somehow just *be there*. Until the day this utopian vision becomes reality, however, we have to find a way to deal with the inevitable problems of computer hardware. Processing complex graphics and images places greater strain on your hardware than almost any other kind of computing, so it's especially important you select the right hardware. A spreadsheet program needs a high-speed processor to rapidly recalculate every number in a five-year financial forecast, and a database program requires a big, fast hard disk to work with immense data files. But a color layout or imaging program needs both, plus high-speed display and tons of memory.

For 15 years, the specialized computers used for color prepress were built around proprietary architectures that locked the user into a specific vendor's hardware and software solution. However, there is now an inexorable trend in color publishing to systems that are built around industry-standard microcomputers, especially Apple Macintosh and Windows-based desktop computers.

But microcomputers have problems working with high-resolution images, in part because the central processing chip must calculate the values of all the pixels that make up each image. Other issues include memory, hard disk storage, data exchange between systems, and the accurate display of color.

In this chapter, we explore the various pieces of hardware you need in order to use desktop computers with maximum efficiency for color publishing. Although each user's specific needs and budget will guide the particular hardware choices, some components are essential in any computer system: a central processing unit, memory, mass storage, graphics card, and display monitor. We discuss scanners and other input devices in Chapter 6, color printers in Chapter 11, and imagesetters in Chapter 12.

The purpose of this chapter is to ensure that you select components *appropriate* to the kinds of publishing jobs you will have, because it's easy to waste money buying the wrong hardware. It's easier still to throw money away on hardware that is insufficient to the tasks at hand, then pay over and over again, in lost time, as you wait for the system to catch up. A thorough understanding of these issues is valuable even for users fortunate enough to be able to delegate responsibility for selecting, buying, installing, integrating, and maintaining hardware.

Central Processing Unit

The Central Processing Unit (CPU) or microprocessor is the essential chip in any computer—a few square centimeters of silicon that have been hard-wired to add zeros and ones together and pass the results to other chips.

The metaphor most writers use to describe a computer's microprocessor is that it is the "brain" inside the machine. Leaving aside for a moment the question of whether a machine can actually have a brain (let the Wizard of Oz decide that one), it might be more fitting to describe the CPU as the *heart* of your computer system.

After all, the CPU pumps data throughout your computer, and data are the lifeblood of computing. The important thing to note about color publishing is that it puts more severe demands on your processor than does almost any other computing task.

Photo: © Intel Corporation

Fig. 5-1
The microprocessor is the heart of your computer, pumping data to the memory chips, support circuits, and peripherals.

Generating the ever-changing screens so that What You See on the screen Is What You Get (WYSIWYG) from your printer places an enormous strain on the CPU chip. Adding full-color photographic images just makes matters worse, which is why image processing tasks are best performed on workstations that use the fastest processor chips available.

Five generations of micros

Since they were introduced in 1984, Macintosh computers have gone through four generations of central processing chips: the Motorola 68000, 68020, 68030, and 68040 series of microprocessors. From their inception in 1981, IBM-compatible personal computers have gone through a similar evolution, based on a series of five Intel microprocessors: the 8088, 80286, 80386, and 80486, and Pentium.

Given that the processing speed of each generation has been at least two to three times greater than its predecessor, today's fastest desktop computers are at least 50 times faster than the original Macs and PCs.

The first two generations of micros are far too slow for any use in color publishing. Third generation machines may be appropriate for working with type, simple graphics, or low-resolution photos, but are not fast enough for use in a serious production environment. Even fourth generation machines (Macs based on the 68040 chip and 80486-based Windows machines), though commonly used by professional designers and desktop publishers, are painfully slow.

The Intel Pentium chip is a fifth-generation processor that follows on the successful 80386 and 80486 chips, but differs from them in a number of crucial areas. For instance, all the chips in the 80x86 series were based on Complex Instruction Set Computing (CISC) technology, although the 80486 includes some aspects of Reduced Instruction Set Computing (RISC) design.

At the most fundamental hardware level, all processor chips operate through a set of instructions that govern where each bit of data is stored and how it is processed. When microprocessors were invented more than 30 years ago, the best way to maximize performance was to keep each instruction as simple as possible, even if that meant a few hundred different instructions in all—a complex instruction set. Today, innovations in chip architecture and machine-level languages make it possibility to achieve higher speeds with fewer such instructions, resulting in processors with reduced instruction sets.

The Pentium chip is a hybrid, built around a core CISC architecture, but incorporating much more RISC design than any previous Intel processor, including features such as *superscaling,* the ability to execute more than one instruction in a single clock cycle. The Pentium chip itself is only a part of a well-designed system—you'll also need a high-speed RAM cache and cache controller to keep the Pentium well stocked with instructions and data. The bus between the cache and main memory should also be as wide and fast as possible, so that the system uses the fewest RAM accesses possible to keep the cache full.

Pentium-based computers provide significantly better performance than their predecessors for working with type or simple graphics, but are still not ideal for dealing with high-resolution photographs. Such machines are fast enough for many users, but not for those involved in such professional image production environments as color trade shops, PostScript service bureaus, or commercial printers.

In a production environment or any situation involving high-resolution color image files, it is most cost-effective to buy the fastest processor available, although it's the most expensive. In other words, for color publishing, buy as much CPU power as you can afford. You can save a little money now by purchasing a slower machine, but you'll end up spending more in the long run as you wait for the screen to redraw.

Co-processors

Because color publishing puts such strain on your computer's central processor, you can speed things up by adding a co-processor chip to take over some of the work. There are two main methods to co-processing: you can add one or more regular processor chips, or you can use a specialized chip known as a *digital signal processor*.

Photo: © Radius Inc.

Fig. 5-2
The Radius Rocket is a NuBus card that adds a 68040 processor to your Macintosh, and supports RocketShare multi-processing software.

Among examples of the first approach are such products as the DayStar Digital 040 family (the Image 040, Quad 040, Value 040 and Turbo 040) and the Radius Rocket, which contain a Motorola 68040 chip, the same processor found in a Mac Quadra.

One unique aspect of the Radius Rocket is its support for RocketShare, a multi-processor software protocol devised by Radius to share intensive imaging tasks among multiple processors. By installing three Rockets in your Macintosh, for instance, or installing Rockets in your Mac and two other Macs (connected via Ethernet), you can rotate or sharpen a large image file almost three times as fast as with a single Rocket.

The second approach involves using a digital signal processor (DSP), a specialized "bit pump" chip ideal for applications such as speech synthesis, voice recognition—and any operation involving moving around billions and billions of pixels.

Fig. 5-3
The Radius PhotoBooster attaches to their accelerated graphics boards and adds a digital signal processor (DSP) chip to speed up image processing in Photoshop.

Photo: © Radius Inc.

The first DSPs came on circuit boards that could be plugged into a NuBus slot on a Macintosh, and required software that would take over specific time-consuming functions in Adobe Photoshop (such as blur, sharpen or unsharp mask filters). With version 2.5 of Photoshop, Adobe broke the program into small modules of code that could be addressed independently. This made it much easier for hardware vendors to develop DSP-based accelerators, because they didn't need to worry about writing custom code.

With the introduction of the Macintosh AV computers (such as the Quadra 840AV), Apple put a DSP chip on the motherboard, thereby boosting speed for Photoshop users without the need for an add-in board. Some third-party vendors responded by releasing accelerator boards with two or more DSP chips for even greater speed.

Photo: © Apple Computer, Inc.

Fig. 5-4
The Macintosh Quadra 840AV contains a DSP chip on the motherboard, and supports the Apple Real-Time Architecture.

At the same time Apple introduced a software protocol, the Apple Real-Time Architecture (ARTA), that assigns all real-time work to supported DSP chips, regardless of whether they're on the motherboard or an add-in board. Through ARTA, the Macintosh processes modem signals, speech, audio, floating-point acceleration, and other real-time tasks with no performance degradation to the main CPU.

RISC—The next generation

Today's Macs and PCs are being superseded by a new generation of RISC-based machines, such as those built around the 64-bit PowerPC chips developed by IBM, Motorola, and Apple. RISC chips have been used in expensive minicomputers for a decade, but only recently has the price dropped enough to make it possible to use them on the desktop.

The first generation of RISC-based personal computers are the Apple Power Macs, based on the PowerPC 601 chip. Available in three models with clock speeds from 60 to 80MhZ (megahertz), these machines are considerably faster than the speediest CISC-based (ie: Pentium) machines available.

Apple has done an excellent job of migrating its customers from the Quadra series to the PowerPC, in part through built-in emulation, which allows you to run old applications at moderate speed without any change to your software. For maximum speed, applications must be rewritten to run in the PowerPC's "native mode", and native versions of all major publishing programs are now available.

Fig. 5-5
The PowerPC chip is at the heart of the next generation of dramatically faster Macintosh computers.

Photo: © Motorola

Even faster versions of the PowerPC family are in the works:

- the PowerPC 603 is a low-cost, low-voltage chip, designed for the next generation of notebook and desktop computers;
- the 604 is a faster version of the 601, offering about twice the speed and able to run at clock rates in excess of 100MHz;
- the 620 is the real speed-demon in the family, running at least twice as fast as the 604, making it about 15 times faster than the Motorola 68040 processor.

In addition to PowerPC-based computers from Apple itself, other vendors have begun offering upgrade boards that add a PowerPC chip to 68040-based Macs. The first company to deliver PowerPC upgrade products was DayStar Digital, whose PowerPro 601 board plugs into the Processor Direct Slot (PDS) on a variety of Quadra models. The board is available in 66MHz and 80MHz versions, and can increase integer performance by a factor of three and floating point performance by a factor of six.

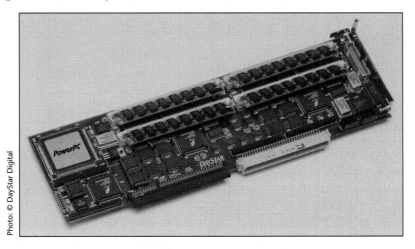

Photo: © DayStar Digital

Fig. 5-6
The PowerPro 601 from DayStar Digital converts a 68040-based Macintosh into a raging PowerPC speed-demon.

The PowerPro 601 works with the Mac's existing memory, but you can also add as much as 128Mb of 64-bit memory to further increase the performance of such "cache busting" applications as Photoshop.

DayStar also makes an optional FastCache PowerPC board, which plugs into the PowerPro to add a 512Kb secondary cache that can increase the performance of FreeHand and Illustrator.

Many software vendors in the color publishing area are already hard at work creating a new generation of applications programs to take advantage of the increased performance and other features of these new chips. To take full advantage of the speed of the PowerPC chip, applications will need to be rewritten or recompiled to run in "native" mode, rather than in 680x0 emulation mode. More than 200 software developers—including Aldus, Adobe, Fractal Design, Frame Technology, Macromedia and Quark—have announced that they are porting their applications to native PowerPC.

Operating systems

The *operating system* (OS) directs the flow of information between the various resources and devices comprising your computer's environment. Operating systems are a complex but essential element in making your computer work. Although, strictly speaking, operating systems are software and might not seem to belong in the hardware chapter, this is the logical place to discuss them.

Fig. 5-7
Computers operate on three levels: an operating system (OS) acts as a master control program; the applications programs run on top of the OS; and data files are created within each application.

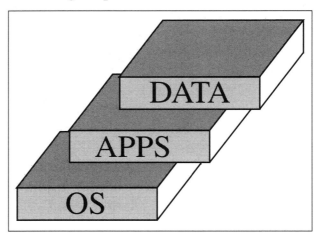

Until now, color publishers have had few serious options in choosing an operating system: the Apple Macintosh System, Microsoft Windows (running on top of DOS), and UNIX. In fact, users have only Windows and Mac OS to choose between, because most software vendors decided (probably correctly) that the potential market for UNIX versions of their products wasn't sufficiently large to justify the significant development costs.

Today the operating system environment is changing—dramatically. There are major innovations in operating system technology that will benefit all computer users, but publishers especially. Many of the problems of color publishing—managing large files, running multiple applications at the same time, tracking many different versions of files, among them—will be substantially reduced under the new operating systems.

One important aspect of this transition is the disappearance of the one-to-one link that formerly connected operating systems and processor chips. During the first decade of microcomputers, for instance, machines containing an Intel processor ran DOS (and later Windows); those with Motorola chips ran the Macintosh OS; and RISC chips were reserved for minicomputers running one of the many variants of the UNIX operating system.

The trend now is to "plug-and-play" connectivity between operating systems and the chips on which they run. For example, Windows NT will run on everything from an Intel 80486 to PowerPC to a Digital Alpha AXP superchip.

Apple Macintosh

The Macintosh operating system, called System, has an intuitive interface known as the Finder. There are a number of features that have distinguished the Macintosh System since its inception, such as the mouse, the use of pull-down menus, and the representation of programs and data files as pictures, or *icons*, stored in *folders*. To copy a Macintosh file, you simply point at its icon with the mouse and drag it to its destination.

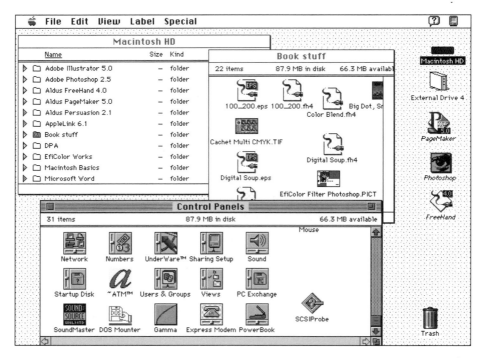

Fig. 5-8
For many users, Apple's System 7 provides the ultimate graphical user interface, a workspace in which actions are intuitive, natural, and consistent.

In 1991 Apple released System 7, an upgraded version of its operating system that features improved support for multi-tasking and easier communications with other systems. A further improvement is the capability to intelligently link diverse applications programs. For example, a photo technician can now retouch a picture in an imaging program, knowing that a page layout in which the picture appears will automatically be updated, regardless of the page layout program being used, and where it is on the network.

For color publishers, the key benefits of System 7 include:

♦   multi-tasking, which allows you to keep your imaging program busy calculating a color correction in the background while you digitize your next image in a scanning program;

◆ 32-bit addressing, which allows the operating system to directly address up to 4Gb of memory, a feature especially important when working with large image files;

◆ Inter-Application Communications (IAC), which lets you write a script, or macro, that transfers information between diverse applications programs—for example, between an imaging program and a picture database application. More important, it also allows your script to instruct other applications programs to take specific actions with the data.

Apple gained a further advantage in color publishing when it released QuickTime, an extension to the System that enables any color Macintosh to automatically compress, decompress, and display video, animation, and sound as part of *multimedia* presentations. System 7 Pro, added more features of interest to publishers, including a powerful task-automation language, AppleScript.

Apple continued to raise the bar in 1994 with the release of System 7.5, which added QuickDraw GX for advanced printing features, a scriptable Finder, PowerTalk colloboration technology, Apple Guide (for step-by-step assistance), QuickTime 2.0, support for Power Macs, DOS/Windows compatibility, and special mobility features for PowerBook users.

Microsoft Windows

When the IBM PC was released in 1981, it was accompanied by a rather crude operating system known as the Disk Operating System (DOS). By the end of the 1980s, computer hardware was improving by leaps and bounds, but PC users were still chained to DOS anachronisms, such as a 640Kb memory limit.

A better solution appeared in mid-1990: version 3 of Microsoft Windows. From the time it was introduced in 1985, Windows offered many of the same easy-to-use features that made the Mac so popular: icons, pull-down menus, and support for a mouse. With Windows 3, however, it finally demolished the 640Kb barrier by permitting applications to address up to 16 Mb of contiguous memory.

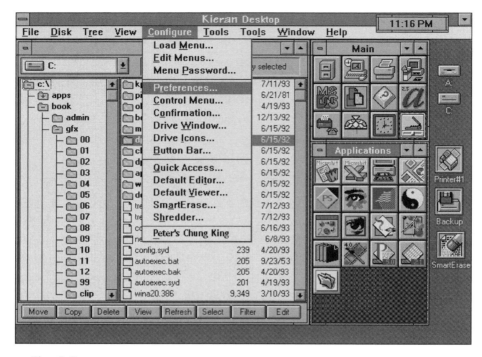

Fig. 5-9
The icons, menus, and graphic user interface of Windows have brought
a Macintosh-like feel to many IBM-compatible PCs.

Windows version 3 also added a feature of great significance to many
publishers—multi-tasking, the ability to run more than one
application at a time. You can have multiple windows open on screen
at once, so that an illustration created in a drawing package in one
window can be seamlessly integrated into a page layout package
running in another. Moreover, you can continue working in an
application in a foreground window while processing continues in
other applications in background windows. Windows got even better
in 1992 with the release of version 3.1, which further improved the
user interface (in other words, made it look more like a Macintosh).

It's important to note that Windows is not a true operating system:
it is a graphical environment that operates on top of DOS. This
presents some problems—DOS was originally designed as a single-
tasking operating system—but millions of people have bought

Windows, and virtually all publishing and graphics programs running on IBM-compatibles do so under Windows.

Microsoft has announced plans for a new version of Windows, code-named "Chicago", that will be a pure 32-bit operating system (rather than 16-bit), which will speed up both the operating system and the applications it supports. This new Windows will run without DOS, and will even support long filenames (a feature the Mac has had since its inception).

During the first half of the 1990s, many large corporations have been "down-sizing" key business applications by moving them from mainframe and minicomputer platforms to the desktop. Some have quickly discovered that features they took for granted on the mainframe, such as security and fault-tolerance, were sorely lacking on PCs. Microsoft's response has been to develop Windows NT, a robust operating system designed for networked mission-critical applications programs.

Windows NT is built around a software concept called "client/server", in which the processing of information is split between the central repository (the server) and the local workstation where the information is being used (the client). Windows NT has so far had a minimal impact on most publishers, in part because of its hardware requirements (32Mb of RAM, for starters), and in part due to the lack of compelling applications software requiring NT. However, because of NT's inherent scalability and its support for multi-processing, it holds the potential to become an important publishing environment in the future.

OS/2

The International Business Machines company (IBM), having recognized the inherent limitations of DOS, in 1987 announced a second-generation operating system, known as OS/2. At that time it seemed natural that PC users, especially those with intensive computing requirements, would grow weary of the memory and single-tasking limitations of DOS, and would migrate to OS/2.

From the outset, OS/2 was designed to meet the heavy-duty

computing needs of large corporations and government departments, and initially it looked as though many such users—especially those with IBM mainframes and minicomputers—would automatically move from DOS to OS/2. However, a number of factors delayed this migration, including technical challenges that slowed delivery of the new system, an on-and-off relationship between IBM and Microsoft, and the incredible success of Windows 3.0 and 3.1.

For many MIS managers, the arrival of third-generation operating systems, such as Windows NT, made the delay permanent. In large organizations, OS/2 remains strong as an environment for custom applications development, but to date it has little or no relevance for most color publishers. Even the release of OS/2 version 2.1 in 1993, which provides full support for Windows 3.1 applications, has failed to increase OS/2's market share beyond its small niche. This is unfortunate, because OS/2 is an excellent operating system, one that could increase the efficiency of many publishing tasks.

UNIX

The UNIX operating system is widely used in minicomputers made by numerous manufacturers. Until the late 1980s, there were two primary obstacles in the way of UNIX becoming an important operating system for microcomputers: its unwieldy interface and the fact that it had at least 17 different "standard" versions. This was acceptable for semi-proprietary high-end prepress systems, but is not well suited to off-the-shelf commercial software applications.

Fig. 5-10
The Magic interface developed by Silicon Graphics provides UNIX users with a friendly interface.

Photo: © Silicon Graphics, Inc.

Within the past few years, graphical shells such as Motif, X Windows, and Magic have been added to UNIX to make it resemble the Macintosh interface, and most of the competing dialects have united, leaving just two main versions of UNIX—with signs that even they may converge.

Until very recently, there seemed to be a good possibility that UNIX would become an important operating system for color publishing, because the minicomputers on which it runs offer the raw horsepower necessary for processing large image files. However, the emergence of competitive UNIX-like operating systems, such as Windows NT, makes this less likely, because users now can obtain the functionality of UNIX without its user-hostile interface.

Photo: © Silicon Graphics, Inc.

Fig. 5-11
With software such as Equal, from Quorum, you can now run Macintosh software on UNIX-based computers.

More important, the raw power of RISC-based chips, such as the PowerPC, make it possible to get the speed of a UNIX-based minicomputer while continuing to use the Macintosh or Windows graphical user interface. For those who are committed to UNIX-based machines, it's now possible to take advantage of the incredible variety of software available for the Macintosh, through Equal, a software emulation technology from Quorum Software.

Macintosh users planning to upgrade to PowerPC-based Macs should take note of the PowerOpen operating system, which is a version of UNIX. Apple has announced it will release an extension to PowerOpen, called Macintosh Applications Services, that will let you run System 7 and compatible applications under PowerOpen.

Which operating system?

For companies and individuals in the process of adopting computer technology, the choice of an operating system is crucial, for it can determine many of your possibilities and limitations for years to come.

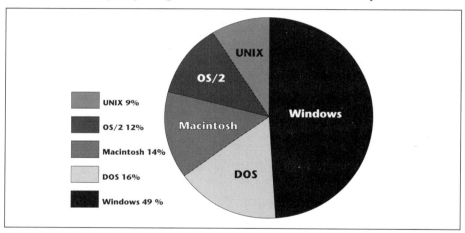

Fig. 5-12
According to market research firm InfoCorp, as of late 1993 Windows and DOS were the most popular desktop operating systems.

The overall strength of DOS and Windows hides one important fact—the domination of the Mac in publishing environments, especially in desktop color. In the early days of desktop color, the Macintosh operating system clearly had the most to offer publishers, because the Mac was the platform on which most of the cool software first appeared—PageMaker, QuarkXPress, Photoshop, FreeHand, Illustrator, and others. However, all these packages have since migrated to the Windows platform, with virtually the same functionality as their Macintosh versions.

One of the key operating system differences concerns the support for color management and multimedia, and it is in these areas that Apple continues to hold a substantial lead. At this writing, for instance, there is nothing on the Windows platform to compete with the Mac's support for color management where it belongs—in the operating system.

Another of the reasons for choosing Windows-based PCs over Macs has also largely disappeared: the price difference. Apple has aggressively reduced its prices over the past few years, to the point where the differential between a Mac and a roughly equivalent PC is 10% or less. And, despite what some Windows users might believe, the Mac interface remains distinctly different, and in the opinions of millions of users, better. Also, in any professional color publishing environment, the computer itself is only a small part of the overall cost. The price of hard disks, monitors, scanners, and printers is essentially the same for both the Windows and Macintosh computers.

The convergence of formerly disparate platforms is another factor that complicates the choice of operating systems. In late 1993, for example, Apple Computer launched a version of the Macintosh that includes a co-processor board and can run DOS and Windows applications right out of the box. Even more shocking (for diehard Macophiles) are the incessant rumors that Apple is planning to license the Macintosh operating system to run on Intel-based computers, thereby creating a market for Mac clones.

Compound document architectures

Before leaving the subject of operating systems, there's one more important issue that needs to be addressed: the emerging trend toward compound document architectures. In the good old days (WordStar 1.1 on a Z-80 CP/M computer), software applications were small and, if truth be told, not really very functional. Early word processing programs, for example, couldn't handle fonts and didn't contain a spell checker, grammar checker, or thesaurus.

The problem is that today's monolithic applications have ballooned in size and complexity to the point where they contain *too many* features—a typical program occupies more than 20Mb of hard disk space and comes with a 1,100-page reference manual. CorelDRAW, for instance, is distributed on two CD-ROM disks (a total of 1,300Mb) and includes seven graphics modules, hundreds of fonts, and thousands of pieces of clip art.

One potential solution is *component software,* in which software consists of many small objects, each one a tool that can be used in any document. In this model, called *compound document architecture,* you won't buy separate applications programs; you'll simply install a new tool, which will work with all your other tools. A color correction tool, for example, will be accessible all the time, regardless of whether you're scanning a photograph, retouching an image, or making color separations.

This new paradigm started with "cut and paste" on the first Macintosh computers, but has grown to become a fundamental change in our understanding of how software operates. With Windows, Microsoft extended the cut and paste metaphor to include support for *dynamic data exchange* (DDE), which allows links between files from different applications. If you place a TIFF image in a page layout, for example, then modify the original image file, the page layout program will notify you of the change and give you the option of having the image updated.

Microsoft later extended this idea into *object linking and embedding* (OLE), which offers even tighter integration between applications. In an OLE-compliant application, double-clicking on an embedded TIFF file provides you with the complete set of tools available in the original imaging application.

In the first version of the OLE specification, the image editing application would be automatically launched so that it took over from the current program. After editing the TIFF file and exiting the imaging application, you would be back in the original page layout program, but with the latest version of the image. With OLE 2.0,

Microsoft enhanced the protocol so that clicking on an embedded TIFF file doesn't hide the current document—it simply changes the menu bar to reflect the options available in the image editing application.

In 1993, Apple released the OpenDoc specification, which competes against Microsoft's OLE 2.0 protocol. OpenDoc is an open, vendor-neutral, cross-platform architecture for documents that contain text, graphics, sounds, QuickTime movies, and other kinds of data.

With OpenDoc, the documents created by today's huge applications will be replaced by collections of components, or what Apple calls *parts*. Each part consists of one kind of content, such as text, a drawing or an image. When you click on content in some part of a document, that part becomes active, which means that a visible border called a *frame* appears around it, and the menu bar changes to reflect the kinds of actions appropriate to that part.

Apple claims numerous advantages for OpenDoc over OLE, including:

- OpenDoc is an open architecture with source code available to users and developers, while OLE is controlled by Microsoft and the source code is not available;
- OpenDoc parts can be any shape and can overlap, whereas OLE objects must be rectangular and can't overlap;
- OpenDoc allows you to link or script any document on your network, but OLE is restricted to documents on the same computer.

A number of vendors, including IBM, Novell, Borland, and WordPerfect have announced they will support OpenDoc on the Windows and OS/2 platforms. Both OLE and OpenDoc are important technologies that have the potential to significantly alter how publishers (and other software users) work with computers.

Memory

In many computer systems, the most cost-effective way to improve performance is to add more Random Access Memory (RAM) chips. You need at least 2Mb to 4Mb of RAM for just the operating system, plus another 2Mb or more for each applications program, plus sufficient memory to hold your entire graphic, image, or other document.

Without sufficient memory, your computer system is forced to use *virtual memory* to "spool" some or all of your work to the hard disk, which significantly slows things down. After all, the hard disk is a mechanical component of spinning metal and plastic, whereas memory chips operate with pulses of electricity that zoom around at the speed of light.

Just how much memory do you need? As an absolute minimum, I recommend 8Mb, even if you are working only with text and simple graphics, rather than with photographic images. However, given that you are reading a book on desktop color, it's safe to assume you would like your documents to contain, at the very least, color graphics, and probably color photographs. In that case, I recommend between 16Mb and 32Mb of memory if you'll be working with low-resolution placeholders, and 64Mb or more if you'll be using actual high-resolution images.

That may seem extreme, but it will significantly improve the overall speed of your system. Besides, RAM is a lot cheaper now than in the old days. When the desktop publishing industry started about ten years ago, RAM chips were about $1,000 per megabyte—20 times more expensive than they are today.

When working with photographic images, a good rule of thumb is to ensure that your system has three times as much main memory as the largest image file you will want to manipulate, plus sufficient memory for the operating system and applications program. This enables memory to hold the original image, the undo version of the image, and the current filter or image transform, all at the same time, thus improving performance by reducing the need for retrieving data from the hard disk. There's another advantage to having tons of RAM—you can keep all your major applications open at the same time, and instantly hop from one to another with a few keystrokes.

RAM disk

To maximize the performance of your desktop publishing programs, you may want to allocate some of your memory as a RAM disk. One of the features built into both Microsoft Windows and Apple's System 7 is support for "virtual memory", which makes some of your hard disk space pretend to be RAM, thereby enabling you to open image files larger than the amount of available RAM. A RAM disk is exactly the opposite: you designate some of your RAM as an additional hard drive, on which you store commonly used data, such as an application's program files. On the Macintosh, you can further improve performance by copying the System folder to the RAM disk.

One very important fact about RAM disks—everything in them disappears when you turn off your computer. Therefore, if you are saving data files to a RAM disk, be sure to copy them to the hard disk before shutting down.

Storage

How big a hard disk do you need? That depends on how much money you have. The bottom line in mass storage—you can never have too large a hard disk. Therefore, you should probably purchase the largest drive you can afford.

Ten years ago, the big news in computing was that IBM had enhanced the original PC with an optional hard disk—with a whopping 5Mb capacity. Nowadays you can't even get Windows or System 7 loaded in 5Mb, let alone any applications software or data files. In fact, many applications programs now require 15Mb or more for themselves plus all the sample files, tutorials, driver libraries, fonts, and utilities. A typical user may have half a dozen such applications, consuming 100Mb or more of hard disk space, not to mention data files.

Nonetheless, hard disks in the 80Mb to 150Mb range are still common for office tasks, such as word processing and spreadsheets. Color publishers, however, even those working only with type, simple graphics, and low-resolution "position only" photos, will require a minimum of 300Mb of storage. If you're working with image files, 600Mb to 1,200Mb (1.2Gb) is a more appropriate hard drive size, though some prepress professionals routinely use workstations with mass storage capacities of 5Gb or more.

Another reason for buying the largest hard drive you can afford is that as the size of a hard disk goes up, the cost per megabyte goes down. A 600Mb drive typically costs about twice as much as a 200Mb drive, although it has three times the capacity. Also, as hard drive size goes up, speed tends to go up. That 600Mb drive will probably be 30 to 50 per cent faster than the 200Mb model.

There are a couple of other facts about hard drives worth noting before you buy. First, there isn't much of a market in secondhand hard disks, so at the outset buy all the capacity you need, and then some. Upgrading your hard disk is not only costly, it can also be quite inconvenient and time-consuming: spending a little more now saves a lot more later.

Many drive vendors emphasize *average access speed:* the time it takes for a drive to reach a specific byte and start reading it. Although access speed is important, a better measure of overall performance is obtained by comparing *transfer rates*, the speed at which data are transferred from the disk to the computer's main memory. After all, when reading a large image file from disk, finding the beginning of the data takes much less time than reading it all from disk into memory.

Storage fault-tolerance

As desktop computers take over prepress tasks previously reserved for dedicated minicomputers, it becomes increasingly important that they be able to withstand the failure of a mass-storage component (such as a hard disk, drive controller or power supply) and continue to perform input/output (I/O) without data loss. There are a variety of methods for achieving such *storage fault-tolerances*, including mirroring, duplexing, and disk arrays, using software only or a combination of software and hardware.

One of the simplest (but least efficient) techniques is *mirroring*, in which the storage sub-system uses a single drive controller to write the same blocks of data to two hard disks. If one fails, the other contains the data intact. This method has two disadvantages: if the controller card fails, the entire system goes down, and performance is impaired because the host CPU must deal with twice the number of I/O operations.

A slightly better approach is *duplexing*, in which two controllers are used to write the same data to two hard disks. This provides a small increase in performance, but you must still shut down the entire system in order to replace a defective drive or controller. Also, as with mirroring, this is an inefficient use of hard disks because you must buy twice the storage capacity you actually require.

It is better still to use arrays of data by arranging, or *striping*, a single data file across a *disk array* of multiple hard drives. To make disk arrays faster and more fault tolerant, a variety of error correction (EC) techniques have been developed so that if one drive in the array fails, the data can automatically be recreated from the others.

Photo: © MicroNet Technology, Inc.

Fig. 5-13
A RAID array not only stores plenty of image data but minimizes the risk of data loss caused by drive failure.

Many professional prepress shops now use a fault-tolerant technology known as RAID (redundant arrays of inexpensive drives), in which software is used to stripe data across multiple drives. There are actually five levels of RAID technology, ranging from simple disk mirroring (RAID 1) to striping data and error-correction information across all drives in the array (RAID 5).

The only disadvantage of using RAID technology is that, for optimal data protection, you must give up some of your hard disk capacity, typically about 20%. When planning your hardware configuration, be sure to add extra megabytes or gigabytes to compensate for the storage space taken up by data redundancy in the RAID system.

Back-up

An untimely collision between a high-speed read/write head and a disk's delicate coating of magnetic material can mean disaster, so back up all data files on a regular basis. Those working on a stand-alone system should use a tape or cartridge backup drive with time-sensitive software that automatically copies all new or modified files from the hard disk at specified intervals.

For computers connected via a local area network, there's often a system administrator somewhere responsible for ensuring that all data files are copied to off-line storage on a regular basis (preferably at least once a day). But just because someone is responsible for it, doesn't mean it actually happens, so be sure to confirm that a prudent network back-up strategy is in place.

One final note. Even tapes and cartridges aren't infallible, especially if you don't keep multiple backups and cycle them from time to time. Be sure to confirm that the backup files are actually readable. You don't want to find out the hard way that your backup tapes contain nothing but garbage, rather than the latest (and only existing) versions of your crucial files.

Now that you've got 53 terabytes (53,000Gb) of on-line storage, how are you going to back it up? Why, onto 53-million little floppy disks, of course. Not!

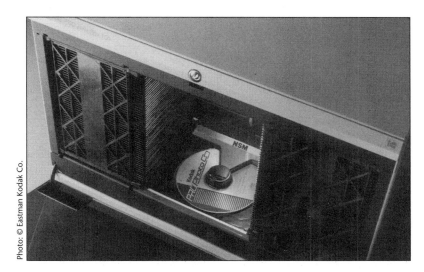

Photo: © Eastman Kodak Co.

Fig. 5-14
One way to store tons of color image data is with a Kodak Photo CD jukebox. There are 100 disks on-line, each containing 650Mb of data—a total of more than 60Gb.

There are a variety of media available for backing up large amounts of data, each with different advantages and disadvantages. Some media are well suited for exchanging image files with service bureaus, color trade shops, and commercial printers, while others are appropriate only for archival backup. Let's take a closer look at the main back-up media for color publishers: magnetic cartridges, optical cartridges, digital audio tape, and compact disks.

Magnetic cartridges

Removable magnetic cartridges are the most common back-up and data exchange medium in the desktop color publishing industry. The major cartridge vendor is SyQuest, and today dozens of manufacturers sell mass storage systems that incorporate SyQuest drives.

The original SyQuest drives had a capacity of 44Mb, with later models extending to 88Mb. For years, the 88Mb mechanisms could read, but not write to, the older 44Mb cartridges, though this problem has been eliminated in more recent versions of SyQuest drives.

Photo: © MicroNet Technology, Inc.

Fig. 5-15
SyQuest removable magnetic cartridges let you store up to 88Mb,
and are a standard format for transporting data
to service bureaus for output.

One of the major advantages of SyQuest drives is that they have
become a relatively standard medium for designers, color separators,
and commercial printers exchanging large publications and image
files. Another advantage, one shared with all other removable media,
is that you get virtually infinite storage capacity, simply by purchasing
more cartridges. Disk-based technologies (such as removable
magnetic cartridges and optical cartridges) also have a significant
speed advantage over tape media (such as digital audio tape), because
the data on a spinning disk can be accessed randomly, while a tape
must be spooled to the correct location before data can be read or
written.

Among the disadvantages of SyQuest drives are reliability problems
with some cartridges, the cost of buying hundreds of cartridges, and
the fact cartridges formatted on some drives cannot be read on other
SyQuest drives. Capacity is another limitation: 88Mb may seem like
plenty of storage, unless you're publishing a 100-page catalog full of

color photographs, with each two-page spread requiring more than 60Mb. Compression technology can help overcome this problem, but at a price—it takes longer to save and open compressed files.

Magneto-optical cartridges

For many color publishers, the medium that offers the best combination of capacity, speed, and cost is the *erasable optical* or *magneto-optical* drive, which achieves very high storage densities by combining a laser beam with an electromagnet.

On a high-intensity setting, the laser writes to the disk by producing a set of heated spots that the electromagnet then magnetizes, converting them into the equivalent of zero and one bits on a standard magnetic disk. On a low-intensity setting, the laser reads the disk by using a variation in the way polarized light reflects from the magnetized spots. Because lasers focus light so tightly, they can store huge amounts of data in a small space.

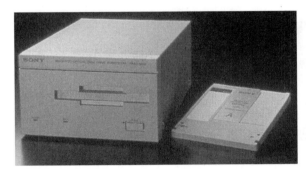

Fig. 5-16
A removable optical drive provides 600Mb of storage per cartridge, which makes them ideal for many color publishing applications.

In general, optical drives offer higher capacities than magnetic drives (typically, 650Mb to 1.3Gb), but tend to be somewhat slower, with average access speeds of more than 30 milliseconds, as compared with hard disk access times of less than 10 ms. However, with the recent trend toward lasers of ever shorter wavelengths, the data density of optical disks is expected to further increase in the next few years, even as their speed increases.

Another potential disadvantage of magneto-optical drives is that, unlike SyQuest removable magnetic cartridges, they are not an industry standard. This is not a problem if your primary objective is backing up a massive hard disk, but it can be a barrier if you want to send large image files to a service bureau, color trade shop or commercial printer, unless of course your service provider also uses the same media.

Photo: © Olympus

Fig. 5-17
Olympus makes a hybrid drive that can read and write both 128Mb optical disks and conventional floppies.

During the past few years, a variety of other magneto-optical drives have emerged, including 128Mb removable optical cartridges. These are too small for most archival storage applications, but are an extremely compact medium for transporting files to and from a service provider.

Digital audio tape

Just as music compact disks (CDs) helped pave the way for inexpensive storage of computer data on CD-ROMs (compact disk, read-only memory), the home audio market has also made digital audio tape (DAT) available as a high-density, low-cost storage medium.

For the color publishing industry, the major advantages of DAT are high capacity and low cost per megabyte. DATs are smaller than conventional audio cassette tapes, but each one can hold up to 2.5Gb of uncompressed data (more than 10Gb with compression). Yes, that's *gigabytes*, as in billions of bytes.

Photo: © Hewlett-Packard

Fig. 5-18
A single digital audio tape (DAT) costs less than $25 and can store 2.5Gb of data, equivalent to about 2,000 floppy disks.

The major disadvantage of DAT is that, unlike magnetic and magneto-optical drives, which are random-access media, DAT operates sequentially. This means that if you wish to retrieve a file that is stored in the middle of a DAT tape, you must wait for the drive to spool to that location, which can take 20 seconds or more, as compared with typical access times of less than 20-milliseconds for disk-based media. This makes DAT drives inappropriate as primary storage devices, although they are ideal for backup of large volumes of data, such as color image files.

As with magneto-optical drives, another potential disadvantage of DAT is that it has not really caught on as a standard medium in the industry for exchanging data. Although an increasing number of service bureaus, color trade shops, and commercial printers have recently added the ability to receive desktop publications on digital audio tape, be sure to check specifically with your suppliers before sending them your files. As long as your color house or service bureau has standardized on the same kind of DAT formatting software, these little tapes provide a very effective way of exchanging thousands of megabytes of image data.

Writable CD

From its inception, CD-ROM technology has been read-only. For distribution of fonts and clip art, nothing beats the cost and convenience of CD-ROM storage, which uses the same optical compact disks popular in home stereo systems. Instead of music, each disk holds up to 650Mb of data, about 500 times the capacity of a typical floppy disk. The cost of a CD-ROM player has dropped to less than $300, complete with interface to your Macintosh or PC.

Fig. 5-19
A CD-ROM disk stores about 600Mb of data, such as fonts, clip art, and libraries of stock-shot images.

Although almost all users of CD-ROMs consider them solely as a source of fonts or picture data, it is getting easier to become a CD-ROM publisher, even if you want to print fewer than 1,000 disks. Three years ago, it cost more than $100,000 to create a master disk from which CDs could be duplicated; today the same master costs less than $1,000, excluding the cost of any retrieval software required. This makes it feasible to create small print runs of specialized collections of data or images on CD-ROM.

In addition, new products have emerged that make it increasingly cheap and easy to write information onto CDs, even if you require only a single disk. This means color publishers now have one more way of storing and transferring large image files.

Photo: © Eastman Kodak Co.

Fig. 5-20 Kodak's writable CD-ROM drive provides an economical way to store up to 600Mb of data.

Kodak, for example, has taken the technology used in its Photo CD products and made it available for corporate publishers, catalog marketers, color publishers, and anyone else who needs to put 650Mb of data on a single disk, quickly and economically. The Kodak Writable CD system is based around the Kodak PCD Writer 200, and lets you produce CDs for less than $25 each. It also features error detection and correction, ISO 9660-compliant formatting software, and a SCSI connection to the host PC, Mac, or UNIX-based computer.

Display

All computer monitors are based on the concept of pixels, or individual picture elements. By turning on and off selected pixels, the monitor can display many different shapes of type and graphics. A black-and-white monitor works with pixels of just one color. To display color graphics, a monitor combines red, green, and blue phosphors at each pixel; by varying the percentages of each color, it can create the appearance of millions of colors.

Photo: © Barco Graphics

Fig. 5-21
The high-end Calibrator II monitor from Barco provides real-time color calibration, and is often integrated into complete prepress systems such as Intergraph's DP/Studio system.

In exploring color pages and graphics displays on video terminals, keep in mind that there are two components in any display system: the monitor itself and the graphics card that drives it. It's important that these two components be matched: it doesn't make much sense to use a monitor capable of displaying millions of colors in conjunction with a graphics card capable of outputting only 256 colors.

There are many different factors that must be considered in selecting the graphics board and monitor for your publishing system. These include monitor size, pixel depth, resolution, acceleration, monitor dot pitch, interlacing and refresh rate, and low-frequency monitor emissions.

Monitor size

Lately, the cost of large color monitors has dropped substantially, making them affordable for an increasing number of designers and illustrators, as well as for people working in color separation trade shops, output service bureaus, and commercial printers.

Most serious color publishers prefer to work with a relatively large display screen—something larger than the 14" monitors commonly used for spreadsheets, data management, and office tasks that aren't nearly as challenging as color publishing. For instance, a 19" monitor lets you see a standard 8.5-by-11-inch page size-as, while a 21" monitor can display an area more than 50% larger.

Photo: © Radius Inc.

Fig. 5-22
A 19" to 21" monitor will let you work comfortably with an entire page (or two-page spread) without having to constantly zoom in and out.

The principle benefit of a large display is that it enables you to see an entire page, two-page spread, or illustration at full size (or close to it), which reduces or eliminates the need for scrolling around. This may not sound like much of an advantage until you actually try it, after which you're unlikely to ever want to go back to a smaller screen size.

Large screens further improve productivity by allowing multiple windows and applications to be open and visible at the same time.

When working on an intricate graphic, it helps immensely to be able to zoom in on a tiny detail while retaining a wide-angle view of how it fits into the overall picture.

The flip side of this benefit is that large monitors can take up ample amounts of desk room, leaving hardly enough for a mouse to squeak by. Among the solutions to the size problem are desk- or wall-mounted arms that suspend the monitor above your work surface. Be sure to use a heavy-duty mounting device, rather than one designed for a regular 14" monitor. Many 19" monitors weigh 90 pounds or more, and if dropped will leave a sizable dent in your floor, not to mention your wallet.

An important factor to watch for is that monitor sizes are usually quoted as the diagonal measure of the picture tube from corner to corner, whereas it's the size of the viewable image that really matters. In most monitors the corner-to-corner size of the image is about an inch or more shorter than the tube, which makes a substantial difference in image area.

Pixel depth

The number of colors a monitor can display is a direct function of the *pixel depth*—the number of bits available for each pixel in the image. A monochrome monitor is limited to one bit per pixel, and therefore displays two possible colors—black and white.

A color monitor in conjunction with an eight-bit graphics card, can display 256 colors or shades of gray. To achieve so-called *true color* requires eight bits per pixel in each of three channels—red, green, and blue. This is *24-bit color*, with a total of 16,777,216 possible colors. (To calculate the origin of all those colors, simply multiply two by itself 24 times: the result is 16.7 million). Note that because a typical 19-inch monitor contains only a million or so pixels in all, even a 24-bit graphics board can show only 1 million colors (from a palette of 16.7 million) at any one time.

Some desktop publishers automatically assume that the more bits per pixel the better, but this is not necessarily true. For publishers working primarily with type and synthetic graphics (created in drawing programs such as FreeHand, Illustrator, and CorelDRAW), there is a significant advantage to working with an eight-bit graphics board: increased speed. For many color publishers, 16 bit graphics boards provide an excellent compromise, offering greater speed than most 24-bit boards while outputting up to 65,536 colors. However, anyone making critical color decisions on photographic images will definitely want to invest in a 24-bit display system.

Resolution

Virtually all monitors employ a cathode ray tube (CRT) with a scanning beam that selectively excites the phosphors at different pixel locations to make them emit light. The latest generation of flat-panel color displays use direct addressing rather than a scanning beam, and the light is emitted by liquid crystals, rather than phosphors. In either case, the resolution or *addressability* of the matrix being scanned is crucial to the quality of the resultant image: the higher the resolution, the better the image quality. This is especially important for color displays, in which there are separate beams for red, green, and blue.

The original Macintosh, with its built-in monochrome screen, was obviously unsuitable for color work. However, the advent of the Mac II brought a flood of color display boards and monitors from such manufacturers as Radius, RasterOps, and SuperMac.

Some monitor manufacturers include software utilities with each display. Radius, for instance, bundles a set of utility programs for tear-off menus (which allows menus to be detached from the menu bar and placed anywhere on screen), a screen saver, a screen capture routine (to save any portion of the screen as a PICT file), and an enlarged menu font for easier viewing.

VGA and beyond

In the IBM-compatible world, the minimum practical graphics display is provided by a Visual Graphics Array (VGA) board, which supports resolutions up to 640-by-480, just enough to display type on-screen with reasonable fidelity. SuperVGA, which extends this to 800-by-600, is better still.

SuperVGA has been largely superseded by the Ultra VGA standard with 1,024-by-768 resolution, capable of displaying 256 colors at once from a palette of 262,144 colors. For many PC color publishers, an Ultra VGA compatible video card and large monitor are probably the most economical choice. This is especially true for those running Windows applications exclusively, because virtually all Ultra VGA cards come with a Windows driver, and support for less popular applications programs is spotty.

Photo: © Matrox

Fig. 5-23
High-performance desktop graphics started on the Macintosh, but are now available for Windows machines through such graphics boards as the Matrox Hiper Plus.

Most 24-bit color display boards support a screen resolution of 72 dpi, which works out to a resolution of 1024-by-768 on a 19" monitor, 800-by-600 on a 16" monitor, and 640-by-480 on a 13" monitor.

The rule of thumb with display resolution is that the higher the numbers, the better. Different manufacturers of large-screen color displays have settled on a variety of resolution levels, most in the 1,000-by-800 range. By comparison, a high-end prepress monitor such as that used on a Hell ChromaCom retouching station, is 19" in size with a resolution of 1,024-by-1,024. Although increased resolution is an advantage, never buy a monitor by the spec sheet, unless you've actually seen it perform, preferably in comparison with competing models.

Acceleration

Life is short, they say, and you're a long time dead. Think of this when you buy a graphics board, and you'll be happy to pay a little extra for one with on-board graphics acceleration.

Photo: © SuperMac Technology, Inc.

Fig. 5-24
For maximum performance you'll want an accelerated graphics board, such as this SuperMac Thunder 24, and a large-screen monitor.

One of the major problems with all graphics boards is the time it takes to move a million or more pixels (which may require more than 24 million bits) from main memory to the monitor. To speed this up, many graphics cards now include on-board accelerators based on specialized chips called application-specific integrated circuits (ASICs).

These accelerator boards improve the speed of QuickDraw, especially for 24-bit graphics-intensive applications, by intercepting QuickDraw graphics functions and simplifying them for rapid transfer to the screen. An accelerated graphics board is one of the most cost-effective enhancements most color publishers can make to their computer systems.

Other display issues

The other key variables to watch for when selecting a color monitor are refresh rate, interlacing, and dot pitch. The refresh rate is the number of times each second the screen is redrawn, and it's important because a screen that redraws slowly will have noticeable flicker.

Early graphics cards refreshed the display only 45 to 50 times per second (expressed as 50Hz, where a Hertz is one cycle per second). This resulted in noticeable flickering of the image, especially under the fluorescent lights common in many offices. As graphics boards improved, typical refresh rates increased to more than 60Hz. Today, the best boards offer refresh rates of more than 72Hz, at which point there is virtually no visible flickering of the image.

In order to increase the resolution of a graphics board, some manufacturers use a technique called interlacing, in which only one-half the scan lines comprising the image are displayed with each refresh cycle. The problem with interlacing is that it tends to cause noticeable flicker, and is therefore to be avoided. In fact, read the fine print on the spec sheet before you buy a graphics board.

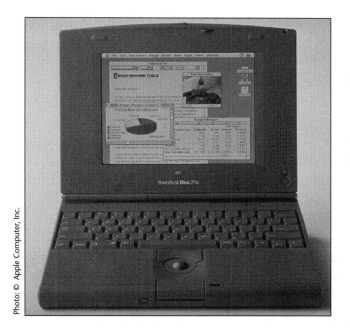

Photo: © Apple Computer, Inc.

Fig. 5-25
This Apple
PowerBook Duo
270C sports a crisp
active-matrix color
screen, so you can
even take color
publishing on the
road.

Ads for some boards proclaim that they "support resolutions up to 1280-by-1024, and provide non-interlaced display". But a careful reading of the specs reveals that the board in question supports its highest resolution only with interlacing, and that non-interlaced display is supported only to a resolution of 800-by-600, which provides significantly less detail.

All CRT-based monitors use red, green, and blue phosphors, and in general the closer together the same-color phosphors are, the clearer and sharper the image will be. Most high-quality color monitors have a dot pitch of .26 to .28 mm, meaning that one blue dot is .28mm from the next blue dot, and so on. Although this should not be the deciding factor in choosing a monitor, you may well find after actually looking at a few similar models that those with the smallest dot pitch have the sharpest image.

As part of today's increasing trend toward environmental awareness, more and more individuals and organizations are looking for ways to reduce the amount of low-frequency radiation emitted by computer monitors. A variety of common-sense measures can be adopted, such as ensuring that you don't sit directly behind or beside a monitor, particularly a large monitor. Very little low-frequency radiation is emitted from the front of a monitor.

For the monitor itself, currently the most stringent requirement is the Swedish Government's MPR II standard, which seeks to drastically lower the levels at which people are exposed to such supposedly benign "non-ionizing" radiation as magnetic fields. If this concerns you, check out the high-end models from the major display makers, most of whom have added MPR II compliance to some or all their monitors. It's important as well to note that when we talk about emissions from monitors they are emissions of non-ionizing radiation, not the ionizing radiation from nuclear sources.

In part because of intense price competition, monitor vendors have been striving of late to differentiate their products based on ease-of-use features. The location and operation of controls for brightness and contrast, for instance, can make or break a potential sale. Some manufacturers have models that include a built-in microprocessor for storing both preset and user-definable settings for recall whenever the display is connected to a video source.

Systems integration

Now that you've specified all the pieces for your ideal color publishing system, how do you put them together?

In the early days of the microcomputer revolution, when hobbyists assembled computers from kits, it was assumed that each user did his or her own "systems integration," that is, ensured that the hardware components worked properly together. Then, as computers became more sophisticated, the emphasis shifted to machines that you could simply plug in and begin using, such as the Macintosh. Typically, however, color publishing systems require components and peripherals from many different vendors, and some users reluctantly find themselves in the role of systems integrators.

There are few solutions to this problem, now that the specialty computer store is virtually obsolete. Any superstore or mail order house will be happy to sell you all the pieces that add up to a color publishing system, but they'll expect you to put them together on your own. Many VARs (value added resellers) provide integration services, with their fees bundled into the overall cost of the system. For many people moving into color publishing, a qualified consultant may be the most cost-effective way of getting the right hardware, and getting it working properly.

One question you should ask whenever configuring or modifying your hardware setup is where the bottleneck is. There will always be a bottleneck, of course—it just moves around every time you add another hardware component. If your system takes a long time to display large image files because the hard disk is too slow, buying a faster hard disk will reduce the time it takes to read files from disk, but now your graphics board will probably be the limiting factor in overall performance. This is a never-ending game, and one that can get very expensive.

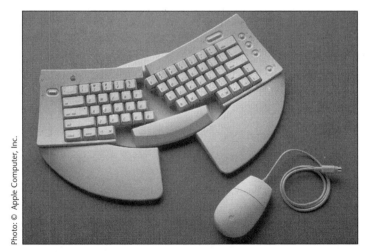

Photo: © Apple Computer, Inc.

Fig. 5-26
The week after you buy your new state-of-the-art computer they'll come up with some cool new gizmo, such as this funky but ergonomically correct keyboard from Apple.

Why hardware is hard

Ever wonder why they call it hardware? After reading the ads, you have probably realized that all currently available computer hardware represents a vast improvement over what preceded it. Tomorrow, however, it will all be obsolete. If you've ever tried to sell used computer equipment, you know that you have to practically pay somebody to haul it away if it's more than six months old.

Buying hardware is always painful—you know there's something faster, more powerful, and cheaper coming out next month. It's really hard to accept that today's state-of-the-art gizmo is tomorrow's quaint antique. That's why they call it hardware.

Color Scanning

"To imagine that which is to be embodied in light,
and shadow, and color—that which is strictly pictorial—
is an accumulative work of the mind."

Eighteenth-century painter Thomas Cole

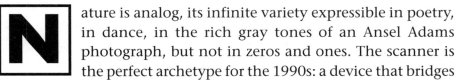 ature is analog, its infinite variety expressible in poetry, in dance, in the rich gray tones of an Ansel Adams photograph, but not in zeros and ones. The scanner is the perfect archetype for the 1990s: a device that bridges the distance between analog and digital, mapping the real analog world into the cool synthetic precision of the machine.

Today, virtually all communications media are in transition from analog to digital. Phonograph records and audio tapes are analog; compact disks (CDs) are digital. The existing telephone system is analog, but is rapidly being converted to digital. Television is analog, but the new high-definition television system will be digital.

Scanners convert *analog* information (light) into *digital* information (computer bits). As discussed in the chapter on halftoning, this conversion requires each tiny picture element, or *pixel*, to be represented by many bits, so that the resulting image file contains enough levels of gray to fool the eye into seeing continuous shades where they do not actually exist.

The underlying rule in color publishing is that, if you want to produce high-quality output, you must start with a high-quality scan. But achieving high-quality scans requires more than plenty of bits: you need precise optics, high resolution and sophisticated software.

And, despite recent innovations in scanning software that enable non-professional users to obtain excellent results, you still need specialized skills.

This chapter explores color scanning, from inexpensive desktop devices used for capturing low-resolution *position-only* images to the high-quality drum scanners found in color trade shops. Our purpose is to understand both the technology and the process of scanning— to become more effective at capturing high-quality color images into the computer, where they can be enhanced, modified, color-separated, and printed. Even if you won't be operating the scanner hands-on, you need to understand the basics of scanning before you commit your images to the scanning process.

A word of warning—handle photographic originals with care. Dust, dirt, smudges, fingerprints or other garbage on the original slide, transparency or print will be difficult or impossible to remove later. Although desktop color software gives you the tools to fix such problems yourself, you need to be a magician to transform marginal input into vibrant output.

Scanner workflow

Working with photographic images is by far the most challenging aspect of the color publishing process, in part because of the file size problem, but also because the human eye is sensitive to incorrect colors, especially in food, flesh tones, and other so-called "memory colors".

Scanning software has improved tremendously of late, making it much easier to automatically obtain images with the correct brightness and contrast, for example. However, most people working with desktop scanners have little understanding of how to select the correct settings for such parameters as tone, cast, selective color correction, unsharp masking, and black generation.

For this reason, many desktop publishers don't attempt to scan and color correct the actual high-resolution image—they leave this complex job to a color trade shop, commercial printer or other color production professional. In fact, there are many different workflow options available to color publishers, and only you can decide which is most appropriate to your skills, equipment, and budget.

Many people find it best to use an inexpensive desktop scanner to create low-resolution position-only images, or *viewfiles*. These low-res images take much less time to scan and consume far less disk storage then their high-res counterparts, but are nonetheless more than adequate for use throughout the design and approval process. In this scenario, high-end scanning doesn't begin until the page design is complete, with all the text, graphics, and keylines in place. At that point, an output service provider (color trade shop, PostScript service bureau or commercial printer) takes responsibility for high-resolution scanning, color correction, proofing, and film output, using the low-res files to show the proper cropping and scaling of each image.

A second option is to work with a service provider from the start. They'll scan the originals at high resolution and provide them as color TIFF files, usually on SyQuest cartridges, optical cartridges, digital audio tapes, or other transportable media. You can then manipulate and enhance these images on the desktop, integrate them into page layouts, and separate them to film on a PostScript imagesetter. One way of saving money when you've chosen this route is to have the images scanned at a professional trade shop, then output the completed pages at a more economical PostScript service bureau.

A third option is to have the service provider scan the originals at high resolution but give you just low-resolution color TIFF viewfiles for design and approval purposes. Using this method, there are two versions of each image, differing only in the scan resolution and file size. The high-res file is retained by the service provider, to be integrated into the page layout at the final prepress stage.

When the design is complete, you send the final pages, on disk, to the service provider, which then replaces the low-res files with their high-res counterparts, either manually or through a semi-automatic link such as the Open Prepress Interface (OPI) or Desktop Color Separations (DCS). This workflow allows you to continue to work with high-end scans, even if you've moved all other page layout and production tasks from traditional to desktop methods.

As the price of high-quality scanners continues to plummet, there's one other scanning option that's becoming increasingly attractive: doing your own high-res scanning on the desktop. With the emergence of desktop drum scanners, it's now possible to capture high-resolution images, retouch and separate them into CMYK format, and place them in page layouts—all on the desktop.

To summarize, as a color publisher, you have a number of choices:

- you can scan low-resolution position-only images on the desktop, and have a service provider manually replace them with high-resolution versions prior to output;

- you can forego color scanning entirely, and pay a color house to scan, process, and separate the images, and provide low-resolution images they will later replace with high-resolution equivalents;

- you can pay the color house to scan the images and give you actual high-resolution image files, which you process and output from the desktop;

- you can do everything on the desktop, including scanning, separating, and outputting the images.

How scanners work

There are many different kinds of scanners (flatbed, slide, drum, and so on), but, irrespective of the mechanical configuration, all are based on the same fundamental principle. An incident light source shines white light through the original (in the case of a transparency) or reflects off the original (in the case of a photographic print or original artwork). The resulting light falls on an array of detectors, each of which captures the data for a single pixel.

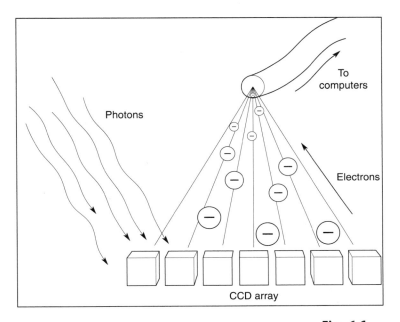

Fig. 6-1
The charge-coupled device detector array inside a desktop scanner
converts light energy into electrical energy

The detectors in most desktop scanners consist of charge-coupled devices (CCDs)—tiny electronic devices that convert bundles of light energy (photons) into bundles of electrical energy (electrons). However, high-end scanners typically use a photomultiplier tube (PMT) rather than a CCD. In general, PMTs have higher resolution and greater dynamic range than CCDs, although recent innovations in CCD technology have increased their resolution so they almost match that of PMTs. PMT-based scanners are also better than CCDs at capturing shadow detail without unnecessary noise.

In the simplest case of a bi-level (black or white) scan, each pixel measures the intensity of incoming photons to determine whether it is greater than or less than a preset threshold level. If it's greater, the pixel emits an electrical charge (an electron). The electrons from each activated pixel are fed to an analog-to-digital converter, which outputs a computer-readable file, usually stored as a TIFF (tag image file format) file.

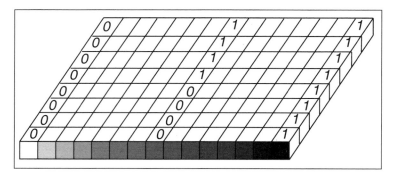

Fig. 6-2
In a gray-scale scanner, each pixel stores multiple bits; the greater
the pixel depth, the more shades of gray can be represented.

In a gray-scale scanner, each pixel is capable of storing more than one bit. Just as in the case of the display monitors, storing two bits per pixel allows four colors or shades of gray (white, black, dark gray, and light gray) to be represented. With eight bits per pixel, 256 shades of gray can be stored, which is the minimum needed to render photographic detail with reasonable accuracy. As explained in Chapter 3, the human eye can detect as many as 100 shades of gray in any part of a scene, which means there must be at least 200 shades of gray between pure white and solid black in order to create smooth blends without banding.

For color scanning, we must capture 256 gray shades for each of the three additive primaries (red, green, and blue), which requires 24 bits per pixel (three times eight). There are two different approaches used by color scanners to achieve this. Some feature a three-pass system in which the detectors move past the original three times (once each for red, green, and blue), with the values from each pass creating one channel in the color image. Unfortunately, tiny tracking errors in the scanning mechanism can lead to misalignment of data acquired during successive passes, resulting in small but potentially noticeable color shifts. This problem can be minimized with good scanning software and motor transport control mechanisms.

Another way of capturing three channels of information is to sequentially illuminate each row with red, green, and blue light during the scanning process, so that only one scan of the original is required. Vendors who use this method, known as *strobing*, claim that it minimizes color shifts caused by tracking errors. Proponents of the three-pass system point out that even small discrepancies in the intensity or angle of the bulbs as they are flashed on and off can also cause noticeable color shifts.

Irrespective of what numbers and charts of scanner performance tell us, nothing competes with the final arbiter, the viewer's eye. The color accuracy of different scanners must be compared relative to one another, based on their varying responses to the same original.

Resolution & dynamic range

The most common basis for comparing scanners is *resolution*, the number of pixels a scanner can see in a given area. Resolution is often expressed as *dots per inch* (dpi), but, as previously noted, a more precise description is *pixels per inch* (ppi), which avoids any potential confusion with halftone dots.

Some scanners use *interpolation*, a technique that allows them to capture files with a resolution higher than their optics (a scanner with an *optical* resolution of 400 ppi, for instance, could, through the use of software, capture an image file with an *interpolated* resolution of 800 ppi). The interpolation routines average an image's bi-level or grayscale values and place new pixels between the existing ones.

Interpolation doesn't add detail to a scan, but smooths it, providing better transitions between grays and reducing the jaggies. Keep in mind that interpolation can significantly slow the image capture process: a scanner that takes less than a minute to scan a 4-by-6-inch photo at its maximum optical resolution of 300 ppi can take more than eight minutes to scan the same photo when interpolation is used to boost the apparent resolution to 600 ppi.

With all the fuss over resolutions, don't automatically assume that it's best to scan at the highest possible resolution. When working with line art, it's important to scan at a resolution of more than 600 to 1,000 ppi, in order to exceed the eye's ability to distinguish fine lines. However, when working with a continuous tone original such as a photograph, the scanning resolution is determined by the 2:1 formula explored in Chapter 3. Because most commercial printing takes place with a line screen of 150 lpi or less, images that are to reproduced size-as should be scanned at a maximum resolution of 300 ppi. It's only when a photo needs to be enlarged for reproduction that a higher scan resolution would be required.

The best way to reproduce good color is to capture it fully and accurately on the input scan. However, this is more than a matter of resolution, and requires that the scanner detect accurately the complete range of colors present, as well as the shades of gray and the detail of lines.

The quality of a color scanner is largely a function of its *dynamic range*, or ability to capture detail in both the highlights (the brightest parts of an image) and shadows (the darkest parts). Dynamic range is measured on a logarithmic scale, where a ten-times difference in brightness between the lightest and darkest parts of an image would be a dynamic range of 1.0, a 100-times difference would be 2.0, a 1,000-times difference would be 3.0 and a 10,000-times difference would be 4.0.

The dynamic range of an original photographic transparency is about 3.0 to 3.5, while that of a print is 1.5 to 2.0. Most low-cost desktop flatbed scanners have a maximum dynamic range of about 1.8 to 2.0, while it's about 3.2 to 3.8 for desktop drum scanners, and about 4.0 for high-end scanners.

In other words, desktop scanners typically have too low a dynamic range to capture detail at both ends of the brightness spectrum. The result is that either the dark areas in the original go black or the light areas go white—it's especially hard to pick up shadow details in dark slides. This problem increases when you correct an image after scanning, because you've already lost information from the high and low ends, so that boosting the brightness forces you to lose even more detail in the light areas.

There are two factors that are crucial to the dynamic range of the image file stored in a computer: the inherent dynamic range of the scanner's light detectors, and the number of bits captured per pixel. Even though PostScript-based systems currently can work with a maximum of only eight bits per pixel (per color), image quality can be substantially enhanced if the scanner captures 10 or 12 or 16 bits per pixel, then uses software to distill this data to eight bits per pixel. In effect, the software looks at the brightness values in each image, then maintains only the eight bits that contain the greatest variation between light and dark.

A typical slide or color photograph with a good range of brightness values would have to be scanned at 12 to 14 bits per pixel per color to capture all the intermediate shadings of color in the original. Most desktop scanners capture only eight bits per pixel, although some scan 12 bits per pixel, then compress the information into eight bits before transmitting it to the computer.

To help solve the dynamic range problem, scanner vendor Leaf Systems recently proposed a new scanning protocol known as High Dynamic Range (HDR), in which scanners would capture 16 bits per pixel per color, resulting in 48-bit rather than 24-bit color. The resulting 48-bit data would be maintained throughout image processing and page layout, and distilled to 24-bit format only immediately prior to output.

Although to date there is little consensus in the industry that HDR is the way to go, Adobe has modified Photoshop (in version 2.5.1) to support 48-bit color. The big problem with going to 48-bit color is that image files become twice as large, thereby exacerbating the performance problem on desktop computers. However, once you know what output device will be used, you can sample the images down to 24-bit color before placing them in the page layout.

Scanners—all shapes and sizes

Because people have a variety of requirements for color production, there is no single scanner that will fit the needs and budgets of all users. Indeed, the scanning market is a continuum of quality and expense that stretches from handheld scanners costing a few hundred dollars to high-end drum scanners costing a thousand times as much.

There are four main configurations for color scanners: flatbed, slide, multi-format transparency, and drum scanners. There are also black-and-white scanner designs, such as overhead and handheld scanners, but these are not well suited for working with color.

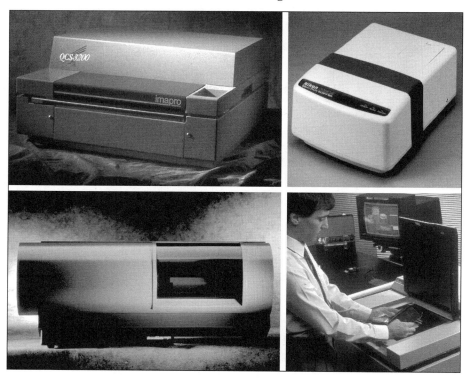

Fig. 6-3
There are many kinds of desktop color scanners, including (clockwise from top left) flatbed, slide, transparency, and drum.

Color scanners come in a variety of formats, including:

- flatbed scanners, which resemble photocopiers: the lid is lifted, the original image placed, face down, on the glass, and the scan begins. Beneath the glass, a motorized scan head on tiny rails travels the length of the page, illuminating the original and measuring the intensity of the reflected light;

- slide scanners that shine a high-intensity light through a 35mm positive or negative film. The light passes through a series of color filters and lenses onto a detector, which converts the light impulses into digital signals. Slide scanners are typically higher resolution and have better detail, bit depth, and focus than flatbed scanners;

- multiple-format transparency scanners, which operate in much the same way as slide scanners, but accept a variety of film formats commonly used in professional photography, from 35mm to 4-by-5-inches. In some cases, their dynamic range rivals that of drum scanners;

- rotary drum scanners, which have long been the mainstay of the professional color house, costing hundreds of thousands of dollars and requiring highly trained operators. Drum scanner technology is rapidly migrating to the desktop, in the form of table-top mini-drum scanners.

There are a variety of ways of connecting a scanner to your computer. The most common is through a SCSI (Small Computer System Interface) connection to your Mac or PC, either directly or through a converter box. Another popular scanner interface is through a GPIB (General Purpose Interface Bus) card that fits in a NuBus slot on a Macintosh. Alternatively, you can connect a scanner through a serial port, although this is much   slower than the other two methods. Many kinds of scanners can be configured as a shared peripheral on a network, though, in most cases, they are stand-alone devices.

Flatbed scanners

At the lower end of the price scale, flatbed scanners are the most popular choice, especially for applications where high-quality reproduction is not required, or where the scanners are being used only to capture low-resolution position-only images that will later be replaced by high-resolution scans.

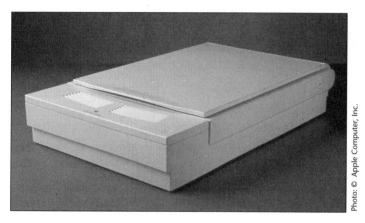

Photo: © Apple Computer, Inc.

Fig. 6-4
Flatbed scanners, such as this Apple Color OneScanner, provide a cost-effective way of getting photographs and original art into a computer.

Many inexpensive flatbed scanners can input only reflective art (prints and artwork), rather than transparencies. Some models allow you to add an optional transparency adapter, although this often compromises image quality. Be aware that many high-quality photographic originals are only available as 35mm slides or 4-by-5-inch transparencies.

The main advantages of flatbed scanners are their relatively low cost and their flexibility for scanning small and large reflective (and optionally transmissive) originals. Among the leading vendors of low-cost flatbed scanners are Apple, Epson, Hewlett-Packard, La Cie, Microtek, Mirror Technologies, Sharp, Tamarack, UMAX Technologies, and XRS.

Photo: © Sharp Electronics

Fig. 6-5
The Sharp JX-610 desktop scanner can be used for either reflective scanning (left) or, with an optional adapter, for scanning transparencies (right).

Many of these vendors bundle their scanners with image capture and manipulation software, typically Adobe Photoshop or PhotoStyler. You should know, however, that some scanner vendors include a full-function version of the software while others provide a "limited edition" version, such as Photoshop LE, which is missing some of the capabilities of the full retail package, such as the ability to create color separations.

In addition to these low-end devices, a number of vendors also make mid-range flatbed scanners, including Agfa, PixelCraft (a division of Xerox), and Scitex.

Photo: © PixelCraft

Fig. 6-6
The PixelCraft 7650C works with images up to 11.7-by-17-inches at resolutions up to 1,200 ppi, and comes with the ColorAccess color separation program.

Slide scanners

Although most commercial photography continues to be shot on 4-by-5-inch transparencies, increasingly, it is being done today with 35mm slides, primarily because of their lower cost. Scanners designed to work with slides (or 35mm negative film) are an excellent way of capturing 24-bit color images for desktop publishing. The major advantage of transparencies as a source for scanned images is that they are capable of a much wider range of brightness, contrast, and color saturation than is possible on reflective materials such as color prints.

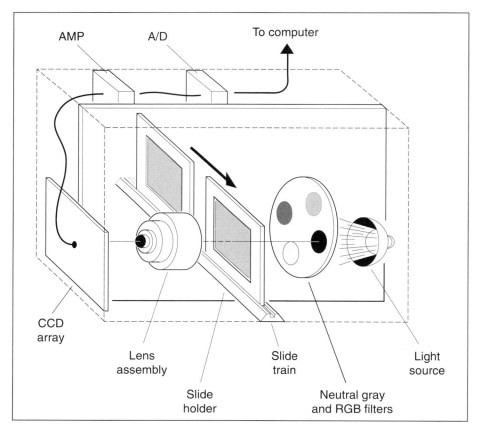

Fig. 6-7
Slide scanners work by passing a slide through an optical path between a CCD detector and a set of RGB and neutral gray filters.

Most slide scanners work according to the same mechanical principle: the slide is held between a light source and an array of CCD detectors, while a set of filters (usually red, green, blue, and neutral gray) rotate in front of the light source. In addition to the quality of the optics and mechanics, the main factor determining the quality of a slide scanner is its pixel depth. The more bits of information captured for each pixel, the greater the dynamic range and hence the quality.

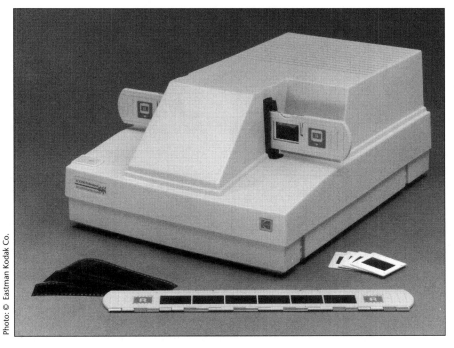

Photo: © Eastman Kodak Co.

Fig. 6-8
The Kodak RFS 2035 Plus is a 35mm slide scanner that can capture an image with resolution and color balance suitable for commercial reproduction.

A secondary benefit of slides is that they are easier than prints to handle, store, and transport. One limitation of 35mm slides is their relatively small size, as compared with 4-by-5-inch transparencies and other larger originals—any enlargement of the image will more easily reveal the underlying grain structure of the photographic emulsion.

Fig. 6-9
The Nikon Coolscan fits in a half-height drive bay in a Mac or PC, enabling you to scan 35mm slides or negative films without giving up valuable desk space.

Photo: © Nikon

One of the more innovative slide scanner designs is the Nikon Coolscan, which is small enough to fit inside a conventional half-height drive bay in any Macintosh or Windows-based computer. It is also available as an external device that attaches to any computer with a SCSI interface.

In addition to the low-cost desktop slide scanners, there are more expensive devices from a number of vendors, including Leaf Systems (a subsidiary of Scitex).

Fig. 6-10
The Leafscan 35 is a 35mm slide scanner that captures 16 bits per pixel per color to provide maximum detail capture.

Photo: © Leaf Systems

Transparency scanners

Because 35mm slides are too small to capture sufficient detail and dynamic range for many commercial photography applications, 4-by-5-inch transparencies are the preferred medium for such users. These larger format transparencies can be input using multi-format transparency scanners, such as those made by Leaf, PixelCraft, Scitex, and others.

Photo: © PixelCraft

Fig. 6-11
A transparency scanner can handle originals from 35mm slides to 4-by-5 inches in size, often with higher quality than a 35mm slide scanner.

One of the most popular scanners in this category is the Leafscan 45, which features a 6,000 element CCD and supports resolutions up to 5,080 ppi. It has a broad dynamic range (to 3.7), and captures 16 bits per pixel per color. The Leafscan 45 connects to Macintosh or Windows-based computers, and lets you set highlight, midtone and shadow values independently for each color.

Another popular mid-range transparency scanner is the PixelCraft ProImager 4520 RS, which accepts originals up to 4-by-5 inches, and comes bundled with QuickScan image acquisition software and ColorAccess color separation software.

High-end drum scanners

Traditionally, color trade shops have used massive rotary drum scanners about the size of a large upright piano. The piano metaphor is apt, because the quality of the separations produced is often a direct result of the skill of the person at the keyboard, regardless of the type of scanner or software used. High-end scanners and other proprietary prepress equipment are discussed in more detail in Chapter 10.

Photo: © Crosfield

Fig. 6-12
This high-end drum scanner is complex, expensive, and powerful, and requires the skills of a trained operator.

There are two different kinds of drum scanners, the huge, expensive kind that you find in a color trade shop, and the smaller, more cost-effective kind that fits on the desktop. Both offer a level of quality that low-cost flatbed and 35mm scanners can't match. For the highest possible image quality (and maximum throughput), nothing can touch the high-end scanners made by Scitex, Linotype-Hell, Crosfield, and Screen.

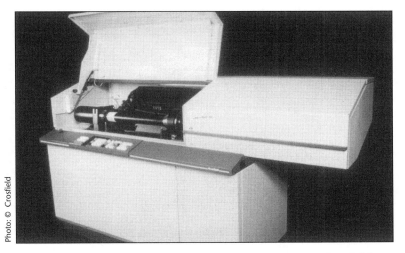

Photo: © Crosfield

Fig. 6-13
This Crosfield drum scanner has both acquire and expose modules, and can be used as part of a high-end prepress system or connected to a desktop computer.

Most high-end drum scanners also function as film recorders. In the early days of digital prepress, most images were scanned directly to film separations: the original was mounted on the scanner's "analyze" drum, blank film was loaded into the scanner's "expose" drum, and the separations were recorded in real time. Although this method is still used in some scanning situations, today it is more common to save the scanned image to a central computer's hard disk, from which it can be sent to the scanner's expose station (or a separate film recorder) either directly or after color correction and image manipulation on a retouching station.

Desktop drum scanners

The most recent innovation in scanning technology is the emergence of desktop drum scanners, which combine the precision of a drum mechanism with the lower cost and standard interface of desktop devices. Also known as mini-drum desktop scanners, they produce output almost as good as that of conventional high-end scanners, while maintaining the flexibility of working on the desktop.

Photo: © Crosfield

Fig. 6-14
The Optronics ColorGetter II Prima is a small drum scanner that bridges the gap between high-end scanners and the desktop.

The first product in this field was the Optronics ColorGetter, which was introduced in 1990 and has since been supplanted by the ColorGetter II Prisma. Some people wouldn't describe a ColorGetter as a desktop device, given that it weighs hundreds of pounds and costs more than $50,000. However, it meets my definition of desktop for two reasons: it fits on top of a large desk, and it connects directly to a Macintosh, Windows-based PC, or UNIX-based workstation.

Other competitors in the desktop mini-drum category include the Screen 1015 and 1030 AI, the ScanMate 5000, and the Howtek Scanmaster D4000 and D7000.

The Screen DT-S1015 is a mini-drum scanner that fits comfortably on a small desktop or table, and supports a maximum resolution of 2,500 ppi. It uses four photomultipliers; three to capture RGB information and the fourth for enhancing sharpness. It also includes a color computer that can convert RGB data to CMYK on the fly, saving the time this would require in Photoshop or some other imaging program.

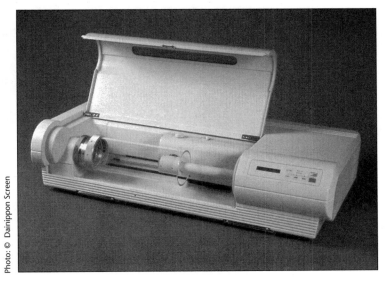

Photo: © Dainippon Screen

Fig. 6-15
The Screen DT-S1030 AI desktop drum scanner comes with "expert system" software that optimizes scanning parameters for each original.

Optional "artificial intelligence" software is available for the Screen 1015, to help inexperienced operators achieve high-quality scans with marginal originals, automatically compensating for under- or over-exposure or for color casts. The software performs a pre-scan to measure the white point and black point in an image, then adjusts the parameters for the actual scan in order to optimize the tonal range being captured. Screen also sells the DT-S1030 AI scanner, which supports originals up to 10-by-12-inches at resolutions up to 5,200 ppi, and has the expert systems software built in.

Photo: © ScanView

Fig. 6-16
The ScanMate 5000 is a desktop drum scanner from Denmark that combines high performance with sleek styling.

The ScanMate 5000 from ScanView is a digital desktop drum scanner that operates at resolutions up to 5,000 ppi, with a dynamic range that is almost as high as that of a conventional high-end scanner. The ScanMate also reflects its Danish heritage, with an industrial design reminiscent of machines that process food rather than digital images. ScanView also sells ColorQuartet, a scanning and color separation program that can be configured to distribute the work among several computers on a network. Alternately, ColorQuartet can run on a Mac containing one or more Radius Rocket co-processor boards, or on a Sun SPARC workstation.

The Howtek Scanmaster D4000 desktop drum scanner uses PMTs to attain high resolution (up to 4,000 ppi) and high dynamic range (up to 3.8). It accepts reflective or transmissive originals up to 10-by-10 inches, and can be interfaced to Macs, PCs, and UNIX-based computers. For maximum tonal range, the D4000 captures 12 bits of color data per channel during the scan, then reduces this to the optimal eight-bit form prior to saving the image to disk.

Howtek also sells a color computer board, the CosMYK 860, which can be installed inside the D4000 to give it capabilities previously available only through the built-in color computer inside a high-end scanner. The CosMYK 860 performs real-time unsharp masking (at 12 bits per channel), data scaling, and color conversion (with user-definable UCR and GCR plus customizable printing ink tables).

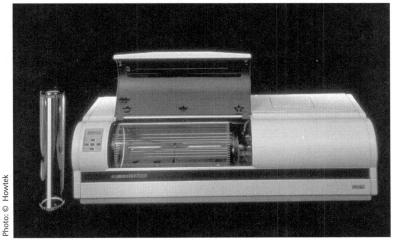

Photo: © Howtek

Fig. 6-17
The Howtek Scanmaster 7000 desktop drum scanner has a built-in color computer and can handle originals up to 18-by-24-inches.

Howtek recently launched the Scanmaster 7000 scanner, which further narrows the gap between desktop and high-end scanners. The $70,000 Scanmaster 7000 is targeted directly at color trade shops, service bureaus, and commercial printers. It can handle originals up to 18-by-24-inches, with UCR, GCR and unsharp masking built into the hardware. The scanner comes with Aurora color scanning software, which controls image enhancement, color correction, auto balance, color-selective unsharp masking, and cast removal.

As we saw earlier, the dynamic range of any scanner is determined primarily by the photomultiplier tubes (PMTs) or charge-coupled devices (CCDs) used to convert light into electricity.

Although some desktop scanners use the newer (and less expensive) CCDs, all high-end scanners use PMTs, which give them greater dynamic range. Although many desktop drum scanners, especially those based on PMTs, now have resolution and dynamic range almost equivalent to conventional high-end drum scanners, they still lag behind in overall productivity, due largely to the fact they are slower.

Some desktop drum scanners have a fixed (non-removable) drum, which means that the scanner is inactive while each original is mounted and removed. By comparison, high-end scanners use removable drums, and each original is not only pre-mounted but often pre-scanned on a separate station to determine scanning parameters prior to being loaded on the actual scanner.

Selecting a scanner

In choosing a scanner, there are many factors to consider, of which the most important is quality. Unlike a hard disk or a computer, where performance can be reasonably well gauged by reading a spec sheet, the quality of a scanner can be assessed only by looking at the image files it creates. This is not so easy to do, especially when you're considering scanners from a number of vendors.

Until recently, it was easy to classify any scanner as belonging to one of two distinct categories: desktop or high-end. The recent emergence of high-quality desktop drum scanners has created a third distinct mid-range category.

To improve your chances of getting the right scanner, attend one of the major graphic arts trade shows, and bring along a typical slide or print that you want to have scanned. Also bring along a supply of SyQuest cartridges or a transportable SCSI hard disk. Ask each of the scanner vendors whose products you're considering to scan your sample and give you the file. Then, back at your own computer, place all the scans in a single page layout document and print them to the same desktop color printer. If you're really picky, you could even have them output to film and have contract proofs made. Another way to interpret the quality of the scans is to open them in Photoshop or PhotoStyler and use the Histogram feature to see how well each scanner has captured the available detail in your original image's highlights, midtones, and shadows.

	Desktop	Mid-range	High-end
Maximum resolution (ppi)	300-600	3000+	3000
Light detectors	CCD	CCD/PMT	PMT
Dynamic range	1.8 - 2.4	3.2 - 3.8	3.5 - 4.0
Quality	Low-medium	Medium-high	High
Productivity	Low-medium	Medium-high	High
Maximum size original	8.5-by-11	10-by-14	26-by-40
Color computer	No	Maybe	Yes
Film recorder	No	No	Maybe
Cost (in thousands)	$1-$10	$25-$70	$100-$200
Operator skill required	Minimal	Moderate	High

Fig. 6-19
Color scanners can be organized into three categories,
according to resolution, cost, and other factors.

There's one other factor to keep in mind. If you're looking at mid-range scanners and have a substantial number of photographs to process, perform a test on a sample image (of appropriate size) to discover how long your imaging program takes to convert it from RGB to CMYK mode. This will affect your decision about whether it's cost-effective to buy a scanner with an on-board color computer capable of color separating scanned images on the fly.

If you're considering low-cost desktop scanners and you will need to scan both reflective originals (artwork or photographic prints) and transmissive originals (slides, negatives or transparencies), be cautious when looking at flatbed scanners with an optional transparency adapter. In some cases, these scanners provide quite good results when working with reflective originals, but quite poor results when scanning transparencies. Carefully test the quality of scans produced with a transparency adapter before you buy one.

High-end scanning

Desktop users can learn a lot by understanding the high-end scanning process as it's practiced by color trade shops and commercial printers. In many ways, high-end scanners operate just like desktop scanners, but there are some important differences, such as resolution—after dealing with typical desktop scanning resolutions in the 300 to 600 ppi range, it's refreshing to move to scanners that have maximum resolution exceeding 4,000 ppi.

More important, high-end scanners are capable of a dynamic range that puts the desktop units to shame. They can scan an original with a difficult range of contrasts and, within limits, capture detail in both the highlight areas and the shadows. A desktop scanner, with its more narrow dynamic range, is usually forced to drop the shadows to black to maintain any detail at all in the highlights. Even with the expanded dynamic range of a high-end scanner, it's essential that a skilled operator set the color controls to emphasize which parts of an image are to be accentuated.

High-end scanners can work with much larger originals than desktop units—often with poster-sized reflective art up to 20-by-24-inches. Typically, they also operate at much higher speeds, their drums rotating at speeds in excess of 800 revolutions per minute. Large illustrations or other artwork can be captured directly on a large drum scanner, whereas they would need to be photographed on a copy stand to create a negative or transparency if a smaller desktop scanner was being used.

In a color trade shop, most jobs begin with preparation of the artwork for scanning. Although an increasing number of originals arrive as 35mm slides, other formats, such as color transparencies and hard-copy photographs from 4-by-5-inches up to 8-by-10-inches, are also common. Transparencies are preferred over reflective art because they tend to maintain a greater dynamic range during the scanning process.

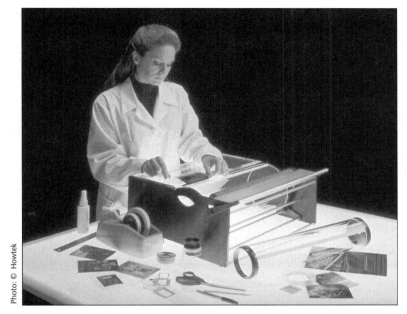

Photo: © Howtek

Fig. 6-19
At a color trade shop or commercial printer, each slide is carefully
mounted on the drum prior to scanning.

The originals are cleaned and carefully mounted on a plastic cylindrical drum, which is loaded into one of two different machines. In a modestly equipped color house, the drum is loaded directly onto the scanner, where it is pre-scanned or probed to determine the proper densities and other parameters. The scanner operator uses a keyboard or control panel to then enter the appropriate scanner instructions, the final scan is performed, and the image saved to disk or tape (or scanned directly to film).

In a medium or large color house with more expensive equipment, the drum is first mounted on a pre-scan station. The operator determines all the operating parameters for the particular job, then transfers them to the scan station across a local area network. Each scanning drum is identified by a bar code, so that as soon as it is mounted on the scanner, the job parameters are loaded and run, and the image data are stored on magnetic tapes or disk packs.

Until very recently, type was scanned into the system from a black-and-white *mechanical* or typeset galley, but today most type arrives as PostScript code, which is uploaded to the high-end system and raster image processed, or *ripped*, to become part of a pixel image. Often, before the layout artist can integrate the type and scanned images into the rest of the page, the images must be cleaned up with retouching tools. This is accomplished by zooming in on individual pixels with pencil, brush or eraser. At the same time, the operator will compensate for any global or local color casts, and will touch up any small problems.

To save time and money on high-end scans, many commercial color publishers rely on *ganging*, in which multiple images are scanned and color-separated at the same time. All the elements to be scanned must be in the same form (transparencies, prints or original artwork), and all must be sized to the same percentage during input.

Most important, the color content of the shots must be similar. All images in a gang must be free of overall color casts, or any color casts present must be uniform throughout all the images. The highlight areas of each image in the gang should be checked to ensure they are uniform in weight, density, and color cast. If an experienced color separator suggests you break a large gang into two smaller ones to allow for cast correction, it is almost certain to be cheaper in the long run to pay for two good scans than for one that is compromised.

If the parameters used in scanning the original do not capture all the color information it contains, fixing the image in the computer later will be difficult, or often impossible. Every brand of slide film, for instance, has a distinct reaction to different colors, a unique *spectral response* curve, which must be compensated for during the color separation process.

The scanner operator normally receives the original with an attached form specifying what the customer wants. This is a crucial communications tool, and it must provide information that is concise, and free from ambiguity.

Such information should include details on:

- the emulsion of the original (such as Kodachrome, Ektachrome or Fujichrome), the emulsion speed, and whether the original is a negative or positive;
- the degree of enlargement or reduction, and any cropping required;
- the desired line screen, and the intended press, paper, ink, and standard dot gain;
- whether sharpness should be increased, decreased or left unadjusted;
- the main area of interest in the original, and whether particular tonal ranges in the original should be emphasized, or "opened up";
- any specific colors that must be matched, and whether local or overall color casts should be partially or completely removed.

Although this kind of form has not yet become a standard practice in desktop scanning applications, savvy users will adopt it as a way of minimizing all kinds of communications breakdowns.

Color computers

Until very recently, one of the main differences between high-end and desktop drum scanners is that only the proprietary high-end devices contained a set of specialized circuit boards, called a *color computer*. A color computer performs three important functions: sharpening, color correction, and color separation. Most important, it performs them in real time (as the scan itself is taking place).

However, in late 1993 even this distinction began to disappear, as some vendors of desktop drum scanners began incorporating color computers into their products. To understand the significance of this transition, let's look at how sharpening, color correction, and color separation affect overall scanning productivity.

Sharpening

Whenever an original image is scanned, some detail is lost. In the terminology of the color trade shop, the image becomes somewhat "soft." In the old days (prior to electronic scanners), an out-of-focus original could be improved through a process known as "unsharp masking," in which the original negative would purposely be duplicated out of focus, to create an intermediate piece of film. The original would then be photographically copied onto a fresh piece of film, with the intermediate film sandwiched between them (as a mask). Because of the diffraction (bending) of light, the result was a sharpened duplicate of the original.

With the advent of electronic scanning, the sharpen function was assumed by specialized hardware built into every high-end scanner. The operator selects the appropriate degree of sharpening (based on the scan resolution, the sharpness of the original image, and the magnification ratio) with the sharpening occurring during the scan itself.

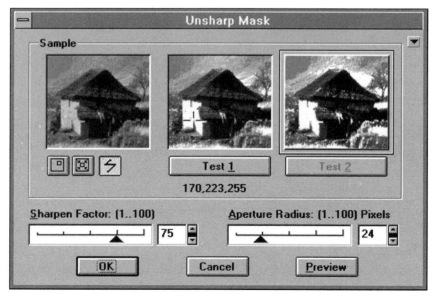

Fig. 6-20
The Unsharp Mask command in PhotoStyler lets you set the intensity and radius of the sharpening effect precisely.

A similar effect can be created with desktop imaging programs. PhotoStyler and Photoshop, for example, provide a variety of different filters, including Sharpen, Sharpen Edges, and Unsharp Mask. In both programs, the Unsharp Mask option provides the most extreme effects, and gives you the greatest control.

Sharpen Edges and Unsharp Mask find the areas in an image where significant color changes occur and sharpens them. The Sharpen Edges filter maintains the overall smoothness of the image, changing only the edges. The Unsharp Mask filter adjusts the contrast of the edge detail, creating the illusion of more image sharpness. It also allows you to specify the radius: if you enter a high value, more of the pixels surrounding the edge pixels are sharpened, while entering a low value ensures that only the pixels closest to each edge are sharpened.

Color correction

Color correction is self-explanatory: it involves altering specific color values in an image to enhance quality. There are two kinds of color correction that can be performed in real time, as the image is being scanned: *global* color correction (also known as cast removal), and *selective* color correction. A third type of adjustment, *local* color correction, involves changing the colors only of specific parts of an image, and therefore must be performed with imaging software (Photoshop or PhotoStyler), or with the retouching programs found on high-end prepress systems.

Before beginning any kind of color correction work, be sure to assess the original image under standardized lighting conditions, such as the 5,000K lighting booths found in print shops and color trade shops. Eastman Kodak makes a set of inexpensive transparent color compensation filters that allows you to quickly find the existence and extent of a color cast.

Global color correction lets you compensate for lighting errors in the original image or errors in photo processing. Unless compensated for, color casts result in a reproduction with improper hue and contrast, and a lack of color saturation. A photograph taken in a typical office, for instance, may be illuminated by a combination of fluorescent lighting (from the light fixtures) and natural lighting (from the windows), resulting in an overall greenish cast that makes people look deathly ill. Color correction lets you compensate by shifting the color balance toward the magenta, thus neutralizing the greenish cast.

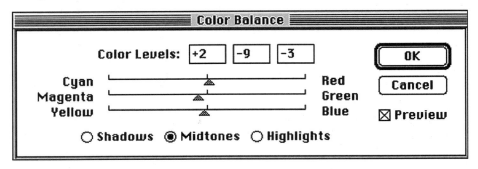

Fig. 6-21
Global correction, such as this compensation for fluorescent lighting, can be performed on a high-end scanner or in a desktop program such as Photoshop.

Global correction also allows you to compensate for deficiencies inherent in four-color reproduction: varying contrast between paper and ink, degradation of the original continuous-tone image as it is converted to a halftone or four-color separation, and contamination of process inks (their inability in the real world to match their theoretical performance).

In addition to control over brightness, contrast, saturation, and hue, you can make a variety of other adjustments, including equalizing the brightness values of colors, inverting colors, and converting a color image to black-and-white. When making color corrections, you will usually want to preview the changes on screen before applying them to your image. Although the screen may not provide a perfect representation of the corrected colors, it will at least show the direction in which color changes are being made.

If your job involves color correcting an image for someone else, talk to them before removing a color cast during the scan, because the color cast may have been intentional, to create a special effect. Once you've decided to remove the color cast, use the color correction filters to decide on the precise adjustments necessary, which can be applied during the scan.

Selective color correction involves changing the intensity of one color within another: for instance, altering only the yellow components of the green tones in an image. For example, if all the reds in a photo seem muddy, the selective color correction controls allow you to remove some magenta from just the reds, without affecting the magenta component of other colors.

Selective color correction is often necessitated by the spectral abnormalities of scanners. The spectral sensitivity of a scanner is different than that of the human eye: the scanner sometimes confuses blue for green, leading to an image that is too blue and not green enough. The experienced color separator knows the problem, and compensates for it with the blue/green correction, in which a small amount of blue is removed during the scan and replaced with a small amount of green. You can make exactly the same correction while using desktop scanners, provided your scanning software includes the necessary controls.

Photo: © Scitex

Fig. 6-22
The dozens of knobs on the front of this high-end scanner allow a skilled operator to control selective color correction precisely.

One of the big advantages of having your photos scanned in a professional color trade shop is that their scanner operators know a lot more about color correction than most desktop publishers. This gap is shrinking as desktop users learn from their high-end colleagues, but it still makes sense to have images scanned by an expert when color quality is paramount.

In some kinds of color separation, the scanner operator is trying to make the color look realistic, which entails balancing the overall cast to a single color element. In pictures of people this color element is usually flesh tones, while in landscape photography it is the color of trees, water, and sky. (In some kinds of ad photography, realism is the last thing they're after.) In product shots, the most important factor is the color fidelity of the image to the actual product.

Color separation

All color scanners, whether desktop or high-end models, capture color as RGB data. At some stage, this information must be converted to CMYK format prior to printing. How color separation (from RGB to CMYK) takes place is crucial to output quality. The color computer built into a high-end scanner performs color separation on the fly (during the scan), and this capability has recently been added to some of the more expensive mid-range scanners.

With desktop scanners, color separation must take place later in the production process, usually in an imaging program (such as PhotoStyler or Photoshop). This isn't a major problem but it can reduce your productivity, especially if a deadline looms and you have a large number of scanned images that need to be separated.

Keep in mind that there's one advantage to maintaining images in RGB format as long as possible, and performing color separation late in the production process. Because a CMYK image file is one-third larger than the equivalent RGB file, it takes longer to open, save, and process.

In the early days of desktop color, the quality of PostScript-based color separations left a lot to be desired, but this issue has disappeared as the quality of desktop systems has increased to match that of traditional high-end systems. For those desktop users who are extremely picky about how their imaging program converts RGB data into CMYK, it is possible to fine-tune the color lookup tables, a process described in more detail in the next chapter.

Productivity

We've looked at three functions that are currently in transition from high-end scanning to desktop processing: sharpening, color correction, and color separation. In each case, the major difference between desktop and high-end systems is no longer quality, it's productivity.

The color computer in high-end scanners performs sharpening, color correction, and color separation in "real time", and this capability is starting to appear in the most expensive desktop-based drum scanners. Most desktop systems, however, perform these functions after the scan is complete, which has an adverse effect on overall productivity. To a certain extent, the productivity constraint of desktop systems is in the process of disappearing, thanks to smarter software and more powerful hardware.

Scanning software

Regardless of the type of scanner you use, you need software to control it, primarily for image capture but also for "cleaning up" scanned images to improve contrast, remove dust or scratches, and crop out unwanted areas. Some scanners come with image capture software, but the quality of these programs can vary tremendously.

For many users, a better solution is to perform scanning with a full-function image editing program such as Adobe Photoshop or PhotoStyler, in conjunction with a software "plug-in" scanner driver. Virtually all scanner vendors now include a disk containing such a plug-in, thereby greatly increasing the ease with which you acquire images. To load one of these plug-in modules, you simply drag the appropriate module into the folder (directory) containing your imaging application, and the next time you load the application there will be an Acquire option in the File menu, customized for your make and model of scanner.

For many publishers, an even better choice is the TWAIN standard developed by Aldus in conjunction with the major scanner vendors. (The official explanation for its name is that it stands between, or *twain*, your computer and scanner, but a reliable source tells me it is actually an acronym for Technology Without An Interesting Name).

An increasing number of scanner manufacturers have made their products TWAIN-compatible, which means that you can work with a variety of different devices without changing drivers. This is especially handy when working on a network to which a large number of different input and output devices are connected.

For those who want increased functionality or ease of use, there are a number of specialized scanning utilities on the market. We'll look at three of these in the next section: OFOTO, Color Access, and MonacoCOLOR.

OFOTO

One of the most innovative scanning control programs is OFOTO, from Light Source, which applies "expert systems" technology to the scanning process through a technique it calls *adaptive calibration*. The key to the process is creating your own calibration loop, simply by printing out a calibration chart (supplied with the program) and scanning it back into OFOTO, which then calculates everything necessary for optimizing output to that printer. The first version of OFOTO was limited to black-and-white scanning, but with version 2.0 the program provides excellent color scanning capabilities.

OFOTO is not designed to replace image editing programs (such as Photoshop and PhotoStyler) or color correction programs (such as Cachet). However, if you routinely have to modify the color of scanned images to match the original, OFOTO can increase your productivity by ensuring that the correct colors are captured during the scanning process.

Fig. 6-23
The color accuracy of images scanned with OFOTO is based on its
"adaptive calibration" technique, in which a test image is scanned,
output, then scanned again.

To make scanning easier, OFOTO automatically:

+ selects the optimal resolution and pixel depth for the output device and the type of image being scanned;

+ removes color casts and adjusts brightness, contrast, and sharpness;

+ straightens out images that have been inadvertently scanned at the wrong angle;

+ removes moiré patterns that normally occur when you scan a previously screened image, such as a picture in a book or magazine.

OFOTO supports Apple's ColorSync, and can peacefully coexist with EfiColor, ColorSense, and other color management systems. It can even do color separations, converting RGB images to CMYK TIFF, CMYK EPS or DCS format. OFOTO images can by imported into PageMaker, QuarkXPress or any application that accepts PICT, TIFF, DCS or EPS files.

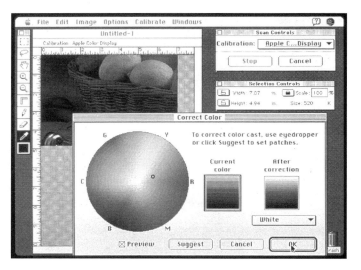

Fig. 6-24
OFOTO
provides basic
color
correction
tools, such as
the ability to
remove
unwanted
color casts.

Interestingly, instead of going along with everyone else in the desktop color industry and using the device-independent CIE color model to achieve its magic, OFOTO uses something called Appearance Equivalency, or AeQ, which is based on human vision rather than on colorimetric values. According to Light Source, AeQ takes into account the context of each color and compensates according to the way people perceive color. Fortunately, you don't need to understand how the software works in order to take advantage of its scanning capabilities.

ColorAccess

There are certain parameters required for scanning any image, such as setting the area to be scanned, the resolution, whether the image is grayscale or color, and so on. These controls are all many desktop publishers need in order to capture images with the level of quality required for their particular applications.

In the professional graphic arts industry, however, a greater degree of control is required. A scanner operator in a color trade shop or print shop, for instance, often needs to adjust the tonal information in an image as it is being scanned, rather than modifying it later on a desktop or high-end retouching station. These are the people who use ColorAccess.

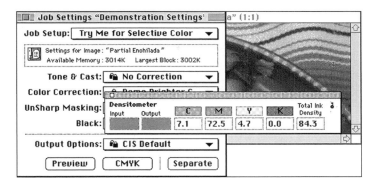

Fig. 6-25
ColorAccess provides a complete set of scanning
and color correction tools, including tone and cast
control, unsharp masking, and black generation.

ColorAccess is a full-function image capture and color separation program from PixelCraft that gives you precise control over all scanning parameters, including selective color correction. Such general-purpose imaging programs as Photoshop or PhotoStyler support global color correction but not selective color correction. In fact, ColorAccess provides a rich set of controls that closely match those found on a conventional high-end scanner.

MonacoCOLOR

A small start-up company, Monaco Systems, recently introduced a scan control program called MonacoCOLOR that automates many of the tasks that previously could be performed only by a skilled scanner operator. Not surprisingly, the author of the program spent years in the printing industry before encapsulating his experience into a software package.

MonacoCOLOR performs color correction and color separation from within Photoshop, running on a Macintosh with at least 4Mb of RAM (and preferably much more if you're working with large image files). The program is compatible with most mid-range scanners (from Optronics, Leaf, Howtek, Screen, and ScanView), plus some desktop scanners.

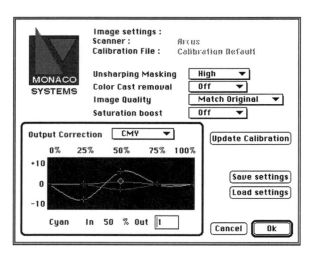

Fig. 6-26
MonacoCOLOR
uses expert systems
technology to
transform a raw scan
so its tonal values
are optimally mapped
to the available
gray levels.

MonacoCOLOR is noteworthy because it uses *intelligent histogram analysis* and color contents analysis on raw scan data so that even an inexperienced scanner operator can get excellent results by pushing one button.

There are three steps in using MonacoCOLOR:

◆   a calibration target is scanned so that the color characteristics of the scanner can be stored in a specification file;

◆   the image is scanned into Photoshop as raw RGB data without any correction;

◆   with a single keystroke, MonacoCOLOR applies the appropriate color corrections, separates the image into its CMYK components, and saves the file in the desired format.

What makes MonacoCOLOR so special that many commercial printers, trade shop owners, service bureau managers, and in-plant printers have been willing to pay $4,000 for the program? The magic is in the way it analyzes the histogram and matches the original image with one keystroke, without any additional manipulation.

As we discussed above, the entire color production process is an exercise in tonal range compression—the human eye can detect many more colors than the printing press can reproduce. MonacoCOLOR looks at the distribution of tonal values in the raw scan data, then decides on an optimal mapping of tones to the available gray levels.

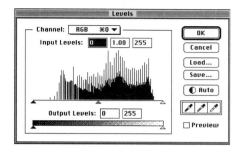 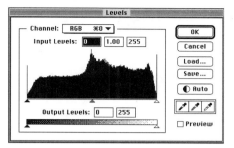

Fig. 6-27
Photoshop histograms taken from an image before (left)
and after (right) enhancement in MonacoCOLOR,
show how it improves tonal mapping.

It automatically performs color correction and unsharp masking, as well as setting highlight and shadow points. The corrected image is then separated, using MonacoCOLOR's custom separation table rather than Photoshop's built-in algorithm.

MonacoCOLOR's batch processing mode simultaneously color-corrects and separates multiple scans, converting from RGB to CMYK in the background. It processes images in the background while your scanner is running, or while you perform other work with your Mac, allowing you the option of allocating processor resources as required.

Is scanning obsolete?

Despite recent innovations in scanning technology, there are three trends that threaten to make scanners obsolete, at least for a large number of desktop publishers: digital cameras, stock shot CD-ROMs, and Kodak Photo CD.

Until very recently, digital cameras were limited to specialized applications, but they are likely to overtake conventional silver-based photography before the end of the decade. Stock shot images on CD-ROM are rapidly altering the economics of commercial photography. Kodak's Photo CD system is already here, and beginning to have a significant impact on the way people get color photographs into their computers.

Digital photography

Although it currently doesn't meet the quality requirements of many professional publishing applications, digital photography is rapidly evolving to the stage where it might make conventional film-based photography obsolete. An increasing number of companies now sell cameras based on digital image capture, including Canon, Leaf, JVC, Kodak, and Sony.

One of the major advantages of digital photography is that it allows professional photographers to continue using much of their existing lighting equipment, studio setups, and lenses. The only major differences are that the camera is hooked up to a computer, and that there is no waiting for film to be developed.

Fig. 6-28
The Kodak DCS 200 is a digital camera, based on a Nikon body, that can directly capture RGB data without film, processing or scanning.

Photo: © Eastman Kodak Co.

Digital cameras have three major advantages:

◆ images are captured instantly, without the delay of film processing, which means that commercial photographers no longer need to shoot dozens (or hundreds) of instant Polaroid photos to fine-tune their lighting setups;

- costs are reduced: you don't pay for film, processing or couriers, and the chances of needing to re-shoot are substantially reduced;

- digital photography is more environmentally acceptable than conventional silver-based film, because there are no chemicals to flush down the sewer.

Digital photography has one major disadvantage: it lacks the resolution and detail we've come to expect from conventional photographs. But there are many business applications in which high resolution is not required—for example, newspaper flyers being printed with relatively low line screens on uncoated stock (often newsprint made from recycled paper). In such cases, the paper stock can't reproduce more detail than today's digital cameras can capture, making digital photography an appropriate image capture method.

Furthermore, many flyers are filled with photographs of vegetables, shampoo bottles, and other small items that are shot with table-top photography and reproduced at small size, typically no more than a few square inches. The resolution of current digital cameras is more than sufficient for such uses.

Photo: © Eastman Kodak Co.

Fig. 6-29
This image, which was captured with a Kodak digital camera, shows a level of quality that is more than sufficient for many applications.

In summary, color scanning continues to become faster, cheaper, and of higher quality, while digital photography, though improving rapidly, is in its infancy. In the longer term (say, five to ten years from now), it would be reasonable to expect that digital cameras will have evolved to become the standard medium for capturing images, both for consumer photography and commercial publishing applications.

Stock image libraries

One side-effect of the recent proliferation of powerful desktop color tools is that high-quality stock shot images are becoming far less expensive, and therefore much more accessible for many publishers. Until recently, for instance, if you needed a high-quality image for use in a magazine, annual report or advertisement, you had two main options: hire a professional photographer or contract with a stock shot agency. Both options could be extremely expensive.

Many professional photographers charge $1,000 or more per day, plus the costs of film and processing, not to mention travel and accommodation when shooting on location. Stock shot agencies

Fig. 6-30 These are just a few of the more than 350 high-resolution stock-shot photos provided on a single PhotoDisc CD-ROM.

charge a usage fee for each image, typically based on the type of publication (in-house newsletter or general interest magazine, for instance), the publication's circulation, and the nature of the image. Most such fees range between $200 and $1,500 per image, which is why the conventional stock shot industry is likely to be decimated by the new CD-ROM stock shot libraries.

One of the many vendors now selling stock photography on CD-ROM is PhotoDisc of Seattle, whose product line consists of a series of CD-ROMs, each costing about $250 and containing approximately 350 high-resolution (18Mb per image), high-quality pictures. For example, many of the images in the color pages of this book are from PhotoDisc, and they are generally considered as good as the images obtained from a traditional stock shot agency. Each image is model released, copyright free (worldwide, in perpetuity), and royalty free—and costs less than a dollar.

Kodak Photo CD

Kodak Photo CD is one of the most important new products since the inception of desktop color. It was designed originally as a consumer product, intended to bridge the gap between Kodak's existing film business and the emerging world of digital photography.

The 1980s saw the emergence of the first digital cameras, which provided very poor quality images and were obviously unlikely to unseat traditional silver-based photographic film. However, it must have been obvious to Kodak's strategic planners that further developments in digital imaging would rapidly threaten their existing film business.

Kodak's response was Photo CD, which enables you to take a roll of unexposed film to your local camera shop or drug store, and a few days later get back both conventional negatives (or slides) and a compact disk (CD) containing digital versions of each image. A single CD holds from 100 to 120 images in compressed format, equivalent to approximately 650Mb of image data. You can start by having a single roll of film transferred to Photo CD, and later store additional pictures on the same disk. Photo CD players, which hook up to either your stereo system (for playing conventional audio CDs) or your television set (for viewing your photos) are now available from Kodak and a number of other manufacturers.

Fig. 6-31
A single Photo CD disk can store up to 120 images in compressed form.

But the real impact of Photo CD isn't as a consumer product: Photo CD is redefining the economics of color image scanning. Today, most color trade shops charge between $40 and $100 per image for high-resolution scanning—just for scanning to disk. Color correction, retouching, proofing, and other services are extra. But most camera stores charge less than $40 for developing a role of 36 exposures (from everyday 35mm film) and saving the images on a Photo CD, which works out to about a dollar per image!

At this low price, Photo CD scans are being created automatically, with the scanner measuring the white point and black point of the image and adjusting the scan parameters accordingly. These image files are appropriate for applications requiring good quality images, but not those where image quality must match that obtained with conventional trade shop scanning. For slightly more money (typically $3 to $5 per image) you can have your pictures scanned to Photo CD at an imaging center, where a skilled technician will manually identify the white point, black point, and other parameters, in order to obtain an optimal image.

Photo: © Eastman Kodak Co.

Fig. 6-32
A complete Photo CD writer includes the scanner (left), control station (center), CD drives, and dye sublimation printer (right).

Although the original Photo CD system supports only 35mm negatives and slides, the newer Pro Photo CD also works with larger film formats such as 2.25-by-2.25-inch and 4-by-5-inch transparencies, the standard media for commercial photography. Because of the larger image format, the disks hold fewer pictures, typically from 25 to 30 images.

To help commercial photographers control they way their images are used, the Pro Photo CD format offers three security features: a special identifier to indicate image ownership and copyright, the ability to place a watermark (such as "PROOF") over an image, and the ability to encrypt high-resolution images to impede unauthorized use.

In addition, Kodak has released specialized versions of Photo CD to meet the requirements of multimedia and catalog publishing applications:

- The Kodak Photo CD Portfolio disk is a new consumer format that allows you to merge Photo CD images with text, graphics, and sound. The original Photo CD format, known as Photo CD Master, stores as many as 100 images in full photographic resolution. By comparison, each Photo CD Portfolio disk can hold as many as 800 TV-resolution images. Both formats can also carry as much as an hour of CD-quality stereo sound, or a combination of sound and images.

- Kodak also sells Photo CD Catalog, which is designed for organizations—such as mail order retailers, art galleries, and real estate brokers—that want to store large numbers of images on a disk and distribute the images widely. A Photo CD Catalog disk can store as many as 6,000 images at video resolution for display on television sets or computer monitors. The images are lower resolution than standard Photo CD disks, and can't be used to make photo-quality prints. They can be combined with text and graphics and organized into chapters and pages to resemble a traditional catalog, and can be searched by keyword with Kodak Browser software, which is contained on each Photo CD Catalog disk.

Kodak has also developed Print Photo CD, a product that allows prepress service providers to store modified images (such as those that have already been color separated) onto a Photo CD disk. Print Photo CD supports standard prepress file formats, such as CMYK TIFF and EPS, and has been endorsed by all four major high-end prepress vendors: Scitex, Linotype-Hell, Crosfield, and Dainippon Screen.

Print Photo CD addresses an important limitation of the regular Photo CD system: the need for saving images after they have been modified or enhanced, whether in a proprietary high-end system or on the desktop. It makes it possible for Photo CD to be used both for capturing images and storing them, and thus helps ensure that it becomes a standard cost-effective way of getting photographs into a computer.

Photo CD compression

One of the most interesting aspects of Photo CD is the way it compresses image data to squeeze the maximum number of photos onto each disk. Photo CD supports five resolutions (with a sixth added to Pro Photo CD):

- base resolution is equivalent to the level of detail on a conventional television set (using the North American NTSC protocol);
- base over four resolution is a medium-resolution position-only version of the image;
- base over sixteen provides a low-resolution "thumbnail" image to be used as an on-screen preview, and for the tiny index prints that appear on the outside of a Photo CD's jewel case;
- base times four is equivalent to the proposed standard for high-definition television, and results in an image that is suitable for reproduction in relatively small sizes;
- base times sixteen is the highest resolution, producing a file that is about 18Mb in size after decompression, suitable for most color publishing applications.

Pro Photo CD adds a sixth resolution—4,096 x 6,144 pixels, sufficient for full-page reproduction at 150 lines per inch. The entire Photo CD system is based on compressing picture data so that the various resolutions are "nested" inside each other. For example, image files stored at the highest resolution contain only that information missing from the next-highest resolution, and so on.

Fig. 6-33
Photo CD images are stored
at five compression levels (six
for Pro Photo CD), as shown
in this file import dialog box
from Photoshop.

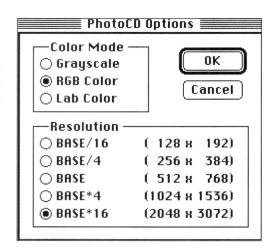

Using Photo CD images

To read the images from a Photo CD disk into your computer, you
need a CD-ROM drive, but not just any drive—it must be compatible
with the XA (extended architecture) standard. Better yet, buy a
"multi-session" CD-ROM drive and you'll be able to take an existing

Fig. 6-34
Photo CD
disks can be
read with any
CD-ROM drive
that supports
the XA
(extended
architecture)
standard.

Photo: © NEC

Photo CD disk back to your photo store to have them add images from one or more additional rolls of film.

An increasing number of popular applications programs have added Photo CD support, including PageMaker, QuarkXPress, Photoshop, PhotoStyler, Fetch, Picture Publisher, CorelDRAW, even GonzoPaint.

In addition, Kodak makes two software packages that read image files in Photo CD format: Photo CD Access and PhotoEdge, both in Macintosh and Windows formats. Photo CD Access can read, display, crop, zoom, rotate, and flip Photo CD images, and export them in PICT, TIFF, and EPS file formats. PhotoEdge has the same base features, and adds the ability to adjust exposure, contrast, sharpness, and tone in the image, though only on a global basis. For local changes, you would still require Photoshop, PhotoStyler, or some other image editing package.

One of the problems that comes with having access to millions of images is knowing how to find the exact image you're looking for. A variety of cataloging programs now exist to help you keep track of images (either your own or those in a third-party catalog such as Kodak Picture Exchange), and we'll take a look at the more popular programs in the chapter on imaging.

Kodak Picture Exchange
As an offshoot of Photo CD, Kodak has formed a global image transmission network designed to provide desktop publishers with instant access to millions of images. Kodak Picture Exchange (KPX) links such distributors of images as stock photo houses with customers they serve, such as graphic designers and publishers.

Each image is stored on the KPX network as a low-res "thumbnail" in Photo CD format, complete with the photographer's name, copyright ownership information, and key words that describe the subject and attributes of the picture. Users will access images by performing on-line searches using key words, while viewing the thumbnails. Once you've selected an image, KPX will alert the image supplier so the required prints or transparencies can be sent directly via courier or through electronic delivery systems.

Photo CD, digital photography, stock-shot CD-ROMs, and new kinds of high-quality low-cost scanners—individually these are fascinating new technological innovations. But a much broader impact will result from their collective effect on publishing.

Desktop publishing brought sophisticated type to the masses. Just as surely, innovations in scanning and imaging will make photographs a routine part of documents of all kinds.

Color Imaging

"Color is the speech of the soul of nature."
Johann Wolfgang von Goethe

orking with color photographic images presents desktop publishers with a dilemma. Images can add powerful impact to a document—a picture, according to the old saw, is worth a thousand words. However, because of the enormous size of image files, working with color photographs puts much greater demands on your computer system than manipulating type or drawings.

Despite this constraint, the use of full-color images in desktop publishing has increased markedly, and will expand further as new tools for capturing and processing photographs become widely available. Desktop imaging programs aren't limited to the graphic arts marketplace, but can be used effectively in corporate communications, engineering, architecture, medicine, science, and fine art.

This chapter explores image editing programs—especially Adobe Photoshop and PhotoStyler—and the tools they provide for working with digital pictures. Typically, imaging programs have four different functions: you can use them to control the scanning process, enhance an image's technical parameters so it will look better in print, alter the content of an image, and create color separations.

Imaging is fascinating and, in some ways, easier than working in a drawing or page layout program. The tools are intuitively designed, so a novice user can create great effects within the first few hours and, with a few days or weeks of practice, gain a level of basic competence. But even expert users will find enough controls and combinations to keep them busy—and interested—for years.

Using an imaging program

Although imaging programs provide a wide range of painting tools for those who want to create pictures from scratch, most people use the programs to work with scanned photographs.

Where do these photographs come from? You can scan them into the computer yourself, pay a color trade shop or service bureau to scan them for you, buy them as stock shot images on CD-ROM disks, or have them digitized by your local photo processing lab and saved on Photo CDs. Regardless of the method you use, imaging programs greatly extend both your ability to get high-quality printed output and the creative possibilities at your disposal.

Before jumping into imaging, it's wise to keep in mind that many image manipulation operations take a long time, even on the fastest computer—be patient if your system seems to be preoccupied. And be prepared to use the Undo command to cancel the effects of a change that is in the wrong direction. If you save frequently, especially with incremental file names for each new version, you will be able to revert easily to any previous version of the file.

The leading imaging programs have a number of features in common, including :

- ◆ selection tools, such as a lasso (for selecting arbitrary shapes) and rectangular and elliptical marquees (for selecting regular shapes);
- ◆ viewing tools, including a grabber (for scrolling through the image) and zoom tool (for zooming in to do detailed work);
- ◆ fill tools, such as a paint bucket and blend tool;

- painting tools, including a pencil, line, paint brush, airbrush, and rubber stamp (or clone) tool;
- editing tools, such as a cropping tool and eraser, plus filters and effects including blur, sharpen, and smudge;
- a text tool, for adding text to an image.

Let's examine them in more detail.

Selection tools

A photograph is often enhanced by cutting away, or *cropping* parts of the image, and it's a good idea to crop as early as possible in the design process, because it can greatly reduce the size of an image file and thus speed up production. Be sure to make a back-up copy of the image *before* you crop it, just in case something goes wrong.

Sometimes you want to alter an entire image, at other times you want to change only a specific part of it. Unless you explicitly define a selection area, any actions you take will effect the entire image. When working with large image files, using the selection tools can greatly increase your productivity. For instance, to find the settings of a particular filter that will produce a desired effect, you can save a lot of time by trying out various settings on a small selection, then applying the optimal settings to the whole image.

There are three ways to define selection areas—regular, freehand, and magic wand—and they can be combined. The regular selection tools are the Rectangle and Ellipse, which allow you to isolate rectangular, square, elliptical, and circular areas. These tools can be used in combination to define an irregular area, usually by holding down the Shift key. For example, you can use the Rectangle tool to define the first part of the selection, then hold down the Shift key while using the Ellipse tool to add or subtract an elliptical area.

Freehand selection tools include the lasso and, in some programs, pen tools that enable you to isolate a specific area by tracing around it. Many people find it easier to define a selection with the pen tool (which acts like the Bézier drawing tool in an illustration program), rather than with the lasso tool, which must be used freehand.

In addition to the rectangle, ellipse, and lasso selection tools, imaging programs contain a magic wand tool that enables you to automatically select irregularly shaped objects by using the changes in pixel values along an edge to recognize the boundaries between foreground and background objects.

Fig. 7-1
A magic wand tool (circled) lets you quickly select an irregularly shaped object (the waves) based on the brightness of adjacent pixels.

Clicking the wand on a particular color tells the program to select all adjacent pixels that are the same or similar color. By changing the sensitivity of the wand, you can control the extent to which neighboring pixels are included in the selection area. Once an area is selected, it can be cut, copied or otherwise modified.

To make best use of the magic wand, remember that imaging packages work with color pictures as though they're composed of multiple 8-bit grayscale channels (three channels for a file in RGB format, four for a CMYK file). Therefore, to fine-tune the settings of the magic wand tool, you need to think in terms of 256 levels of gray. A black pixel has a brightness value of 0, a white pixel is 255, and a midtone 50% gray is 128. For example, if you click on a midtone 50% gray pixel with a magic wand sensitivity setting of 20, all adjacent pixels with brightness values between 108 and 148 will be included within the selection area. If you want to limit the selection to similar hues, you can work in a single channel.

Painting on the desktop

Painting on the desktop with digital tools has evolved to the point where artists and illustrators are putting down their brushes and picking up a pressure-sensitive stylus. When you paint in a pixel-based program, you change the color values of pixels, with the number of colors available varying with the pixel depth of the image.

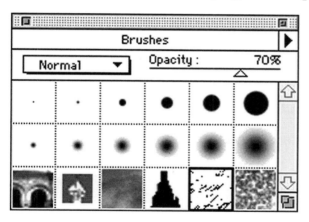

Fig. 7-2
The brush palette in Photoshop shows (top to bottom) hard-edged, soft-edged and custom brushes.

An eight-bit image, for example, has a palette of up to 256 colors, while a 24-bit image has a palette of 16.7-million. If you edit a 24-bit image on a computer system containing an eight-bit graphics board and monitor, you can still create 16.7-million colors in the image (and the final output), even though you will be able to see only 256 colors on screen.

Although most people working with imaging software start with photographs that have been scanned into the computer, some prefer to begin with a blank screen, onto which they paint with electronic brushes. You can choose virtually any color, and create custom palettes of exactly the shades you desire. You can apply electronic paint with brushes that mimic traditional bristles, even simulating the effects of fade-out and drying. Or you can select any portion of an image and use it as a custom brush or texture.

For maximum flexibility, and to most closely mimic the effects and feel of real brushes, many electronic artists prefer to work with a pressure-sensitive stylus, such as the cordless models from Wacom and Calcomp.

Fig. 7-3
Photoshop gives you complete control over the diameter, hardness, spacing, and other aspects of each brush stroke

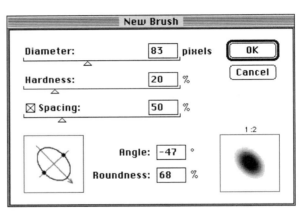

Although such general-purpose image editing programs as Photoshop and PhotoStyler provide painting tools, an artist concentrating on painting on the desktop will prefer a specialized program, such as Painter from Fractal Design.

Cloning

Cloning, the replication of any part of an image, is one of the most powerful capabilities of imaging programs. It follows directly from the concept of a custom brush pattern made from the image itself. You click to identify a source area, from which pixel values will be copied, then click and drag (as if painting) over the areas you want to fill with the cloned pixels.

Fig. 7-4
Photoshop's clone tool has been used to duplicate parts of the lunar
crater (left) to create a new landscape (right).

It takes practice to use the cloning tool effectively, but it's worth the
effort, because cloning can help you fix many kinds of problems in
photographs, including dust, scratches or small tears. Cloning can
also be used selectively to restore parts of an edited image to its
original state, as well as for creating special effects, such as an
Impressionist painting style.

Gradients

A *gradient*, or *vignette*, is a visual effect in which the foreground color
makes a gradual transition to the background color. Even when
working on high-end prepress systems, producing smooth, seamless
gradients without banding can be a complex and time-consuming
procedure.

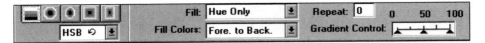

Fig. 7-5
The gradient fill tool in PhotoStyler provides control over the gradient shape, color model, fill color, number of repeats, and the start, end, and midpoints.

In an imaging program, creating a gradient is simply a matter of selecting the foreground and background colors, then clicking and dragging the mouse to indicate the beginning and end points of the vignette. A gradient can be a linear fill (from one point to another in a straight line) or radial fill (from a center point outward in all directions). The default settings produce a gradient with its midpoint, or *skew*, halfway between the foreground and background colors, but you can alter this so that the transition occurs closer to one point or the other.

Typically, default settings produce a vignette that blends directly from one color to another—a vignette from red to yellow, for instance, would have orange in the middle. Alternately, you can blend around the color wheel, in either direction. For instance, the color spectrum at the top of page 76 was created by choosing red as both the start and end points for the blend, then selecting a clockwise spectrum gradient.

Resampling

You can control the resolution of an image by *resampling* it—changing the amount of information used in the image. Resampling allows you to discard information that doesn't appreciably improve the output quality of the image. The amount of information needed depends to a large extent on the resolution at which you plan to output the image, how it was scanned, the quality you want to achieve, and the screen ruling used to produce halftones and color separations. The benefit of resampling is that it permits you to work with the smallest possible file sizes, based on your device and quality requirements.

Resampling can also save time if you receive low-resolution view files from a color trade shop or service bureau to be used for position-only purposes during the design, layout, and approval process. Sometimes these files will contain far more color information than you need, because the trade shop may consider a 150 dpi image to be "position-only," although a resolution only half that (75 dpi) is adequate for many layout purposes and results in files just one-quarter the size.

Never resample down an image for use on a low-resolution device such as a desktop laser printer, then resample up the same image for output to a high-resolution device. Every time you resample down, some color information in your original is deleted. If you resample up, *interpolation* is used to insert additional color information, resulting in an image that is not as sharp as the original. Interpolation fills in the missing information by comparing the color values of pixels adjacent to the pixel being calculated and averaging the results.

Photoshop and PhotoStyler provide three different methods of resampling, allowing you to choose an appropriate balance between speed and quality:

- *nearest neighbor* is the fastest but lowest quality method, because it creates new pixel values simply by copying the values of adjacent pixels;

- *bilinear* is somewhat slower—the value of a new pixel is calculated by drawing a straight line between the brightness values of two adjacent pixels, and selecting a point halfway along this line;

- *bicubic* is the slowest (and highest quality) method—the brightness values of the two adjacent pixels are joined by a cubic curve (which more closely mimics human light perception), and the value for the new pixel is obtained halfway along this curve.

Working with type

Imaging programs can be used to create many wonderful colored type effects, but it's important to remember that they're severely limited in the way they handle type. Unlike a drawing program, which represents type as lines and curves, imaging programs treat type as if it's made up of pixels. As such, it is rendered at the resolution of the image (which is often much lower than the resolution of your output device), and it can't be edited once placed. After you create and deselect the type, it becomes part of the image, and you can change the type only by editing the pixels that comprise the characters.

Fig. 7-6
Two close-up views of a letter "A" show how bitmapped type without anti-aliasing looks jagged (left), but improves with anti-aliasing (right).

When creating type in an imaging program, be sure to specify that the characters are to be *anti-aliased*. Anti-aliasing is a software technique for improving the quality of images by blending the edges of a bitmapped image into the surrounding colors. It is especially useful for hiding the sharp staircase edges often visible in bitmapped type—it makes the edges of each character seem smoother, so they blend into the background.

Channels

Most imaging programs let you work with the individual *channels* that make up a photograph, with each channel similar in concept to the individual plates used in the four-color process. A grayscale image contains a single channel; an RGB image has three channels; and a CMYK image has four channels. Additional channels can be added to manipulate the image and to store *masks*, which isolate part of the image so that it can be modified without altering the rest of the picture. This leaves plenty of room for experimenting.

Fig. 7-7
Does this grayscale image look slightly unusual? That's because it's
actually one of the four channels (in this case, the magenta) that,
together, comprise a CMYK image.

If you want to manipulate a specific part of an image while leaving the rest untouched, you simply create a new channel in which the image is converted to black-and-white. It is very easy to use the magic wand tool to select a discrete white area. You then change everything except your selection to solid black, thus creating a mask. Once the object is selected, the mask channel can be reincorporated into the full-color editing channel, and the defined object will remain highlighted as the current selection. You can then modify the selection any way you want, completely independent of the rest of the image.

Masks are commonly used to create a *close-cut*, in which a specific object is isolated from the rest of the picture. The photo editor for a tabloid newspaper, for instance, might close cut around an image of a lizard so it can be enlarged, then cut and pasted into a background image of a city ("Genetic Disaster: Lab Mix-Up Creates Ten-Ton Lizard!").

Fig. 7-8
A mask isolates the background elements in an image so the foreground can be edited independently, or vice versa.

Most full-function desktop imaging programs support both RGB and CMYK on-screen editing, a feature previously seen only on high-end systems. By editing CMYK values on-screen, you improve color accuracy between the scan, the display and output, because CMYK scans don't need to be converted to RGB for display, then converted back to CMYK for output. Keep in mind that color monitors are RGB devices, so even though the image is stored and manipulated as CMYK data, the monitor can display only RGB.

Image enhancement

Image *enhancement* is anything you do to adjust the technical properties of a picture so that it will look better when printed. This includes modifications to exposure, brightness, contrast, and so on, but not to the actual *content* of a picture.

The exposure in many photographs, even those taken by professional photographers, needs to be adjusted prior to printing or the pictures will appear too light, too dark, or with insufficient contrast. The essential ingredient in photographic reproduction, whether in black-and-white or color, is *tonal range*. Most pictures contain few if any pixels that are pure white or solid black—most of the tonal information is in the midtones.

Tonal range compression is the single most important issue in reproducing photographic images. The entire color production process is an exercise in skillfully reducing the total tonal range of the image, from the original to the scan to the monitor to the final printed page. An original scene in nature contains much more tonal information than can be captured on film, and the film in turn contains more tonal information that can be captured by the scanner, and so on throughout the print production process.

The human eye can distinguish literally millions of colors; the best photographic film can capture tens of thousands of colors; but process color printing can reproduce only a few thousand colors. Therefore, the task of image enhancement is to modify the tonal values in the original so that as much detail and tonal structure as possible are retained in the final printed piece.

Fig. 7-9
Changing the contrast and brightness of an image can bring out hidden details.

This is accomplished with three main tools, which are common to all major desktop imaging programs: brightness/contrast, levels, and curves. Most people new to electronic imaging would assume that the brightness and contrast settings are the appropriate place to modify an image that is either too light or too dark. In fact, the brightness/contrast tools often reduce, rather than increase, the image's tonal range.

The reason can be seen in the *histogram* of pixel values corresponding to any photograph. A histogram is simply a chart showing the number of pixels at each of the 256 gray levels in the photograph. Normally, you would work with a composite histogram of the red, green, and blue channels, but you can also create a histogram for any one channel, or for a grayscale image.

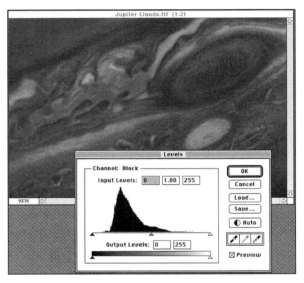

Fig. 7-10
The histogram of this photo of Jupiter shows that almost all the pixels are darker than a midtone, and that there are no pure highlight or shadow pixels.

The left side of the histogram shows the pixels with dark color values (near 0), the middle those with medium values (near 128), and the right side those with light values (near 255). The Y-axis represents the number of pixels with that value. In Photoshop, pointing the cursor at a specific part of the histogram shows the color level (from 0 to 255) for that point, the number of pixels at that level, and the percentage of pixels with color levels darker than the current one.

The histogram can also be used to define an image's black point (shadow) and white point (highlight), which can improve tonal balance. Although most imaging programs can select the black point and white point automatically, you can often get better results by choosing them manually.

To set the white point manually in Photoshop or PhotoStyler, select the eye-dropper (densitometer) tool, and point the cursor at one of the image's white highlights. Whatever the CMY values for that point (such as 1, 0, 2), they will be changed to 0 as the image is neutralized (its lightest points become pure white). The same operation can be performed to balance the black, by locating the darkest point in the image and neutralizing it.

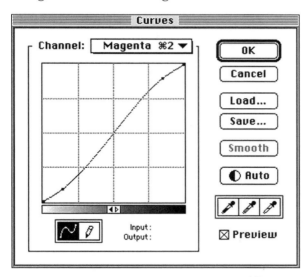

Fig. 7-11
In this example, Photoshop's Curves dialog box is being used to enhance an image by increasing magenta in the shadows while reducing it in the highlights.

In Photoshop, tonal values can also be optimized with the Curves dialog box, which allows you to adjust the brightness, contrast, and *gamma* of an image at any point along the gray level scale. The gamma of an image is the relationship between the output density and the original density across the midtones.

The x-axis of the graph represents the original brightness values of the pixels, from 0 to 255 (input levels); the y-axis represents the new brightness values (output levels). The diagonal line shows that by default every pixel has the same input and output value. By adjusting the setting in the Curves dialog box, you can bring out hidden detail in an image, alter the color balance or apply color corrections.

Image manipulation

Unlike image enhancement, in which only the technical properties of images are adjusted, image *manipulation* involves modifying the actual content of pictures to create totally new images. We've seen the results of image manipulation in advertising, such as the car rental company ad that boasts its unlimited mileage policy by showing a car sitting on the moon. It's a lot less expensive to create an artificial reality in a digital prepress system than to actually transport a car to the moon.

Fig. 7-12
Scientists have tried for centuries to fix the leaning tower of Pisa, but it took only a few minutes in a desktop imaging program.

If you want to create a montage with absolutely invisible seams, there are a few rules you must follow. First, make sure that each of the original images is at the same resolution and has approximately the same degree of sharpness. If not, use the resample command and blur/sharpen filters to modify one or more of the original images.

Next, when selecting an object that will be cut and pasted into another photo, always use your imaging program's "soft edge" or "feather" capability to define a gradient between those portions of the image that are fully selected (the part being cut) and those not selected (the background). This ensures that the final montage will have a seamless blend between foreground and background. Finally, look out for potential problems caused by color casts. When combining two or more images, make sure they are free of any noticeable color casts or adjust one or more images so that the casts are the same.

Photoshop, PhotoStyler and other imaging programs come with a variety of *filters*, which let you soften or sharpen the focus, apply special effects, fracture, offset, outline or otherwise modify an image. Many filters work by evaluating the brightness values of pixels in a selection, then changing the values. Typically, filters work with one pixel at a time, evaluating its brightness relative to surrounding pixels and calculating its new brightness value, then moving on to the next pixel in the image.

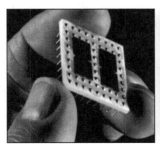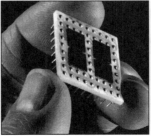

Fig. 7-13
Starting from an original photograph (left), we can see the effects of the Blur (center) and Sharpen More filters (right).

Fig. 7-14
An original image (top left) has been modified with ripple, sphere
and solarize filters.

Filters can be organized in various categories:

- Sharpen—A *sharpen* filter brings a selection into focus and improves image clarity by increasing the contrast between adjacent pixels. Scanning "softens" or blurs images, making sharpening necessary, either during the scanning process itself or through a filter. An *unsharp mask* filter mimics the traditional prepress production by producing exaggerated density at the borders of a color change.

- Blur—A *blur* filter softens the image by reducing contrast between adjacent pixels. For more intense blur effects, use the Gaussian blur filter, named for the bell-shaped (Gaussian) curve it produces in the map of color values.

- Two-dimensional—Among the many 2-D special effects filters are options for crystallize, diffuse, emboss, extrude, fragment, mosaic, solarize, twirl, wave, and zigzag.

- Three-dimensional—Among the 3-D effects are sphere, pinch, punch, ripple, and polar coordinates.

The only way to get really good with filters is through hands-on practice, playing with various combinations of settings to see what they produce. Again, work with low-resolution images or just a small selection from an image to get the settings right, then go back and apply them to the actual high-resolution file.

Image compression

Pixel-based image files are large, oversize, husky, big, extensive, gargantuan, jumbo, hefty, giant-size, immense, Brobdingnagian, colossal, and humongous. As we saw in the chapter on scanning, a full-page color image takes up 30Mb or more of disk storage and, in most cases, would be impractical for transmission by modem. Our first line of defense against the file size problem is compression. Getting complex images down to manageable size has become more and more important as desktop publishing moves toward the ever greater use of color.

There are a variety of Macintosh and PC-based utilities available, such as StuffIt, ARC, and ZIP. These provide *lossless compression*, in which every byte in the original file is present after the file has been compressed and subsequently decompressed, but they lack the power needed for commercial prepress.

The standard in compression of image data is called JPEG, for the Joint Photographic Experts Group. JPEG compression reduces image files to 10% of their original size or smaller, but the files can later be decompressed with little or no detectable loss of detail or color quality. This is a very significant improvement in storing images. It means you have all the high-resolution color data you need while actually working with the image, but allows you to store on disk and transmit to other sites a compressed file with more than 90% of the data removed.

When the image is compressed 20:1, a color expert will recognize the loss in image detail and dynamic range, but most observers will not, especially in a high-contrast image. Although the degree of compression that a given image can withstand varies according to its content (and the eye of the observer), it appears that, in general, almost nobody will be able to detect a 10:1 compression.

The JPEG standard specifies a *lossy* or "non-lossless" algorithm, meaning that some image data is lost. However, the loss occurs only on the first compression and decompression cycle. Once an image has been compressed, any subsequent compression/decompression cycle will be practically lossless.

Fig. 7-15
A black-and-white TIFF file (left) shows only slight degradation after being compressed 10:1 and decompressed (right).

JPEG programming is designed to identify and ignore pixels that contributes little to the overall quality of the image, such as any large area of mostly uniform color. At small compression ratios of 10:1 or lower, these changes are virtually impossible to detect—as you can see in the color images on page 89, which show the same photograph before and after moderate and heavy compression. JPEG technology is available both as software (built into imaging packages such as Photoshop and PhotoStyler) and as hardware.

Most users will find it more cost-effective to use software-based compression tools, but those willing to pay for extra performance will want to investigate hardware-based compression products. Digital Signal Processor (DSP) chips can compress or decompress a typical color image in a few seconds or less. With JPEG compression it becomes practical to store large image files on floppies, move them around on networks, and transmit them over telephone lines. The ultimate goal remains to perform such operations in real time, so that compact files on disk can be viewed instantly and edited at their full resolution on screen.

Some JPEG compression packages, such as PicturePress from Storm Technology, are available in both a software-only version and as a NuBus card with features targeted at professional users, such as the ability to directly manipulate the variables controlling the JPEG algorithm. You can customize the quantization tables for chrominance and luminance, choose independent vertical and horizontal subsampling rates, and generate custom Huffman-encoding tables, which compress more data, albeit at slower speeds.

Most users probably won't want to customize their quantization tables, but this is a valuable tool in the hands of a skilled professional. By controlling the amount of quantization applied to the chrominance and luminance, you can achieve acceptable quality with higher compression rates than would otherwise be possible. For example, an image with little contrast but a wide range of colors can lose more luminance data and less chrominance data than a high-contrast image in which a few tones predominate.

Another factor that enhances JPEG performance is selective compression, in which lower compression ratios (and, hence, better image quality) are used for the parts of the image that contain the area of interest, while higher compression ratios are used for image portions that contain less important elements. In a typical shot for a sales catalog, for example, the product would be less compressed (higher quality) than the backgrounds.

An important advantage of the JPEG protocol is that it's supported in PostScript Level 2. When a JPEG-compressed image is sent to a PostScript Level 2 output device, decompression takes place in the printer, which means document transmission takes much less time.

Keep in mind that whatever the other benefits of compression, it will not improve times for the actual manipulation of the pixels that comprise an image, because the files have to be decompressed before they can be manipulated.

Adobe Photoshop

Adobe Photoshop is the best-selling imaging program on the Macintosh platform, and is a leading competitor in Windows-based imaging. Photoshop is more than a product—it's a little industry, employing thousands of people producing plug-in modules, special effects filters, books, magazine articles, training courses, videos, and much more.

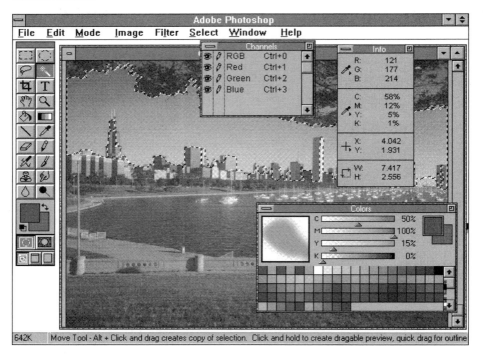

Fig. 7-16
Photoshop provides pop-up palettes for channels, density information and colors, and runs equally well in both Macintosh and Windows environments, with complete file exchange between them.

Photoshop 3.0 is a multi-faceted program—you can use it for scanning, painting, image enhancement and manipulation, color correction, and color separation, all in 24-bit color. Among designers and photographers it is known as a creative tool, but people working in color trade shops and commercial printers consider it a production tool.

Photoshop has very robust file import and conversion features. You can import and export Encapsulated PostScript (EPS), PICT resources and files (including 32-bit), TIFF, Scitex, MacPaint, TGA (Targa), PIXAR, Pixelpaint, Compuserve GIF, and Amiga IFF/ILBM. It even supports Thunderscan, for all those color enthusiasts creating separations from the roller of a dot-matrix printer.

Color models

Photoshop lets you view and edit images in a variety of color and black-and-white modes, with the default mode determined by the image—grayscale images appear in monochrome and color images in RGB color. You can override these defaults for special effects. To colorize a black-and-white photograph, for example, you change the mode from grayscale to RGB and, to create color separations, you simply change the mode from RGB to CMYK.

If you're working with multimedia or other video-based applications, take note of Photoshop's ability to convert images to "indexed color" mode, which stores only eight-bit color data (256 colors). When you convert an RGB image to indexed color, Photoshop builds a color table, which stores the colors in the image, to a maximum of 256 colors. If a desired RGB color is not present in the color table, the program matches the requested color to the closest color in the color table or simulates the requested color using the available colors.

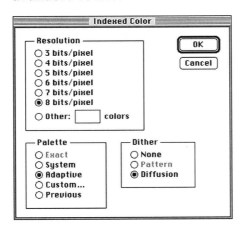

Fig. 7-17
The Indexed Color dialog box in Photoshop allows you to specify the bit depth of an image, and the color palette to be used.

One of Photoshop's more unusual features is its support for the CIELAB model. CIELAB images use three channels to represent color, one for luminance (brightness) information, and the other two for chrominance (color) information. The "L" channel is luminance, the "A" channel ranges from green to magenta, and the "B" channel ranges from blue to yellow.

CIELAB mode is useful when you want to edit the luminance of an image (or part of an image), without altering its color values. Because CIELAB is a device-independent color model, it is recommended for moving images between computer systems, or when printing to a PostScript Level 2 output device. In fact, CIELAB is used internally by Photoshop when converting images between RGB and CMYK modes, because its gamut encompasses both RGB and CMYK gamuts.

Duotones

One unique Photoshop feature is its ability to create accurate duotones (and such similar effects as tritones and quadtones) with any Pantone spot or process color ink, and preview the results on-screen and in color.

Duotone effects enable you to increase the tonal range of a grayscale image. Although a grayscale image may contain up to 256 levels of gray, a printing press can reproduce only about 50 levels of gray per ink. By printing a grayscale image with two, three or four inks, you can significantly expand the range of tones visible on the printed page.

For instance, printing a duotone with black and gray inks allows you to set the black ink to capture shadow detail while the gray ink reproduces midtone and highlight areas. More frequently, duotones are printed using a spot color for the highlights, resulting in a significant increase in tonal range. Duotones, tritones (made with three inks) and quadtones (four inks) can also be created with process colors, as shown in color on pages 90 and 91.

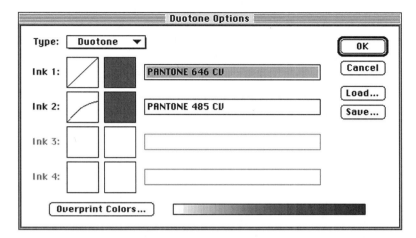

Fig. 7-18
Photoshop's duotone feature is unique among desktop programs, and such effects are difficult, even on high-end systems.

Filters

One reason for Photoshop's success is that it has been bundled with many desktop color scanners, which has led to a large installed base. Another important factor is the availability of many plug-in filters, such as special effects filters that allow you to transform ordinary photographs so they resemble paintings. Starting with Photoshop 3.0, you can even preview the effect of a filter before applying it.

Photoshop's full range of filters, painting, drawing, and selection tools provide a tremendous degree of artistic control and precision. Filters include sharpen, edge sharpen, blur, Gaussian blur, despeckle, motion blur, add noise, diffuse, facet, star lens, mosaic, trace contours, and convolution. And if none of these quite fit the bill, you can create custom filters, or buy them from third-party vendors.

In addition to the many image filters provided with Photoshop, you can devise your own by experimenting with the values in the Image Filters Custom dialog box. You create special effects by changing the brightness values of pixels according to a mathematical *convolution kernel* that you specify. For example, you can define a filter that displays a selection in high relief or a filter that creates a motion blur effect.

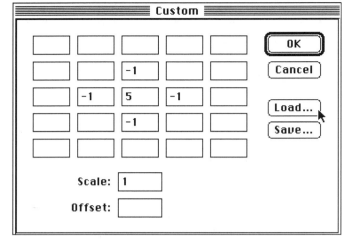

Fig. 7-19
You can create
custom
Photoshop
filters by
varying the
numbers in the
matrix to define
a unique
mathematical
convolution.

Color correction

Photoshop provides a number of tools for color correction. New in Photoshop 3.0 is selective color correction, which lets you specify the exact amount of ink used on a printing plate, to compensate for the "contamination" of colors in any ink. Magenta ink, for instance, always contains some cyan. By setting the ink densities in the selective color correction dialog box, you can precisely control the colors that will appear in the final printed image.

One of the more useful features in Photoshop is the Variations window, which makes the color correction process much more accessible to non-professional users. For many years, color correction has been a complex process requiring enormous skill and an intimate understanding of color theory. Many images require color correction, either because of lighting conditions in the original image or because of constraints imposed by the printing process.

The Variations dialog box shows the current image surrounded by six alternate versions, one each with increased red, green, blue, cyan, magenta, yellow, and blue. To remove an overall cyan cast from an image, for instance, you simply click on the More Red option. You adjust exposure by clicking on a variation that is lighter or darker than the current image.

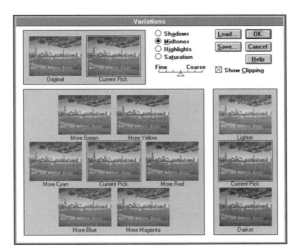

Fig. 7-20
Photoshop's Variations feature lets you visually adjust color balance, making it easier for non-professional users to achieve reasonably good color correction.

Layers

One of the most important additions to Photoshop 3.0 is the layers palette, which lets you work with transparent sheets of acetate that float above an original background image. You can draw, edit, and paste on separate layers, or try out different combinations of images or placement of graphics, text and special effects until you get exactly the effect you were looking for. You can independently set the opacity of each layer, to quickly create transparency effects.

Photoshop lets you print to any PostScript color or black-and-white printer, with control over halftone frequency, screen angle, and dot shape. Another important output feature is "intelligent resampling" which lets you reset resolution or image size to values appropriate for printing.

Color separations

To print color separations, you must convert an RGB, indexed color or CIELAB image to CMYK mode (with the exception of CIELAB images printed directly to a PostScript Level 2 printer). Before color separating any image, it's a good idea to save the original file, just in case you want to re-separate it later. Don't convert back and forth between RGB and CMYK modes: every time the image is converted, color values must be recalculated, resulting in color shifts.

When you convert an RGB image to CMYK, Photoshop first converts the RGB values to CIELAB values according to the settings in the Monitor Setup dialog box, then builds a color table, which it uses to calculate the optimal CMYK values. You can save multiple color tables and use them with other Photoshop files, which comes in handy if you frequently print images using different printers, presses, inks or papers.

You can print separations directly from Photoshop, or save them as CMYK TIFF files or encapsulated PostScript (EPS) files for placement in graphics and page layout programs. Many graphics applications, such as Adobe Illustrator and FreeHand, use the EPS format to transfer drawings between programs. PostScript print files can't be displayed on screen on a Mac or Windows-based PC, but an EPS file bundles the PostScript code with a low-resolution screen preview—typically a PICT file on a Mac and a TIFF file on an IBM-compatible. The preview allows you to place the image on the page with appropriate sizing and scaling, and gives you an idea of what it will look like when it is printed.

Another export option in Photoshop allows you to save a CMYK document as five separate EPS documents for placement in DCS-compatible page layout programs such as QuarkXPress, PageMaker, and Ventura.

PhotoStyler

Professional color imaging started on the Macintosh, but with PhotoStyler 2.0 it has now arrived in full force on the Windows platform. For designers, desktop publishers, photographers, and people working in production environments, the ability to perform high-quality image editing under Windows is no longer in question. The key issue now is productivity.

Imaging productivity

PhotoStyler 2.0 is designed from the ground up to maximize the productivity of those working both in design and production

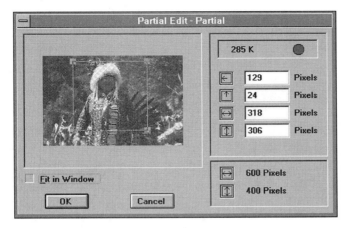

Fig. 7-21
PhotoStyler's Partial Edit feature lets you open and edit any portion of an picture, which can save you considerable time when working with large image files.

environments. The program completes image enhancement and manipulation tasks much faster than was previously possible, especially when working with very large image files.

For instance, a typical imaging task would involve opening a 10Mb TIFF file to remove a speck of dust or small scratch on the original image. In Photoshop and most other image editing programs, you would have to open the entire file, just to fix one small aspect of it. The Partial Edit feature in PhotoStyler can substantially speed up this kind of operation: you open only the portion of the image you need to work on, then, when you're finished, PhotoStyler automatically glues it back into the complete image.

Small details that can increase your productivity abound. The File Open dialog box, for example, allows you to open a copy of a file, rather than forcing you to waste time saving a copy to disk. It even allows you to open multiple files, simply by holding down the Control key while you select them.

User interface

One of the most dramatic enhancements in PhotoStyler 2.0 is the user interface, which includes an on-screen tool ribbon that keeps almost every major function at your fingertips, without the necessity of scrolling through seven layers of menus.

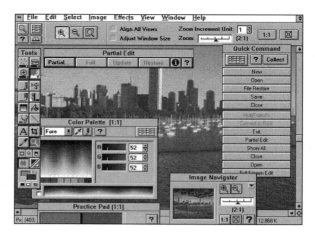

Fig. 7-22
PhotoStyler gives you instant access to (clockwise from top right) a quick command palette, image navigator, practice pad, color palette, partial edit palette, tool bar, and tool ribbon.

For instance, the Quick Command palette enables you to customize the program so your most frequently used tools are readily at hand. And almost all dialog boxes include multiple preview windows that eliminate time-consuming trial and error adjustments.

The toolbox has been reorganized with tools grouped according to function: all the selection tools, for example, are visible at once. You can even customize the toolbox by simply dragging and dropping the tools you want into the place you want them. This lets you group tools according to their function or the specific workflow processes you employ.

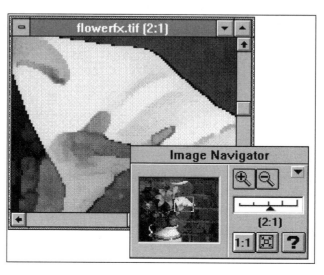

Fig. 7-23
PhotoStyler's image navigator makes it easy to move around quickly in a large picture without getting lost.

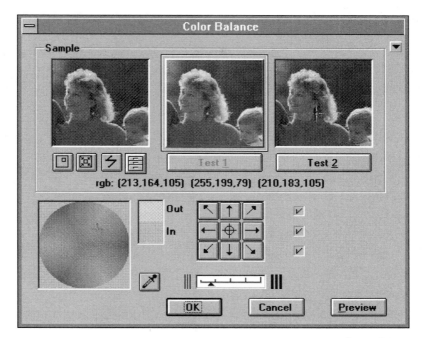

Fig. 7-24
Multiple preview windows in dialog boxes
help you quickly enhance and manipulate images.

Another real time-saver is the Image Navigator, which provides a thumbnail birds-eye view of the active image—you can keep track of where you are in the whole image while zooming in to edit pixel by pixel. It also lets you quickly select where to go in an image without panning, scrolling, or zooming in and out.

Image editing

PhotoStyler comes with a complete array of flexible, interactive tools for color correction, conversion, separation, image editing, retouching, and composition. Built-in filters include sharpen, blur, edge trace, add or remove noise, emboss or relief, mosaic, motion blur, pinch, and whirlpool, and you can define and save custom filters. A magic wand tool lets you quickly select parts of an image to create masks, which can be added, subtracted or inverted from other images.

Many of PhotoStyler's dialog boxes provide multiple previews that make it easy to try out filters, effects or color corrections. You can see the original image plus two test versions that can be independently adjusted. This provides an easy way to compare changes before committing them to the original image, and saves you the hassle of making a change, applying it to the image, hitting Undo to reverse the effect of the change, then starting all over again.

When merging two or more images, PhotoStyler gives you complete control over how transparent or opaque the pixels will be. In fact, you can adjust the transparency for any number of discontinuous color ranges along the RGB spectrum. You can even drop out a single color—black, white or any other color—simply by clicking on it, which is very helpful when compositing images that have solid backgrounds.

PhotoStyler comes with a built-in Album utility that, at first glance, looks like a ho-hum image browser. But lurking behind this plain exterior is a very powerful program. In addition to letting you hunt for missing files by name, file type, date and other parameters, Album lets you convert any number of files from one type to another (such as from Kodak Photo CD to TIFF), with a single command. None of the files have to be loaded for this to work, which can be a real time-saver.

PhotoStyler supports 14 libraries of process colors, more than any other desktop imaging program. You can also create custom color libraries. An image stored in indexed color mode has a color palette containing a fixed number of colors, usually 256. Although other image editing programs let you edit the definitions of these colors through look-up tables, PhotoStyler goes much further. You can easily step through the colors in the palette to edit them, find all occurrences of a particular color or range, invert colors, and redefine colors so they blend smoothly from one selection to another. This lets scientists perform powerful kinds of image analysis, while helping designers and artists create distinctive special effects.

Another PhotoStyler feature that helps you get the right colors is its support for the HLS (hue, lightness, saturation) color model, in addition to the RGB, HSB, and CMYK models. The HLS model lets you isolate and work with specific properties of a color, such as adjusting its hue without altering its lightness and saturation, in order to provide more realistic color effects.

Color separations

Nothing in an image editing program is as important as the quality of the printed output, whether directly from a color printer or as film separations that will be printed on a press. This is where PhotoStyler 2.0 really shines.

PhotoStyler is tightly integrated with PageMaker 5.0, enabling you to pre-separate color images as CMYK TIFF and DCS files which can then be placed in PageMaker. PhotoStyler also lets you export EPS and DCS files with a "clipping path" that makes the background of an image transparent, so you can place an irregularly shaped picture in PageMaker and easily flow text around the shape. And because PhotoStyler supports Object Linking and Embedding (OLE) as a server, you can place an image from PhotoStyler into PageMaker, FreeHand, Persuasion or other OLE-compliant applications and have it automatically updated should it change.

PhotoStyler's Print Preview dialog box shows you all the elements that will be printed on the page, complete with printer's and crop marks, labels, and tiling breaks. This enables you to verify every detail of the page before printing it, thereby saving plenty of time and money.

Color management

The Kodak Precision color management system is a central component in PhotoStyler 2.0, providing Windows-based color publishers with high-quality color matching and color separation capabilities until recently available only on the Mac. PhotoStyler 2.0 comes with a set of device profiles, or Precision Transforms (PTs), for popular scanners, monitors, color printers and proofers, plus special PTs for artistic effects. It also includes the Color Configure utility, which creates different configurations of PTs for each input and output device in your system.

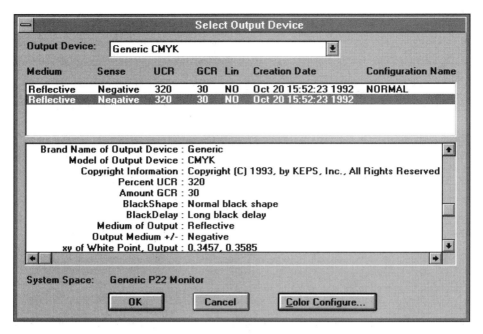

Fig. 7-25
The Kodak color management system built into PhotoStyler
allows you to define the properties of each input
and output device in your system.

PhotoStyler uses the PTs and color processor to color-correct images as they are opened, imported, exported, previewed, edited or output. This enhances the color quality of the images, and ensures predictable, repeatable color. It's easy to take advantage of Precision's enhanced color management capabilities. When you first install PhotoStyler, it asks you to specify the components of your system, such as the monitor, scanner, printer, and so on, then loads the appropriate profiles. If you're using devices for which there are no built-in profiles, PhotoStyler substitutes the generic RGB (monitor) and CMYK (SWOP printer) profiles.

When using PhotoStyler, there are two different places where the "magic" of color management takes place. First, whenever you display an image on your monitor, the Precision CMS ensures that the on-screen colors match (as closely as possible) those that will be obtained from the selected output device. This does not involve changing the underlying pixel values in the image until you save the image to disk. Second, when you color-separate an image, or print an RGB image to a CMYK device, Precision ensures that the results most closely match the colors in the original image.

Micrografx Picture Publisher

Micrografx Picture Publisher is a Windows-based image editor that combines a full set of image enhancement and manipulation tools with an intuitive user interface. Picture Publisher 4.0 was introduced in 1993, and now supports CMYK TIFF files, 8-bit masks, and a variety of color management systems and third-party plug-ins (including Adobe Gallery Effects and Photoshop plug-ins).

Fig. 7-26
Picture Publisher provides a complete set of image editing tools, with pullout menus (center left), a QuickZoom window (top right), and info palette (bottom right).

One of the most interesting features in Picture Publisher 4.0 is an innovative capability called Object Layers, which lets you treat portions of any bitmapped image as discrete objects, with complete control over their size, placement, transparency, rotation, and layering. Objects are completely editable, and you can group, ungroup, duplicate, delete, apply special effects or anti-alias any object. Even after "pasting down" part of an image, you can move it at will without leaving a gaping hole where the pixels used to be.

This image-object capability redefines the way you work with images, giving much greater flexibility and control when you are combining pieces from multiple files to create a montage. It seems destined to become a permanent part of all pixel-based imaging programs.

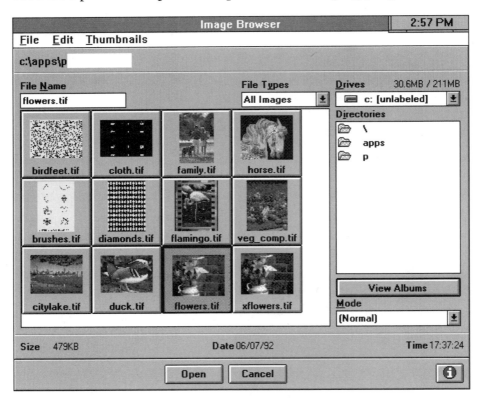

Fig. 7-27
Picture Publisher comes with an image browser that lets you store groups of related images in "albums," and search through low-resolution thumbnails.

Other features in Picture Publisher 4.0 include:

- an image browser that provides low-resolution thumbnails and a key-word search capability;
- a visual color correction tool that lets you improve the contrast, brightness, and color balance of images by comparing on-screen previews that reflect a variety of different parameter settings;
- FastBits, which lets you select and edit one small part of an image without having to load the entire file into memory, with the program automatically combining the edited portion back into the main image file;
- a low-res image open option that allows you to apply color correction and other global editing commands to a screen resolution image, then record a macro that can be played back to apply the desired changes to the original high-resolution image.

Live Picture

Live Picture, distributed in North America by HSC Software, is a radical new image manipulation program based on a mathematical imaging technology called Functional Interpolation Transformation System (FITS), developed by French mathematician Bruno DeLean.

Live Picture lets you open a 300Mb file on a standard Mac Quadra, rotate and scale it, paint on the image with 48-bit color, montage multiple images together—not quite in real time, but very quickly indeed. Unlike today's imaging technology, which is based on moving huge amounts of pixel data from one place to another, Live Picture uses the concept of a "virtual image" that can be automatically rendered to the required resolution for output to the screen, film or printer.

The first thing Live Picture does is convert incoming image files (from TIFF or other common formats) into an internal file format called IVUE. Once an image is in IVUE format, Live Picture uses a resolution-independent RIP to create virtual images of the file on screen. All functions within Live Picture use mathematical expressions to describe all operations, layers, and images. These expressions, which are stored in a FITS file, represent all the work done by the user, without actually performing such functions on the original pixel images. Instead of a single Undo command, for example, Live Picture provides an infinite, progressive, selective undo capability.

When it's time to output a file for printing or film separations, the FITS file automatically assembles and manipulates (RIPs) the original pixel data to create a TIFF or other file format. A number of companies have released high-powered hardware-based RIPs to speed the output process, though this can still take some time, especially when imaging large files at high resolution.

It's too early to tell what effect Live Picture will have on the imaging world, but at first glance this looks like a revolutionary technology for speeding up the image manipulation process and encouraging creative exploration.

A similar technology has been developed by The Human Software Company as part of its ColorExtreme image editing product. When opening large image files, it creates a copy of the image data in a proprietary format that can be quickly manipulated. In addition to creating color separations from desktop and high-end formats, ColorExtreme has one feature not found in Photoshop or Live Picture: selective color correction, which enables you to adjust the CMYK composition of any specific color (or range of colors) without affecting all other colors in an image.

Specialized imaging software

In addition to the general-purpose imaging programs already described, there are many, more modest, software packages designed to perform only one or two specialized functions. In most cases, these outshine Photoshop and PhotoStyler in carrying out the particular function for which they have specifically been designed—for example, scan control, color correction, or image database management.

Among the specialized packages that serious color publishers will want to consider are:

- Cachet, from Electronics For Imaging, for color correction;
- Fetch, from Adobe, for image management;
- Gallery Effects, also from Adobe, which allows you to quickly convert a photograph into a charcoal sketch, watercolor, oil painting or other graphic style;
- Kai's Power Tools, from HSC Software, which makes it easy to produce all kinds of unusual and creative visual effects;
- Altamira Composer, an innovative Windows-based imaging program;
- PhotoMatic, from DayStar Digital, a scripting utility to speed up repetitive image editing tasks.

Cachet

Color correction of images is as much an art as a science—as anyone who tries it quickly learns. Cachet is an innovative program that enables those without a technical background in color prepress to produce good color corrections. It is designed for the mass of people who want to improve the quality of their scanned images, but don't have the time to obtain a Ph.D. in color science or complete a five-year apprenticeship in a trade shop.

Cachet is based on the idea of using a reference image (that has already been printed and found to produce high-quality output) as an on-screen guide to correcting the colors in a subject image. The software is accompanied by a book containing reference pictures, plus a disk of the corresponding scanned images used to print the pictures.

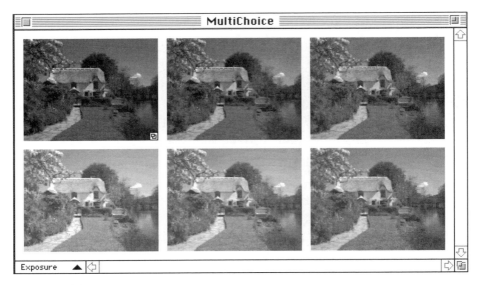

Fig. 7-28
The MultiChoice tool in Cachet makes it easy to choose the optimal adjustment to an image's exposure or other parameters.

You operate Cachet by viewing two images on screen: the subject photo you wish to color correct, and one of the reference photos. Your task is to make the subject photo look like the reference photo. The advantage of this approach is that you don't need a calibrated monitor and controlled room lighting—as long as the subject photo looks like the reference photo on screen, it will print with the appropriate colors.

When Cachet was introduced in 1992, it had two unique features, both of which have subsequently appeared in competing products:

- Cachet's multi-choice tool gives you on-screen previews of how the subject image would look as a result of making a specific change in brightness, contrast, color cast or other parameters;
- Cachet was the first image editing program built on top of a full-function color management system (EfiColor), but color management is rapidly becoming a standard feature in all major imaging, drawing, and page layout packages.

Cachet lets you manipulate contrast, color saturation, and tonal curves directly, although most novice users will prefer to use its multi-choice tool. In addition to the subject photo, Cachet displays on screen six alternative versions of the same image, each slightly different. For example, if your original image is too dark, you select "lightness" from a menu, which then displays three progressively lighter and darker versions of your original image.

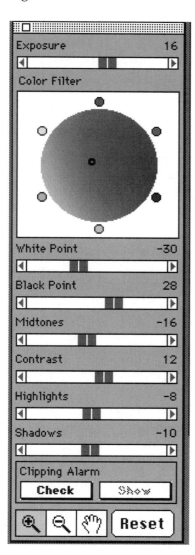

One of these six alternates is probably closer to what you have in mind than the others; clicking on that image applies its levels of brightness adjustment to the subject image. The six alternate images are then updated to present a new range of progressively lighter and darker choices.

Selecting from the multiple-choice picture palette automatically updates the values in the various brightness, contrast, and other color controls. Therefore, as you use Cachet, you begin to learn what effect each of the traditional controls would have on a given image.

Fig. 7-29
By adjusting the parameters in the MultiChoice tool, you can both color correct the image and learn how to correct similar images.

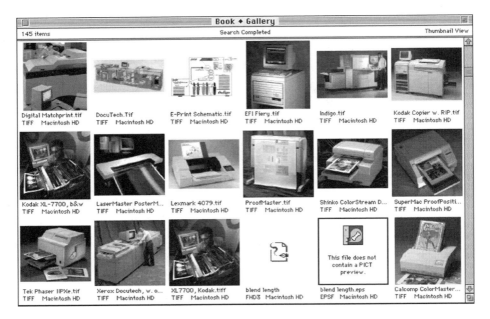

Fig. 7-30
Fetch is ideal for organizing the hundreds of TIFF, PICT, and EPS files
required for a large publishing project, such as this book.

Fetch

Adobe Fetch is the first full-function image database—it's one of
those programs that may seem rather obvious at first but, once you've
been using it for a while, makes you wonder how you ever got along
without it.

Fetch was engineered to make it easy for people in both the design
and production sides of color publishing to keep track of the
thousands of different files they work with every day—images,
graphics, logos, clip art, animation, and video clips. It is a multi-
user, multi-volume database—users anywhere on the network can
retrieve files, whether they're stored on-line or on archival media.
Fetch supports all major Macintosh-based file formats, including AIFF,
AIFC, FreeHand, Persuasion, EPS, GIF, PICS, PICT, TIFF, QuickTime,
Photo CD, SND, and SoundEdit.

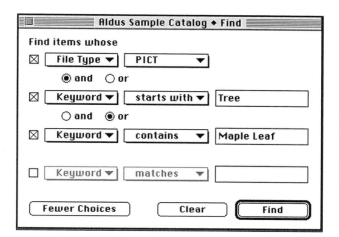

Fig. 7-31
Fetch makes it easy to search for images according to file name, file creation or modification date, and one or more keywords.

A single Fetch catalog can contain more than 100,000 items, and you can quickly browse through them in a visual gallery format or as a file list. You can search for items by specifying keywords, file types, filenames, and volumes. If you select an item that is stored somewhere other than on the current hard drive, Fetch prompts you to insert the required cartridge or tape, then automatically finds the requested file. Once a file has been found, it can be previewed at full size and resolution without launching its source program.

As color publishers continue to build their libraries of drawings, images, clip art, and other visual materials, Fetch and other multimedia image databases are certain to become essential software tools.

Gallery Effects

Gallery Effects is a library of professional-quality special effects for grayscale and color images. It provides 16 "master effects" that look hand-created, but can be applied to any image—such effects as watercolor, charcoal, graphic pen, dry brush, and emboss. Each of them includes individual controls that you can preview; you can save as many as 25 custom settings per effect.

Gallery Effects filters make it easy to alter a photo so it looks as if it were created by hand with pencil, chalk, charcoal, watercolors, oil

Fig. 7-32
Aldus Gallery Effects lets you instantly turn an ordinary photo (left) into a watercolor (right).

paints or other media. A variety of these effects are shown in color on page 94.

Kai's Power Tools

One of the more innovative Photoshop plug-ins is a clever program called Kai's Power Tools, from HSC Software. Written by Photoshop guru Kai Krause, these handy little filters and utilities are available for both Mac and Windows, and allow you to create all sorts of outrageous visual effects, from gradients and textures to ray tracing and fractals.

Kai's Power Tools include a Texture Explorer (for creating textures, backgrounds, and materials), Gradient Designer (providing an unlimited palette of gradient designs), Gradients on Paths (which wrap and blend around a free-form user path or text selection), and

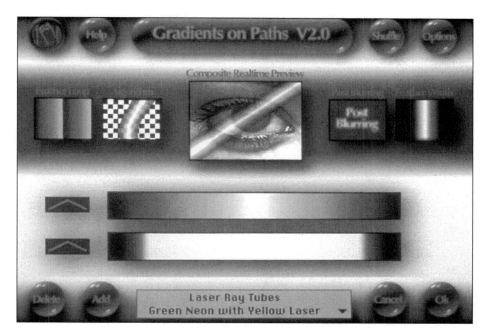

Fig. 7-33
In addition to providing tools for wild imaging effects such as gradients on paths, Kai's Power Tools features one of the more unusual user interfaces ever seen.

the Julia Sets fractal explorer. It also comes with 29 filters, including Glass Lens, Hue-Protected Noise, and Sharpen Intensity.

Altamira Composer

Photographic imaging on the Windows platform recently took a giant step forward with the release of Composer, from Altamira Software.

Composer uses a method called *dynamic alpha channels* to enable artists to treat images, and selected parts of them, as objects that have shape and transparency and are arranged in layers. You can select and move these "image objects" by pointing and clicking, and they can be cut out, saved, and reused in libraries. In addition to moving them vertically and horizontally, you can move them up

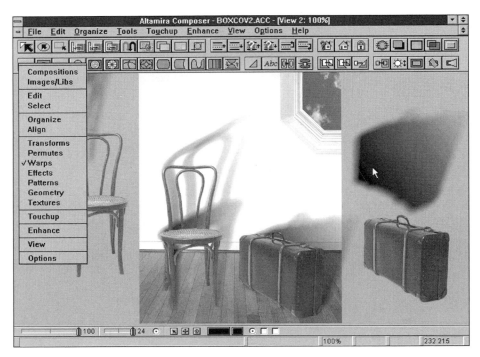

Fig. 7-34
Composer lets you create photographic montages in which each
component remains distinct, and can be edited independently at any
time.

or down in the stack, covering up or revealing other image objects.
A "color lift" tool allows you to create a new image object by selecting
a range of colors to lift from another object.

PhotoMatic

Macintosh Photoshop users working with large image files, or those
performing repetitive image editing tasks, will want to check out
the PhotoMatic plug-in from DayStar Digital. PhotoMatic is a
scripting utility that lets you record a series of actions in a "watch
me" mode, so they can later be replayed. It comes bundled with
AppleScript and works with any Open Scripting Architecture
compliant system.

A script can be applied to one image at a time, or to a series of images through an included batch-processing application. PhotoMatic can even be used on a remote Mac on a network, freeing the local Mac for other tasks.

Integrating images into page layouts

Most page layout programs have almost no image editing controls, so you need to perform all image enhancement and manipulation operations from within an imaging program, then export the finished picture and place it in your layout.

When it comes to exporting pictures from your image editing program so they can be imported into a page layout package or other application, you should be aware of one major difference between the EPS and TIFF file formats—file size. An image of the same size, pixel depth, and resolution is likely to occupy twice as much disk space when stored as an EPS file than if it is being stored in the TIFF file format.

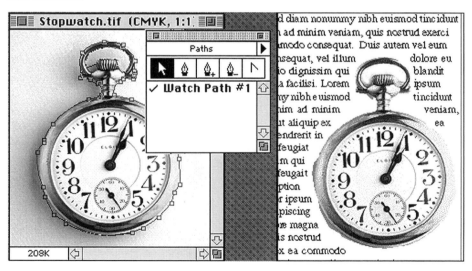

Fig. 7-35
After specifying a clipping path in Photoshop or PhotoStyler (left), you can save the clipped image as an EPS file, which can be imported into a page layout program, with text wrapped automatically around the clipped image (right).

However, there's one situation where EPS files offer a major advantage over TIFFs—when you need to import an irregularly shaped image but don't want its background to hide other items on the page. This is where the PostScript *clipping path* feature comes in handy. Both Photoshop and PhotoStyler let you define a path surrounding the part of the image you want to have appear in your page layout.

When you save the image as an EPS file, you have the option of specifying a clipping path, which makes all pixels outside the path transparent. When this EPS file is imported into your page layout program, only the part of the image within the path will be visible.

Integrating photographs into page layout presents another problem whenever a page or spread contains two or more photographs taken under vastly different lighting conditions.

The human eye has an uncanny ability to detect color imperfections in any reproduction, especially for "memory colors"— trees, sky, water, and people's faces. When a single color image appears on a page, the reader's eye will quickly adapt to the content of the image, unless its colors are really unusual. However, when two or more images appear together on a page, much greater care must be taken to ensure that the memory colors are consistent from picture to picture.

This ideal, which is very important to the uninterrupted perception of the reader, is difficult to attain unless the photographs were taken on identical film, under the same lighting and exposure conditions. In the high-end prepress world, experienced scanner operators have learned how to alter the colors as they are being recorded to compensate for differences between original photographs. Desktop equipment has made the tools widely accessible—but what's commonly missing is the ability to use the tools with sensitivity and skill.

Intellectual property rights

Scanners and image editing software have made it increasingly easy for people to manipulate pictures, so much so that some people have forgotten that intellectual properties, such as photographs and illustrations, are protected under copyright law. Even copies and derivatives of an original work are covered. In the United States, works created prior to 1978 are generally protected 75 years from their publication date. Those created since 1978 are governed by a somewhat more complex set of statutes, but it's safe to assume they remain protected for many years to come.

American copyright law derives from language in the U.S. Constitution authorizing Congress to "promote the Progress of Science and useful Arts, by securing for limited Times to Authors and Inventors the exclusive Right in their respective Writings and Discoveries". There are some exceptions to copyright protection, however. Textures, colors, designs based on simple geometric shapes and other generic patterns are considered to be in the public domain, and thus not copyrightable.

Congress has since recognized that some copying is essential, and has developed a four-part "fair use" test:

+ purpose of use—copying for educational or non-profit use is generally viewed as more acceptable than copying for profit;
+ nature of the copied work—newspapers are expected to be copied more than original paintings, and copying an out-of-print work is generally more acceptable than copying something hot off the press;
+ amount of use—in general, the larger the portion of the original that is copied, the greater the likelihood of infringement, although courts also take into account whether the portion copied was the artistic heart of the work;
+ economic impact—courts tend to be most punitive when the copying has done economic harm to the creator of the work while having enriched the copier.

Eventually, the law will need to change to keep up with technological innovations such as image manipulation software. In the meantime, the simplest way to assess liability is with the "recognizability" test— the more a fragment or derivation of an image is recognizable as such, the more likely it is that the original creator's rights have been infringed.

Fig. 7-36
The image on the left is an original photograph.
Is the image in the middle a "derivative" of this original?
What about the image on the right?

But at what point does an image becomes sufficiently modified that it is no longer the same image, and cannot be considered a copy or even a derivative of the original? No matter where you draw the line, someone will come along with an image editing program and move it.

The end of photographic evidence

What does a photograph mean? Does it capture a moment in time, something that really occurred, or is a photograph just pixels, a not-quite-random collection of zeros and ones?

In the days before electronic imaging, a photograph was considered a representation of something "real," a record of events that actually existed in a particular time and space. This interpretation was quickly rendered obsolete, first by high-end electronic prepress systems, which made it possible to seamlessly alter the content of an image, then by desktop systems, which made that cheap and easy to do.

We've become jaded during the past few years by ads showing artificial worlds in which cars fly through outer space and people walk inside computer chips. To create a picture that will sell a product, commercial artists have used specialized imaging tools that were formerly available only on high-end systems, but are now accessible from any desktop.

These provide users with a powerful tool—the ability to build visual worlds that would be difficult or impossible to create in reality. After all, if the ad calls for a tiger stepping out of a courier package, it's easier to shoot each image element separately and glue them together electronically, than it is to ask the tiger to hold still while you adjust the lights. These synthetic worlds are so real, in fact, they force us to redefine our everyday interpretation about what a photograph means. For example, image editing tools are rapidly eroding the notion of photographic "evidence" in courts of law.

It is virtually impossible to detect many of the changes possible with digital photography. And although modifying an image may be standard practice in the advertising industry, many observers question whether it should have any role at all in news photography. In some cases, such as commercial or advertising photography, removing scratches or specks of dust from an image would be considered insignificant enhancements of the original picture.

In other situations, such as news photography or in a court of law, the same modifications could well be considered unethical or illegal. It all depends on the context, and on the viewers' expectations of the photographs as a "true record" of actual events.

Such capabilities are very new, and our framework for dealing with them has not kept pace. Many questions remain unanswered:

- Should a newsmagazine's photo editor retouch a shot of the Queen of England because the camera angle makes it look as if a tree is growing out of the royal nose?

- Is a renowned geographic magazine within its rights in moving a few Pyramids over a little so they fit better on the cover? Should it be required to tell its readers the image was modified?

- Should retouching be used at all in a daily newspaper?

There are no simple answers to these questions, but the issue of reality versus photography is worth careful consideration—before we quickly forget which is which.

Color Drawing

"The possibilities of color are wonderful."
American painter Robert Henri

n recent years, the world of commercial art has been turned upside down by the increasing sophistication and popularity of such computer-based illustration programs as Adobe Illustrator, FreeHand, CorelDRAW and Micrografx Designer.

These graphics, or *drawing,* packages are distinct from the *imaging* programs discussed in the previous chapter. The essential difference is that drawings are composed of lines and curves that are represented in the computer as mathematical formulas, whereas images are made up of millions of tiny pixels. Illustrations created in drawing programs are also called "synthetic" artwork, to distinguish them from "natural" photographic art.

When desktop publishing first started in 1985, the emphasis was on page layout, and the big news was that you could combine text and graphics into complete pages without manual cutting and pasting. Two years later, Adobe Systems released Adobe Illustrator and suddenly an entirely new set of powerful tools was readily at hand. Other software soon followed: FreeHand, CorelDRAW, and Micrografx Designer. Today, these four still dominate the market for microcomputer-based drawing software.

Page layout programs provide line, box, and ellipse drawing tools but, typically, little more. A draw program, on the other hand, allows you to turn a sketch into a logotype, create eye-catching headline type, or give a vivid picture of rearranged floor plans without actually moving the furniture. Most publishers will find it essential to have a drawing program in their repertoire of software tools.

Fig. 8-1
This simple graphic took less than one minute to create in a PostScript-based drawing program, but would have been impossible by hand.

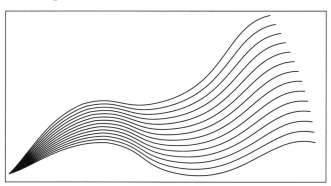

This chapter looks at how drawing programs can be used to create all kinds of logotypes, technical and scientific illustrations, commercial art, maps, and many other kinds of visual materials— all in full color, of course.

Drawing on the desktop

As explained in the previous chapter, there are some kinds of visual effects that can be created only in such bitmap (imaging) programs as Adobe Photoshop or PhotoStyler, which provide the artist with an electronic palette of brushes and other tools for creating original images and modifying scanned photographs. However, there are three major problems with bitmap programs:

- a typical picture contains millions of pixels, each many bits deep, and thus requires heavy-duty processor speed, memory, and storage;

- the parts of a picture are not represented as distinct objects and thus cannot be individually edited;

- resizing, stretching or rotating a bitmapped image will always result in distortion.

The solution, when you need to create line art graphics, illustrations, technical drawings, logotypes, and fancy typographic effects, is to use a drawing package. In such packages, the objects can also be re-sized without any loss of detail. Line segments are represented, not by a series of dots, but by mathematical formulas, so they can always be printed at the ultimate resolution of the output device—whether it's a 300 dpi desktop laser printer or a 3,000 dpi imagesetter.

People use draw programs to create everything from postage stamps to billboards, including:

- the medical illustrator who creates precise anatomical color graphics, separated onto different layers according to function;
- the advertising typographer who creates unique variations on hundreds of typefaces, then fine-tunes them for use in headlines;
- the graphic artist who uses a blend tool to create elegantly fluid logotypes in which type and other graphic elements seem to be in motion relative to one another;
- the fabric designer who draws a tiny motif, then automatically generates a perfectly tiled full-width fabric pattern, with infinite color changes a few clicks away;
- the woodworker who drafts the plans for a cedar blanket box, then uses the symbol library feature to print out a detailed parts list to take to the lumber yard.

The lines and curves used in drawing packages give you tremendous flexibility and control in creating complex illustrations that can be modified or reshaped. And the objects you draw can be filled with a color, pattern, or graduated blend of colors.

The PostScript language

Since its emergence less than ten years ago, the unifying factor in desktop computer illustration has been the PostScript language. Graphics programs built around PostScript let the artist achieve (and sometimes surpass) the quality of artwork created by hand. Lines are smoother, tints can be applied easily and evenly, and continuous-tone gradients are smooth as silk.

But PostScript drawing programs are much more than replacements for existing illustration tools. They are a whole new medium—a new language. They have both led to and inspired a new breed of designers and artists of all ages and from all backgrounds who have learned this new dialect and are creating innovative art with drawing programs.

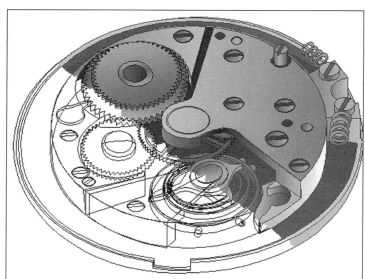

Fig. 8-2
This cutaway view of a complex graphic reveals the lines, curves, and gradients typical of drawing programs.

PostScript drawing programs let you:

- create fluid curves, smooth arcs, and perfectly straight lines, even if you can't *draw* a straight line;
- manipulate type to create outline, shadow, skews, distortions, and other effects;
- print type and graphics at the highest resolution possible on any PostScript output device;

- automatically trace around bit-mapped images to create a graphic that can be further edited or enhanced;
- select and cut masks to allow editing of specific parts of a graphic;
- color a drawing using hues specified in any of the major color models;
- maintain palettes of colors to be used repeatedly.

All this creative freedom is a direct result of the fact that the graphics are drawn as paths (lines and curves), not dots. For those who like to write their own computer programs, the PostScript language makes it possible to construct very complex shapes with just a few command lines. Even here, drawing programs can be a big help. By reading the PostScript code created by a drawing program, a programmer can pick up useful tips and tricks about writing PostScript code.

For example, use your draw program to construct a page that contains nothing but a large Helvetica "A." Print the graphic to disk as a PostScript file, then print out the PostScript code, using your word processor or editor. You'll find that it consists of five or six pages of descriptions of various PostScript parameters, ending with a few lines of text that refer to Helvetica and "A."

Go back into the graphic with your drawing program and add some more text or change the font, then print the graphic to disk again. This time, when you compare the PostScript code with that from your first try, you will find it modified to reflect the changes in the graphic. Repeat the process while adding some lines and curves, modifying rotation, scaling, gradient fills, blends, arrays, and many other effects. After each modification, examine the resulting PostScript code, making note of how your drawing program has described each graphic in the PostScript language.

Most people, of course, don't want to actually write a program—they just want to draw on the screen. Even if you can't draw a straight line, you can direct the software to keep it perfectly straight, simply by holding down a command-key. Curve-shaping tools make it just as easy to recreate complex shapes or patterns without the plastic

French curves used in traditional drafting. Those experienced with desktop page layout will find many of the concepts familiar, although there are a number of distinctions to master.

PostScript objects

All drawing programs work with individual *objects*, with each object described mathematically in the PostScript language. This results in very compact storage of the various pieces that make up illustrations, including the complex patterns, shapes, and gradients that are the hallmark of contemporary graphic design.

For example, the colored illustration on page 96 which contains complex lines, curves and gradients, required only 1.2Mb of memory in the FreeHand file. By contrast, when it was raster image processed (ripped) to create a bitmap, the resulting file required more than 20Mb.

The objects you create in a draw program can be any color—all the drawing packages discussed in this chapter support the essential color models, including RGB, HSB, and CMYK. They also support both spot color and process color specification systems such as the PANTONE MATCHING SYSTEM, Trumatch, and Focoltone.

Creating objects from lines and curves in the major drawing programs couldn't be easier—you simply click and drag. A constrain key helps you draw perfectly vertical or horizontal lines, or create exact circles and squares. In any drawing program, the lines and curves you create define *paths*. These paths can be open (having two end points) or closed (completing themselves, with no endpoints). They can be *stroked* (drawn) and filled with a color or pattern, or can be used to mask other graphic elements.

You create paths with a freehand pen tool, with a polyline tool, or with any tool that operates like a pen or pencil. Objects that you draw contain *control points* that allow you to quickly modify the shape of the object. Many computer-based drawings making use of specialized curves known as *Bézier curves*, named for the French mathematician who worked out the original calculations for drawing complex shapes.

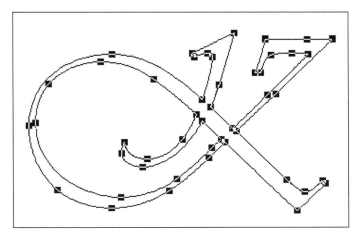

Fig. 8-3
A logotype created as a single PostScript object in a drawing program, reveals the individual control points that define its curves.

A Bézier curve can be modified after it's drawn by relocating individual anchor points, or by dragging the handles attached to each anchor point. Moving the handles changes the angle at which the line approaches the anchor point. Although each of the major drawing programs handles Bézier curves in a slightly different manner, they all support this feature. Bézier curves are an important tool for the artist, because the shapes are much more fluid than in previous kinds of computer drawings.

The number of segments that PostScript needs to represent a path depends on the complexity of the path, the size, number, and sharpness of curves, and the resolution of your printer. A path that

Fig. 8-4
The same logotype can be altered with Bézier curves, where the length and position of the handles determine the shape of each curve.

requires more line segments than PostScript can handle with available memory will produce a "limitcheck" error that prevents your graphic from printing. To overcome a limitcheck error, or to speed up printing, add more memory to your printer, and change the settings to increase the *flatness* of complex elements in illustrations.

PostScript output devices render curves as a series of very short straight lines. The flatness setting changes the minimum length of these lines. By increasing flatness, you reduce the quality of the curve. Flatness applies only to graphic elements, not to imported EPS image files. The flatness required to print a complex path with acceptable quality depends on the resolution of your printer. For a specific graphic at a given flatness setting, printing to a high-resolution imagesetter produces a much smoother image than printing to a desktop laser printer.

Fig. 8-5
This newspaper illustration, created in FreeHand for the 1992 Summer Olympics, shows how outline and fill can be used
to add dimension to a drawing.

Outline and fill

One of the most useful aspects of drawing programs is that the pattern and color used to fill any object can be different than the those used for its *stroke* or outline. This enables you to create artwork in which each shape has a distinct border—which makes it easy to mimic the effect of stained glass, for example.

Another important use for colored outlines is in creating the chokes and spreads used for color trapping. As explained in Chapter 2, color traps are small overlaps between objects with different colors, designed to bridge the inevitable misregistrations that occur during the printing process.

Take as an example the simple graphic shown at the top of page 97. If we print this drawing without specifying any trap, the result will be a small "light leak" as shown to the right of the original graphic. Because the foreground object is composed of a single color, as is the background color, we can easily trap this by either spreading the foreground or choking the background.

The rule of thumb in trapping is that the lighter tone expands into the darker tone; in this case, that means the stroke around the foreground object will take a color closer to the foreground than to

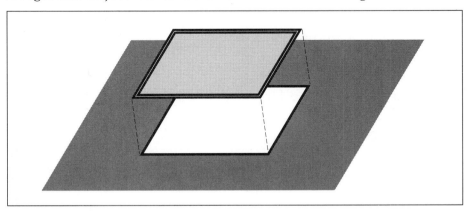

Fig. 8-6
Simple traps can be created in a drawing program by increasing the width of an object's stroke, and giving it a color in between the foreground and background colors.

Illustration: © Courtland Shakespeare

Fig. 8-7
This illustration by Courtland Shakespeare contains elements created in
Adobe Illustrator and CorelDRAW, combined with a background in
Adobe Photoshop. It would be exceedingly difficult to trap
conventionally or in a drawing program.

the background. Such a trap can be constructed equally well with
conventional techniques (by a film stripper on a light table) or in a
drawing program.

However, when it comes to more complex illustrations (such as
those with multi-colored foreground objects against a background
gradient fill), it quickly becomes possible to create graphics so
complex that they would be almost impossible to trap
conventionally.

Before getting too carried away building traps in complex
illustrations, it's best to stop and consider whether trapping should
be performed at all in drawing programs, or whether it's best done
in dedicated trapping software. With the emergence of such
specialized desktop trapping software as Adobe TrapWise and
IslandTrapper, plus trapping routines built into high-end RIPs and

Fig. 8-8
Drawing programs allow you to manipulate type to create a variety of special effects.

page assembly stations, many savvy designers are beginning to question whether they should spend any time at all making traps.

Although some artists will insist on creating their own traps, in many cases they could more productively and more profitably pay

Photo: © Pixar

Fig. 8-9
This modification of the Adobe Systems logo was created in Pixar Typestry, a 3-D type rendering package.

someone else (working in a color trade shop or high-end PostScript service bureau) to take care of trapping. This issue is explored in more detail in Chapter 12.

Working with type

One of the great benefits of PostScript is that it has made it relatively easy for designers to treat type as a graphic element—to stretch, skew, rotate, flip, mask, swirl, and distort it in every conceivable way. The downside, of course, is illegible design—pages in which type appears at every angle except horizontal.

Drawing programs allow you to work with any typeface, whether PostScript or TrueType, and convert the characters from text into graphic outlines, which can then be modified as if they were freehand lines and curves. For instance, the original letterforms can be altered to create a distinctive logotype.

For even more exotic effects, you can create type in such three-dimensional rendering programs as Adobe Dimensions or Pixar Typestry, then save it in EPS format for importing into a drawing or page layout program.

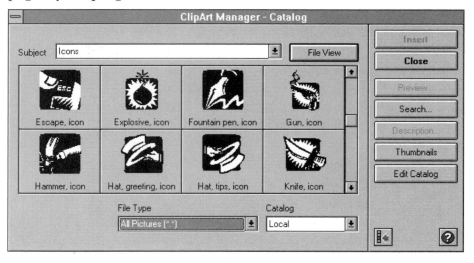

Fig. 8-10
Micrografx Designer comes with more than 13,000 pieces of clip art, plus a clip art manager to help you keep track of it all.

Process-colored type, especially in small point sizes, must be properly trapped or the characters will be noticeably distorted by even slight misregistration on press. When the only thing on the page that needs to be trapped is the type, and it is set against a background of a single color, the traps can be built in the drawing program, but when other objects on the page require trapping, it is best left to a dedicated trapping package.

Clip art

Most of the major drawing programs come with libraries of clip art, and although some of the pieces are in black-and-white, all comprise objects that can be individually colorized. In the early days of computerized drawing, a lot of clip art was of rather poor quality, but today most of it is quite usable.

Some designers and graphic artists are rather snobbish when it comes to clip art, considering it beneath them. Those who believe that are missing out on some real treasures, and probably wasting time and money. For example, if you need to create a presentation that describes your organization's computer networks, you could start by drawing from scratch a symbol for every piece of computer and office equipment in the company.

Or you could use the clip art that comes with your drawing program or the clip art offered by the countless vendors whose ads are found on the back pages of all the popular desktop publishing magazines. Simply by combining various objects and drawing different kinds of solid and dashed lines to connect them, you can quickly create your own impressive illustrations.

Layers

Working with oil paints, watercolors, or other traditional media, an artist can subtly change a picture by recognizing how underlying colors will be affected when new colors are placed on top. But PostScript drawings work in opaque layers, from back to front.

By deconstructing a drawing into multiple layers, you can more easily isolate and control individual elements, and reduce the time

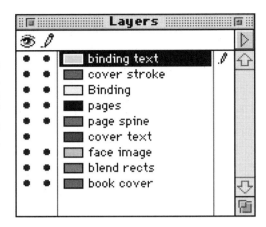

Fig. 8-11
The layers in a drawing can be individually viewed, edited, and printed, which can you save a great deal of time when working with complex illustrations.

needed to display and print the graphic. Each object is displayed and printed as if it were on a separate layer, in front of, or behind, all other objects in the drawing. In other words, an object on top (unless it's transparent) completely obscures whatever lies beneath it; therefore, as an artist you must think in terms of opaque paint, rather than transparent watercolors.

Spot color and process color

You can assign color values to objects as you draw them, or after you have finished the linework, using either the process color system or spot colors. When working with process colors, you assign percentages of cyan, magenta, yellow, and black to objects in the illustration, often with the help of color tint books available from graphic arts supply stores.

If you are debating whether to use spot or process color when both are available, remember that the overall objective is to produce the minimum number of pieces of film (and printing plates). Thus if your document contains only two colors, it will be cheaper to produce with spot color than with four-color process, but if you have defined 37 different colors, it obviously makes more sense to use four-color process so that you have four pieces of film, rather than 37.

All the major draw programs now support the Pantone color matching system, and some support other color specification systems, including Trumatch and Focoltone.

To use the color matching feature, pick the ink color you want in a swatch book, such as the PANTONE MATCHING SYSTEM (PMS) Color Formula Guide (available from graphic arts supply stores or directly from Pantone). When you specify a PMS color on screen, your monitor will attempt to display the closest match based on look-up tables for each kind of display, but it won't be nearly as accurate as the swatch books. If you are printing spot color overlays, your printing company will mix the appropriate ink, based on the labels you assign each layer, such as "Dark Green PMS 343".

When working with process color, you can create custom colors, either by specifying their CMYK values or by fiddling with the color controls in any of the other color models your software supports, then converting back to CMYK. If you use certain colors regularly, create a document that contains them. As long as that document is open, you can quickly duplicate the colors in other documents.

Drawings and page layout

Although some drawing programs have recently added the ability to create multi-page documents, they are still better suited for individual logotypes, graphics, and other illustrations. The standard way of integrating drawings with the other components of a page is through the encapsulated PostScript (EPS) file format.

Virtually all drawing programs allow you to import and export graphics as EPS files, which have much of the same code as the illustration printed to disk, but with a few important differences:

- A PostScript file printed to disk contains all the information needed by any PostScript printer to produce the desired graphic or page, including page size information, fonts, and TIFF image files, a header used by the printer and, in some PostScript files created on the Mac, a copy of the Apple LaserPrep file.

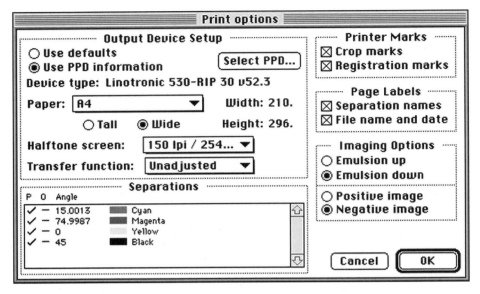

Fig. 8-12
When printing a PostScript job to disk, you need to specify the
intended output device, screen angles, and separation parameters. If
you don't specify screen angles, the imagesetter's default angles will be
used, which is often what you want, especially if you're using supercell
screening. But you definitely want to specify screen frequency.

♦   By contrast, EPS files are used primarily to transfer graphics
    between different software programs. They cannot be printed
    directly because they do not contain page setup information;
    may or may not have the necessary TIFF files; and do not
    contain headers. Moreover, unlike PostScript files printed to
    disk, EPS files may or may not contain a PICT (for Mac) or
    TIFF (for DOS or OS/2) screen image of the illustration.

Unlike a PostScript file written to disk as a print file, you cannot
print an EPS file simply by sending it to an output device—it must
be output from a PostScript application program. Here are some of
the other rules you must follow to avoid problems when working
with EPS files:

♦   be sure to include imported EPS files on disk when you send
    the complete page layout to a service bureau for output;

- all fonts embedded in an EPS file must be available to the page layout application whenever outputting the finished pages, whether to disk, paper, or film;
- any chokes and spreads defined in a drawing program must be of the correct size for the specific paper and printing conditions: they cannot be modified in the EPS file.

There is another potential problem when you work with EPS files that have been created with spot colors, rather than process colors. When you place spot color EPS files in your page layout, it's important that the page layout program recognize the spot colors, especially when the same spot colors have been used for text on the pages. This feature was introduced in PageMaker 5.0, and has been incorporated into version 3.3 of QuarkXPress.

Although the PostScript language is the very heart of desktop publishing, neither the Macintosh not Windows-based computers use PostScript for representing information on screen: the Mac uses Apple's own QuickDraw (or the new QuickDraw GX), while Windows applications use the Windows graphics device interface (GDI).

If you're using either the Mac or Windows, you have to be aware of a couple of problems. First, what you see on screen is not exactly what will be printed on paper. Second, when creating an EPS file in a drawing program, you must bundle with it a low-resolution preview for display on screen—a TIFF file for PC-based applications, and a PICT or TIFF file for Macintosh. When you place an EPS file in your page layout program, what you see on screen is just the low-resolution preview, not the actual PostScript graphic.

Adobe Illustrator

Among professional designers and illustrators, Adobe Illustrator is one of the most popular drawing packages on the market. It provides a complete set of drawing tools and, with the release of Illustrator 5.5, has numerous significant features for color publishers; these include floating palettes, enhanced gradient fills, layers, and character and paragraph styles.

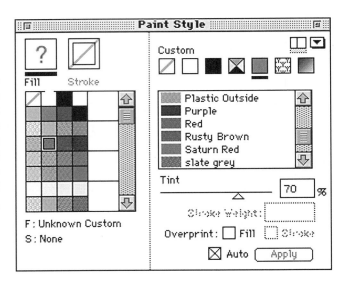

Fig. 8-13
The Paint Style palette in Illustrator 5 makes it easy to mix CMYK colors and create custom patterns and gradients.

Other important features of Illustrator include:

- very smooth on-screen drawing, a property that is hard to quantify but frequently mentioned by Illustrator users as one of its greatest strengths;

- the fact that its native file format is EPS (after all, Adobe also invented the PostScript language), which makes it easy to import and edit drawings created in many other drawing packages;

- a charting tool, which many illustrators never use, but others find invaluable for creating the kind of "infographics" used in USA Today and many other newspapers and magazines.

Prior to version 5, one of Illustrator's major weaknesses (compared to its primary competitor, FreeHand) was that you had to create drawings in line-art mode, then shift to preview mode to see colors or fill patterns. This has finally been rectified, much to the relief of Illustrator users everywhere. Illustrator 5 also added multiple levels of undo and redo, support for pressure-sensitive pens, and a floating Layers palette, which allows you to create and name as many layers as you require, move objects from layer to layer, change the order of layers, and print and preview only selected layers.

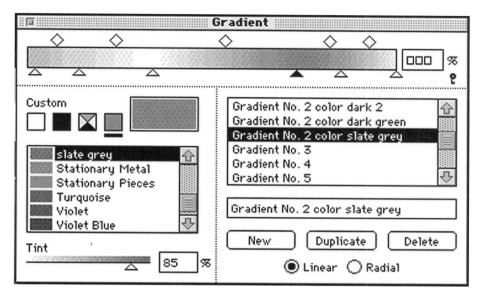

Fig. 8-14
Illustrator 5 includes a flexible gradient palette that allows you to create color blends tuned for the least possible banding.

One of the most substantive enhancements to Illustrator 5.5 is that Adobe has taken the concept of plug-in filters popularized in Photoshop and extended it to drawings. Filters can be used to:

- automatically create complex shapes, such as polygons, stars, and spirals;
- dynamically alter an object's color with such effects as Invert, Adjust, Mix, and Blend;

Fig. 8-15
Illustrator's Pathfinder filters can define the interaction of two objects (left), such as their intersection (center) or the result of subtracting the foreground object from the background object (right).

◆ perform special effects such as Calligraphy (which distorts a path so that it appears to be drawn with a calligraphic pen), Drop Shadow, and Roughen (which adds points to a path, then randomly distorts it).

One of the biggest improvements in Illustrator 5.5 is its handling of fonts. Previous versions forced you to add fonts to the Fonts menu one at a time through a dialog box. The new Character palette makes fonts and formatting available all the time, allowing you to quickly fine-tune horizontal scaling, baseline shift, and automatic kerning. Illustrator 5.5 also comes with 120 Adobe PostScript Type 1 fonts.

Illustrator has been integrated somewhat with such other Adobe programs as Premiere and Photoshop. For example, if you Option-double-click a placed Photoshop EPS file in Illustrator, Photoshop is automatically launched (assuming you have Photoshop on your system) so you can edit the EPS file. Unfortunately, Illustrator doesn't show you any changes to the EPS file until you save, close, and reopen the Illustrator document.

For Illustrator users who also work with Photoshop, the Color Matching dialog box in Illustrator's File Preferences menu can improve the consistency of your color output. If you use the same settings in Illustrator's Color Matching dialog box and in Photoshop's Monitor Setup and Printing Inks Setup dialog boxes, an image displayed on-screen in either program and printed from either program will match.

Fig. 8-16
This graphic was easy to create with the Pathfinder filters in Illustrator 5, but would have required hours of tedious cutting and pasting in previous versions.

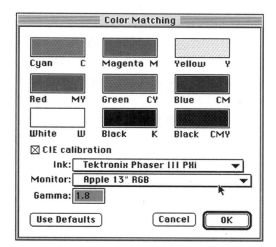

Fig. 8-17
Illustrator's Color Matching
dialog box lets you adjust
the colors displayed on-
screen so they more closely
match printed colors.

To create color separations, you use the Separator utility that comes
with Illustrator. Creating color separations involves opening a color
EPS file in Adobe Separator, setting the separation operations, then
printing or saving the file. The first step is to specify the appropriate
PPD (PostScript Printer Description file) for your intended output
device.

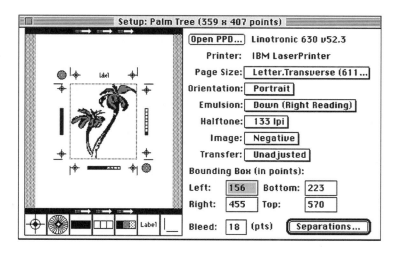

Fig. 8-18
Adobe Separator provides complete control over the color separation
process, including settings bleeds, crops, printer marks, screen
frequency, and transfer curves.

A PPD contains important information about an output device, such as its resolution, line screen rulings, screen angles, and page sizes. Before printing or saving the file, you can also change your artwork's imageable area, specify bleed settings or a border around the artwork, and add or reposition register marks, color bars, gradient tint bars (gray wedge), and crop marks. When specifying the page size, you can change the Offset value to alter the placement of the page and thereby save film or paper.

FreeHand

FreeHand is a popular full-function drawing program that competes head-to-head with Adobe Illustrator. FreeHand version 4 maintains the program's reputation for excellent functionality and sophisticated text manipulation, while remaining relatively accessible and easy to use.

FreeHand introduced a number of features that have now been adopted by competitive drawing packages, including flexible control of layers, pressure-sensitive stylus support, and multiple levels of undo. Other innovative FreeHand features include:

- a style palette that allows you to format an object quickly, simply by clicking on the appropriate style—in creating a map, for instance, you just draw a path for a road, then instantly format it as a four-lane highway;
- the ability to create drawings on multiple layers, making it very easy to view, edit, and print just those portions you're currently concerned with;
- the ability to output color separations directly from within the program, rather than having to use a separate utility, such as Adobe Separator;
- tight integration with PageMaker, within which you can Option-double-click on a FreeHand drawing in order to launch FreeHand and edit the drawing.

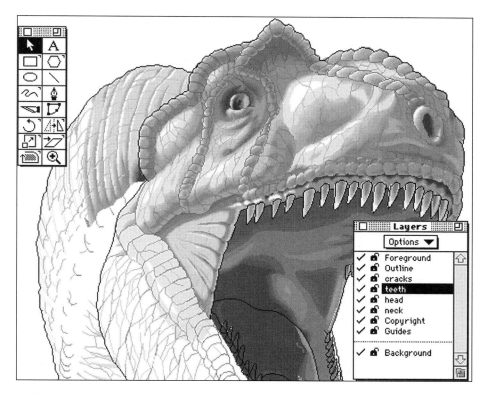

Fig. 8-19
This extraordinary drawing-in-progress was created in Aldus FreeHand
by Steve Cowden, and makes extensive use of layers to isolate
individual elements.

Some of the most important improvements in FreeHand 4 are in the
user interface: many dialog boxes have been replaced with floating
palettes that are always available. The Inspector palette, for instance,
replaces more than 35 dialog boxes, including the old Elements Info
command. The Inspector contains five icons that allow you to modify
settings for objects, fill patterns, stroke, text, or document setup.

Using the Document Inspector, you can quickly add, delete, and
rearrange pages—FreeHand 4 can create documents containing as
many pages as will fit on the 56-square-inch pasteboard.

Color tools

FreeHand 4 sets a new standard for ease of use in specifying and applying colors in a drawing program. Virtually every aspect of working with color has been implemented through a "drag and drop" interface. For example, once a color has been specified in the Color Mixer palette, it can be dragged to the Color List for future use, or simply dragged and dropped onto part of a drawing. Dropping the color inside an object applies it as a fill (even if the object wasn't previously selected), while dropping it on the object's boundary applies it as a stroke. Holding down the Option key while you drop creates a radial fill, while holding down the Control key creates a graduated fill.

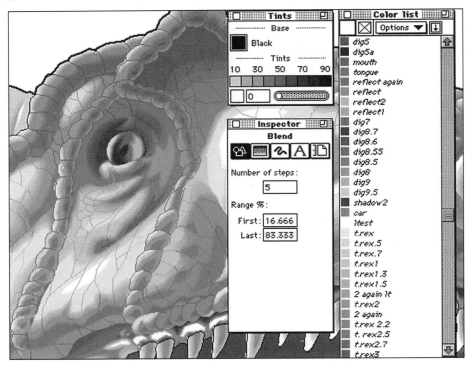

Fig. 8-20
Steve Cowden used FreeHand's Color List feature (with more than 70 colors) to add realistic shading to this prehistoric beast.

Any color in the Color List can be redefined by specifying a new color (in the Color Mixer) and dropping it on an existing color in the list. Any objects using the original color will instantly be changed. If an object has been colored directly by mixing a color in the Color Mixer (without including it in the Color List), it can be grabbed from the Fill or Stroke Inspector and dragged to the Color List for future use, or dropped on the Color Mixer for editing.

Creating percentage tints of any defined color couldn't be easier: simply drag and drop colors to and from the Tints palette. To apply a color to the stroke or fill of multiple objects, select the objects and drag the color to the appropriate swatch in the Fill or Stroke Inspector.

The power of FreeHand's color tools is further magnified by the program's support for styles. This makes it very easy to define a style for any kind of object, then change the color of all similar objects instantly by redefining their style.

Text tools

The text tools in FreeHand have been so substantially improved that they rank on par with those in many page layout programs. Text can be typed directly onto the page or into an existing path, text blocks can be linked, and text can flow from one path to another (for example, from inside a circle to along a curve, then around a square). Font, size, and style can be selected from the floating Type palette, while the Type Inspector allows you to adjust paragraph-level formatting, including tabs, indents, space before and after a paragraph, alignment, letter and word spacing, and hyphenation.

In fact, some of FreeHand's text controls go beyond those found in page layout programs. In addition to left, right, center and decimal tabs, FreeHand supports wrapping tabs, for wrapping text in the columns of a table. For any text block, you can specify not only the number of columns but also the number of rows and the direction in which the text flows. The rows and columns can be automatically balanced, either by adjusting leading or altering point size (with control over how far point size can be changed). FreeHand even supports hung punctuation—the ability to hang quotation marks,

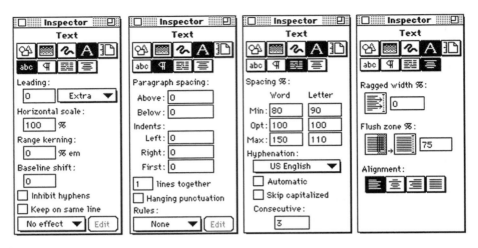

Fig. 8-21
The Text Inspector in FreeHand provides instant access to settings for
leading, scaling, kerning, spacing, hyphenation, and alignment.

periods, and other punctuation marks outside the margins—a feature
not yet available in page layout software.

With its improved text capabilities and multi-page features,
FreeHand 4 might seem to be treading on ground previously reserved
for page layout programs. Indeed, if you're constructing a one-page
flyer or simple newsletter, you can probably get away with doing
the whole thing in FreeHand, rather than importing the text and
graphics into PageMaker or QuarkXPress. However, attempting more
complex projects will quickly remind you that FreeHand was
designed for drawing, not page layout. It lacks paragraph styles,
search-and-replace, and the diversity of file import filters found in
most page layout programs.

Another difference between the realms of page layout and drawing
is that most graphic arts professionals work with only one page layout
program—you rarely meet someone who regularly creates
publications using both PageMaker and QuarkXPress. However, many
illustrators and designers work with both Illustrator and FreeHand,
because of each program's unique features and strengths, although
even this trend has diminished since the most release of Illustrator
5.5 and FreeHand 4.

FreeHand 4 can import and export files in Illustrator 1.1, 88 and 3 formats, as well as EPS, PICT and RGB formats. In fact, FreeHand 4 can even import its own EPS files.

CorelDRAW

Among Windows-based drawing packages, the undisputed leader in terms of market share is CorelDRAW, which is based around a set of full-function drawing tools but also includes modules for charting, presentations, and image enhancement. Version 5 of the CorelDRAW package even comes with Corel Ventura, a full-function page layout program, but the drawing module continues to be the core program in this impressive graphics toolkit.

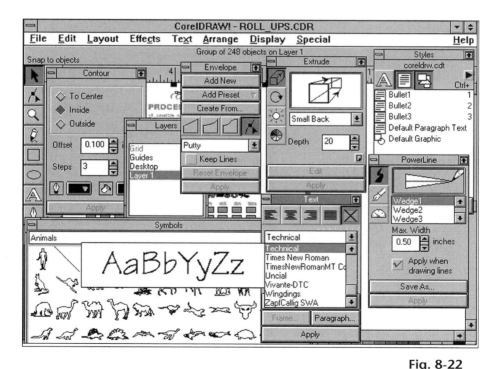

Fig. 8-22
Although CorelDRAW's "roll up" palettes provide quick access to tools, your screen can get somewhat crowded if you display (clockwise from top left) the Contour, Layers, Envelope, Extrude, Styles, PowerLine, Text, and Symbols roll ups simultaneously.

CorelDRAW's strong point is the ease of use—you don't need to be a professional graphic artist to create good-looking drawings, and its small number of tools gets you to a moderate level of program-use competence relatively quickly. It's also considered a good value because of the bundled fonts and clip art, plus the charting and presentation modules, though its real strength lies in the core drawing tools.

CorelDRAW provides support for all the major color models, including RGB, HSB, and CMYK, plus spot and process color matching systems from Pantone and Trumatch. It also features a complete set of printing and color separation controls.

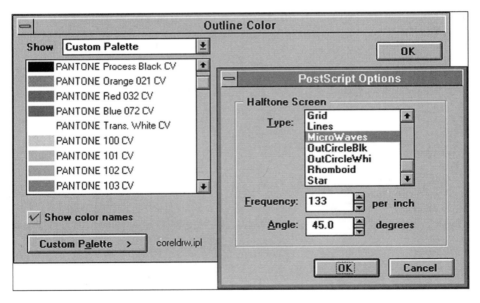

Fig. 8-23
In addition to support for most major color specification systems, CorelDRAW 4.0 lets you specify such halftone parameters as screen type, frequency, and angle.

Although some professional graphic artists may prefer FreeHand or Illustrator, others have become dedicated CorelDRAW fanatics, pointing to unique features such as its extrude, envelope, and other commands that allow quick and easy creation of objects that appear three-dimensional.

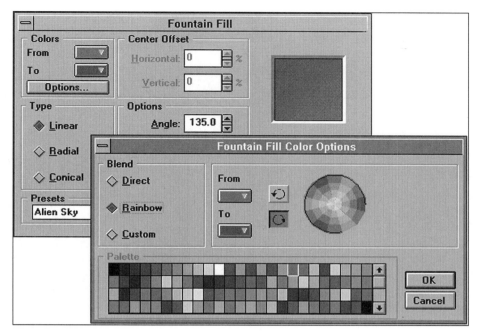

Fig. 8-24
CorelDRAW provides flexible tools for creating fountain fills (gradients),
including custom rainbow blends.

Another area where CorelDRAW really shines is in creating linear, radial and conical fountain fills (gradients). In addition to regular color blends and rainbow fills (using the HSB model), CorelDRAW allows you to create custom fountain fills using multiple colors.

Serious CorelDRAW users should check out Chris Dickman's *Mastering CorelDRAW* Journal, which is packed with hands-on tips and tricks. For a free sample issue, phone 1-800-565-0815.

Micrografx Designer

Micrografx Designer is a Windows-based drawing package that has introduced a number of important innovations in computerized drawing. Despite its technical prowess, it has not fared well in the marketplace against such competitors as CorelDRAW, but deserves consideration by the person seeking a full-function drawing program

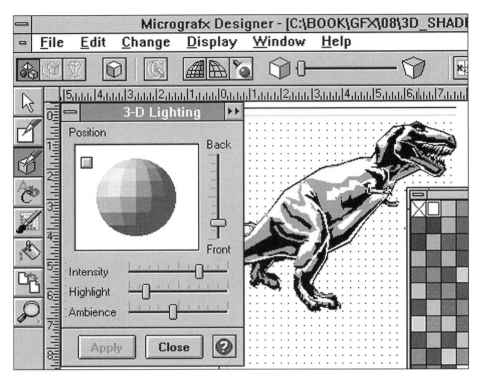

Fig. 8-25
Although it's primarily a two-dimensional drawing program, Designer
4.0 includes many 3-D functions, such as rotation, light source control,
and smooth shading of complex objects.

that has overlap capabilities with computer-aided drafting packages.
Designer was the first PC-based PostScript drawing package to support
multiple layers, automatic dimensioning, built-in color separations,
and a graphic search-and-replace function that operates on drawings
the same way a word processing program works with text.

Micrografx Designer 4.0, which was released in 1993, adds a
number of features, such as the ability to automatically draw complex
three-dimensional shapes. Its 32-bit graphics engine creates drawings
with resolution up to 25,400 dpi, and lets you create and edit objects
to a precision of 1 micron (one-thousandth of a millimeter). In
addition to RGB, HSB, and CMYK color models, Designer supports
the PANTONE MATCHING SYSTEM, Trumatch, and Focoltone.

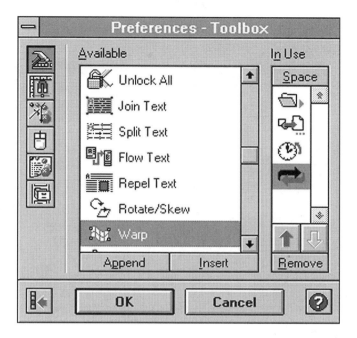

Fig. 8-26
Micrografx Designer lets you customize almost any aspect of its user interface by selecting the tools and functions that will appear in the toolbox.

Designer 4.0 features a streamlined user interface with an interactive tool ribbon, context-sensitive pop-up menus, and a hint line that provides useful suggestions about any tool, as you move the mouse over it. The program comes with 280 PostScript Type 1 fonts (and matching TrueType fonts), and a library of more than 13,000 pieces of clip art, plus 200 images (on CD-ROM). You can give your imagination free reign with fonts, such as skew, stretch, warp and fill text, and still edit the text.

Other important features in Designer 4.0 include:

- 29 drawing tools, plus such functions as warp, array, and extrude;
- styles, which let you quickly copy attributes from one symbol to another;

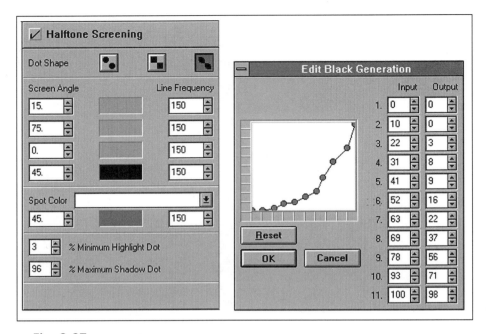

Fig. 8-27
The SmartSep utility that comes with Micrografx Designer provides
complete control over halftone settings (left), and supports calibration,
ink correction, and black generation (right).

- ◆ sophisticated type manipulation, including flowing text
  inside a symbol and flowing text from one container to
  another;
- ◆ support for multiple views and multiple open documents;
- ◆ PhotoMagic, a surprisingly powerful built-in image editing
  module.

Micrografx Designer comes with a sophisticated color separation
utility, SmartSep, which supports spot and process color separations,
and performs undercolor removal, gray component replacement,
trapping, and black boost. It also includes a utility for printer
calibration.

Drawing conclusions

Now that drawing programs are increasingly powerful, inexpensive, and easy to use, what trends will define the evolution of these products over the next few years?

One way to get a sense of where professional drawing software is headed is to look at such low-cost drawing programs as Adobe IntelliDraw and Shapeware Visio. The major benefit of these programs isn't their feature set, it's the fact that casual users can quickly create good-looking drawings without spending weeks learning how the program functions.

IntelliDraw, for instance, is "intelligent" in the sense that after you've drawn a line connecting two objects, it is automatically redrawn if you decide to move or otherwise alter one of the objects. IntelliDraw is available for both Macintosh and Windows, and features "smart" clip art that can be altered and combined into countless variations.

Visio, from Shapeware, is based on the idea of stencil palettes that help you create diagrams and drawings. It comes with 17 stencils containing more than 300 predefined shapes. Shapeware also sells Visio Shapes, specialized stencil add-ons designed for specific drawing tasks such as bathroom and kitchen layout, chemical, electrical, and mechanical engineering.

Clearly, we can expect the new drawing tools found in low-end packages such as Visio and IntelliDraw to appear soon in the mainstream drawing programs. Similarly, the shift from single-page to multi-page orientation is likely to become widespread.

Other likely trends in drawing software include:

- bundling ever-increasing libraries of clip art and fonts, to the point where buying a drawing package may be one of the more economical ways of acquiring a font library;
- an increasing overlap between draw programs (which, historically, have been limited to a single page) and page layout programs (which work with many pages but have provided only the most rudimentary drawing tools);

◆ distribution on CD-ROM and, ultimately, electronic distribution.

Desktop drawing tools have opened a world of graphic creativity to a large audience, many of whom have no formal artistic training. The ability to draw any shape, to color it any way, and to combine it with existing electronic artwork, provides countless new possibilities for expression.

At the same time, these tools have revolutionized the work of professional illustrators. Never before have they had such a rich palette of tools or been so intimately involved with producing the finished piece, not just its creating it. The results of these trends are beginning to be seen everywhere, in advertising, commercial and technical illustration, industrial design, and fine art.

Color Page Layout

"In color are to be found harmony, melody, and counterpoint."
French poet Charles Baudelaire

Color page layout is the domain of integration: it's where text, drawings, and photographs are brought together to create complete pages, and pages organized into long, complex documents. Page layout programs combine meticulous control over positioning type with the ability to import and organize a wide variety of drawing and image file formats.

When desktop publishing began a few short years ago, the very fact that you could easily combine text and graphics on a page was considered revolutionary. Today, page layout programs are much more sophisticated, and are used for producing virtually every kind of publication, from one-page black-and-white flyers to full-color glossy catalogs hundreds of pages long.

Indeed, the rapid success of black-and-white page layout and the subsequent demise of traditional typesetting should have everyone currently employed in traditional color publishing looking over their shoulders, because desktop tools are about to take over virtually all color publishing.

In this chapter we look at the major page layout programs—PageMaker, QuarkXPress, and Corel Ventura—and compare their capabilities for producing full-color publications. No single program will best meet the needs of all users, so we examine their similarities and differences, to help you select the most appropriate software. Among the parameters that must be considered in assessing color page layout programs are the quality of typography, support for graphics and images, and ability to work with different color models. We also explore how page layout programs can be linked to high-end systems for scanning, proofing, and film output.

The domain of integration

Page layout programs aren't designed to create every element on the page: their purpose is to take text (created in a word processing program) and integrate it with graphics (created in a drawing program) and photographs (scanned and enhanced in an imaging program).

The integration of some kinds of simple documents doesn't even require a page layout program—it can be adequately performed with today's high-powered graphical word processing packages. However, to create more complex documents, such as brochures and magazines, you need a full-function page layout program.

For example, if your document contains one or two small TIFF files that are placed in ordinary rectangular keyline boxes, any graphical word processor will suffice. On the other hand, if you're working with esoteric file formats, have text flowing around irregular shapes,

Fig. 9-1
The page layout market encompasses everything from graphical word processors to design-oriented desktop publishing programs (PageMaker and QuarkXPress) and packages for producing structured documents (Ventura and FrameMaker).

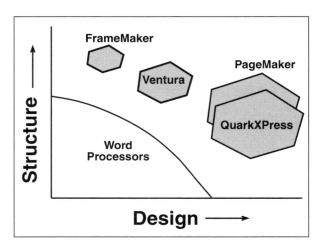

or need to adjust the brightness and contrast of imported image files, you require the added capabilities of a full-featured page layout package.

An essential aspect of any page layout program is its ability to import the widest possible array of files, in both native formats and in file formats (such as ASCII, RTF, and EPS) designed for exchanging data between different programs. Support for many import and export filters is an important indicator of the probable suitability of a page layout program for heavy-duty page production.

Typography

When PageMaker 1.0 for the Macintosh was released in July 1985, it featured typographic capabilities that were both sophisticated and crude—sophisticated in that PageMaker was the first microcomputer application program to provide control over such typographic fundamentals as leading, tracking, and kerning; crude in that it lacked many other typographic essentials, including *ligatures* (composite characters, such as ff).

Things have changed a great deal in the intervening years. Today, all page layout programs (and even some word processing packages) have much more sophisticated typographic controls than that first desktop publishing program. All major page layout programs provide control over *leading* (the space between lines), *kerning* (tightening the space between specific pairs of characters so that they fit together well, particularly at larger point sizes), and *tracking* (overall tightening or loosening of letter spacing that affects all characters equally). But the programs differ in the level of control they offer over each of these parameters.

Some type effects, such as gradient fills or using type to mask parts of an image, can't be achieved in a page layout program. They must be created in an illustration or imaging program, then exported as an EPS file or other format to be imported into the page layout.

Page layout programs now support Adobe Multiple Master font technology, which uses two or more variations of a typeface (such as the compressed and extended versions) to automatically calculate all the intermediate *instances* in the face. In some Multiple Master typefaces, each variation is *optically scaled* rather than stretched linearly, so that the thickness of stems and the shapes of serifs are modified to maintain the essence of the original typeface.

The success of desktop publishing has spawned a dynamic new market for digital type, which has given desktop designers access to literally thousands of distinct typefaces. There are now more than 10,000 PostScript typefaces on the market—Adobe alone now has more than 1,000 faces in its library. This has produced a wave of incredible typographic innovation, but it sometimes backfires, as when novice publishers use too many faces on the same page, or combine faces that clash with one another.

Fig. 9-2
The person using this computer is clearly font impoverished—there are only 100 or so typefaces available.

Although it's now easy for desktop publishers to acquire many fonts, it's not as easy to acquire the skills needed to use fonts properly. Typography is an art, and one that some publishers simply have not taken the time to learn, to their detriment and that of their readers.

PostScript versus TrueType

Although the PostScript font format helped get the desktop publishing industry rolling, it now has a competitor: the TrueType font format promoted by Microsoft and Apple. There are advantages to both the PostScript and TrueType font formats. Both treat fonts as outline shapes that can be precisely scaled, stretched or rotated. Both are device-independent, which means that characters can be proofed on a low-resolution desktop laser printer, then output at much higher resolution on an imagesetter without any change in the size, spacing or position of the text—only the resolution has been increased.

However, PostScript continues to have some major advantages for professional publishers, including the fact that it is a complete page description language, whereas TrueType is limited to describing fonts. (Microsoft and Apple have developed TrueImage, a page description language to compete against PostScript, but PostScript is firmly entrenched in the electronic publishing industry.)

Another important consideration is that virtually every service bureau in North America has invested substantially in building a library of PostScript typefaces, and would not take well to the idea of having to buy TrueType equivalents of each face. Many desktop publishers routinely solve this problem by sending their service bureaus all the fonts contained in their documents (although this is usually a violation of the relevant font license agreements.)

The one market segment in which TrueType is winning is the office environment, where users are primarily concerned with having access to low-cost type that looks good at the relatively low resolutions of office laser printers (300 to 600 dpi). TrueType has become particularly well entrenched in the office market since the arrival of Windows 3.1, which enables users to embed TrueType fonts in documents, making it possible to print and, in some cases, edit them, even if those fonts are not on the system. Moreover, shortly after shipping Windows 3.1, Microsoft began selling low-cost packages of TrueType font, which had the effect of lowering all font prices, even those of PostScript fonts.

In a way, the battle between the PostScript and TrueType font formats is reminiscent of a similar battle waged almost a century ago, when the typesetting industry was controlled by the Linotype Company. In the early 1900s, Monotype emerged as one of many competitors to Linotype and, like the others, was forced to create its own library of typefaces, because each typesetting machine would only work with its own faces.

The competition between Linotype and Monotype resulted in the production of hundreds of new typefaces, many more than would have emerged if Linotype's monopoly had been maintained. Similarly, the arrival of TrueType in the late 1980s had two immediate effects: it forced Adobe to unlock the encryption of its fonts, and it resulted in a rapid decline in the price of fonts. Desktop publishers everywhere are the ultimate beneficiaries of this competition.

Color models

Page layout programs must support as many color models as possible, so you can create page elements (type, lines, and tint areas) in the model appropriate to your output method. The type and other elements in a layout can be colored using any of the models supported by your applications program: RGB, HSB/HLS, CMYK, and the PANTONE MATCHING SYSTEM.

For best results, use the color model appropriate to the task at hand:

- If the piece is going to be printed as a four-color process job, specify all the colors, from the beginning, in terms of their CMYK values. Use a process color guide, such as those available from Focoltone, Trumatch, and Pantone (their *process* color guide).

- If the piece will be printed with spot colors, specify each color in terms of its PMS number or other solid color standard. You can start with the Pantone color library when defining spot colors and, if the one you need is not available, define a custom color using any of the color models. Your printing company can then apply a pre-mixed or custom-blended ink for that spot color.

	PageMaker	QuarkXPress	Ventura
RGB	◆	◆	◆
CMY	◆	◆	◆
HSB/HLS	◆	◆	◆
PMS	◆	◆	◆
PANTONE Process	◆	◆	◆
PANTONE ProSim	◆	◆	
PANTONE ProSim Euro	◆		
PANTONE Process Euro	◆		
Trumatch	◆	◆	
Focoltone	◆	◆	
Toyo	◆	◆	
Munsell	◆		
DIC	◆	◆	

Fig. 9-3
Support for color models and color matching systems
varies between the main page layout programs.

Another important aspect of color support concerns color management systems. Starting with version 3.2, QuarkXPress now supports the EfiColor color management system (CMS) from Electronics for Imaging, which was covered in Chapter 4.

The arrival of color management systems in page layout programs is going to make it much easier for publishers to achieve consistent, predictable color matching throughout the production cycle. However, for the potential benefit to be realized, it's essential that color management tools be implemented at the operating system level, so they are applied identically in all applications programs, whether for drawing, imaging or page layout.

Color separations

Because pages (and the graphics and images they contain) must be separated into their cyan, magenta, yellow, and black components before being printed on press, color separation is an important aspect of page layout. But in discussing the ability of page layout programs to produce color separations, it's important to distinguish between different kinds of separation capabilities.

Today, all page layout packages allow you to specify the color of type and linework (ruling lines and boxes) created within the program, and to separate these into their spot or process color components prior to printing. You can also place in your layout any graphics created in drawing programs and exported as EPS files, and all three major programs (PageMaker, QuarkXPress, and Corel Ventura) can separate these graphics into their CMYK components.

A more challenging task for page layout programs is to color separate photographs, a capability that until recently was excluded because of its cost and complexity. A typical strategy for getting around this problem has been to either pre-separate the images (in an imaging program prior to importing the images into the page layout package) or post-separate them as part of complete pages (in a stand-alone utility such as Adobe PrePrint).

QuarkXPress 3.2 was the first page layout program to support color separation of photographs, through its built-in EfiColor XTension. PageMaker 5.0 is not able to do this, although Adobe has announced that color management will be added in the next major release. Corel Ventura does not currently support photographic color separation, but it seems likely it will do so once its major competitors have added this feature.

A word of warning: you must distinguish between what is technically feasible and what will maximize your productivity. Although your page layout program may be capable of separating photographs into their process color components, it will usually take much longer than performing the same operation in Photoshop or PhotoStyler.

In general, you are better off placing pre-separated images into page layouts, rather than forcing your layout program to separate them. It will take a little longer on the front end (during scanning or in an imaging program) but can save a substantial amount of time on the back end (when outputting to an imagesetter or desktop color printer), especially if you are working with large files.

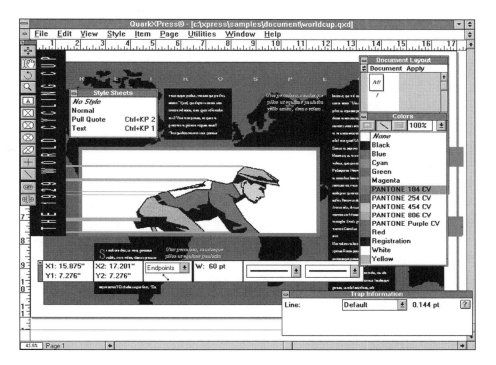

Fig. 9-4
QuarkXPress is now available in a Windows version that is virtually identical with its Macintosh counterpart.

QuarkXPress

QuarkXPress is a full-function page layout package that provides a complete range of tools for the color publisher. It offers advanced typographic controls, multiple master pages, style sheets, and support for a variety of color models.

For years QuarkXPress was available only for the Macintosh, but in 1993 a Windows version arrived, at which point Quark began to learn some difficult lessons about multi-platform software support (lessons that Aldus had learned almost five years earlier). For example, the first Windows-based version of QuarkXPress (release 3.1) could import page layouts created on a Macintosh, but layouts created on a PC could not be imported into Quark on the Mac. This was pretty lame, given that very few service bureaus at that time had Windows-based computers connected to their imagesetters, and that PC pages were routinely saved as PostScript print-to-disk files so they could be transferred to a Macintosh for output on an imagesetter. The problem was corrected with QuarkXPress 3.3, which is virtually identical on both platforms.

QuarkXPress 3.3 adds a few new features, such as variable-shaped text boxes, multiple-item undo, support for the Toyo and DIC color models, JPEG and Photo CD import filters, and a kern/track editor. It also borrows from PageMaker the ability to automatically add to the color list any colors in an imported EPS file.

One of the most important enhancements in the Macintosh version of QuarkXPress 3.3 is its support for Apple Events scripting, which allows you to write custom scripts to automate time-consuming tasks, such as opening all documents in a folder or applying uniform layout settings to a document. You can, for example, write a mail-merge script (in AppleScript or UserLand Frontier) that imports selected data from a database program into a QuarkXPress document and then prints customized letters using the data. You can even write scripts that launch other applications (as long as they support Apple Events), and then work with them in conjunction with QuarkXPress.

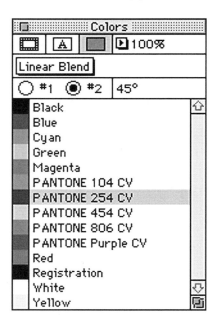

Fig. 9-5
The color palette in QuarkXPress provides one-stop control over most color features, including adding, removing, and altering color values.

Color features

QuarkXPress provides a rich set of color features. It allows you to apply color to characters, lines, and rules, to box backgrounds and frames, and to imported black-and-white pictures. You can apply only those colors contained in a document's color palette, but can quickly add new colors to a palette. You can edit existing palettes, and append colors from other documents' palettes. When you create a document, it automatically includes the default color palette, which you can fine-tune to your taste.

The preset default color palette contains nine colors: black, white, red, green, blue, cyan, magenta, yellow, and registration. The registration color enables you to print characters and items to which it is applied on all color separation films. For example, you can apply the registration color to cut or fold marks, so that they appear in the same position on every color separation film when you print a page. The default on-screen display color for the registration color is black.

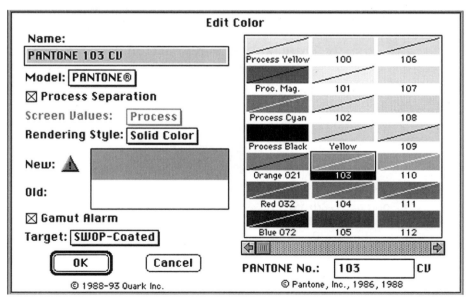

Fig. 9-6
When viewing spot colors in the QuarkXPress Edit Color dialog box, a line through a color indicates it can not be exactly matched with process colors.

You create and edit colors using the Edit Color dialog box , which enables you to use a color wheel or numeric fields to select and work with colors. You can begin by selecting a Pantone color and edit it using another color model. To apply color to characters and pictures, use the Color command in the Style menu; to items, via the Color pop-up menu in the Item Specifications dialog box; and to rules, via the Paragraph Rules dialog box. You can switch from one color model to another while creating or editing any color. If you modify a color after applying it to characters or items, QuarkXPress automatically updates the color wherever it is applied, according to the changes you have made.

When you create or edit a color, you can specify it as either spot or process color. QuarkXPress prints items that have been given a spot color on an individual spot color plate; items to which you apply a process color are printed on four process-color separation plates. Note that if CMYK is the selected model, you can specify a color using the definition fields only, rather than the color wheel. When you import an EPS graphic into a document in version 3.3, any spot colors in the EPS file are automatically added to the Color scroll list.

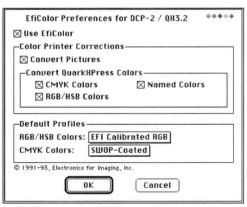

Fig. 9-7

Support for the EfiColor color management system in QuarkXPress lets you select the color profile for your monitor and output device, in this case offset litho printing on coated stock with SWOP-standard inks.

One of the most significant color features in QuarkXPress is the EfiColor XTension, which is a version of the EfiColor color management system described in Chapter 4. Once you have calibrated each input and output device in your publishing system (and purchased or constructed a device profile for each device), the

EfiColor XTension converts the colors generated by your scanner or monitor into the CIE color model, and from there into the color space of the target printer or other output device. The XTension comes with 20 profiles, and you can purchase others from EFI.

Whenever you're faced with representing color in XPress, such as the Get Picture, Edit Color or Page Setup dialog boxes, the EfiColor XTension adds drop-down menus from which you can choose the appropriate device profile. One limitation here is that the EfiColor XTension can't work with colors in imported EPS files.

One side-effect of having EfiColor built into QuarkXPress is that you can now color-separate RGB TIFF images at print time without the need for a stand-alone separation utility such as Adobe PrePrint. As mentioned previously, in most cases it will be far more efficient to pre-separate RGB TIFFs in an image editing program, such as Photoshop, rather than produce separations from within XPress.

One useful QuarkXPress feature is the Collect for Output command in the File menu: it copies a document and its associated graphics files into a single user-specified folder, which would typically be on a transportable drive, such as a SyQuest cartridge. It also generates a detailed report of printing-related information so that service providers don't need to waste time tracking down missing files, and customers don't need to pay to have a job output more than once. The report includes information about the version of QuarkXPress used to create the document, any XTensions required to output it, the number of colors, fonts used in the document, and fonts used in any graphics that have been placed in the document. For legal reasons, the fonts themselves are not copied to the destination disk.

Quark XTensions

The idea of extending the functionality of a piece of software by "plugging in" additional modules is one of the most powerful concepts in microcomputer software. The plug-in approach was introduced with Adobe Photoshop; indeed, one of the key reasons for Photoshop's success is the ease with which third-party users can write custom scanner drivers and other enhancements.

In the page layout market, the availability of plug-ins called *XTensions* has been crucial to the success of QuarkXPress, and a similar technology, called *Additions*, has now been added to PageMaker.

If you know how to write computer programs in any C or C++ language, you should have no trouble writing a custom XTension, either for your own use or for the commercial market. Among the XTensions available are:

- Visionary, from Scitex, which provides a link between desktop page layout with QuarkXPress and high-end imaging on a Scitex color prepress system;

- XData, from Em Software, which automates the production of recurrent documents by taking data from any database or spreadsheet file and mapping it through a template in XPress, thereby producing hundreds or thousands of customized documents;

- Workflow Administrator, from North Atlantic Publishing Systems, which allows you to keep track of revision levels, workgroup users, file status, and schedule dates for all the text files, graphics, and images you use in QuarkXPress documents.

These are merely the tip of the iceberg, and the number of useful extensions continues to grow. To use an extension, simply copy the extension file into your QuarkXPress program folder and launch QuarkXPress. That's all there is to it. Once it's loaded, an extension's features—new windows, menu commands, tools or others—are seamlessly integrated into XPress. The kerning and tracking editor that comes bundled with QuarkXPress is one example of an extension that many people use.

The rapid proliferation of XTensions has resulted in an independent organization, XChange, which has published a few XTensions of its own but is known primarily as a one-stop shop for third-party XTensions. You can reach XChange at 1-800-253-8472.

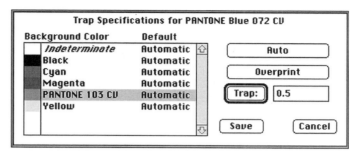

Fig. 9-8

The Trap Specifications dialog box in QuarkXPress lets you specify automatic or manual trapping for each spot and process color.

Trapping in QuarkXPress

For a few years, QuarkXPress led the page layout programs employed in the professional graphic arts industry—in part because of such rarely-used features as incremental rotation of graphics. For some designers, this obscure feature was like a fire engine—something that you don't have much use for on a daily basis, but when you need it, you really *need* it.

The rudimentary trapping feature built into QuarkXPress is another example of this phenomenon. Although Quark can't trap the EPS graphics placed on the page, and can't trap complex situations such as side-by-side gradient blends, many desktop publishers now rely on the program for trapping, sometimes with disastrous results. For instance, any last-minute alteration, such as changing the paper stock or the type of printing press, would necessitate a modification to the trapping values.

Also, although simple pages can be trapped directly within a page layout program, any page that contains complex linework, placed EPS graphics, or type against a color gradient must be trapped conventionally (photographically or on a high-end prepress system) or in a stand-alone trapping program (such as TrapWise and IslandTrapper, which are discussed in Chapter 12). Even where it is technically possible to trap within a page layout program, most users will find that the most productive approach is to leave trapping until the final stage of the production process.

To set traps within QuarkXPress, select the Colors dialog box in the Edit menu. Selecting Colors when no document is open changes the trapping values for colors in the program's default color palette. In the Colors dialog box, select from the Color list an object color for which you want to specify trapping values. Click on Edit Trap to display the Trap Specifications dialog box. QuarkXPress also provides a trapping palette that can be displayed on screen at any time, offering even more precise control over complex trapping situations. As well, it allows you to set traps for each particular object, rather than just for a particular color.

The Trap Specifications dialog box shows the trapping values specified for the object color selected in the Colors dialog box and each of the colors in the Background Color column. The Value column lists the trapping value specified for each background color, with Automatic indicating that object color and the background color's trapping relationship is determined by the program's built-in automatic trapping algorithm. Overprint indicates that the object color is not knocked out of the background color's separation film. A numeric value indicates a trap value has been specified between the object color and the background color.

To specify a trap amount between the object color and the selected background color, enter a value in the Trap field and click Trap. You can enter trap values from -5 to 5 points, in increments of .001-point (although, in practice, trap values are usually kept within -1 to +1 points). A negative trap value chokes (reduces) the knockout area on the background color's separation film; a positive value spreads (enlarges) items on the object color's separation film so that they overlap the background color.

The automatic trap value for a given combination of object and background colors is determined by the amount of black in the two colors. The object color and background color are first converted to CMYK values, and the black values of the two colors are compared. If the black value is greater in the object color than in the background color, the background color is choked. If the black value of the object color is less, the object is spread. The amount of trapping is determined by the difference in the two black values.

When creating traps in QuarkXPress, there are a few operating principles to keep in mind:

- color characters are always trapped to the background of the text box that contains them;
- process colors are trapped according to the CMYK values associated with their color, although they print on the process separation film;
- if the background of an object is Indeterminate (containing multiple colors, as in a color photograph), automatic trapping knocks out the object's background without trapping.

A similar trapping feature has been added to PageMaker 5 as an Addition, and it sports a few enhancements not available in QuarkXPress, including the ability to trap a compound foreground object properly against one or more background objects. More complex trapping situations, however, should be trapped manually or through a dedicated trapping program, such as TrapWise.

QPS

Quark Inc. has also developed an ambitious workflow program, known as the Quark Publishing System (QPS), designed to help newspaper and magazine publishers keep track of the many text and graphic files they create with every edition. QPS is based on the concept of a database, using the client-server technology that is allowing many large organizations to replace centralized mainframe computers with networked microcomputers.

QPS allows writers, editors, and layout artists to work on a publication simultaneously through a single networked system. It consists of three main applications—QuarkDispatch, which controls the system and handles file management; QuarkCopyDesk, a word processing and editing program; and QuarkXPress, for page layout. In addition, three QuarkDispatch modules (Administrator, Planner, and FileManager) allow managers to configure the system to their requirements.

With QPS version 1.1, Quark added a number of features, including:

- an increase in the QuarkDispatch server capacity from 50 users to 70;
- a new query definition interface that lets users tailor their queries to as many specific sections and file types as desired;
- user control over passwords.

Despite these enhancements, QPS still has a number of limitations. For example, it is designed specifically for the needs of newspaper and magazine publishers, and is ill-suited to the requirements of groups working on newsletters, training manuals, brochures, ads, and many other kinds of documents. Also, it is a closed system that requires you to work entirely within QPS, which means you can't easily integrate QPS-based layouts other word processing programs.

Adobe PageMaker

Adobe PageMaker is the package that started the desktop publishing revolution in July 1985. Since then, PageMaker has undergone numerous revisions, adding more features each time while retaining its intuitive look and feel. With version 5.0, PageMaker has now largely matched and, in some cases, exceeded QuarkXPress (version 3.3) in feature set, productivity, and ease of use.

PageMaker now has many of the features that were long sought by loyal users. The program can rotate text and graphics to any angle, in increments of a hundredth of a degree—and rotated objects remain fully editable. You can have multiple publications open at once, and even drag and drop graphic and text elements between them.

One of the most important innovations in PageMaker 5 is a powerful control palette, which was present in a lesser form in PageMaker 4.2 on the Macintosh but absent from previous Windows versions. The control palette lets you specify precisely the position, height, width, and scaling of all elements for accurate placement on the page. You can quickly change typography (at both paragraph and character levels), create and apply paragraph styles, and rotate, skew, and reflect objects.

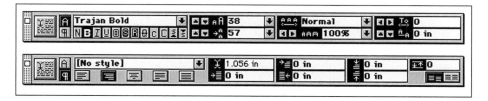

Fig. 9-9
The PageMaker control palette provides instant access to almost every imaginable typographic option.

Other important features in PageMaker include:

- a Library palette that not only lets you save text, graphics, and entire pages for use in other documents, but allows you to search for objects based on names, keywords or other text;

- interruptible screen redraw, which permits you to move on to the next operation without waiting for PageMaker to redraw the screen;

- the Panose font-mapping system, which allows automatic or manual mapping of fonts across the Windows and Macintosh platforms, eliminating problems caused by missing or mis-named fonts.

Color features

PageMaker supports more color models and color libraries (color matching systems, such as those from Pantone, Trumatch, and Toyo) than any other page layout program. Before selecting a color from a library, ask your commercial printer which color matching systems they support, which they prefer, and why. Base your color selections on printed swatch books, not on the appearance of colors on your monitor.

You can apply spot or process colors (and *tints*, or percentages, of spot or process colors) to text, linework (lines, rectangles, and ellipses), monochrome or grayscale images (such as TIFF files), and EPS graphics imported into PageMaker. With linework, you can apply different colors to the object's line and fill.

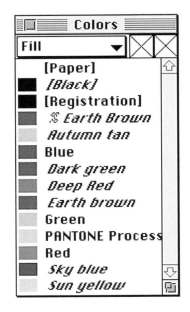

Fig. 9-10
The color palette in PageMaker lets you
quickly create, edit, and delete colors.

PageMaker's color palette brings together most of the program's color controls in one place. The color palette automatically contains three colors—Paper, Black, and Registration—which can't be removed. Paper refers to the color of the paper on which you will be printing; its value is the only one you can change.

An object placed behind a paper-colored object won't print where the paper-colored object overlaps it—the paper-colored object *knocks out* the other object. Instead, the color of the paper you're printing on shows through. Black refers to a preset and unchangeable color value (100% process black), which, by default, knocks out graphic objects it overlaps but overprints text. Registration is not a color, but rather an attribute you can apply to objects, such as crop marks, that are to appear on each separation.

The color palette makes it easy to apply, alter, and delete colors:

- when working with rectangles or ellipses, the Fill/Line menu allows you to specify whether color should be applied to the object's line, fill, or both;

- a % sign in front of a color in the color palette indicates a tint;

- by default, the color palette lists three spot colors—red, green, and blue—which you can remove if you're specifying your own colors;

- the palette also lists colors you've set as program defaults, plus colors you've created on the page, and spot colors included in any placed EPS graphics.

Process colors created in a FreeHand EPS graphic are also listed in the color palette, but not process colors in graphics created in other applications. PostScript does not have a standard way of describing process color information, so PageMaker's color palette can't list process colors imported from other programs.

An EPS symbol in brackets at the beginning of a color name indicates an EPS color, which can be applied to objects within PageMaker, but not edited. If you're planning to alter the colors in an EPS graphic from within PageMaker, create it using spot colors, rather than process colors (in your drawing program). You can alter spot colors in a placed EPS file in PageMaker, but not process colors.

Printing capabilities

Printing is another area in which PageMaker has been substantially improved. Printing is fast; you can specify any selection of pages to print; and you can print in the background (while working on other tasks). There are more printer's marks available—crop and registration marks, color-control strips, density bars, and plate identification.

To avoid problems when printing, be sure to distinguish between the Separations option in the Color print dialog box and the For Separations option in the Options print dialog box. Use the Separations option when you want to print color separations directly from PageMaker: it creates process color separations and/or spot color overlays for each color in your publication. This is the option to use whenever you want to output film separations, for instance when your document contains CMYK TIFF images.

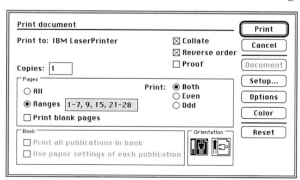

Fig. 9-11
PageMaker's print setup dialog box lets you specify page parameters, printer's marks, and printing non-contiguous pages.

On the other hand, the For Separations option is available only when you select "Write PostScript to File" in the Options print dialog box. This creates a file that includes OPI (Open Prepress Interface) comments, and should be used when you want to work with the publication in a separation program such as Adobe PrePrint. You would use this option, for instance, if your document contains TIFF files in RGB format, which must be separated into their CMYK components to be printed.

There are a few other printing enhancements that service bureaus and color trade shops will appreciate:

- a Printer Styles Addition lets you queue several publications with different print settings for batch printing;

- print dialog box settings can be defined, saved, and applied as needed;

- you can generate a report on every print job, including the filename, the name of the person who created the file, and the total printing time.

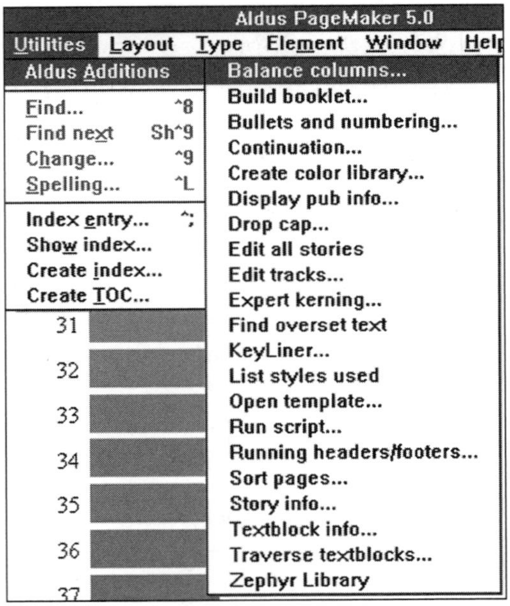

Fig. 9-12
The 20 additions built into PageMaker provide features that, as XTensions, would cost QuarkXPress users hundreds of dollars more.

Additions

With PageMaker 5, Adobe has substantially beefed up the Additions technology introduced in the previous version, both in terms of the free Additions that come built into the product and the increased support Adobe provides to third-party developers to encourage them to write useful enhancements to the base product.

There are more than 20 Additions built into PageMaker, including:

- Build Booklet, an imposition tool that arranges pages to correspond with printing signatures or multi-page spreads for printing 2-, 3- or 4-up booklets and brochures;
- Bullets & Numbering, which automatically inserts a special character or number (plus a tab) at the beginning of each item in a list;
- Create Color Library, which exports the entire contents of the color palette to a file that can be used by other PageMaker publications;
- Display Pub Info, a very handy utility that displays or prints detailed information about a publication's fonts, styles, and file links—very useful to anyone sending files to a service bureau for output;
- Edit Tracks and Expert Kerning are two Additions that provide advanced users with very precise control over these typographic attributes;
- Keyliner, which automatically creates a keyline box (with specified line weight and offset) around any object;
- Sort Pages, which lets you re-order and re-number the pages in a publication, and shows thumbnail views of each page.

There are actually three different kinds of Additions you can create, depending on your requirements and programming skills:

- scripts, which use text-based commands to automate tasks that could otherwise be accomplished with the keyboard or mouse;

◆ loadable modules, which appear in the Additions submenu on the Options menu, and combine commands and queries with more sophisticated routines written in the C language;

◆ stand-alone modules, which run independently or in conjunction with another application, such as a spreadsheet or database.

Scripts and loadable modules enhance capabilities from within PageMaker, while stand-alone modules rely on Dynamic Data Exchange (DDE) for communicating with other Windows applications, or Interapplication Communications (IAC) for working with other Macintosh applications under System 7.

One of the key differences between Additions and XTensions is that it takes programming skill to write a loadable or stand-alone Addition (or a Quark XTension), while even novice users can use text-based commands to create scripts that automate repetitive procedures within PageMaker. You can type a script right in PageMaker (or any word processor), then invoke it simply by selecting "Run Script" from the Additions submenu. This is an important feature—you can take advantage of it even if you don't have programming skills, and it can significantly increase your productivity by speeding up many kinds of recurrent tasks.

You can also send scripts to PageMaker as AppleEvents from Frontier, HyperCard or QuicKeys. It's much faster than the Run Script Addition, and even works across a network. For instance, this was the method used in producing this book: many tasks, including placing and resizing graphics, creating keylines, and inserting photo credits were automated with Frontier scripts.

Another difference is that XTensions modify the core code of XPress, which means they will not necessarily be compatible when QuarkXPress is upgraded; Additions, by contrast, are isolated in a module called the Additions Manager and will continue to function properly in future versions of PageMaker. While XTensions can be designed to appear in any of Quark's menus, Additions can be added only to PageMaker's Utilities menu.

In addition to the Additions incorporated into PageMaker, independent developers have created others, including :

- Sonar Bookends, from Virginia Systems, which can automatically create a detailed index in PageMaker, without the need for manually marking key words;
- Marksmaker, from Sundae Software, which saves you money by combining multiple pages onto a single sheet of film, automatically adding the proper crop and registration marks, guides, and color ramps;
- Screen Machine, from Fast Electronic Sales, which lets you incorporate 24-bit digitized video images directly into PC or Macintosh PageMaker documents.

To make it easier for PageMaker users to gain access to useful Additions, Adobe has helped found an independent organization, the Adobe Developers Co-op, which sells more than 40 Additions from a variety of third-party developers. For a complete list of third-party Additions, contact the Co-op at 1-800-685-3547.

Adobe PrePrint

Adobe PrePrint is a Macintosh color separation utility that adds to the capabilities of such layout programs as PageMaker or QuarkXPress. PrePrint allows you to generate quality four-color separations of text, illustrations, and photographs—directly from the desktop. You can separate an entire publication at once, without splitting it into single-page files.

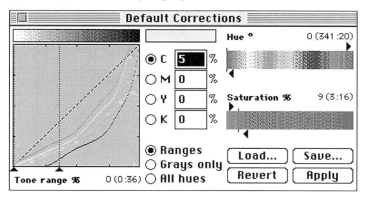

Fig. 9-13 Aldus PrePrint is a full-function color separation and print control utility.

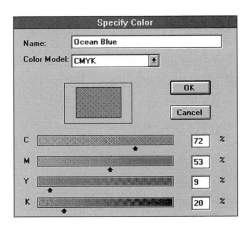

Fig. 9-14
Corel Ventura allows you to
specify colors in RGB, CMY,
CMYK, and Pantone spot and
process color systems.

Alternately, you can start with one or more TIFF image files or with any color file saved in the PostScript/OPI format.

You can output color separations to any PostScript-compatible imagesetter, or as black-and-white or color composites to a color PostScript printer. Files are printed to disk for transport to your service bureau, and image masks can be included in your separations for use with traditional stripping methods. PrePrint supports DCS and CMYK TIFF files, and can directly separate any PostScript-language file that conforms to Adobe's document and color-separation conventions.

Corel Ventura

From its inception in late 1986, Ventura Publisher was the first full-function desktop publishing program on the PC platform, running under the now-obsolete GEM environment. However, it was soon eclipsed by the Windows version of PageMaker, and when Ventura Software was a few years late in recognizing and responding to the impact of the Windows environment, its product was mortally wounded.

Ventura was rescued in late 1993 by Corel, and, after a maintenance upgrade (Corel Ventura 4.2), has been properly redesigned from the ground up and released as Corel Ventura 5.0.

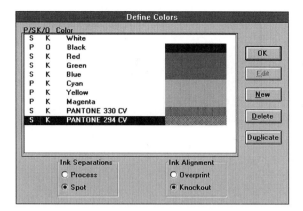

Fig. 9-15
The Define Colors dialog box in Corel Ventura lets you specify whether each color should overprint or knock out the colors beneath it.

Even after being ported to the Windows environment, Ventura used a rather strange method of keeping track of fonts: Every time the program was launched, it would build a series of "width tables" containing font metrics for every font on your system. Unfortunately, if you happened to have a great many fonts, the process could take ten minutes or longer. Version 4.2 finally resolved this problem. Other enhancements in Corel Ventura 5.0 include:

- built-in utilities for scanning and color separation;
- inclusion of the Adobe Acrobat Reader, and the ability to export documents in Acrobat format;
- 10,000 pieces of clip art and 300 fonts (from the same clip art and font libraries bundled with CorelDRAW);
- Ventura Database Publisher, a stand-alone module for producing recurrent content-driven publications;

Ventura Publisher was the first page layout program to focus on the production of entire documents, rather than of individual pages. It borrowed (from Microsoft Word for DOS) the concept of *style sheets*, in which paragraphs are identified with distinct names (called *tags*), which, with a single action, can be altered throughout the entire document. The concept of styles has since been adopted, not only by such competitive page layout programs as PageMaker and QuarkXPress, but by most major word processing packages as well.

FrameMaker

FrameMaker is an integrated word processing, drawing, and page layout application from Frame Technologies. It is targeted at business and technical users who create "demanding" documents: typically, those that have a long life cycle, are frequently revised and updated, and contain complex formatting. They are often very long and require automatically numbered sections, complex page and document layout, and contain tables and illustrations, cross-references, footnotes, indexes, and multi-level tables of contents. Until recently, such documents were produced almost exclusively in black-and-white, but even they are being caught up in the overall trend to color.

Early versions of FrameMaker were almost devoid of color capabilities, but this deficiency has been resolved with FrameMaker 4.0, which adds support for the HLS, RGB, and CMYK color models, as well as the PANTONE MATCHING SYSTEM. The program can now print (to a PostScript printer) spot and process color separations of EPS, DCS, and CMYK TIFF files. FrameMaker 4.0 also features an improved user interface, more powerful formatting tools, improved information management capabilities, and an extensible architecture.

In some respects, FrameMaker resembles Corel Ventura, but it adds many other capabilities, including:

- hypertext links between different parts of a document;
- cross-platform support between the Windows, Macintosh, and UNIX (Sun and HP workstations running X/Motif) environments;
- an extensible architecture using a C-based applications programming interface that enables systems integrators, independent software vendors and corporate developers to create custom extensions to FrameMaker;
- support for electronic distribution of documents through the optional FrameBuilder utility.

Image replacement protocols

The color publishing process can be divided into two distinct domains: working with color photographs, and everything else. As we saw in Chapter 3, the problem with color image files is their size—a full-page photo takes up more than 30Mb when stored at a resolution appropriate for high-quality output.

In its early days, desktop publishing was an ideal way to produce type and linework but rather poor at handling photographic images. To solve this problem, and avoid the complexity and processing requirements of working with high-resolution image files, many publishers adopted a two-part solution. First, desktop graphics and page layout programs were used to create all the type and linework, including *keylines* (boxes indicating where images were to be placed). Then, photographic images were scanned and corrected, using high-end prepress systems, and stripped into position by hand during the film assembly stage. In many cases, publishers would paste into each keyline a photocopy of the actual image, marked "for position only", as a guideline to the operators in the color trade shop.

As the quality and power of desktop color systems increased, some publishers began doing everything on the desktop—scanning, image enhancement, color separation, drawing, and page layout. But they quickly ran into a major productivity barrier: working with large image files could tie up the entire system for hours.

The solution many publishers now use is the electronic equivalent of the original *position-only* pictures. The idea is to distinguish between the original high-resolution images and low-resolution place-holders that can be used throughout the design and approval process.

Scanned images are sent directly to a central file server, and kept there until ready to be sent directly to the final output device. Meanwhile, a low-resolution position-only file is used in the desktop page layout program, and linked to its equivalent high-resolution file for automatic picture replacement immediately prior to final output. This method can greatly increase productivity, because the position-only image files moving around the network are small, typically only 1% the size of their high-res equivalents.

During the past few years, two image replacement methods have emerged: the Desktop Color Separations (DCS) color separation protocol, and the Open Prepress Interface (OPI) workflow protocol. Both solve the same problem, but take somewhat different approaches. Most color publishers will use one protocol or the other, although it is possible to construct prepress systems that make use of both DCS and OPI. (In addition to these software protocols, there are also hardware links for physically attaching desktop systems to high-end prepress equipment.)

Despite their differences, both specifications exist for the same reason—to produce plate-ready color separations of entire publications, including photographs. DCS is a desktop-only solution, while OPI offers paths to both desktop and high-end systems. The similarities and differences between the two will concern any desktop publisher working with color, whether adding a single spot color to a company newsletter or producing a dazzling, full-color catalog with high-quality photographs.

Desktop Color Separations (DCS)

DCS is a separation protocol: it governs how RGB image files are converted into CMYK format, and links the high-resolution separation files with a master low-resolution position-only file. The DCS protocol was invented by CyberChrome, first implemented on the desktop as part of QuarkXPress, and later adopted by PageMaker.

DCS allows you to convert an RGB image into five files—four EPS files (one for each of the CMYK separations), and a low-resolution PICT file to be used as a position-only place-holder. The key to working with DCS is that color images are pre-separated, so the page layout application does not need to know how to convert RGB values into their CMYK equivalents—it simply passes the individual cyan, magenta, yellow, and black separations through to the output device as part of the complete page.

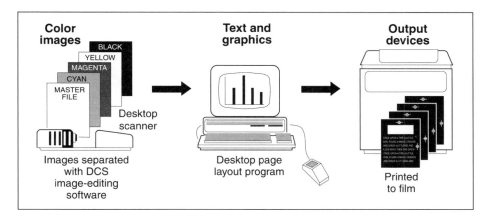

Fig. 9-16
A publisher with a desktop scanner can use DCS to go directly from original images and page layouts to final film from a service bureau or other output provider.

To produce a publication containing color photographs you simply scan each color photo with a desktop scanner either directly to DCS format, or to produce a TIFF (tag image file format) file, which you then separate, using a DCS-compatible program such as Photoshop or PhotoStyler. This gives you five EPS files for each image: one main file plus one each for the cyan, magenta, yellow, and black separations. The main file includes a low-resolution screen image, information for printing a composite page proof, and a set of comments that link the file to the four separation files.

You then import the main DCS file for each image into a DCS-aware page layout program, such as PageMaker or QuarkXPress, which can produce color separations of text and graphics. When the layout is finished, simply print separations from the page layout application to any PostScript-language imagesetter—your application will read the DCS comments attached to the main files and replace each main file with the four corresponding separation files. The resulting output is full-color separations, plate-ready for your commercial printing company.

There are three operations you can perform on the low-resolution place-holder file within your page layout program, that will automatically be applied to the equivalent high-resolution file prior to output:

- cropping, which removes unwanted areas, and can be done without harming either the image quality or your productivity;
- scaling, which forces your page layout program to recalculate every pixel in the image, thereby reducing quality and slowing the output process;
- rotation, which also reduces both image quality and productivity.

The main advantage of the DCS protocol is that you can work more quickly with low-resolution than with high-resolution files. Also, the images have been pre-separated prior to being placed in the page layout, so there is no need to separate them immediately prior to output. This can mean significant time savings when outputting final film on deadline.

Its major disadvantage is that the four EPS files occupy about twice as much space on your hard disk as the equivalent TIFF file, tripling storage requirements if you scan to a TIFF file and keep it on disk after converting it to DCS format.

Another potential pitfall in working with the DCS protocol stems from the fact that the images have been separated early in the production process, and, in most cases, have already been converted to halftones. Altering printing parameters such as the line screen (due to changing from coated to uncoated stock, for instance), means that the DCS files will have to be created again, either from the original TIFF files or by rescanning the original images.

The DCS protocol has recently been upgraded to version 2.0, which stores separated images in a single file (rather than five linked files), and supports documents that include both process and spot colors.

Open Prepress Interface (OPI)

The OPI protocol was invented by Aldus Corporation for use with PageMaker, but has since been adopted by QuarkXPress. Unlike DCS, which is a color separation protocol, OPI is a workflow protocol.

In the OPI workflow, you scan each color photo on the desktop to produce a TIFF file or, for higher quality, pay a color prepress shop to scan your original on its drum scanner as a high-resolution image and provide you with a low-resolution TIFF file for screen display. Instead of separating the images at this time, as you would with DCS, you place the TIFFs directly into an OPI-compatible page layout program such as PageMaker or QuarkXPress.

While in your page layout program, you can also specify color page elements as desired, and import any other color EPS or TIFF files. When the layout is complete and you are ready to produce separations, print the file to disk, which saves it in OPI format. OPI consists of PostScript-language comments that provide information about the placement, sizing, and cropping of color images included in the publication.

Just as with the DCS method, the low-resolution files placed in your page layout application can be cropped, scaled, and rotated, and the equivalent operations will be performed on the high-resolution file automatically prior to output.

You then use an OPI-compatible separation utility, such as Adobe PrePrint, to generate the separations from the OPI file through a PostScript-language imagesetter. You can also upload the file to an OPI-compatible prepress system from Agfa, Chelgraph, Crosfield, Diadem, DuPont-Camex, Eastman Kodak, Hell Graphic Systems, Howtek, Networked Picture Systems or Screaming Color.

If you print separations through an OPI-compatible high-end color prepress system, the low-resolution versions of the TIFFs will automatically be replaced by their high-resolution counterparts. In either case, the resulting output is full-color separations of the entire page, plate-ready for your printing company.

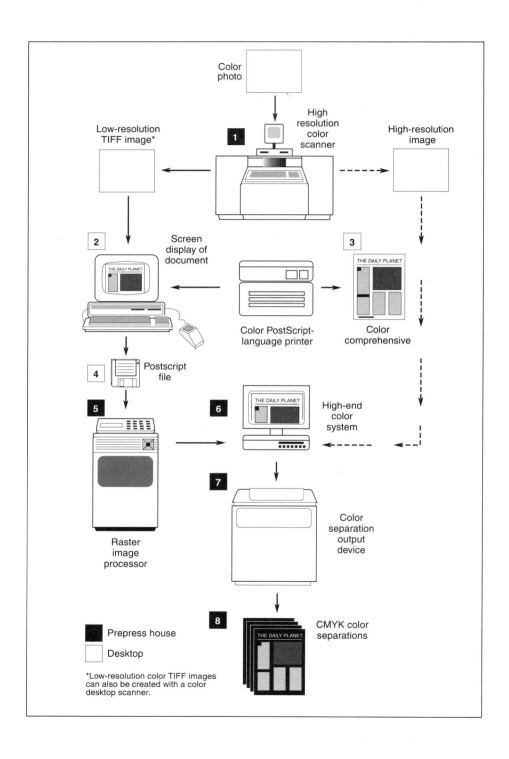

Color
photo

High
resolution
color
scanner

1

Low-resolution
TIFF image*

High-resolution
image

2

Screen
display of
document

Color PostScript-
language printer

3

Color
comprehensive

4   Postscript
file

5

6   High-end
color
system

Raster
image
processor

7

Color
separation
output
device

8   CMYK color
separations

■ Prepress house

□ Desktop

*Low-resolution color TIFF images
can also be created with a color
desktop scanner.

Workflow strategies

For many color publishers, linking desktop and high-end systems provides the best of both worlds: you get the flexibility and control of the desktop, plus the productivity of the high-end. Today there is a thriving market for products that link the two, from both the high-end systems vendors and a variety of third parties.

Both DCS and OPI have their advantages and disadvantages. DCS produces five EPS files per image, thereby consuming more disk space than OPI, which must store only one TIFF file per image. Because the DCS method uses pre-separated images, any changes to them means separating and placing them again. With OPI, photographic images can be altered after the page layout stage but before separations are made.

Because DCS works only with pre-separated images, you must commit to specific separation parameters (such as paper type and press characteristics) before beginning the page layout. These parameters, however, may change during the design process, perhaps requiring you to separate and place the DCS images again. This is not a problem with OPI, which works with unseparated images.

Both DCS and OPI allow you to combine desktop-published documents and color photographs on the same set of plate-ready separations. DCS works well as a desktop-only solution, but forecloses the possibility of combining desktop layout with high-end color output.

OPI offers significant flexibility as a post-processing tool that lets you choose desktop color technology for a quality mid-range solution or high-end prepress technology for a high-end solution.

Together, these specifications are making it easier for desktop publishers to include color photographs in their documents, without

Fig. 9-17 (opposite)
The OPI protocol is more complex than DCS, but gives you greater flexibility, and makes it easier for color separation and page layout to occur simultaneously

the hassle of dealing with huge image files. As these picture replacement protocols become a standard part of all publishing systems, page layouts are certain to be enlivened with more and more photographic images.

A spectrum of color production tools

Desktop color is not a single tool or technique—it is an approach. It encompasses prepress solutions in which the desktop component varies according to the requirements of each job: some projects can be produced entirely from the desktop while others require that page layouts created on the desktop be integrated with images scanned and corrected on conventional high-end prepress systems. For many users, the key issues are productivity and cost, and they've found that using OPI or DCS saves them both time and money.

Image quality is another reason for using an image replacement protocol. If color quality is a major concern, and you have not mastered the skills of color scanning, image enhancement, and color separation, you might be better to use the services of a color trade shop or service bureau. In effect, you are letting the professionals perform the most difficult and hardware-intensive part of the color prepress process, while retaining control over page layout.

Maximum savings are achieved because you create and modify the type, graphics, and page design, using desktop color software. Maximum quality is attained because the really difficult part of the job (color imaging) is being performed by highly-trained professionals using extremely expensive equipment.

High-End Color Systems

"Colors speak all languages."
Joseph Addison

High-end color electronic prepress systems (CEPS) are specialized computers used for scanning, enhancing, retouching, correcting, and color separating full-color artwork and photographs. They have become indispensable for producing high-quality documents, advertising, and packaging.

With the exception of short-run color publishing produced on color copiers, making a large number of duplicates of a color original requires a printing press. But a printing press needs plates (usually), and plates require final film (usually). To make the film, photos must be scanned, color corrected, retouched, merged with text and drawings, and assembled into pages. These are exactly the functions high-end prepress systems perform, in deadline-oriented production environments.

In the past decade, the market for high-end professional color systems has been shared primarily by four companies—Linotype-Hell, Scitex, Crosfield, and Screen. "High-end" describes both the price and performance of these systems. Many of the recent "innovations" on the desktop, such as image cloning, the magic wand tool and color maps, have been standard features on high-end systems for years. Only twenty years ago, high-end prepress was the "coming revolution" threatening to displace traditional camera-based color separations, but today its own future is threatened by lower-cost systems on the desktop.

This chapter focuses on high-end prepress systems and the color trade shops that use them. It includes summary information on each of the major vendors, as well as their links to the desktop. It also describes the services and operations of a typical color house, with suggestions for desktop users who want to integrate high-end color into their publications.

There are a number of ways in which high-end color prepress systems are similar to desktop systems. However, high-end systems typically:

- are faster, sometimes a lot faster;
- have greater resolution and dynamic range, and hence higher quality;
- are more complex to operate;
- can handle larger original and output sizes;
- cost more, often a lot more.

Fig. 10-1
During the past two decades, color prepress shifted from photographic to high-end systems, but desktop tools are now taking over.

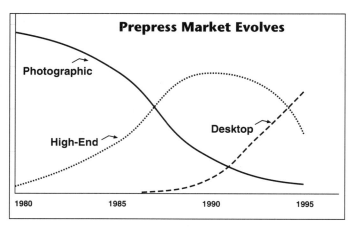

Prepress Market Evolves

Photographic

High-End

Desktop

1980   1985   1990   1995

A radical change is occurring in color production, with major consequences for the high-end prepress industry. People who own high-end systems are, for obvious reasons, less than thrilled by the recent explosion in desktop color production—they've invested millions of dollars in systems that are rapidly being rendered obsolete. Some of these people may take exception to my prognosis, insisting that desktop systems lack the quality or productivity of high-end solutions, but the pace of change on the desktop is relentless.

For those working with desktop color tools, linking to high-end prepress systems offers an opportunity to get the best of both worlds—the productivity and quality of the high-end plus the flexibility and control of the desktop. For existing providers of high-end color prepress services, the emergence of powerful desktop hardware and software offers a severe challenge—to rapidly reinvent themselves or find their businesses decimated by the new technologies.

Who buys high-end prepress systems?

There are four main markets for high-end prepress systems—color trade shops, PostScript service bureaus, commercial printers and in-plant printers. For years, the largest segment of this market has been the color trade shops, but now the greatest growth in market share is among commercial printers.

Color trade shops have always cost-justified the purchase of high-end equipment with the increased revenues that can be generated. But today, there are two factors rewriting the cost-effectiveness equation—increased competition from desktop systems, and the need for much shorter payback periods as a result of rapid technological innovation.

Let's look at each of the major kinds of customers for high-end color prepress systems, with an eye to understanding what they must do to cope with the transition toward total desktop color.

Color trade shops

Color trade shops, also known as film houses, color houses or separation houses, provide scanning, image enhancement, page assembly, film output, and proofing services. Trade shops are fascinating places—many operate three shifts a day, seven days a week, cranking out the film separations and color proofs so essential to commercial printing.

Typically, the owners of a color house have invested in specialized prepress equipment, most of it from a single vendor whose products are often completely incompatible with those from other vendors. For instance, until recently a scan performed on one brand of scanner might not work with a competing brand of film recorder, because the pixels were rectangular, rather than square.

A successful color house has also invested substantial money in training the people who operate the equipment. The prepress process has traditionally required many skilled, highly-paid technicians precisely cutting, aligning, taping and copying pieces of film. A typical color trade shop:

- sells proofs, but manufactures film;
- outputs a hundred or more sets of color separations and proofs per day;
- has gradually adopted desktop color, at least for type and page layout;
- interprets "desktop" to mean Macintosh, and does not see Windows as a serious platform for color publishing.

Although color houses provide a diverse assortment of value-added services based around the prepress process, their bread and butter comes from making *quads*—the sets of four color-separated films, ready to be stripped into complete *flats* from which the printer will make the printing plates that go on press.

Most large prepress houses run 24 hours a day, producing color separations and stripping them together. Just as the night shift ships its last set of quads, the couriers start arriving with raw material for the day shift—new originals, new disks, new problems.

The production manager receives production reports, along with any noteworthy dockets, from the night shift supervisor and in consultation with the sales department, prepares a schedule for the day. They have at their disposal some very expensive equipment and highly skilled scanner operators, photo retouchers, and film

Photo: © Quantel

Fig. 10-2
Color trade shops provides many services, including scanning, image enhancement, page assembly, film output and proofing.

strippers, all of whom work under the daily pressure of deadlines and inevitable breakdowns.

One of the reasons color trade shops are willing to spend so much money on high-end prepress systems is that their customers expect, and demand, rapid turnaround, even on jobs involving hundreds of scanned images. In trade shops dedicated to servicing the advertising industry, for example, turnaround times are measured in minutes and hours, not days.

A large group of production managers supervise and coordinate all aspects of the workflow. At any one time, there may be more than a hundred jobs in various stages of production, from initial scanning and page layout through proofing, client approval, and final output. A variety of customized forms are attached to the job docket at different stages, such as color correction or image assembly, so the client can be billed correctly for the work performed.

Some desktop publishers are just beginning to incorporate full-color images into their publications, and are starting to rely on trade shops for scanning and film output. Others have evolved beyond

Fig. 10-3
Experienced trade shop personnel add value to the prepress process by helping clients properly interpret film proofs before the job goes on press.

the stage where they require the services of trade shops, relying instead on desktop scanners or Photo CD for input, and PostScript service bureaus for output.

Many trade shops have traditionally specialized in certain kinds of work—magazines, catalogs, advertising, inserts (newspaper flyers), and so on. Among the thousands of color trade shops in North America:

- some specialize in producing advertisements of the highest possible image quality, where color must be matched exactly, regardless of the cost;

- some are dedicated to the publications market, such as catalogs and newsmagazines, where both quality and the ability to produce relatively large volumes of work at reasonable prices are important;

- some focus on the newspaper insert market, where the emphasis is on producing hundreds of separations per day at the lowest possible cost.

It's important for desktop publishers planning to make use of the services of a trade shop to know which of these markets a given trade shop has focused on, so you can select a shop whose equipment, quality standards, workflow, and pricing match your needs.

Working with a color shop

If you're buying prepress services, there are a few guiding principles that can save you time and money. When Benjamin Franklin observed that "time is money", he might have been thinking about his newspaper's color prepress department. Turnaround times have been halved in most metropolitan film shops during the past few years, with two-day or three-day service replacing the old one-week turnaround. Of course, you can get complex color corrections, proofs, and separations overnight if you're willing to pay the price.

When using the services of a color house, it's important to understand the basis on which they charge—failing to do so can be expensive. Many color houses use automatic systems in which the operators hit a control key to mark the start and finish time for each element of each job. If you ask for a certain visual effect without specifying a time or dollar limit, you may get the effect you're looking for but at a price that will leave you in shock.

One way to increase throughput when using the services of a color house is to set up your originals precisely (on a layout dummy) so they can be scanned directly into your page layout, thereby reducing film stripping costs.

If you're working on a project with long lead times, negotiate with your film supplier early in the game, to get discounts not available on last-minute deadlines. Another way of saving money without giving up quality is to work out an annual commitment with your color separators, in which they gain a steady stream of work at predictable times and you get improved service and lower costs.

The future of trade shops

The picture does not look bright for the color trade shop industry as a whole. One by one, the functions that they used to specialize in—page assembly, scanning, image enhancement, imposition, trapping and so on—have migrated to the desktop. The main value many trade shops add today (other than their speed in outputting high-quality film) is that they think in CMYK. Scanner operators, film strippers, page assembly artists, retouchers—all understand what halftone densities are required, dot by dot, in each piece of film in order to produce good-looking color on press. This is something most desktop users don't understand well, if at all.

On a certain level, that's not about to change. A manager putting together a colorful business proposal does not want to know about UCR, GCR, tangent angles and frequency-modulated screening.

But as color production shifts from craft to routine procedure, we increasingly find skills embodied in the software that formerly were the privileged domain of highly trained individuals—as the system becomes expert, the user doesn't have to be. Unfortunately for the people who work as prepress technicians and operators, many of their valued skills are in the process of being converted into "features" that will be used to sell some new software package, and will cost them their jobs.

PostScript service bureaus

Unlike traditional color trade shops, which have existed for decades, PostScript service bureaus are a relatively new phenomenon. The PostScript language itself was invented only in the early 1980s, and the first high-resolution PostScript output device, the Linotronic 100 imagesetter, was released in 1985. Thus, the service bureau industry was born. Within a few years, PostScript imagesetters had increased in precision to the point where they could produce high-quality color separations, and the service bureau market expanded rapidly.

Although some service bureaus have concentrated on the black-and-white market, cranking out large volumes of pages at relatively thin margins, most have set their sights on color production. The better ones have acquired drum scanners (used high-end scanners from defunct trade shops, or new desktop drum scanners), and have added conventional film proofing services.

Unfortunately, many service bureaus have very little understanding of color theory and even less hands-on experience with scanning, color correction, color separation, trapping, and imposition. This is starting to change, of course, so that in the next few years it will become increasingly difficult to distinguish between color trade shops and PostScript color service bureaus. We look at PostScript service bureaus in more detail in Chapter 12.

Commercial printers

For years, many large-scale commercial printers considered color prepress a necessary evil. They had built symbiotic relationships with one or more color trade shops, and were happy to have someone else worry about scanning, proofing, and film output. When these printers incorporated color prepress services into their shops, it was only to provide customers with one-stop shopping, so they wouldn't take their printing business elsewhere. They considered their "prep" departments cost centers, not profit centers.

For other printers, however, prepress has always been an integral part of the service they offer their clients, not to mention an important source of profits. Such printers are the wave of the future— as desktop tools take over, an increasing number are looking to color prepress as an essential element in their survival.

Photo: © Heidelberg

Fig. 10-4
Printing companies make money only when the presses are rolling, but increasingly must offer prepress services to get the job done.

More and more customers now demand the convenience and single-point accountability of having their printer work directly from digital files, thereby making the printer responsible for every stage of the process, from film output to proofing to the final printed sheet.

From the printer's point of view, increased competition from color trade shops and PostScript service bureaus for the prepress part of the business means that if they don't capture the job early in the production cycle, they will never see it. This makes commercial printers an increasingly important market for both high-end and desktop color prepress equipment.

In-plant printers

Many large corporations and government organizations do so much printing that they find it cost-effective to have complete prepress and printing capabilities in-house. Until recently, most of these in-plant printers could produce only black-and-white documents, or those containing black plus one spot color.

However, the emergence of highly automated multi-color presses, combined with increasing demand for full-color printing, has led some in-plant printers to add process color printing capabilities. Naturally, because they're doing the printing in-house, they want to do the color prepress in-house as well. For this reason, in-plant print shops also represent an important market for both high-end and PostScript color prepress systems.

The evolution of high-end prepress

High-end prepress is a recent innovation—until the late 1960s, all prepress functions were performed manually. Before the advent of electronic scanners, photos were color separated in a graphics camera, and color correction and retouching were done by hand, by skilled craftspeople, in a process known as *dot etching*. The photographs were then assembled—in another mechanical process, *film stripping*—into finished pages.

To understand where the professional color prepress industry is headed, we must look at where it has come from. The history of the prepress industry can be compressed into three distinct phases:

- from the 1890s (when color halftoning was developed) to the late 1970s (when the first digital prepress systems were released);
- from the 1970s to 1992, the golden age of high-end electronic prepress systems;
- from 1992 to the present, the age of desktop color.

The first phase was based on photographic technology, with color separations created in a large graphic arts camera by sequentially exposing the original image through three or four color filters.

The second phase began with the invention of the first Scitex prepress system (the Response 200) in 1979, and was based on the concept of electronic dot generation, in which halftone dots are created by grouping together many individual pixels.

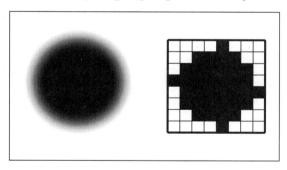

Fig. 10-5
High-end prepress systems replaced conventional photographic halftone dots (left) with digital halftone dots (right).

The third phase, which just recently started, is also based on the concept of electronic dot generation, but makes use of industry-standard desktop hardware and software, rather than the proprietary tools of yesteryear.

Until very recently, desktop tools were clearly inferior to high-end equipment, but that is no longer the case. In fact, the major difference between desktop and high-end systems today is that high-end equipment is substantially faster. But there's a new reality in prepress hardware, a reality many of the high-end vendors have been reluctant to accept—desktop hardware is rapidly catching up.

Without exception, all the major vendors of prepress equipment have been loudly proclaiming their evolution from proprietary to "open" desktop systems. In fact, they have no other choice, and are being dragged, kicking and screaming, into the brave new world of open systems.

For many years, the high-end vendors were able to charge for specialized color retouching and layout software, embedded in proprietary hardware. But now the underlying computer hardware is becoming a commodity, at the same time as the high-end retouching software is under attack from extremely functional desktop programs such as Photoshop. Indeed, Photoshop has had such a dramatic effect in the color prepress world that it can be considered an *enabling technology*, an essential component in the revolution that is altering the business landscape, both for those who make high-end equipment and those who buy it.

The transition from high-end to desktop color is occurring in phases, starting at the back end of the prepress process and moving to the front:

- first came PostScript imagesetters, which in their earliest form could not remotely compete with the quality of traditional drum-based film recorders, but since the arrival of drum imagesetters (with supercell screening) now provide a level of quality every bit as good as the traditional equipment;

- next came the page layout programs such as PageMaker and XPress, whose capabilities now match or exceed those of proprietary high-end page assembly stations;

- image editing software such as Photoshop and PhotoStyler have not yet exceeded the functionality of high-end retouching software, but they are quickly closing the gap;

- desktop drum scanners have now almost matched the quality of high-end scanners, though there are still significant differences in speed and overall productivity.

High-end prepress equipment

To understand the high-end prepress market, you've got to think about throughput. For many commercial printers and color trade shops, productivity is just as important a factor as image quality. Some of the larger trade shops, for instance, produce thousands of sets of film separations each week. In the PostScript service bureau business, it's not unusual to wait an hour or sometimes much longer for a single set of separations to output, but companies in the trade shop industry simply can't afford that much time.

For this reason, all the major prepress systems vendors have taken a modular approach in designing complete "solutions", usually by making a dozen or more highly specialized machines, each optimized for a single function. This approach works well only in large shops, where there is sufficient work to justify the expense. Smaller shops tend to use more general-purpose prepress equipment and rely on their operators to manually perform tasks that could be automated.

Each of the main prepress vendors has taken a slightly different approach to equipment functionality and process workflow, but we can get a fairly good idea of how specialized these machines are by examining each component in a typical high-end system:

- The core of any electronic prepress system is the *central processing unit* (CPU). The vast majority of existing prepress systems are built around proprietary processor architectures, although market pressures are forcing vendors to gradually move toward standard computing platforms. Typically, these systems run some variant of the UNIX operating system, though often with circuit boards or buses (electrical pathways) that are available only from a single manufacturer.

- The *mass storage* sub-system, consisting of an array of hard disk drives and associated back-up drives, is connected via the bus to the central processor. The disk controller circuits are very important, because they govern the speed with which data can be read from, and written to, the hard disks. Keeping in mind the size of high-resolution image files, it's easy to see why high-end prepress systems typically contain many gigabytes of on-line storage, backed up by terabytes (thousands of gigabytes) of tapes, disks, or other off-line archival storage.

◆   All prepress systems are built around some kind of *network*, which links the various hardware components and peripherals. Again, because of the file size problem, the network can often be the bottleneck in the system, and must be carefully considered when designing workflow procedures. Most prepress systems use Ethernet, but there is increasing competition from FDDI (fiber distributed data interchange) and other high-bandwidth solutions.

◆   There's at least one and often multiple *input/output stations*, which let the system operator control the flow of work from one device to another. With two I/O stations, one can be used to control input while the other is used for output.

◆   No prepress system would be complete without a *scanner*, which is typically used both for input and output. When operated in *analyze* mode, the scanner is an input device. When used in *record* mode, it is an output device. Some trade shops use a dedicated *film recorder*, also known as a *laser plotter*, for film output, rather than the record module of a scanner.

The components listed so far are all essential—every high-end prepress system includes them. Larger color trade shops typically have other specialized devices, such as:

◆   a graphic workstation used only for line files containing tints, linework, and logos;

◆   an image workstation that handles all imaging tasks, including retouching, silhouetting, cropping, and special effects;

◆   an image data executing station to move image post-processing tasks off-line, so the image workstation operator can continue working while files are being output;

Photo: © Dainippon Screen

Fig. 10-6
A page geometry
station, such as the
TaigaPrep station from
Screen, identifies
where scanned
images will be placed.

♦   a pre-scan station to measure density values and set up the
parameters for each job before it gets scanned at high
resolution.

Although the overall quality and productivity of a prepress system
are dependent on every one of these machines, the greatest emphasis
is on input and output. As we saw in the chapter on scanning, unless
you capture the widest possible range of tonal information in the
original photograph, there is little you can do later in the prepress
process to improve the quality of the image. This is one area where
conventional high-end scanners have a significant advantage over
desktop scanners—they have a greater dynamic range, which means
they can capture a wider range of tonal values.

Also, high-end scanners support larger original sizes, which is
important when working with large drawings or other original
artwork, and always support removable drums, an absolute
prerequisite for high productivity. Regardless of hardware issues, the
major difference between high-end and desktop scanners is the skill
of the operator, which is by far the most important determinant in
overall image quality.

The other essential part of any high-end prepress system is the
film recorder. All high-end film recorders are based on a drum
mechanism, and include a way of automatically punching a set of
holes in the film to ensure consistent registration during plate-
making and printing. The key characteristics of any film recorder

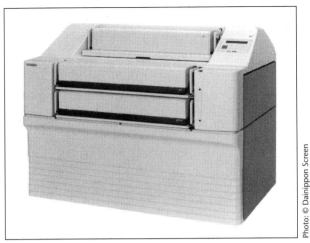

Fig. 10-7
The MT-R1120 is a large-format film recorder that can be used in either a PostScript environment or as part of a Screen prepress system.

Photo: © Dainippon Screen

are precision and repeatability, which are crucial to the quality of film separations.

After all, if the film is no good, there's very little that can occur during plate-making or printing to improve the quality of the final printed piece. This is why there has traditionally been such a strong symbiotic relationship between color trade shops and commercial printers, and why most printers initially had such a strong aversion to working with film produced on PostScript-based systems.

Desktop to high-end links

As the prepress industry migrates from proprietary high-end systems to desktop technology, it is going through a transition phase in which various kinds of hardware and software *links* play an important role. The rationale for using links is that they make it possible to combine the speed and quality of high-end scanners with the flexibility and control of desktop microcomputers. More than 20 companies now sell some sort of desktop-to-scanner link, including all the major prepress vendors. There are two main kinds of links:

- *Direct links* typically consist of a cable and two circuit boards—one connects to the color computer inside a high-end scanner and the other resides in a Macintosh or Windows-based PC. The desktop computer controls the scanner, and contains a very large hard disk for storing the scanned images. The problem with most direct links is that the desktop computer can't be used for anything else while the scanner is in use.

◆ *Indirect links* use an intermediate storage medium (such as high-density disks or tapes) or a powerful computer (typically a UNIX-based minicomputer) to connect the scanner with the desktop machine. Moving large image files around on transportable media is one of the cheapest ways of bringing high-end scanning quality to the desktop, but is rather inefficient, because of the time it takes to read and write the files. Indirect links that use an intermediate computer have the advantage of quickly releasing the desktop computer for other tasks during scanning and film output. They usually provide the greatest productivity but are the most expensive.

Most high-end prepress vendors would have you believe that links will be a permanent part of the new color landscape—that, no matter what happens with type and illustration, color images will always be scanned and separated at the high end. In fact, it's not likely to turn out that way.

In my opinion, links are nothing more than a temporary way of taking advantage of proprietary high-end scanners before they are superseded by the next generation of high-quality desktop scanners. As desktop microcomputers continue to threaten application areas long reserved for minicomputers and mainframes, micros will be used as the front end for all publishing activities, regardless of whether they include professionally scanned or separated color images.

High-end systems vendors

From their established positions at the high end, the makers of professional color prepress systems have seen the beginnings of the desktop color industry with a mixture of hope and trepidation. They hope that, by bringing their products downstream, they can significantly expand their market by capturing a number of first-time color users. But they are justifiably concerned about the long-term prospects for their bread-and-butter market—the professional color house.

During the past 15 years, four companies have risen to the forefront in the electronic prepress industry—Scitex, Linotype-Hell, Crosfield, and Dainippon Screen:

- Scitex was founded in 1968 in Israel, and began by making color separation equipment for the textile industry;
- Linotype-Hell, based in Germany, is the result of the merger of Linotype (one of the first typesetting companies) with Hell Graphics Systems (one of the first high-end prepress vendors);
- Dainippon Screen, based in Japan, began in 1943 and is one of the world's largest vendors of conventional graphic arts equipment;
- Crosfield, based in England, was founded in the 1970s and is now jointly owned by DuPont and Fuji.

In addition to these four main vendors, there are other companies selling high-end prepress equipment for specialized tasks. Quantel, for instance, is a British company that has built a reputation for the unparalleled speed of its image retouching and page layout stations, such as the Paintbox and Printbox. Kodak, with its Prophecy system, and Intergraph, with DP Studio, also have achieved some success in the high-end market.

Scitex

Scitex manufactures a complete line of scanners, image processing stations, film recorders, and PostScript imagesetters, and was one of the first high-end vendors to sell products linking desktop and high-end systems. As far back as 1988, Scitex was selling a desktop-to-high-end link (Visionary), and although the company still makes proprietary equipment, most of its products have evolved toward PostScript-based prepress.

Scitex makes two high-quality flatbed scanners that connect directly to the Macintosh, the Smart 340 and 720 PS. The Smart 340

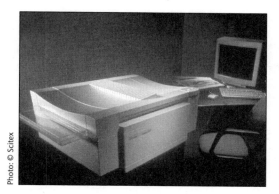

Fig. 10-8
The Scitex Smart 340 scanner can handle color reflective and transmissive originals up to 11-by-17-inches.

is a large-format CCD-based scanner that supports desktop file formats (TIFF, EPS) as well as proprietary Scitex formats. It can handle reflective and transmissive originals up to 11-by-17-inches at resolutions up to 2,630 ppi. The Smart 340L version has been optimized for scanning linework.

The Smart 720 PS is a flatbed color scanner that uses robotics to increase productivity. An automatic loader holds up to 120 35mm slides or negatives (though the scanner also supports 4-by-5-inch transparencies). The operator can crop, scale, rotate, and set color and tone parameters for one image in the foreground while the scanner scans another image in the background.

Scitex has also upgraded its imaging and page layout workstations. The speed of the Prismax II has been boosted with an accelerator board, enhanced picture memory, and a RAM disk.

Fig. 10-9
The Scitex Performance series workstations are packed with memory to enable real-time manipulation of large image files.

Fig. 10-10
The Scitex Dolev 100 imagesetter uses the same marking engine as the Dolev 200, but uses a Harlequin RIP (rather than Adobe) and is therefore less expensive.

Photo: © Scitex

In addition to the Prismax II, the Scitex Performance series of workstations includes the enhanced Blaze II, and the new PrisMagic. The PrisMagic comes with 256Mb of RAM, and provides real-time creative retouching, color correction, and page assembly. The Prismax II and Blaze II come with 384Mb of RAM, and include a four-channel retouching accelerator and a Picture Memory board.

All three systems maximize speed by working with images in RAM, so that retouching operations are performed instantaneously, both on the display and on the high-resolution image. Any function can be applied locally or to the entire image, and brushes can use vector limits or alpha channel masks.

As part of the migration of its products from proprietary formats to the desktop, Scitex has announced support for Kodak's Print Photo CD format. The Scitex ResoLUT image processor can read Photo CD images in their native YCC format, convert them to RGB or CMYK, and transfer them to a Scitex Prismax or Whisper workstation. ResoLUT can automatically perform a number of operations on an image, including determining highlight and shadow points, sharpening, color correction, detail enhancement, scaling, and tone reproduction.

To enhance file management in desktop environments, Scitex has introduced the Ripro Server, a UNIX-based image server built around an IBM RS 6000 RISC workstation. The Ripro Server supports Scitex and desktop file formats, and works with both Scitex APR (automatic picture replacement) and OPI. Scanned images can be simultaneously

Fig. 10-11
The Scitex Star PS has been upgraded from a '486 processor to a Pentium chip, more than doubling the speed of many functions.

Photo: © Scitex

accessed by Macintosh, PC, and UNIX applications programs for retouching and page layout.

On the output side, Scitex makes a wide selection of imagesetters and RIPs, from the entry-level Dolev 100 imagesetter with a Harlequin software RIP to the huge 440F, which can output a double-page broadsheet newspaper spread. With all its output devices, Scitex offers three imposition software options, all based on the Impostrip software from Ultimate Technographics.

At the lower end of the spectrum, the Dolev 100 is a compact, internal-drum imagesetter that can output 14-by-20-inch pages at resolutions up to 2,540 ppi. The Dolev 100 is sold with a Harlequin software RIP.

Scitex has also upgraded its RIPs and other output devices. For example, the Star PS page assembly and stripping workstation has been upgraded from a '486 processor to a Pentium chip, more than doubling the speed of many functions. The Star PS is based on an IBM PS/2 computer running the AIX operating system and X Window graphic interface. It uses an Adobe PostScript interpreter and can be connected to any Scitex desktop-based system for additional page assembly or color correction. One of the interesting features of the Star PS is that allows post-RIP editing—users can edit a PostScript file prior to final imaging.

Scitex has also developed a Unified File System (UFS) that lets users read and write removable storage media (such as SyQuest cartridges and digital audio tapes) between Macs and a variety of Scitex stations, including Whisper, Star PS, and Dolev PS systems. As an option to its RIPs, both on the PC and Macintosh platforms, Scitex offers the Full Auto Frame (FAF) trapping utility, which automates most trapping procedures. FAF allows previewing of trapped files and final edits prior to imaging.

Scitex has a variety of halftoning products, collectively called Class Screening, to meet the needs of different printing environments. In addition to their conventional screening (which produces round, square, gravure, diamond and composite dot shapes), Scitex offers:

- GeometricDOT, a screening method for creating elongated dots that resemble conventional elliptical dots but minimize rosette patterns, thereby giving the appearance of higher line screens than those actually used;
- High Definition Printing, a method of producing ultra-fine line screens (up to 600 lpi) which maintains tonal gradation by generating a coarser line screen in the highlight and shadow areas;
- FULLtone, a frequency modulated technology that varies both dot size and dot spacing, and that can be proofed using conventional materials.

Linotype-Hell

Linotype-Hell is a company with roots back to the earliest days of both typesetting and color prepress. Ottmar Mergenthaler, who founded the Linotype Company, invented one of the first typesetting machines more than 100 years ago, and Linotype developed the first PostScript imagesetters in 1985, thereby fueling the desktop publishing revolution.

Hell Graphic Systems was among the earliest developers of electronic prepress equipment. Its founder invented and patented color screening techniques that were used for decades by all high-end color prepress vendors. In 1991, the two companies merged to form Linotype-Hell, which has since managed to combine the strengths of both firms to capture a dominant position in the PostScript color production arena.

Photo: © Linotype-Hell

Fig. 10-12
Linotype-Hell's new DaVinci series combines the flexibility of PostScript-based systems with the productivity of proprietary high-end prepress systems.

Linotype-Hell has introduced a new generation of high-end prepress equipment—the DaVinci system. Unlike older high-end color prepress systems, which were based on proprietary hardware and software formats, DaVinci is centered around an open VME bus architecture, and uses two Motorola 68040 processors as controllers.

The DaVinci workstations are available in two versions. The RS (retouching) model includes two 1.2Gb hard disks (one for the system files and the other for data), plus a 150Mb backup tape drive and a 19-inch monitor. The CP (color page production) model includes a 3.5Gb data disk, a 600Mb optical disk, a digitizer, and a pressure-sensitive pen. Page geometry information can be imported from desktop page layout programs or from digitized mechanicals. Page elements can then be resized, rotated, flopped, grouped, aligned or otherwise distorted.

Photo: © Linotype-Hell

Fig. 10-13
One of the key features of DaVinci is an elegant user interface that provides instant access to commonly used tools.

The workstations can support as many as four additional dual-SCSI interfaces for extra storage, including the Megashuttle removable disk drives popular on Linotype-Hell's older ChromaCom systems. Files can be output in TIFF, DCS, or ChromaCom format, using a variety of popular networking protocols, including TCP/IP, NFS, and the emerging FDDI/IFEN high-speed fiber-optic ring network.

Among the key features that make DaVinci stand out from its competitors (and previous Linotype-Hell products) are:

- a graphical user interface based on the OSF/Motif standard that provides point-and-click operation, thumbnail previews of image files, and many other ease-of-use features familiar to Macintosh and Windows users;

- automatic conversion of type to vector data as it is imported into the workstation, which makes advanced coloring and trapping possible;

- object orientation, which stores each object and each action (such as a color correction) as discrete objects, thus enabling an unlimited number of undo and redo operations;

- a high-speed post-processing method, called *lamination*, in which the objects representing each of the changes to a file are applied to the original high-resolution image and the resulting image file is written to disk, either as an EPS file or in ChromaCom format.

In conjunction with DaVinci, Linotype-Hell introduced a number of other products, including a dedicated imposition station, Signastation (which we examine, with other imposition products, in Chapter 12), and upgrades to its scanners and RIPs.

The popular high-end ChromaGraph DC-3000 scanner line has been extended with the introduction of three new models, all of which can scan both reflective and transparent originals. The S3500 scanner accepts originals up to 17.7-by-20 inches, has a rotation speed of 15 revolutions per second (rps), and allows enlargements up to 2,000 percent. The S3700 is identical except that it also provides support for

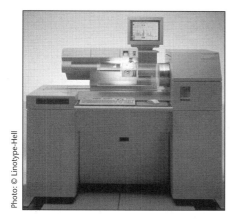

Fig. 10-14
The Linotype-Hell S3800 scanner
supports larger original sizes, greater
enlargement and faster rotation
speed than its predecessors.

Photo: © Linotype-Hell

the ChromaSet scan preparation system and reading bar-codes. The
S3800 accepts larger originals (up to 25.6-by-20 inches), can enlarge
up to 3,000 percent, and has a higher rotation speed (22.5 rps).

The top-of-the-line S3800 also comes with powerful new scanning
software, NewColor 3000, which extends the operator's ability to
specify corrections and adjustments that will take place in real time
during the scan. These include color correction based on the
luminance, chrominance, hue (LCH) model (which enables color
corrections in a user-definable color range without affecting any other
colors in the scan); color-specific unsharp masking (which allows

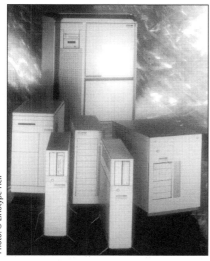

Fig. 10-15
The LinoServer family includes a
variety of Unix-based image servers
with various storage and connectivity
options.

Photo: © Linotype-Hell

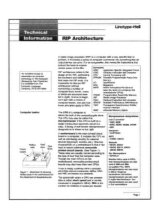

Fig. 10-16
Linotype-Hell publishes a comprehensive series of technical bulletins, covering everything from film chemistry to color models and ink densities.

different colors in an image to be scanned with different levels of sharpness or softness); and automatic print adaptation (which enables the scanner to simulate many different printing conditions).

The LinoServer 5000 is a UNIX-based file server that can be used in Macintosh, PC, and UNIX networks, and supports a number of picture replacement schemes, including OPI, DCS, and LinoPicture Includer protocols. It can be configured with a variety of high-capacity storage and back-up devices. All LinoServers are based on a "Symmetric Multiprocessor Technology" that allows you to add additional CPUs as needed to boost system performance.

The RIP 60 is Linotype-Hell's first RIP based on Hyphen's PostScript-compatible interpreter. It is available with an Extended Power Option (XPO) containing a digital signal processor (DSP) chip that significantly increases the speed of processing continuous tone images.

There's one other Linotype-Hell product many desktop color users should know about. The company publishes an excellent series of technical bulletins on prepress production, edited by Jim Hamilton, which are available free to their customers, or to others for a modest subscription fee (phone 1-800-842-9721).

Screen

Screen USA is a division of Dainippon Screen, which in addition to making electronic prepress products is one of the world's largest providers of conventional graphic arts equipment and supplies.

Photo: © Dainippon Screen

Fig. 10-17
The Screen TaigaSPACE system includes scanners, large-format film recorders, and image retouching and page layout stations.

Screen makes high-end scanners, film recorders, and page makeup stations, but they also make film processors, platemakers, step-and-repeat machines, densitometers, contact printers, and other prepress equipment.

Although it was late in picking up on PostScript-based publishing, Screen has more than made up for its slow start by releasing a number of sophisticated prepress products that work with desktop hardware and software.

On the input side, Screen makes a variety of high-end drum scanners, including the Scanagraph SG-7060P, which automates many scanning tasks, including focusing, aperture selection, and light-source switching. It features faster drum rotation, high-intensity light source, and magnifications up to 3,000%. The SG-7060P can be used as both a stand-alone scanner and for input to a desktop or high-end prepress system, such as Screen's TaigaSPACE system. It can also be connected directly to Screen's MT-R1100 film recorder for simultaneous scanning and film output.

The Screen Scanagraph SG-737 scanner incorporates a data preset function for simplifying scanner setup and automating the production of recurrent scans. Setups for as many as 64 jobs can be stored on a floppy disk and retrieved as required. The proper size aperture for each magnification is selected automatically, which saves time and ensures accurate centering in the light path. The SG-737 can be connected to a variety of peripherals, including the ST-90 scanner setup unit, the AV-200 autovignetter, and an automatic film processor.

Screen also makes two desktop drum scanners, the DT S-1015 and DT S-1030 AI, which provide direct SCSI connection to Macintosh or Windows-based computers.

In 1993, Screen introduced an entirely new concept in high-end prepress, which they call the TaigaSPACE system. The Japanese word *taiga* means big river, the metaphor Screen uses to describe the way its system efficiently handles large volumes of image data.

TaigaSPACE is a scalable, open, modular architecture. On the upstream side, the system includes the TaigaPage layout and image retouching station, TaigaPrep for input of mechanicals, TaigaLine for processing linework, and TaigaMask for silhouetting. Downstream, TaigaSPACE uses the Sun SPARCstation 10 running the Solaris operating system and the TaigaPress application program to integrate the massive amount of data required for high-volume, high-quality prepress production.

Screen makes a variety of imagesetters, including the DT-R2035, the DT-R1065, and the MT-R1120. The DT-R2035 is a high-speed external drum imagesetter that can output film at 5.9 inches per minute at resolutions up to 4,064 ppi. It features automatic internal punching and automatic film handling, and can handle film as large as 13.5-by-20-inches.

The DT-R2035 is available with Adobe's CPSI RIP with PixelBurst, or Harlequin's Scriptworks RIP, and is normally connected to the RIP via Ethernet. The film recorder does not need to buffer the output

Photo: © Dainippon Screen

Fig. 10-18
The Screen DT-R2035 is a drum imagesetter that supports resolutions up to 4,064 pixels per inch.

from the RIP; instead, as one film is being exposed, a second can be ripped and processed immediately, thus saving time. The recorder has a stop-start feature to keep pace with the RIP. The DT-R1065 is similar to the R2035, but supports film sizes up to 22-by-25.5-inches.

The MT-R1120 is an external drum machine that can be used with Screen's TaigaSPACE prepress system or in a pure PostScript environment. It can output film up to 32-by-44-inches, making it possible to output an entire flat of eight letter-sized pages at once, at resolutions of 2,000 or 4,000 ppi. It features fully automatic film handling and an optional on-line film processor. Screen also owns Island Graphics, maker of Island Trapper, a desktop trapping program described in Chapter 12.

Crosfield

Crosfield started in the United Kingdom in the 1970s, and is now owned by DuPont and Fuji, with Fuji marketing Crosfield products in Japan, DuPont selling them in North America, and a joint venture (DuPont Fuji Electronic Imaging) selling them in the rest of the world. Crosfield's scanners have long been known for quality and productivity.

The most recent addition to their scanner product line is the Magnascan 200i, an entry-level drum scanner. The 200i supports transmission or reflection originals with a maximum size of

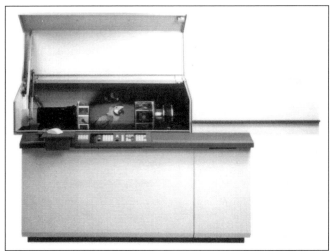

Fig. 10-19
The Crosfield
Magnascan
scanners provide
the quality and
productivity
required in the
color prepress
industry.

Photo: © Crosfield

10-by-10 inches at resolutions up to 4,000 ppi, recording up to 4,096 gray levels per color.

In the early days of PostScript color systems, Crosfield developed the MagnaLink bridge between its high-end systems and Macintosh-based image editing and page layout. This has since been enhanced with the MagnaLink 600 option for Crosfield scanners, a SCSI-2 interface that supports virtually all standard desktop and high-end file formats, and can be further accelerated with a Rocket Radius board to allow simultaneous scanning and image editing. With MagnaLink 600, image data can be scanned directly to the local Macintosh hard disk, to removable media, or across a network to a disk drive located on a remote workstation.

Crosfield recently introduced a series of color workstations that use RISC technology to achieve significant speed increases. The 9600R is an entry-level system with a 2Gb hard drive and image database software. The 9700R comes with a 6Gb drive, Studio Palette interactive editing software for continuous tone images, and Studio ColorfFil, a linework editing package. In addition to increased speed, the 9600R and 9700R have an image merge and dropout capability, called ImMerge, which enables complex drop shadows and image merging to be incorporated into the final page.

Photo: © Crosfield

Fig. 10-20
The Crosfield 9600R and 9700R workstations use high-speed RISC technology to dramatically increase the productivity of stripping and page assembly.

In the imagesetter department, Crosfield has developed the MS850-M, which can handle film sizes up to 32.6-by-40.5 inches, allowing impositions of eight-up letter-sized pages. The MS850-M is driven by Crosfield's MagnaRIP raster image processor, a software-based PostScript RIP running on a Sun SPARCstation.

Crosfield has also added trapping as an option to its MagnaRIP and MS750 RIPs. The MagnaRIP auto-trap function applies trapping after the image has been ripped, which improves productivity and makes it easier to view and apply traps. Color trade shops and PostScript service bureaus will also want to take a look at Crosfield's ImageBureau software, which streamlines page production by using the OPI picture replacement method to isolate high-resolution images from page layout until the final output stage.

Photo: © Crosfield

Fig. 10-21
The Crosfield MagnaRIP (in the foreground) can apply trapping to pages and graphics before they are imaged in the film recorder (in the background).

High-end prepress in transition

Vendors of high-end prepress equipment face an uncertain future. On the one hand, the rapid growth in color publishing provides them with many new potential customers. Some direct-mail companies, for example, are now buying high-end systems so they can bring catalog production in-house.

On the other hand, nobody in their right mind would start a color trade shop today and equip it exclusively with high-end equipment.

PostScript color publishing is the new reality. To succeed, vendors of high-end equipment must abandon the idea of selling complete systems, and focus on making desktop-compatible products that can compete head-to-head against innovative products, both from the established vendors and bold new start-ups.

The next few years will present severe challenges and great opportunities for all the companies that buy high-end equipment, whether they are commercial or in-plant printers, PostScript service bureaus or traditional color trade shops.

The integration of printing and prepress represents a tremendous opportunity for commercial printers, both to increase revenues and to form tighter bonds with their clients. The successful printers will build "transparency" into their relationships with major clients, so that buying prepress and printing services requires just a single click of the mouse. At the same time, this transition presents a major technical challenge, as printers are forced to understand, not only the skills of the color separator, but also the complexities of computer hardware and software.

Increasingly, in-plant printers will be caught in a different dilemma, as the need to reduce costs pressures them to bring more and more prepress functions in-house. At the same time, drastic reductions in the cost of prepress services from outside suppliers will force in-plants to bring their costs and service levels in line.

The PostScript service bureau industry is poised for a massive shake-out, as over-supply and increasing price competition make life difficult or impossible for small shops without the financial or technological capital to remain on the leading edge. Some service bureaus will enhance their competitiveness by buying high-end prepress equipment and transforming themselves into color trade shops, but they will have to target their market niches precisely or form strategic relationships with one or more commercial printers to make this approach pay off.

The color trade shops are perhaps the most seriously threatened segment of the prepress industry, faced with incessant technological innovation and competition from every side. But they are not without options—there are still market niches that could keep savvy trade shops very busy. For example, commodity four-color color separations will soon be a big business, but profitable only for suppliers who can produce film in very high volumes and with very thin profit margins.

Prepress for non-print publishing will also be a growth industry, producing color graphics and images for electronic distribution through media such as on-line computing services, CD-ROM disks, and personal digital assistants (hand-held communications devices).

Evolving to total desktop color

Although desktop systems have made great strides in the past few years, they are still in the early stages of evolution. High-end prepress systems, by comparison, have already evolved substantially and will have to be significantly more cost-effective to compete against upstarts from the desktop.

What are the relative strengths and weaknesses of these competitors, and how will their market positions change over the next few years? Today, high-end equipment has two main advantages over desktop system: greater quality in scanning, and higher productivity overall. Desktop systems, however, offer much lower costs plus greater flexibility and control.

For those concerned with throughput of large volumes of color pages, high-end systems are still the way to go, because of both the raw horsepower of the equipment and the way high-end architectures have been designed. However, the processing speed of desktop computers is rapidly catching up to proprietary systems, while desktop imaging programs are emulating the very architectures that have worked so well for high-end vendors (such as working in real-time on a screen-resolution version of an image and later applying all changes to the high-resolution image in a separate "execute" step).

Given these trends, today's high-end vendors have limited flexibility in evolving their systems to meet the threat from the desktop. One option would be to maintain their emphasis on speed, selling proprietary or semi-proprietary equipment to trade shops and other environments willing to pay for extremely high performance.

Another option would be to focus on migrating their high-performance input/output peripherals to desktop systems. As the speed of off-the-shelf microprocessors continues to soar over the next few years, virtually all color prepress activities will move to industry standard open platforms. But even as these super-charged desktop computers take over the majority of image processing and page layout tasks, they will still need high-quality peripherals for getting data into and out of the system.

Whatever happens to the market for prepress services, it seems clear that they will soon take place almost exclusively on systems based on industry-standard non-proprietary hardware and software. Certainly there will be a place for the high-end vendors to sell products with superior quality and throughput, but the era of traditional one-vendor prepress systems is over.

HiFi color—hope for the high-end

Why are there four process colors? Why not five, or six, or eleven? As we saw in Chapter 1, by combining percentages of cyan, magenta, and yellow, we can create thousands of different colors. The addition of black not only increases the number of colors that can be reproduced, but makes possible enhanced contrast, crisper type, and better detail in the shadows.

It follows that using still other process colors—in addition to cyan, magenta, yellow, and black—would further increase the range of possible colors. In fact, we have known for decades that the gamut of the lithographic printing method could be measurably increased by adding other inks in exactly the parts of the color chart that are difficult to attain with combinations of cyan, magenta, and yellow.

This new set of printing processes, known as *high-fidelity* color, should not be confused with the often-used method of printing both process and spot colors on the same sheet, for instance on a job that includes photographs and custom corporate logo colors. As of early 1994, high-fidelity or *HiFi* color was virtually nonexistent in commercial printing, though experiments were being conducted by a number of companies, including Crosfield, Fuji, Kodak, Pantone and Scitex.

There are three main approaches to increasing the gamut of color printing:

- combine process and spot colors in a single image by using a "touch plate" that applies a highlight color only to those parts of an image that require it;
- use a "bump plate" to overprint a second coat of cyan, magenta or yellow ink over the basic CMYK separations;
- expand the set of process inks by adding colors, such as orange and green, that maximize the press gamut.

Each of the vendors exploring HiFi printing has adopted a different approach.

DuPont, for example, has developed a process called HyperColor, that increases the saturation of process colors by creating a second separation for 100% density areas in yellow, magenta or cyan. The additional separations are used to make bump plates that add increased color in those areas, producing a continuous tone look with no rosettes at line screens up to 300 lpi.

The HyperColor software is available as an upgrade to the Crosfield ML600 system, which provides a link between Crosfield's high-end scanners and desktop systems. After the original artwork has been scanned, the HyperColor software automatically calculates the necessary separations and outputs them as two TIFF files. Separations can be output on any PostScript imagesetter.

Linotype-Hell's HiFi experiments have focused on increasing the number of inks by adding orange, green, and violet (OGV) to the traditional CMYK. This method was originally developed by the German scientist Harold Kupper, who found that he could increase the number of distinct colors in the press gamut by about 20% overall, with an increase of about 80% in the blue part of the spectrum.

Linotype-Hell has modified Kupper's model to further increase the gamut in the reds and greens, and its expanded colorant set, called VSF, will be released as a set of scanner color tables that will allow the scanner operator to produce separations for five, six or seven inks according to the content of various types of images. Each image would have to be scanned twice, first for CMYK and then for any additional colorants to be used.

Scitex has taken a similar approach, except that it uses red, green, and blue as the additional colorants. Using the ResoLUT image processor or a Color Imaging Station, the Scitex operator creates two sets of film from each RGB image. The first is a set of conventional CMYK process colors separations, the other a set of RGB films. The resulting seven-color printing has expanded color gamut and dynamic range.

Pantone has decided to develop a HiFi printing method based on six, rather than seven colors, in part because of the large number of six-color presses in use, and in part because they believe that by carefully choosing the six colors it's possible to get output with a wider gamut than seven-color CMYKOGV or CMYKRGB.

The key to the Pantone method, called Hexachrome, is starting from scratch by throwing out the cyan, magenta, and yellow inks while retaining the black. Pantone's method uses black plus five other colorants (which it hasn't yet revealed), and is designed to expand the press gamut to include as many PANTONE MATCHING SYSTEM spot colors as possible.

The fact that it only requires a six-color press could be a major advantage, as it makes Hexachrome more cost-competitive in the inevitable shake-out that will occur as each of the vendors tries to get its method defined (by the marketplace) as the hi-fi standard.

Pantone has worked with Kodak to create a device profile for the Kodak PCS-100 color station, making it easy for its users to work with color-accurate high-fidelity printing.

HiFi color is not an important commercial technology yet, but its future looks bright. Desktop publishing technology is rapidly making four-color printing a commodity, and companies that make expensive, high-quality products will continue to need distinctive eye-catching printed materials to market their wares. Therefore, it seems likely that high-fidelity color publishing will become an important niche.

During the next few years, color trade shops and other providers of high-quality prepress services will have to re-invent themselves in order to stay alive. One fact that should give them some peace of mind is that they'll no longer be forced to use proprietary hardware and software to achieve the quality or productivity their customers have come to expect.

There will always be a high-end, but the new high-end will look strangely like the best desktop systems available today—high-quality industry-standard peripherals attached to powerful desktop processors running off-the-shelf, shrink-wrapped software.

Color Printers

"All colors will agree in the dark."
Sir Francis Bacon

Until a few years ago, color printers were expensive, complex devices limited to specialized applications in engineering, medicine, and science. Today, you can find inexpensive desktop color printers in all color trade shops, most design studios, and an increasing number of offices. In the design and prepress industries, color printers are used to create an intermediate print as part of the production process. In office publishing, and in short-run, on-demand publishing, the output from the color printer is the final product.

Most color publishers don't get to see the final result of their design efforts until paper emerges from a printing press after a long, sometimes arduous, journey through the prepress process. Part of this process involves making proofs in order to predict the appearance of the final printed piece—contract proofs are typically film proofs created from the final film that will be used to print a job. Increasingly, however, desktop color printers are being used to create inexpensive pre-proofs for use throughout the design and approval stages.

For those producing short runs of tens or hundreds of copies, desktop color printers serve a different role—rather than providing intermediate output prior to going on press, they *are* the press. We have already seen how the rapid emergence of high-quality software tools has made it increasingly easy for people to create full-color documents on their desktops. Now that desktop color printers are plummeting in cost while increasing in quality, it's becoming quick, easy, and inexpensive to produce full-color pages in small quantities.

You can put color on paper in numerous ways, with a variety of different inks, toners, waxes, and dyes. Each technique has advantages and disadvantages of cost, quality, speed, durability, and other factors. In this chapter, we explore the various methods for printing color pages directly from the desktop, and highlight their strengths and weaknesses.

But first, a word about print quality. Assessing the quality of print samples is a subjective process. In my opinion, the best way to compare color printers is to compile a collection of output samples. You can amass a portfolio of sample pages from a hundred or more different color printers, simply by asking for them at graphic arts trade shows and by responding to ads from the various manufacturers.

As you collect each sample, take a few minutes to label it with the name of the manufacturer, printer model, print technology and media used, printer cost, media cost, and the date it was printed. Better still, prepare a sample file on diskette or cartridge and, wherever possible, have it output on the various printers so you can compare different versions of the same image. For best results, your sample file should contain text, synthetic graphics, and a photographic image, preferably of a person (so you can assess the quality of flesh-tone reproduction).

Print technologies

There is no ideal printer—different people have different concerns and priorities, and each printing technology has its merits and limitations, whether in price, quality, speed or media cost. Indeed, media cost is a crucial, though often overlooked, factor. Over the lifetime of the printer, you will spend much more on paper and supplies than the original cost of the printer.

Photo: © Canon

Photo: © 3M

Fig. 11-1
Color printers vary in size and price from Canon's $600 desktop
bubble-jet BJC-600 (left) to 3M's $300,000 Digital Matchprint (right).

The principle factor that determines the quality and cost of color output is the underlying technology used in the printer. Most of today's digital printers use one of six methods to put color onto paper:

- **bubble jet printers** offer low cost plus the convenience of printing on any paper stock, and are used for both presentations and for producing design comps;

- **thermal wax printers** are inexpensive and well suited to corporate communications tasks, though of limited use in color prepress;

- **dye sublimation printers** provide excellent quality continuous-tone output, but are more costly to use because they require special photographic media;

- **electrostatic printers** include huge color plotters, and toner-based color photocopiers that are costly to buy, but are among the fastest and cheapest in terms of per-page output;

- **ink jet proofers** can print on any stock, and can be fine-tuned to closely match the colors from a conventional film proof or the actual press sheet;

◆   **electrophotographic printers** are the most expensive and highest quality, and are the only digital printers capable of producing halftone dots that match those on the final printed sheet.

Bubble jet printers

Bubble jet technology is a relatively inexpensive way to create color output, producing vivid colors on plain paper. Among the vendors offering bubble jet printers are Apple, Canon, Hewlett-Packard, and Lexmark, all of whom use a marking engine made by Canon.

The major advantages of bubble jet printers are that they can print on plain paper and are relatively low in cost, for both the printer itself and per page. Most use four inks (CMYK), so they can produce a true black (not a composite black created by combining cyan, magenta, and yellow). Because each colorant is in a separate cartridge (unlike thermal wax printers, which use three-color or four-color transfer ribbons), it is less costly and less wasteful to print such documents as proposals, where many pages contain black only, and where there is just the occasional color diagram or photograph. On the other hand, they cost more per page for color-intensive documents.

Another benefit of bubble-jet printers is that, typically, they are small and quiet. Their main disadvantage is that the print quality is suitable for comps, not prepress proofs—not surprising, given their low

Fig. 11-2
The Lexmark 4079 JetPrinter is a bubble-jet printer that can be used with Macintosh or Windows-based computers.

Photo: © Lexmark

Fig. 11-3
The Apple Color Printer is a tabloid-sized color ink-jet printer.

Photo: © Apple Computer, Inc.

cost. Some bubble-jet printers, such as the low-cost Canon BJC-600, are limited to letter-sized pages, while most also support tabloid size.

The Canon CJ-10 is a unique bubble jet device that combines a 400 ppi color scanner, printer, and photocopier in one desktop-sized box. For bright, well-saturated colors, the CJ-10 should be used with special paper or card stock, though it can also print on plain paper. What makes the CJ-10 stand out from other bubble jet devices is that it combines printing, scanning, and photocopying in a single machine, and provides excellent output quality. The major limitation is that it's rather slow, compared to some other color printers.

Fig. 11-4
The Canon CJ-10 combines a 400 dpi color scanner, copier, and printer in a single peripheral.

Photo: © Canon

Tektronix makes a series of printers based on a variation of bubble jet technology known as "phase change" printing. The Phaser III PXi and Phaser 300 use solid ink to create bright colors on plain paper. The ink changes phase quickly, starting as a solid before being melted in the printhead, then changing again from liquid to solid on the page. These printers provide good image quality, broad color gamut, and low per-page costs. The latest phase change printer, the Phaser 300i, is twice as fast as previous models, and offers even better print quality.

Although phase change technology is conceptually similar to bubble jet, the ink doesn't have time to bleed into the paper, so printed colors remain brilliant and well defined on almost any type of paper, from paper towels to 120lb. card stock. Also, the Phaser 300i is unique in its ability to print on any size media from 4-by-6-inches to 12-by-18-inches.

Thermal wax printers

Since they were introduced by QMS in 1988, thermal wax printers have captured a significant share of the low-end color output market, in part because of falling prices. The first such devices were in the $30,000 range, while recent thermal wax printers are less than $2,000.

Fig. 11-5
Thermal wax printers, such as this Calcomp ColorMaster Plus, use opaque waxes that are ideal for producing overhead transparencies.

Photo: © Calcomp

Among the leading vendors of thermal wax printers are Calcomp, QMS, Seiko, and Tektronix.

In a thermal wax printer, a colored ribbon (CMY or CMYK) is placed against a metal drum, which has been divided into a grid of individually addressable pixels, typically 300 per linear inch. Each pixel for a given color heats up, melting the wax into the paper. The major advantages of thermal wax printers include their relatively low cost and the high *opacity* of the wax, which makes them ideal for creating overhead transparencies. Depending on the make and model, the disadvantages of some thermal wax printers can include problems with speed and quality, plus the need for special paper.

Some low-cost thermal wax printers are able to work with only 8-bit color (256 colors) rather than 24-bit color (16.7-million colors), and each manufacturer of 8-bit printers uses a proprietary halftoning method, or screening algorithm, to create the appearance of more than 256 colors. Although the technology behind screening may be complicated, the results are easy to observe, simply by looking closely at output samples from a number of different devices.

For example, print a sample page on three different 8-bit thermal wax printers, all with 300 dpi resolution, using a variety of plain and special papers. Examine the samples closely and you'll see that some printers produce much smoother color blends than other, almost identical, printers. You'll see marked differences in the quality of color blends, caused by the use of more or less sophisticated dithering algorithms.

These algorithms, which are based on a technique called *error diffusion*, are actually an example of the same frequency modulated screening technology discussed in Chapter 3.

Some thermal wax printers offer the option of using either three-color (CMY) or four-color (CMYK) ribbons. Three-color printing is faster and slightly less expensive, but a four-color ribbon is recommended, especially when working with a lower quality printer or when printing pages with large amounts of black type or visuals (as when printing a business report or proposal with only occasional use of color graphics).

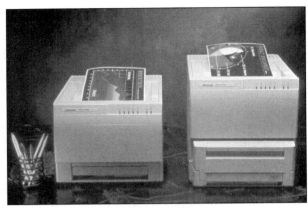

Fig. 11-6
The Tektronix Phaser 220i color printer is available with a second print tray for large-volume printing on a network.

Photo: © Tektronix

The advantage of three-color printing is that it's faster and slightly less expensive, but a four-color ribbon is recommended if your pages contain both graphics and black type.

A recent innovation in the thermal wax area is a pre-coating technology, for use with plain laser printer papers, developed by Tektronix and used in its Phaser 220 series color printers. The Phaser 220 normally uses a three-color ribbon. With plain laser papers, it uses a three-color ribbon with an additional coating or transparent base wax that is applied only to those parts of the page that will later receive one or more colored waxes.

Under a microscope, ordinary office bond paper reveals a landscape of mountains and valleys. The base wax fills in the valleys, leaving a flat smooth surface to which the colored waxes can more easily adhere.

Dye sublimation printers

For color publishers requiring digital color pre-proofs of photographic images, the best balance between quality, cost, and other factors is found with dye sublimation printers. Dye sublimation devices are similar to thermal wax printers, in which heat is transferred to a ribbon permeated with a special wax, that then melts onto the paper. The difference is that the heating array in a dye sublimation printer is much more precise, and can heat the dyes in the transfer ribbon to one of 256 levels.

Photo: © Eastman Kodak Co.

Fig. 11-7
A dye sublimation printer uses special photographic paper and vibrant dyes to create bright, deeply saturated, continuous tone prints.

Some dye sublimation printers offer the choice of three-color ribbons (CMY) or four-color (CMYK) ribbons. Three-color printing is faster and slightly less expensive, but a four-color ribbon should be used when optimum print quality is required. A CMY ribbon contains three dye layers, which means that at each pixel there are 256 possible states of cyan, 256 of magenta, 256 of yellow. The total number of possible colors is 256 times 256 times 256, which is 16.7-million (or, to be precise, 16,777,216). The fluid color of the liquid dyes in combination produces the continuous tone effect by which dye sublimation prints are often identified.

Because of the near-photographic quality of the output, dye sublimation printers are especially popular among color publishers working with images, as opposed to just text and drawings. Among the vendors selling desktop dye sublimation printers are 3M, Kodak, Mitsubishi, RasterOps, Seiko, Sharp, SuperMac, and Tektronix.

Not all dye sublimation printers are created equal—you have to be aware of a number of factors in order to get maximum quality and productivity. For example, many dye sublimation printers don't

Fig. 11-8
The SuperMac
ProofPositive dye
sublimation printer is
available in both letter
and tabloid sizes.

Photo: © SuperMac Technology, Inc.

support PostScript. If you're considering a PostScript dye sublimation printer, you must choose between models with a built-in hardware RIP and those that work with a software RIP.

For optimal speed, a PostScript printer with a hardware RIP should also contain a RISC processor and at least 16Mb of RAM. Adding more memory allows larger input buffers and faster throughput; some dye sublimation printers support up to 64Mb. Font support is essential, both for PostScript and TrueType. If you use many fonts, make sure the printer has a built-in hard disk or a SCSI port.

Many manufacturers, including 3M, Kodak, Seiko, and SuperMac, have opted for a software RIP, which can be easily upgraded. Dye sublimation engines are expensive and will likely last several years: with a software RIP, you can stay current with improvements in RIP technology without having to ditch your printer.

Connectivity is another important variable. The best dye sublimation printers not only connect to Macs, PCs (DOS, Windows, and OS/2) and UNIX workstations, but support them all simultaneously, automatically switching between interfaces without user intervention. If you use a network, make sure the printer allows you to add an optional network card.

Photo: © 3M

Fig. 11-9
The 3M Rainbow is one of the most popular dye sublimation printers used by service bureaus and color trade shops.

For the best color quality, look for printers that are Pantone certified and that support Adobe's PostScript Level 2 language. Some printer vendors provide additional color matching capabilities, such as Tektronix with its TekColor PS color fidelity software. Tektronix also includes Photofine rendering software with its dye sublimation printers to improve the quality of fine lines.

The primary advantage of dye sublimation printers is image quality—they produce continuous tone images that closely resemble photographic prints. Ironically, this can also be a disadvantage, because the dye sublimation prints often look better than the actual printed sheet: they can appear excessively shiny with vibrant colors.

Another disadvantage is that, although dye sublimation printers produce excellent photographic images, they are not as adept at rendering fine lines, such as the serifs in small type. Furthermore, dye sublimation printers work only with special photographic paper, and, therefore, cannot replicate the way colors will appear when printed on ordinary paper, especially on uncoated stock.

Dye sublimation proofers are less expensive than color copiers, high-end ink jet printers, and electrophotographic devices, but more costly than thermal wax and bubble jet devices. Per-page costs are typically lowest for solid wax printers and color copiers, and highest for dye sublimation printers.

Fig. 11-10
The Shinko ColorStream/DS dye sublimation printer provides letter-sized output at 300 dpi.

One color printer that doesn't fit neatly into a single category is the Seiko Professional ColorPoint 2PSF, which incorporates a new print head technology that enables it to operate as both a thermal wax and a dye sublimation printer. The user can switch from one to the other, depending on whether the current job requires the extra quality of dye sublimation or the lower cost of thermal wax.

Laser printers

Now that it's relatively easy to create full-color publications directly from the desktop, the race is on for ways to produce hundreds or thousands of copies of these publications, without resorting to conventional printing presses. Color laser printers that also perform as copiers, such as those from Canon, Kodak, Xerox, and Minolta, dominate this short-run color market.

The high-speed black-and-white copier has been a major factor in the rapid growth of printed business documents for the past 20 years—one of the reasons we're all drowning in paper, although there are a number of applications in which data can be processed and exchanged electronically, without ever appearing on paper.

But there are many situations in which the printed word must be just that: printed. It is, after all, portable, browsable, and reusable. And with the recent surge in desktop publishing and photocopying, the printed word is everywhere (unfortunately, it's usually in the same 35 fonts).

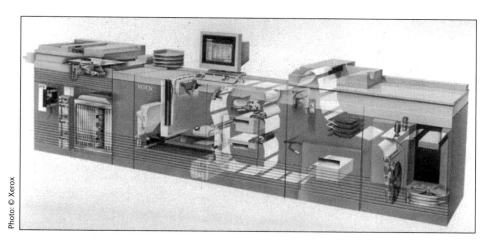

Photo: © Xerox

Fig. 11-11
Black-and-white digital printing presses, such as this 135
page-per-minute Xerox DocuTech, will soon offer full color.

Color copying is used by in-house reprographic centers, copy shops, advertising and public relations firms, graphic art and design companies, sales and marketing organizations, real estate agencies, as well as packaging, fashion, and interior designers. Many of them still use black-and-white copiers as well, for speed, economy, and paper-handling options missing from today's color copiers.

Although there are desktop color copiers that cost less than $10,000, some cost ten times that, depending on output quality, speed, and connectivity options. Color copiers are crucial to the proliferation of color publishing, because the per-page cost is low enough to encourage users to freely include color in their documents.

The emergence of high-speed low-cost color copiers opens up a new era in color publishing, in which relatively large quantities of color documents can be created directly from the original data, without an intervening prepress stage. They will help usher in an age when color business documents will be the accepted standard.

Color copiers print with a technology known as color xerography, quite similar to that used in conventional black-and-white copiers. The major difference is that four toners are used, one each for cyan, magenta, yellow, and black.

Fig. 11-12
Color copiers, such as those from Xerox, Canon, and Kodak, are used both for creating pre-proofs and for printing short-run color publications.

Photo: © Eastman Kodak Co.

By default, the marking engines in most color copiers are dithered devices, but they are capable of printing continuous tone output when connected to a RIP (raster image processor), such as the Fiery controller from Electronics for Imaging (EFI) or controllers from SuperMac, ColorAge Incorporated (CAI), ColorBus, DiceNet, and others.

The Fiery Color Server transforms the copier from a halftone device into a continuous tone printer by adding special control electronics and up to 128Mb of RAM, which enables it to drive supported copiers at their maximum resolution and speed rating at all page sizes. It

Fig. 11-13
EFI Fiery is a raster image processor (RIP) that connects to color copiers from Canon, Xerox, and Kodak to convert them into continuous tone printers.

Photo: © Electronics for Imaging

Photo: © ColorAge, Inc.

Fig. 11-14
EFI fired up the copier RIP business with the Fiery, but now has competition from such products as the ColorQ 3000 RIP from CAI.

contains a RISC processor, plus an internal hard disk to handle large image files and for spooling multiple jobs. The Fiery can be connected to Mac, PC, and UNIX networks, and supports all major networking protocols, including TCP/IP. It comes with software utilities for scanning, spooling, downloading PostScript and TIFF files, and calibration.

ColorAge Inc. (CAI) has developed an innovative approach to networked color print servers, exemplified by the ColorQ 3000. Based on a high-speed Intel Pentium chip, the ColorQ 3000 is PostScript Level 2 compatible and supports Novell and AppleTalk networks. It also provides tools for color calibration and PANTONE MATCHING SYSTEM spot color matching. In addition to supporting digital color copiers from Canon, Kodak, and Xerox, the ColorQ 3000 works with Xerox Versatec plotters as well as film recorders from Agfa and Management Graphics.

Canon also makes its own controllers for the CLCs, both for halftone and continuous tone output. It was the first company to develop digital color copiers that connect directly to Macs and PCs, and continues to have the largest portion of the market, although competition has increased recently with the arrival of new products from Xerox and others. The Canon Color Laser Copier (CLC) 350 and 550 machines follow on the successful CLC 300 and 500 models,

Fig. 11-15
The Canon CLC-550 color copier can be connected to a network and shared as a color scanner, copier, and printer.

Photo: © Canon

but with one major enhancement—the ability to print duplex (on both sides of the sheet). Kodak sells the same series of copiers under the ColorEdge name.

Xerox has three CMYK copiers/printers that compete in this category. The 5775 SSE is a composite device that copies, scans, and prints at 7.5 pages per minute. It accepts input from a variety of sources, including TIFF and PostScript files, and supports a maximum resolution of 400 dpi.

The Xerox 4700 is a high-volume dedicated color printer, rated for up to 80,000 pages per month. It prints 300-dpi letter-sized color pages on plain paper at 7.5 pages per minute, and can be hooked up to any PC, Mac, or UNIX-based system. The 4700 can also print on tabloid (11-by-17-inch) paper, and is designed for printing multiple copies of a document and printing collated copies of multi-page documents. It simultaneously spools incoming print jobs, RIPs and formats the data, and prints, which means that the printer works non-stop when the input queue is kept full of incoming jobs. The 4700 uses the XScript language, which is Xerox's emulation of PostScript, and also supports HP-GL and the Xerox Distributed Print Mode (XPD) command set.

The newest color copier from Xerox is the MajestiK, which offers an unprecedented level of quality for a color copier. It is a 6 ppm CMYK device that can be connected via RIPs from EFI, SuperMac,

Photo: © Xerox

Fig. 11-16
The Xerox MajestiK is a color copier that outputs up to six pages per minute, and can be connected to Macs, PCs, or UNIX-based machines.

and other vendors. The odd spelling of "MajestiK" reflects the fact that it was designed to be economical for producing regular (black-only) pages, in addition to full color.

MajestiK is designed to reproduce full-color photographic images with the vivid hues, highlights, and tonal gradations normally associated with offset printing, made possible through a new ultra-fine (seven-micron diameter) toner. It has a resolution of 400 dpi at 256 gradations per color, resulting in 16.7-million colors, and supports paper sized up to 11-by-17-inches.

QMS, the company that first brought PostScript to desktop color printers, recently introduced a PostScript color laser printer targeted at the office market. The QMS ColorScript Laser 1000 is a plain-paper, letter-sized device with 300 dpi resolution and sells for about $10,000.

The ColorScript 1000 uses a special photo-conductive belt that makes four passes (one for each process color) to build up the image on a transfer drum, from which the image is then transferred to the paper in a single pass. The ColorScript 1000 supports PostScript Level 2 as well as HP PCL 5 and HPGL protocols, and can output two full-color pages per minute. A variety of optional network interfaces are available for 10BaseT, thin or thick Ethernet, and Token Ring.

Although even the fastest color laser printers/copiers are currently limited to speeds of less than ten pages per minute, there are no fundamental technical barriers to attaining much higher speeds, and in the next few years speeds in excess of 50 pages per minute are likely. At that point, the floodgates will burst open, and a new era of on-demand, short-run color publishing will arrive. The arrival of high-speed full-color laser printers will rapidly decimate the conventional short-run color printing industry.

Ink jet printers

High-end ink jet color printers, which typically cost $50,000 or more, have little in common with the bubble jet printers described previously. The major manufacturers in this category are Iris Graphics (a division of Scitex) and Stork. Technically, high-end color printers are different from their low-end cousins in that they blast a continuous stream of ink toward the page, then use deflectors to steer some of it to ink reservoirs, which then return the unused ink to the appropriate container. By contrast, inexpensive bubble jet printers send bursts of ink on demand.

The Iris SmartJet 4012 is a continuous tone color printer with 300 dpi resolution, but because it can place between zero and 31 tiny (15-micron diameter) droplets per color in each pixel, it has an

Fig. 11-17
The Iris SmartJet 4012 ink jet printer can produce accurate digital color proofs on virtually any paper stock.

Photo: © Iris Graphics

apparent resolution of between 1,500 and 1,800 dpi. The Iris 3024 handles paper up to 24-by-24-inches, while the Iris 3047 can do so with paper up to 34-by-37-inches.

Strictly speaking, "paper" is not the right word: one of the major advantages of the Iris devices is their ability to print on virtually any paper stock, which makes them an appropriate choice for color proofing when connected to either a high-end or desktop system. Iris also sells a special RIP, the Trans4, which lets you adjust the color lookup tables to fine-tune the printed output so it more closely matches the final printed sheet.

Electrostatic plotters

Until recently, electrostatic plotters were used only for black-and-white output, but, like all other media, they are making the transition to color. This market was originally developed by Xerox Engineering Systems, with the Versatec series of plotters.

Calcomp, for example, makes a series of color plotters, such as the 68000GA, that are used primarily for creating posters, banners, signs, and other large-format prints. These plotters have also proven valuable as proofing devices for showing page impositions for printed signatures of up to 16 pages (eight-up per side).

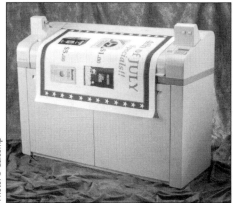

Photo: © Calcomp

Fig. 11-18
Large-format color plotters can be useful both for creating poster-sized prints and for proofing page impositions.

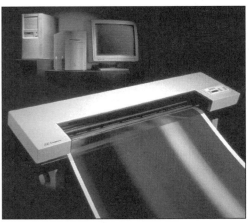

Fig. 11-19
The LaserMaster
DisplayMaker is a
large-format digital printer
that can output posters,
signs, and displays up to
36 inches wide.

Photo: © LaserMaster

LaserMaster sells a large-format color printer, the DisplayMaker, that offers a new level of price-performance for really big color prints. Costing less than $20,000 (about one-half the price of most electrostatic plotters), the Macintosh-based DisplayMaker works with all popular desktop applications programs.

Electrophotographic printers

The major competitors in this category are Kodak Approval and 3M Digital Matchprint, both of which cost approximately $300,000 and provide extremely high quality halftone proofs on any paper stock.

Fig. 11-20
The 3M Digital
Matchprint
produces contract
proofs with a dot
structure that
closely
approximates the
printed sheet.

Photo: © 3M

The main advantages of these devices, other than their high quality, is that their output consists of halftone dots exactly like those on the printed sheet. In this respect they are closer than any other digital printer to traditional film proofs. Another advantage is that prints can be created on the same paper stock that will be used for the actual printing job, thereby ensuring a closer color match.

According to color trade shops that have installed Approval or Digital Matchprint devices, a big part of the payoff comes from the fact that operators working on image editing stations can see the results of their work within about 20 minutes, rather than having to wait hours for a conventional film proof.

Slide film recorders

There's one other popular way of getting output from desktop systems—as 35mm slides that can be projected with a conventional slide projector. If you only output slides on an occasional basis, a low-cost recorder from Mirus or Polaroid will probably be most cost-effective. Professional output providers or those creating large volumes of slides will be better off with the heavy-duty recorders from Solitaire, MGI, and Symbolics.

A film recorder works just like a camera, but instead of pointing at the scene to be photographed, the camera inside it points at a cathode ray tube (CRT). The one major disadvantage of slide film recorders is that after exposing the film you must send it to a photo lab to be developed (unless you produce so many slides that you can cost-justify an E-6 developing system). This is not a major problem in

Photo: © Mirus

Fig. 11-21
The Mirus FilmPrinter turbo II is a 36-bit slide film recorder that allows you to image a 35mm color slide in about a minute.

any large city, where most photo labs provide one-hour service, but it is not as convenient as getting final output right at your desk.

Digital color presses

All desktop color printers share the same limitation—they're too slow for duplicating more than a dozen or so copies of a page. It will take even today's fastest color photocopiers, which are currently constrained to producing less than ten pages per minute (ppm), a few years to reach speeds of 50 or more ppm.

Digital color presses, such as those released in 1994 by Xeikon, Indigo, and Agfa offer a solution to this bottleneck. These devices represent a whole new category in the printing industry—highly automated, self-contained presses small enough to be used in a typical office environment. There are enough of these machines in the field now to begin to assess their quality, speed, and cost-effectiveness.

Although some early machines had problems with image quality, this has not been a major issue for many prospective purchasers. The market segments being targeted are more concerned with speed, the ability to print short runs, and the cost (approximately comparible with litho printing), to care much about the fact that print quality is not quite as good as most conventional printing.

Indigo E-Print 1000

The E-Print 1000 is a revolutionary sheetfed digital color offset printing press developed by Indigo, a Dutch company with research and manufacturing facilities in Israel. It can print up to six colors on a standard A4 letter-sized sheet at a rate of up to 4,000 single-color impressions per hour (67 per minute). An in-line booklet maker can automatically gather, fold, staple, and stack finished documents up to 100 pages in length.

The first step in printing a job on the E-Print is loading the electronic files (from a desktop or high-end prepress system) into the machine's RIP, from which they are imaged onto a reusable digital electrophotographic offset plate. The plate cylinder is electrostatically

Fig. 11-22
The Indigo E-Print 1000 is a digital color printing press that can output
1,000 four-color pages per hour.

Photo: © Indigo

charged, ink is applied from one or more nozzles, the ink is transferred to an offset blanket, and then all the ink is applied to the page. Each sheet can be printed on both sides in succession, before being moved to the booklet maker for binding.

One of the more radical aspects of the E-Print's design is that, in theory, it can handle a completely different image on every revolution, thanks to a patented liquid known as ElectroInk. In practice, this would require a RIP substantially faster than any currently on the market.

In a conventional offset press, the ink on the impression cylinder splits in two, with one half of the image being transferred to the paper while the other half remains on the cylinder. ElectroInk, by comparison, contains a dispersion of tiny colored polymer particles that, on contact with paper, instantly harden to form a thin laminate. The result is greater edge definition, or *acutance*, of halftone dots,

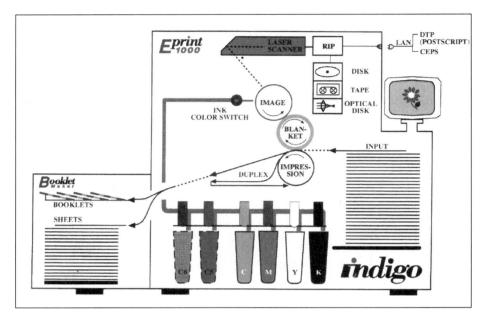

Fig. 11-23
After being ripped, data is sent to the laser imager, which controls the application of inks (CMYK plus up to two spot colors) from the ink supply below.

which means little or no dot gain (because the ink doesn't flow onto the paper, it bonds to it). Inks are available for SWOP and other process-color standards, plus spot colors, metallics, and fluorescents.

Another important component in the E-Print 1000 is the optional imposition and binding module, which outputs completed booklets without manual intervention. Unlike a conventional press, which prints the same page over and over then collates and binds the sheets, the E-Print prints each page sequentially. Keeping all these pages available for imaging requires substantial memory and processing horsepower. The E-Print 1000 comes with a Sun IPX or IPC workstation and a dedicated controller containing 640Mb of RAM, and uses a proprietary compression scheme that reduces image file size by a factor of five.

The E-Print 1000 has a resolution of 800 spots per inch, which, under normal conditions, would be insufficient for high-quality color output. However, as a result of its ink and offset technologies, and exceptional registration, it can print at line screens of 133 to 150 lines per inch. A stripped-down configuration of the E-Print 1000 (single color, one side only) costs about $200,000 while a complete system supporting six colors, duplex printing, electronic collation, personalization, and the booklet maker is around $400,000.

Xeikon DCP-1

The DCP-1 is a digital color web press from Xeikon n.v. of Belgium, capable of printing up to 70 full-color letter-sized pages per minute. It uses electrophotographic technology to print on A3-sized paper (12.6-inch web width) with eight identical printing units (CMYK on each side of the paper). Each unit exposes an image area onto the paper web, following which toner is applied and permanently fixed to the paper by a non-contact hot fusing system. After fusing, the printed web passes to a sheeter and stacker.

Unlike a conventional printing press, the DCP-1 comes in a fully enclosed cabinet, and the operator doesn't have to mount plates or adjust ink settings. It has a resolution of 600 pixels per inch, but supports 64 gray levels at each spot by varying the amount of toner. This enables it to produce color pages with quality acceptable for many kinds of publications, though not appropriate for *National Geographic* or other glossy magazines.

The DCP-1 has four 54Mb image buffers, one for each color printing unit. It's LED (light-emitting diode) imaging system is driven by a PostScript Level 2 interpreter running in an 80486 or Pentium-based PC. The user interface runs under Microsoft Windows. One interesting feature of the DCP-1 is that a limited area of each page can be updated during the printing process, thereby allowing some customization of each document for purposes such as sequential numbering or direct mail applications.

The DCP-1 is targeted at short-run full-color printing in quantities from 100 to 5,000 copies, and is priced at approximately $210,000 for a base configuration.

Photo: © Agfa

Fig. 11-24
Agfa ChromaPress is a complete digital color printing system, based on
the Xeikon engine.

Agfa ChromaPress

Agfa has taken the Xeikon engine and combined it with a powerful
front end to create the ChromaPress system, a complete computer-
to-paper system for short-run, on-demand color printing.

Jobs to be printed are fed (across a network) to a press server, where
they are prepared for ripping. The server automatically imposes
(assembles) multi-page documents and adjusts for page counts,
formats, and trim sizes without the need for conventional film
stripping. The server also provides system management functions
such as job tracking, print queue management, and print engine
status and control.

Input to ChromaPress is via PostScript or Agfa's ChromaPost
workflow management module, part of a series of extensions to

Fig. 11-25
Digital proofs aren't ready to eliminate conventional film proofs, but
they can save time and money during the design and layout stages.

PostScript that include OPI comments (for automatic picture
replacement) and ColorTags (for color management). In this sense,
ChromaPress builds upon the basic Xeikon marking engine by
integrating important color matching and image file management
functions.

The ChromaPress system includes an Agfa-developed PostScript
RIP running the AgfaScript interpreter, which is based on a multi-
processor, multi-tasking hardware design. One unusual characteristic
of the RIP is that it supports RGB to CMYK conversion, eliminating
the need to color separate image files. Rasterized jobs are sent to the
print unit over a dedicated high-speed interface.

Digital proofs

What is a proof? Until the arrival of desktop color, the word "proof" meant a film proof, made from the same film used to make the plates with which the job was going to be printed. Today, however, some desktop publishers consider a print from a cheap thermal wax printer to be a "proof" of how the final printed piece is expected to look.

Whether we like it or not, digital proofs created directly from Macintosh and Windows-based computers are here to stay. In fact, any digital color printer can be used as a proofing device, though there can be substantial variations in quality between different kinds of printers. Direct digital color proofs (DDCPs) have already become an important part of the design and approval process, and are moving ever deeper into actual print production.

In both the design and print production communities, digital proofs present a challenge and an opportunity. The challenge is in learning to interpret them properly, especially with cheap pre-proofs from thermal wax printers or intermediate proofs produced on dye sublimation printers, rather than with contract digital proofs created on more expensive ink jet or electrophotographic printers.

The opportunity comes from the fact that digital proofs allow you to create working composites, or *comps,* prior to plotting film, which results in significant savings, especially if you end up making changes to the job prior to going on press. After all, if reviewing a film proof leads you to decide to make changes, you end up throwing away both the proof and four pieces of film. With digital proofing, you still toss away the proof, but no film is produced until you're confident (based on the digital proof) that everything looks right.

Before you go shopping for a printer to be used for creating color proofs, there are many factors to consider, including the quality and color fidelity of the output, the type of paper or other media supported, the printer's original cost and the per-page cost, and the printer's support for color calibration.

Limitations of digital proofs

Regardless of the type of digital proof, they have many potential pitfalls you should be aware of when making decisions about color. Most of these problems are tied to the fact that final film is produced after the digital proof is made, which means the film can contain many defects not visible on the proof.

For instance, because the raster image processor (RIP) used to create the film is usually different than that used to create the proof, the screen angles, screen frequencies, and dot shape can vary between film and proof, which may result in color shifts, moiré patterns, and other unpleasant effects on the printed page. Remember, a RIP is simply hardware or software that converts PostScript lines, curves, and images into bitmaps, or raster patterns, at the resolution appropriate to a specific film recorder.

The imagesetter and film processor are other potential trouble spots. If the film cassette runs out after imaging three of the four film separations, and the film in the new cassette stretches slightly as it's loaded, one piece of film will be out of register. Or if the person operating the photo processor decides to replenish the developer in the middle of a set of separations, one piece of film will have the wrong dot density. Also, there are many ways one or more of the film separations can be damaged or mishandled, such as by scratches or exposure to heat.

Because of these limitations, many publishers are successfully using digital proofs throughout the design and approval stages, then having a conventional film proof made before going on press. Although digital proofing technology is maturing, many commercial printers continue to insist on a film proof before putting a job on press. Even when the client does not require a film proof, savvy printers will include the cost of one in their quote, just to insure against the horrendous expense of re-running a botched job.

Where's the dot?

There's one other problem with most digital proofing methods, at least from the commercial printer's point of view: they do not contain halftone dots. With the exception of the latest (and most expensive) digital proofers, such as the Kodak Approval and 3M Digital Matchprint systems, most digital proofers, such as dye sublimation printers, create continuous tone output.

The results may look good, but are of little use to the press operator, who makes assessments of quality not on subjective grounds but on how closely the halftone dots on the press sheet match those on the proof.

Digital Matchprint and Approval are the first digital proofers to solve this problem, by creating color prints with the same halftone dot structure found on the film (and press sheet). They also have the advantage of being able to print on whatever stock will ultimately be use in the actual printing.

Despite the limitations of digital proofing, it seems clear that it will become increasingly popular over the next few years, and that, in some applications, it will eliminate the need for film proofs. Yes, there will always be ways for things to go wrong between the digital proof and the printed sheet, but for many publishers the savings in time and money will be worth the risk.

Output Service Providers

"When I choose a color, it is not because of any scientific theory.
It comes from observation, from feeling, from the
innermost nature of the experience in question."

Henri Matisse

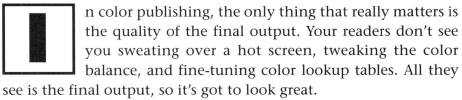n color publishing, the only thing that really matters is the quality of the final output. Your readers don't see you sweating over a hot screen, tweaking the color balance, and fine-tuning color lookup tables. All they see is the final output, so it's got to look great.

A few color publishers create short runs of their final printed pages through high-speed color copiers, but most continue to rely on the traditional printing process. With the exception of the nascent direct-to-plate and direct-to-press technologies previously described, commercial printing requires plates, and before you can make plates you need film. This is where output service providers fit in: their job is to take your electronic files and turn them into plate-ready film.

Although it is becoming increasingly difficult to tell them apart, there are two main types of service providers: conventional color trade shops and PostScript service bureaus. Color trade shops have been making film since the inception of full-color printing a century ago and, in order to remain competitive, virtually all have now added PostScript capabilities. Typically, trade shops have complete proprietary high-end prepress systems and provide scanning, color correction, film output, and proofing services, whereas many service bureaus just provide film output.

Service bureaus are an essential part of desktop publishing, specializing in high-resolution output from such popular Macintosh and Windows-based applications programs as PageMaker, QuarkXPress, FreeHand, Illustrator, CorelDRAW, Photoshop, and PhotoStyler. Some provide only film and paper output from imagesetters, while others sell color pre-proofs made from thermal-wax, dye sublimation or other digital printers, plus such related services as scanning, file conversion, and page layout.

An increasing number of service bureaus now provide color scanning, either with desktop flatbed or desktop drum scanners. A small percentage have even purchased traditional high-end drum scanners and connected them directly to desktop computers in order to get the best of both worlds.

All service bureaus and color trade shops have at least one PostScript imagesetter—a high-resolution laser printer that translates electronic files onto paper "camera-ready" pages or directly onto film. For black-and-white publishing, the imagesetter creates a single piece of film or paper per page. For publishing with spot color, it produces one piece of film or paper for each color, while for process-color publishing it produces four pieces of film per page.

Fig. 12-1
Service bureaus and color trade shops are usually packed with expensive hardware, from monitors and workstations to scanners and imagesetters.

Photo: © Scitex

An imagesetter is an expensive piece of equipment, typically $50,000 to $200,000. Even publishers who pay someone else to output film for them should still pay attention to imagesetter technology, because it is an essential component of color quality. The information in this chapter will make you a more informed consumer of output services, and help you anticipate potential technical and communications problems.

Shake-out in the prepress industry

Despite the fact that the desktop output industry is less than ten years old, it is already in the throes of an economic and technological shake-out. If you have PostScript files you want output to film, there are now three different kinds of companies who want your business: service bureaus, color trade shops, and commercial printers.

Bad news for service bureaus

This shake-out does not bode well for the service bureau industry. As bureaus have become more common, competition has increased to the point where many now sell film output at prices that provide very little margin for profit, or room for error.

In most large North American cities, for example, you can get letter-sized pages output to film for less than $10 each, sometimes for $5 or less. This means that a complete set of film separations

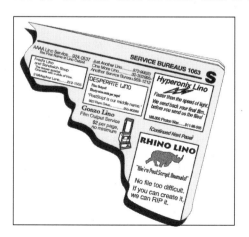

Fig. 12-2
The explosion in PostScript service bureaus has led to vicious competition, with some bureaus providing film output for less than $5 per page.

costs $20 or less, compared to the $100 or more you would pay at a traditional color trade shop. Naturally, this has forced some bureaus out of business, while others have found specialized niches.

Some bureaus compete successfully on price, but that strategy requires them to output tons of film on very thin margins. Others have settled on a value-added strategy: they charge considerably higher rates but provide many additional services, such as PostScript error detection and correction, cleaning up typography, building traps (chokes and spreads), and handling page imposition.

For some service bureau owners, color is a great opportunity. It's bringing a broader range of customers to desktop publishing, often willing to pay a premium price for color. Many new services can be marketed alongside color desktop publishing, including film, slide, and paper output, color copies, design, training, and consulting.

Bad news for trade shops

Many traditional color trade shops are just now learning how to compete against the emergence of desktop color service bureaus; the color houses have different origins, work with different technologies, and, in the past, have always dealt with customers who were printers and typesetters, not independent desktop publishers.

On the other hand, trade shops possess crucial color skills and often have the capital to properly implement desktop color systems. A Macintosh-based color prepress system, complete with imagesetter and digital proofer, might cost $200,000 or more, which seems quite expensive to most computer users, but sounds like a real bargain to a color trade shop planning to use it instead of a high-end color prepress machine costing well over $1-million.

The first barrier most trade shop personnel must overcome is the lack of computer skills. For many years, the prepress craft was seen as just that—a craft. The only computers to be found in many color trade shops were in the accounting department. This is changing, but not fast enough. To survive and thrive in the world of desktop color, a trade shop must know a lot more than its customers about computerized prepress.

Trade shops that resist the conversion from manual to electronic stripping in order to protect their employees' jobs are doing them a disservice. Soon there will be almost no manual prepress jobs left, and all the good electronic prepress positions will have been taken by people who have been retrained to work with computers.

Another potential pitfall for color trade shops is failing to understand the new dynamics of market segmentation. The emergence of high-quality desktop color systems has forever changed the economics of the prepress business and made it much easier for new competitors to enter the market. Many of these new competitors have lower overhead costs, so they can "skim" the market, going after only the price-sensitive jobs that do not require the extreme productivity or quality of high-end systems. For years, these jobs have been the bread and butter for many existing color trade shops, who will now have to migrate to niche markets willing to pay extra for the added value available only from high-end systems.

Bad news for commercial printers

Many factors now are reshaping the printing industry, including desktop prepress and production, the transformation of four-color process printing into a commodity, and the gradual transition to on-demand printing and, ultimately, to electronic delivery of information.

I am convinced that, in the next few years, the printing industry will swallow large parts of the prepress industry. I'm not suggesting that the typical corner service bureau or even the mid-sized color trade shop is about to become extinct, but they are heading to the endangered species list. Within the next three years, virtually every commercial printer in North America will be able to accept all kinds of publications in electronic form, perform the necessary prepress operations, and deliver finished printed pieces to the customer. They'll need to offer such services, just to survive.

From the customer's point of view, the driving force behind this transition is convenience (high quality, low prices, and quick turnaround are assumed). Most customers want to hand over a disk, cartridge or tape containing all their files and get back completely finished printed materials. This is where the commercial printers have a long-term advantage.

Consider the costs of getting started in the service bureau, color trade shop or commercial printing business. You don't need much equipment to get started in a service bureau business—often just an imagesetter, photo processor, densitometer, and a few Macs and PCs. In many cases, the total start-up costs could be $150,000 or less, which explains the incredible number of new companies in the industry, and the recent wave of intense competition and price-cutting.

By contrast, most high-end color trade shops have spent $2-million or more on equipment, albeit at a time when desktop color prepress was not a viable alternative. Although the high-end vendors continue to sell their costly scanners, film recorders, retouching/layout stations, and other products, such equipment is being bought primarily by companies that already have a substantial investment in high-end systems. In other words, today, as desktop tools are poised to take over the field, nobody is starting a color trade shop built around high-end proprietary hardware and software.

To put the cost issue in a broader perspective, however, a typical medium-sized commercial printer has invested $5-million or more in presses, plate-makers, binding machines, and other equipment. Unlike high-end electronic prepress systems, which are rapidly losing value because of the desktop prepress revolution, most printing presses continue to be amortized over a decade or more.

In other words, an imagesetter represents a large proportion of the start-up costs for most service bureaus, is a medium-sized cost for most trade shops, but is a negligible cost for most commercial printers. Given these factors, and demands from customers for one-stop convenience, it seems likely that during the next few years a significant portion of the market for output services will shift from stand-alone service bureaus to value-added commercial printers.

Lest the above analysis give printers too rosy a view of the future, consider some of the issues the printing industry will have to confront during the next few years:

- High-speed digital color printers: By 1997 many large offices will contain a networked digital printing press (and bindery) capable of outputting a one-of-a-kind full-color 50-page double-sided document every 60 seconds.
- Environmental legislation: The number and complexity of environmental regulations in the printing industry is about to go stratospheric, and with it the costs of compliance.
- Electronic delivery: Eventually, digital information has to be delivered digitally and printed locally on demand, if at all, so it's time to expand our idea of "document" to include things that never appear on paper, and are never the same twice.

Service bureau relationships

One of the main trends in the transition from traditional publishing to the desktop has been that designers have been forced to accept ever-increasing responsibility for the production process. Only a few years ago, this would have been unthinkable: the designer was responsible only for the *aesthetic* of the piece, and was expected to hand art boards over to graphic arts professionals, who would then assume total responsibility for shepherding the job through the prepress and printing process.

Now the writer, illustrator, designer, scanner operator and layout artist may well be the same person, who turns the work over to a service bureau only at the film separation stage, then hands the film to a commercial printer to litho thousands of copies. Therefore, it's essential designers understand and accept some responsibility for what happens at the service bureau.

When the client receives a printed piece that looks like garbage, the last thing they want is to be stuck in the middle of an argument between the designer and service bureau about who's responsible. In effect, designers working with computers must accept responsibility, not just for aesthetics, but for pragmatic aspects of print production, such as color trapping.

The pendulum has swung too far. Designers are paid to create effective visual communications, not to figure out how to construct chokes and spreads. Print production is a complex field, best left to the experts in the color trade shops and print shops. Naturally, there are some highly skilled desktop "super-designers" who insist on doing everything themselves, from scanning to page layout through to trapping, imposition, and color separations. However, for most designers, it's time the pendulum swung back so they can get on with the job of innovating new forms of visual expression.

Selecting a service bureau

Many service bureaus are firmly rooted in the tradition of black-and-white publishing, with little if any experience in color prepress, though they may "forget" to tell you that. Other service bureaus started as offshoots of traditional trade shops, and have developed extensive skills in both color prepress and imagesetting.

A good service bureau must be competent in many different areas. Here is a shopping list to review if you're contracting work to a service bureau, and a quality checklist if you're operating a service bureau.

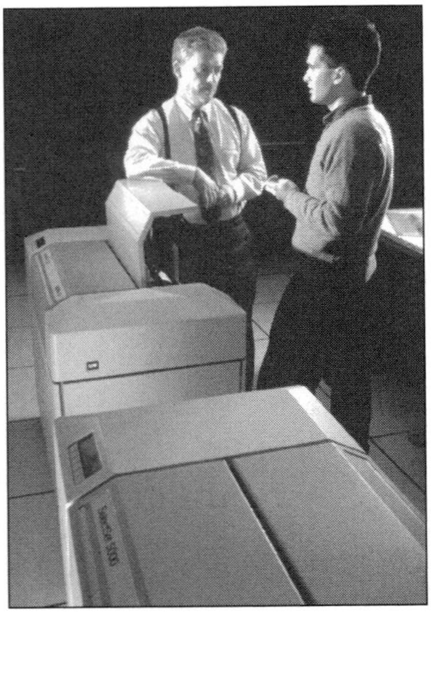

Fig. 12-3
The communication skills of the people working in a service bureau are every bit as important as their technical skills.

Photo: © Agfa

Communication: Communication is the single most important issue when working with a service bureau—communication between people, not just between computers and peripherals. Over and over again, knowledgeable users emphasize that, when color is involved, it's particularly important that the service bureau understand each job well enough to be able to anticipate potential breakdowns before they occur. When any aspect of a job is not completely understood, the service bureau personnel must be able to explain the problem clearly and communicate possible courses of action, potential advantages, and drawbacks. Simple things, like answering phone messages promptly and delivering the finished product on time, are an important aspect of this communications process.

Output quality: The precision and repeatability of halftone dots in the film separations will have a significant impact on the overall quality and color fidelity of your publications. Some aspects of halftone quality can be gauged with a densitometer and a proof, but the real test occurs when the plates are on the press. After running a handful of desktop color jobs through the service bureau and having them printed, you will get a better sense of where your negative film stands in terms of halftone quality. For quality color separations, up-to-date hardware is essential, especially the imagesetter and RIP. If you have a large number of pages to separate, look for a service bureau that has more than one imagesetter, and works multiple shifts.

Technicians: A crucial but often overlooked factor in your success is the skill of the operator behind the imagesetter, the person who ensures that all controls are properly set, and that established procedures for maximizing quality are being followed to the letter. Although many service bureau personnel are self-taught, you are usually better off with someone with an in-depth knowledge of photo-chemistry, combined with at least three years of hands-on desktop computer experience.

Applications experience: If service bureau personnel are really knowledgeable about the specific applications programs you are using, such as PageMaker or QuarkXPress, you can send them the native applications files, rather than the PostScript files output from your application. If there is a particular graphic preventing the job from imaging, the service bureau technician will be able to go into your application and correct or remove the problem, allowing the rest of the job to be processed properly. This would be impossible, or at best very difficult, if they had only the PostScript file. Experience with the appropriate *platform* is also essential: many service bureau personnel are very skilled with the Macintosh but know little or nothing about Windows-based color publishing.

Problem-solving ability: Pages that, in theory, should output perfectly are often difficult or impossible in practice. The expert service bureau technician should have a diverse repertoire of tricks for coaxing difficult pages to output, including hacking some PostScript code where necessary. Solving PostScript errors requires perseverance and ingenuity, because imagesetting is a relatively new field, and there are countless variables to be considered.

Price and service equation: This is listed last because it is very difficult to correlate the price paid with the quality of the separations or the service. The successful service bureau owner must charge for the use of all that expensive equipment, while providing value-added services that, in some measure, compete against the corner bit-buckets offering imagesetter pages at fifty cents apiece.

How do you find the bureau that best provides the kinds of services you require? One way is to look through the ads that appear near the back of each issue of the leading electronic publishing magazines, including Publish, Pre, Graphic Arts Monthly, Graphic Monthly, and others.

For a list of its members throughout North America, contact the Association of Imaging Service Bureaus (AISB) at 919-854-5697. To find bureaus that have demonstrated some proficiency in outputting PageMaker and FreeHand files, contact those that belong to the Adobe Imaging Service Bureau program. The Adobe service bureau list is available from Adobe Customer Support. Corel and Quark also have authorized service bureau programs.

Fig. 12-4
When sending a job to a service provider for output, you'll need to fill in a form full of questions about your files, fonts, and requirements.

Working together

The word "partnership" is overused in business these days, but it couldn't be more appropriate for describing the relationship between a service bureau and its customers. Each side has rights and responsibilities, and to ensure problem-free service, it's important that you, as customer, include a detailed order form with each job.

At a minimum, the order form should include the following information:

- your name, company name, telephone and facsimile numbers (and, where necessary, pager and cellular phone numbers);

- the film specs, including line screen, screen angles, and crops (the North American standard is film that is right-reading, emulsion down—but check with your commercial printer before specifying film requirements);

- the names of all fonts, placed EPS and TIFF files, and any other files required for output;

- whether files are in their native file formats or written to disk as PostScript (if sending native files, first make sure your bureau has exactly the same version of any application programs you've used);

- when the output is required (most service bureaus can provide immediate rush service, but you should expect to pay extra for the privilege);
- the name and telephone number of the printer you will be using, plus information about any unusual aspects of the job.

Once you've selected a service bureau, sit down and talk with people there about your expectations, project specifications, timelines, budget, and other details. Don't be afraid to ask about their experience or recommendations in any aspect of the job. If they use any terms that you don't completely understand, ask for clarification. Once you've found a bureau you trust, set up an account with them, to get better service, better pricing, and the convenience of having them courier film and proofs directly to your print shop.

According to service bureau operators, designers new to color work often have unrealistic expectations about how long things take, or how many details must be covered in producing high-quality separations. To keep your friendly neighborhood imagesetter operator happy, do not, for example:

- expect a perfect match between your monitor and the proof;
- plead with them to print your 75Mb file in five minutes;
- insist that colors printed using four-color process exactly match PANTONE MATCHING SYSTEM spot colors;
- rely on the service bureau to discover overlooked parameters, such as missing fonts and image files;
- send extremely complex files without printing a low-resolution black-and-white proof, then disclaim responsibility for wasting hours of their time and film.

Wherever possible, involve your service bureau operator as early as possible in the creative process, to avoid building production constraints into the graphic design. In drawing programs, for instance, the curve flatness settings and the use of grouping, layers, and other features can dramatically increase the time it takes for a page to output. Other things to watch for include rotated pattern fills, EPS files embedded within other EPS files, and drawings containing a large number of blends. In some cases, a small change to the drawing's structure will not be visible to the reader, but will reduce the print time from hours to minutes.

File transfer issues

To output your job, the service provider needs your files. There are two distinct problems that must be resolved: the format of the data and the physical media on which the files are transferred.

There are two ways of sending desktop publications to an output provider: as PostScript files printed to disk, and as native application files (those created directly by the applications program). The advantage of sending PostScript files is that it works cross-platform, and the service provider need not have the applications program used to create the document—they can download the PostScript data directly to the imagesetter. The advantage of sending native application files is that it saves the user one step, because each file doesn't have to be written to disk as PostScript. This also makes it possible for the service provider to make any minor changes to the file needed to make it run properly (as long as they have the correct version of the applications program).

Some service providers actively discourage clients from submitting native application files, because it takes longer to open the application and start the file printing. However, if you have a lot of files to be output, it could take hours of your time to write them all to disk as PostScript. Remember, the service provider exists to provide *service*. If it won't accept your application files and you don't want to have to create PostScript print files, start shopping for a new service provider. Don't be surprised, however, if service bureaus charge $50 or so per hour for writing your application files to disk.

Be aware that there are potential problems in sending native application files, and these should be discussed with your service provider prior to sending them. For instance, there are many possible differences between your system and the service bureau's in such areas as font versions, kerning and tracking controls, trapping settings, and halftone screen values, among others. Another factor to consider is whether you want the staff at the service bureau, however well intentioned, monkeying around with your precious files.

One other note: when you print the PostScript to disk, be sure to include any downloadable fonts. Doing so will increase the size of the file, but removes any potential incompatibilities that occur when you and your service bureau have different fonts (or different versions of the same fonts). This is probably a technical violation of the license agreement that came with your fonts: someone at the service bureau could poke around in the PostScript code and use a utility program to retrieve those fonts and convert them into usable form. In real life, however, nobody has time for such shenanigans. Furthermore, including the fonts in a PostScript dump is better than the alternative—providing the service bureau with the actual PostScript fonts.

Files can be transferred on various kinds of disks and tapes, or transmitted via modem. However, color drawings can be a few megabytes in size, while color image files can be many times larger still, so you must pay close attention to the capacity of your disks or tapes, and the compression and decompression of files.

In many cases, individual color graphics or spot-color page layouts will fit on a floppy diskette, so they can be easily copied and delivered to the service provider. The use of such compression programs as StuffIt (Macintosh) and PKZIP (IBM-compatible), further extend the capacity of floppies, so that an 800Kb disk will store 2Mb or more of data. Naturally, the service bureau needs the appropriate decompression program to open the files. Furthermore, these programs do not provide sufficient compression for working with large image files.

The removable 44Mb and 88Mb hard disk cartridges made by SyQuest have become a standard for transporting large image files from desktop to service bureau: virtually every service bureau in North America now supports them. Magneto-optical drives have greater storage capacity (they hold approximately 650Mb to 1.3Gb each), but are not quite as widely used, so make sure your intended service provider has the appropriate drive unit before sending optical cartridges.

Portable external hard disk units are another way to get higher capacities while getting around the device-dependency of removable cartridges. Available in capacities of 300Mb, 600Mb, and up, they cost from $500 to $1,500 and are well suited to transporting color images. They are much bulkier than cartridges, however, because they contain the entire drive mechanism and power supply. Portable drives connect to your Mac or PC through a SCSI port, which provides a measure of device independence in moving data from the desktop to the service bureau. Never cart around your original data files: a portable hard disk should contain only a copy of data from your main hard disk, plus any required system files.

Although it's impractical to transmit large image files by modem, telecommunications can be a significant advantage in moving some files from designers to service bureaus, especially such small ones as missing fonts. As communications speeds increase and image files shrink through compression, many color publishers are becoming more comfortable with using modems as a medium for exchanging data with service providers.

Meanwhile, improved modems and error-correcting circuitry are increasing the speed of file transfers over ordinary telephone lines. Before the end of this decade, the widespread use of Integrated Systems Digital Networks (ISDN) and other high-capacity connectivity methods will provide publishers with a data superhighway with sufficient bandwidth to handle large image files.

Service bureau horror stories

At most service bureaus, between 5% and 10% of jobs arrive incomplete, usually as a result of missing fonts or graphic files. Technicians will sometimes spot the problem before the job is run, otherwise the first indication of trouble comes when somebody notices they have a few dozen pieces of film with type set in Courier.

If a job won't output on a given imagesetter, don't blame the service provider personnel, even if you are subsequently able to get the file to print at a different service bureau. There are some jobs that are destined not to print, for reasons unknown to mere mortals. Any

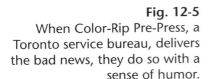

Fig. 12-5
When Color-Rip Pre-Press, a
Toronto service bureau, delivers
the bad news, they do so with a
sense of humor.

number of factors, individually or in combination, can prevent a complex page from imaging properly, or at all.

Based on conversations with many service bureau operators, the most frequently cited reasons for a job not printing are:

*   weird files: designers are free to use applications programs to construct whatever kinds of graphics and pages they want, even if they might be particularly difficult for PostScript to image;

*   bugs in the imagesetter's PostScript interpreter (the RIP);

*   exceeding device limits with an overly complex file or graphic, such as a page layout file containing numerous EPS graphics, or EPS files embedded within other EPS files;

*   insufficient memory (RAM) in the RIP to store all downloaded fonts and prep files, or insufficient virtual memory to handle complex graphics;

*   bugs in the graphics, imaging or page layout programs used to create the file;

*   device-dependent code (not conforming to the PostScript standard), used intentionally by some applications programs for image scaling and rotation, or for custom screens or gray response curves.

There are countless things that can go wrong in outputting PostScript files, and every service bureau owner has a collection of disaster stories of jobs doomed to fail, because of technical snafus, user error or both.

Many disasters involve files so complex they cause the RIP to crash. There are many ways to create such files (Hey, kids, don't try this at home):

- Trace a complex illustration with a thick pencil, scan it, then use the auto-trace feature in your drawing program to convert the original bitmap into a vector file. If you set the trace parameters for maximum sensitivity, you can create a file with thousands of control points (where only a few dozen are necessary). This file will take forever to be processed by the RIP (if it can be processed at all).

- Create a really complex pattern in your drawing program, then shrink it to microscopic size and use it as a fill pattern inside a masked object. To really slow down the RIP, create a few dozen of these, and use them all on the same page.

- Place ten overlapping copies of the same large TIFF file on a single page, cropping each differently. To a PostScript RIP, the fact that most of each image has been cropped out is irrelevant: it still needs to interpret the value of each pixel, which means interpreting the images hidden by the rest of the page.

Another way to overload the RIP is to insist on outputting a complex eight-page flat as a single piece of film, rather than splitting it into single pages that could be assembled by a film stripper. Instead of building a huge file that is too complex to image, make use of the film stripper's skill.

Wherever possible, do little or no image cropping or resizing in your page layout program. Performing these operations in an imaging program, prior to importing the picture into a page layout, can significantly reduce the size and complexity of your PostScript files. In draw programs, simplify all unnecessary detail, reducing graphics elements to the smallest number of points required to maintain the desired level of quality.

Think like a RIP

In a good trade shop or service bureau, the technicians know many tricks that will make it possible to output difficult jobs, their solutions often based on the error messages generated by the PostScript interpreter. These messages are returned by the printer on the communications channel where the program originated. This is fine for a stand-alone user, but causes big problems on a network. If an application has sent its stuff and then signed off, any subsequent error in processing will not be reported back to the application. The user is left wondering what happened.

Many serious color service providers use an error reporter to help track down problems that are slowing or stopping a file from imaging. Utilities such as the PostScript Error Reporter from PinPoint and the Advanced PostScript Error Handler from Systems of Merritt, provide a detailed interpretation of the error messages, with some suggestions for correcting the identified problem. You'll also find that every professional output provider will have a well-thumbed copy of Adobe's *PostScript Language Reference Manual*, the definitive guide to the PostScript language.

Many service providers, and the desktop publishers who keep them busy, also use a handy utility called LaserCheck (also from Systems of Merritt), which lets a low-res PostScript desktop laser printer mimic an imagesetter, enabling you to proof a file before committing it to film. LaserCheck works by intercepting the low-level PostScript page set-up commands, then scaling the image to fit on the physical page used by the laser printer. Important job information is printed around the edge, including data on the fonts used, allocations of memory and processor time, and device parameters.

These clues are often useful for finding out why a given file may not print properly (or at all). Indeed, the use of a utility like LaserCheck is highly recommended for novice color publishers, to minimize the likelihood of surprises when generating your first color separations. Even experienced color publishers may find it cost-effective to use LaserCheck as a proof before going to the imagesetter.

There are many kinds of problems a utility like LaserCheck can't solve, including those caused by files containing exceptionally complex PostScript objects. A number of vendors now are researching *pre-flight* software that would test all incoming PostScript jobs to flag potential problems prior to output. The software would use "expert systems" technology to identify sections of code identified as likely sources of errors that might slow or hang an imagesetter. Pre-flight software could help avoid the waste of costly materials, and catch problems that might otherwise crash the imagesetter.

All PostScript drawing, imaging, and page layout programs give you the ability to create jobs so complex they can never be printed. The key to designing files that will output easily is to *think like a RIP*. Every time you construct a graphic or lay out a page, you're actually writing a PostScript program, so keep in mind that it will ultimately have to be interpreted, and make things as simple as possible.

Imagesetter technology

The key piece of equipment for any service provider is an imagesetter: a precision photographic printer that uses a laser (or light-emitting diode) to expose photosensitive paper, film or plate material, which is then processed chemically.

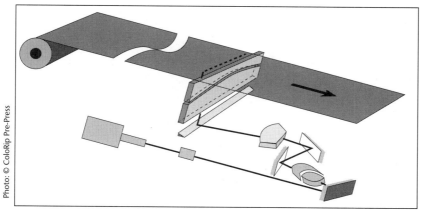

Photo: © ColoRip Pre-Press

Fig. 12-6
First-generation imagesetters were based on a flatbed capstan advance mechanism.

An imagesetter costs between $50,000 and $200,000 and requires a skilled operator, especially for color work. There are some smaller and less expensive imagesetters targeted at design studios, but these lack the precision necessary for producing quality color separations. In describing the workings of imagesetters, we refer to their output as "film" although the output media could well be photographic film, resin-coated (RC) paper or plate material.

An imagesetter must place a tiny spot of light in a specified position, with an accuracy of at least .003 inches, then place another spot just as precisely on the next piece of film. Building an imagesetter is difficult: it must work with great precision, and be fast enough to record many jobs each day.

There are three components to an imagesetter system: the raster image processor (RIP), the imager, and the photo processor. PostScript imagesetters have evolved rapidly during the past ten years.

The first imagesetters used a flatbed imaging system with a capstan (rubber roller) advance mechanism, and were better suited to monochrome and spot color output, rather than process color work.

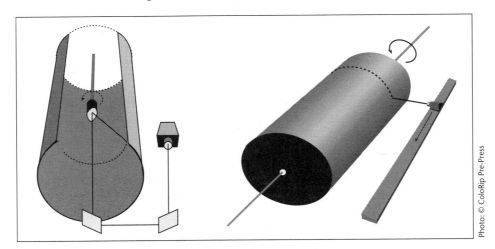

Photo: © ColoRip Pre-Press

Fig. 12-7
The film in a drum imagesetter can either be wrapped around the inside of the drum (left) or along the outside (right).

A major problem was repeatability: because they used imprecise film transport mechanisms, a dot produced on one separation was often displaced slightly from the same dot on another separation.

More advanced imagesetters soon arrived on the market, based on the same kind of drum mechanism used in high-end film recorders. The major advantage of drum-based imagesetters is greater mechanical precision, which ensures that each of the four separation films is in perfect register, with halftone dots in exactly the right size, shape, and location. In addition, many drum imagesetters have adopted the precise punch registration systems used on conventional film recorders.

Photo: © Optronics

Fig. 12-8
A large-format drum imagesetter, such as the Optronics ColorSetter XL, can output an entire flat up to 40-by-50 inches as a single piece of film.

In recent years the size of drum imagesetters has increased to the point where many can now output an entire eight-page flat as a single piece of film. The SPrint 120 from Orbotech, for instance, can output as many as ten complete flats, each 40-by-32 inches, per hour. Meanwhile, as some imagesetters have become larger, others have become smaller and moved to the desktop.

Fig. 12-9
Like everything else, drum imagesetters
are moving to the desktop, such as this
ID36 model from ECRM.

Photo: © ECRM

Some corporate publishers with in-plant print shops now use desktop imagesetters with a maximum film size slightly larger than a tabloid page, which perfectly matches the capability of their small one-color and two-color presses.

We can expect future imagesetters to continue the trend toward better precision, more automatic operation, lower cost, and higher

Fig. 12-10
A raster image
processor, such as this
Linotype-Hell RIP 60,
converts PostScript lines
and curves into bitmaps
at the resolution
appropriate to the
imager.

Photo: © Linotype-Hell

speed. A great deal of research continues to be directed toward "dry" imagesetters that won't require liquid chemical developing; the technology looks promising for some black-and-white applications, but so far the resolution and precision aren't sufficient for color work.

The raster image processor

The raster image processor (RIP) converts the PostScript data from a desktop publishing system (the lines and curves that make up graphics, plus the bitmaps that make up halftones), and renders it as a series of pixels matched to the resolution of the specific imager being used.

Although most early RIPs performed their calculations with specialized chips and circuit boards, most now do all the work in software, and run on standard Macs, PCs, and UNIX-based microcomputers. In recent years, the performance of software RIPs has increased to the point where they have overtaken hardware RIPs as the standard. Software RIPs are also commonly used in slide file recorders, digital proofers, color copiers, and desktop trapping programs.

The RIP begins by breaking the PostScript file into individual objects (a *display list*), which it processes, one by one, until it has built a complete high-resolution bitmap. The RIP then passes the bitmap to the imager, or *marking engine,* which generates the actual spots on the paper or film.

Speed is crucial when outputting color publications, because CMYK separations require the production of four times as many pieces of film as black-and-white. Until recently, the speed of the RIP was the limiting factor in the output system, because RIPs could rarely keep up with the laser imager. But during the past few years, the emergence of much faster RIPs has shifted the bottleneck to the imager, which now often has trouble keeping up with the flow of data from the RIP. Even though some models of imagers are now twice as fast as those of just a year or two ago, they still have not kept pace with the latest high-speed RIPs.

Photo: © Linotype-Hell

Fig. 12-11
The image recorder, such as the Herkules from Linotype-Hell, contains a laser and optical system, which produce dots on photosensitive film or paper.

The laser imager

The laser imager weighs hundreds of pounds and takes up as much space as a medium-sized photocopier. It is connected directly to the RIP and, typically, has a panel display that lets the operator select the desired resolution and other parameters.

One common type of imager uses lenses and mirrors to modulate (turn on and off) a tiny beam of light from a gas laser, thus converting the data into spots exposed onto photosensitive paper or film. Another type of imager uses a simpler laser diode that is electronically modulated. Typically, imagesetters produce a spot between 15 and 50 microns in diameter (a micron is one millionth of a meter). PostScript imagesetters tend to produce digital halftones with a *hard dot* that is crisper and more sharply defined than the *soft dot* characteristic of traditional photographic halftones.

In addition to spot size, the other variables crucial to the performance of the laser imager are accuracy and repeatability. *Accuracy* refers to the imagesetter's ability to place a pixel in precisely the correct location, and is typically plus or minus two microns on an imagesetter designed for color separations. *Repeatability* is a measure of the imager's ability to place a pixel in exactly the same location, time after time, and is typically within 25 microns over the full exposure area of the imager. Repeatability is essential to producing color separations: the halftone dots in the cyan, magenta, yellow, and black films must be accurately positioned with respect to one another; otherwise color shifts will occur on the printed page. Although a number of factors contribute to the accuracy and repeatability of an imagesetter, mechanical design is one of the most important for producing consistently high-quality color separations.

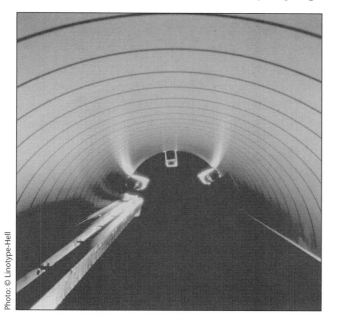

Photo: © Linotype-Hell

Fig. 12-12
This view inside a Linotype-Hell imagesetter shows the laser imager exposing the film wrapped onto the drum.

Imagesetter media (photographic film and paper) are specially designed to be sensitive in the part of the color spectrum emitted by the laser, which varies between manufacturers. There are countless subtle differences in the properties of the leading photographic films, whether from Kodak, 3M, Fuji, Agfa, or other manufacturers. Similarly, there are subtle but important differences in the response curves of the various processing chemicals commonly used. These result in measurable differences in the exposure times required, and in the resulting dot densities. Many service bureaus have eliminated the problem of film and processor variability by standardizing on a single brand.

In most imagesetters, the media are stored in two cartridges: an input cartridge for unexposed media, and a take-up cartridge for media already exposed to the laser beam. After a job has been exposed, the film is cut and the take-up cartridge removed from the imagesetter and inserted into the photo processor. Many imagesetter manufacturers now offer on-line processors that automatically receive exposed film from the imager for processing.

The photo processor

In some service bureaus, the photo processor is treated with disdain, as if film processing has become a no-brainer for even the most simple-minded human or machine. In fact, nothing could be further from the truth—the processor determines dot densities.

Fig. 12-13
A deep-bath photographic processor, such as this Agfa RapiLine unit, is an essential component in the film production process.

Photo: © Agfa

When creating color separation films, a change in dot size of less than 3%—in any one or more of the films—will result in a noticeable reduction in color fidelity. But variations of 5% or more occur routinely in some service bureaus, either because they lack deep-bath chemical processors or because staff don't know how to operate them in a stable and consistent manner.

The photo processor uses a three-stage system. The film is first bathed in developer to darken only those areas of the film exposed to the laser beam. The film then passes through a bath of fixer, which stops the development process, stabilizes the blackened areas, and dissolves unexposed light-sensitive material from the film. Finally, the film is washed with water to remove the final traces of chemicals, and heated to remove moisture. The dried film or paper is then cut into individual pages, either automatically or by the operator.

Desktop imposition

Now that desktop publishing has taken over page production, the next frontier is the use of desktop computers for *imposition*: arranging pages in the proper sequence for printing on the press. Imposition has traditionally been a manual process in which individual pieces of film were precisely taped or *stripped* together on a light table. Electronic imposition software will further reduce the demand for highly skilled (and highly paid) film strippers.

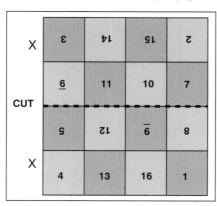

Fig. 12-14
The gripper edge is marked with an X in this typical "work and turn" imposition for a 16-page form with three right-angle folds.

Until the advent of desktop publishing, film strippers performed three main tasks: page assembly, flat assembly, and trapping. Page assembly has long since been taken over completely by PageMaker, QuarkXPress, and Ventura. Desktop imposition and trapping programs are now poised to carry out the rest of the job, automatically trapping finished pages and assembling them into complete *forms*, or *flats*.

Before we delve too deeply into how desktop imposition programs work, let's review the specialized terminology of the film stripper:

- a *signature* is a group of pages printed on the same sheet of paper, which after folding will appear in the correct sequential order and alignment;

- a *flat* (or *form*) is a group of pages that will all be printed on the same plate;

- *creep*, also known as *shingling* or *pushout*, occurs in signatures that are *saddle-stitched* (wire stapled together); as pages are stacked inside one another, rather than on top of one another, those on the inside of the booklet are forced further away from the binding than those on the outside;

- *bottling* is a slight skewing of pages as they are folded, especially apparent on web presses as pages are folded into one another toward the inside corner, with the result that inside pages are not completely vertical;

- a *reader's spread* is a pair of pages positioned across the binding edge, or gutter, from each other after a publication is assembled;

- a *printer's spread* is a pair of pages positioned across the fold from each other on the press sheet;

- a *dummy* (or *imposition chart*) is a sheet of paper folded to show how pages should be positioned on the plate to meet press and bindery requirements.

Photo: © Orbotech

Fig. 12-15
A large imagesetter, such as this Orbotech SPrint 120, can output a fully imposed punch-register flat every four minutes.

Watching a skilled film stripper at work is impressive. Small metal clips are inserted into the punch holes in each piece of film, and pieces of film and *rubylith* (an opaque masking material) fly here and there as the stripper uses a razor-sharp knife (or a computerized ruby cutting machine) to cut each element precisely to size. Little pieces of tape hold the various components together. When all the elements for each flat have been stripped together, it is ready for plate-making, which is typically the responsibility of the print shop.

Putting technical issues aside for a moment, the key question with desktop imposition is responsibility. Until recently, it was not a matter for debate: whether it was a color trade shop or a commercial printer, whoever made the film was responsible for imposing the pages properly. This always required close communication among the client, the company outputting the film, and the printer.

The fact that desktop tools are now capable of complex imposition jobs does not mean that desktop publishers should take over this crucial, and often complex, function. Nor does it eliminate the need for timely communication and coordinated actions among publishers, film providers, and printers. Indeed, it makes them even more essential.

A good rule of thumb for publishers without the time and inclination to become deeply immersed in the printing process is that imposition should take place as close to the final output device as possible. This means that, except for desktop publishers who have their own imagesetter, imposition should remain the responsibility of the output service bureau, color trade shop or commercial printer. The printer should also retain responsibility for imposition in magazine publishing, in which virtually all the ad pages arrive as final film (although this may change in the future as advertisers and agencies begin to provide ads in electronic form).

Fig. 12-16
A large-format plotter, such as the Calcomp ProofMaster, can be used to review a fully imposed flat prior to outputting film.

Photo: © Calcomp

On the other hand, there are many situations in which there are significant benefits in having the person responsible for front-end layout also take responsibility for creating impositions. For instance, this can save a lot of money when publishing books, such as novels, that have simple formatting. Other jobs that can be cost-effectively imposed by their originators include directories, price books, part lists, and other repetitive documents, as well as training manuals and technical specifications, which often run to hundreds or thousands of pages.

The downside of having desktop publishers create their own impositions is that if it isn't done properly, the commercial printer will need to cut apart the film and manually strip the pages together without registration marks, a costly and time-consuming procedure.

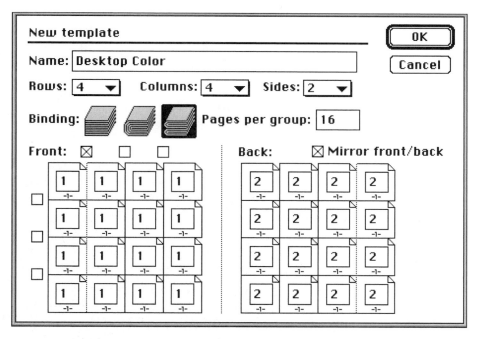

Fig. 12-17
PressWise is a full-function program that provides complete control over all aspects of imposition.

Competition in desktop imposition

Desktop imposition is a relatively new field, with the first programs introduced in 1988, but the field has expanded significantly of late to include at least a dozen competitors. Packages fall into two categories: stand-alone programs, and those that work only as XTensions (to QuarkXPress) or Additions (to PageMaker). They can be further divided into full-function packages (Impostrip, PressWise, Preps, and Island Imposition Publisher), and rudimentary imposition utilities (INposition, and Printer's Spreads).

PressWise, from Aldus, is a full-function Macintosh stand-alone imposition package that works with PageMaker and QuarkXPress files, as well as with any EPS files that conform to Adobe's Document Structuring Conventions. PressWise comes with a variety of common signature formats, and you can create your own. One of its more interesting features is the ability to skip prep and font downloading, saving time when the prep files or fonts are already resident in the RIP. PressWise provides details on every page in an imposition.

PressWise 2.0, which was released in early 1994, supports web-fed and 40-inch sheet-fed presses, up from the 25-inch presses supported in the first version of the program. It can handle up to 64 pages per form, 128 pages per signature, and comes with extensive page positioning controls. It supports automatic configurations for perfect-bound, saddle-stitched, stacked-web, and loose-leaf binding methods, and can open multiple PostScript files at once.

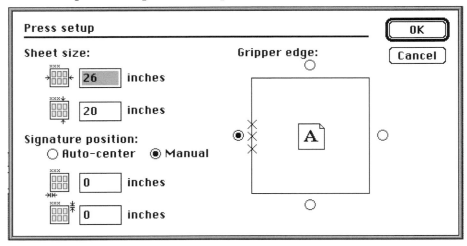

Fig. 12-18
PressWise provides complete control over press parameters, including paper thickness, signature position, sheet size, and gripper edge.

Impostrip, from Ultimate Technographics, was the first desktop imposition program, and is now available in versions for the Macintosh, DOS, Windows, and UNIX-based systems. It is a stand-alone package that works with files that have first been printed to disk. You begin the imposition process by specifying such job parameters as binding style, creep, and the number and size of signature pages. The next step is to specify the parameters for individual signatures, such as the number of pages (a 28-page document, for example, might consist of three eight-page signatures and one of four pages).

Preps, from ScenicSoft, was initially developed for the Windows platform but is now also available for the Macintosh. This full-function program includes advanced features for web printing, such as the ability to select individual webs and create multiple web signatures.

You can place different page sizes within one signature. Preps supports both OPI and DCS protocols, so it will separate color files when it prints the signatures. It includes high-end color features, such as UCR and GCR support, plus the ability to alter the press ink color specifications based on their CIE chromaticity values.

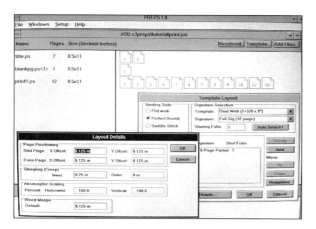

Fig. 12-19
Preps was developed by ScenicSoft for the Microsoft Windows and Macintosh environments, and is available from other value-added integrators such as Intergraph.

Island Imposition Publisher is a stand-alone Macintosh program developed by Farrukh Systems of England and distributed in North America by Island Graphics. As with many of the other imposition programs, Imposition Publisher requires that you print your document to disk as a PostScript file, either as separate pages or as a range of pages. You then tell the program which PostScript files to use in the imposition, and apply one of many built-in signature layouts or create your own.

INposition, from DK&A, is an XTension that lets you define and print impositions directly inside QuarkXPress, without having to first print pages to disk. You begin by setting up a *plate style* by specifying the number of pages per plate, the imposition order, and the locations of press marks, binding, and plate margins. The next step is to define a *publication style*, with the appropriate binding method, paper thickness, and so on. One of the major advantages of INposition is a publication palette that allows you to view a job either as printer's spreads or reader's spreads, which makes it easy to double-check a publication before printing.

In addition to these software programs, there's one other imposition solution that's in a category of its own: Signastation from Linotype-Hell. Signastation runs on an 80486-based computer under the NeXTstep operating system, and consists of four main modules: electronic flat assembly, electronic imposition, automatic film saving, and step-and-repeat.

Like most imposition products, Signastation requires that files first be printed to disk. They are then previewed on screen (using Display PostScript); because all files are ripped to the screen prior to being sent to an imagesetter, the likelihood of error is decreased.

The next step is to select one of the built-in signature templates, or design one from scratch. You can view the resulting signatures as an actual flat or as thumbnails, and each signature can be edited as required. Signastation also includes a film optimization feature designed for large-format imagesetters, which automatically calculates the placement of pages in order to put the maximum number of pages on a single sheet of film.

Fig. 12-20
Signastation is a specialized imposition computer from Linotype-Hell that also includes film optimization and step-and-repeat functions.

Photo: © Linotype-Hell

Color trapping

Color printing is a mechanical process, which means that, by definition, it's imperfect. A modern sheet-fed press can print 8,000 to 12,000 impressions per hour, and a web press can print between 25,000 and 40,000 impressions per hour. As paper moves through the press, ink is applied to it, but the ink isn't always in precisely the right place. One or more inks may appear slightly misaligned—out of *register*—because of problems with film, plates, paper, press or operator. These misalignments can result in tiny background-colored shapes, called *light leaks*, that reduce the overall quality of the printing. In fact, the eye can detect even very small spaces between colors—gaps as small as .002 inches.

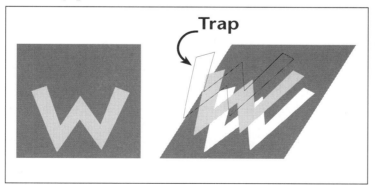

Fig. 12-21
Traps are small areas of overlapping color that compensate for registration errors on press.

For many years, prepress professionals have solved the misregistration problem by building *color traps* into their pages. Trapping lets you compensate for potential gaps by making small adjustments—*spreads* and *chokes*—to color areas on the final film. A spread is created by slightly enlarging a lighter foreground object, a choke by slightly shrinking a lighter background color to create a small overlap.

The size of chokes and spreads is crucial: they must be large enough to compensate for variations on press, but not be so large they form a noticeable outline around objects. Typical sizes for traps range from 0.003 inches (about .25 point) for high-quality printing on coated stock, to 0.05 inches or more for printing on newsprint.

Type of paper	Minimum	Maximum
Sheet-fed offset on coated stock	.1 pt	.3 pt
Sheet-fed offset on uncoated stock	.5 pt	.8 pt
Offset web on newsprint	.4 pt	.7 pt
Flexographic web	.7 pt	5.0 pt
Screen printed T-shirt	1.0 pt	5.0 pt

Fig. 12-22
The optimal trap thickness varies primarily with
the printing method used.

Another important trapping control is *overprinting*. Normally, a foreground color created in a desktop drawing program will automatically *knock out* the color underneath it, leaving a hole the same size and shape as the foreground object. Without knockouts, for example, a red object printed against a blue background would appear purple. But it's the knockouts that force you to use trapping, and all desktop drawing programs allow you to set an object to overprint. If you can design an illustration so that the colors are created through overprinting, you don't need to trap it.

Trapping fundamentals

Although the only way to become really conversant with trapping is through experience and observation, there are a few guidelines worth following:

- The goal behind any trap is to maintain the integrity of the edges being trapped. For the purposes of trapping, the darker color defines the edge of an object.

- When working with spot color inks (either spot-on-spot or spot-on-process), make the trap outline the same color as one of the objects it touches. When working with process color inks only, give the trap a third color that combines those of the touching objects.

- In general, use a .25 point area of overlap. The appropriate amount of overlap will depend on the printing press, paper type, and total ink coverage, so be sure to consult your commercial printer when deciding on trap widths.

- In imaging programs, type is often improved by using *anti-aliasing* to soften the edges where a dark foreground object (such as a character) abuts a lighter background.

- Solid black elements (type and rules) should always overprint; don't produce traps for these. Trapping small serif type is difficult because the trap has to be large enough to avoid gaps, without destroying the shapes of the characters. Because registration is a real problem with thin lines, always use plain overprinting black (no other colors) for them.

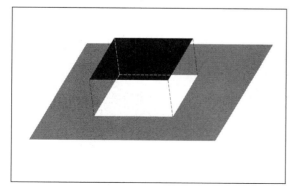

Fig. 12-23
One solution to the trapping problem is to ignore it completely, aligning objects to "kiss fit", and ensuring very tight registration control on press.

Mechanical trapping

Until the 1970s, trapping was a photomechanical process in which a skilled film stripper used a graphic arts camera to selectively expose portions of the film in order to build chokes and spreads. This works well for simple pages, but not for those containing complex artwork created on desktop systems, especially illustrations with small type or gradient fills (blends or vignettes). Indeed, the emergence of desktop drawing programs has made it easy to create artwork that is completely impossible to trap using conventional techniques.

Photomechanical trapping will become rare as desktop trapping programs take over in the next few years, although there will probably always be some jobs that can be done most efficiently using traditional techniques.

Bitmap trapping

Electronic prepress systems make a second approach to trapping possible: a skilled color technician works with images as bitmaps (pixels), and changes the pixel values according to the color printing process and the specific printing conditions for each job.

High-end prepress systems, such as those described in Chapter 10, can be used to produce high-quality color traps, but they require expensive hardware and a highly skilled operator. The prepress operator identifies which areas on a page require trapping, specifies the characteristics of each trap (its location, color, and width), then generates the traps and transfers the page to the next stage of the production process. The traps are constructed at the full resolution of the image, using color lookup tables that have been fine-tuned to produce reliable trap colors.

On desktop computers, Photoshop can be used to construct bitmap traps, but it lacks the color lookup tables of the high-end systems, and cannot handle huge image files productively.

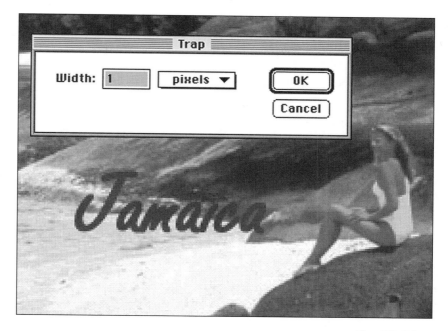

Fig. 12-24
Adobe Photoshop can be used to construct
bitmap traps on the desktop.

One major advantage of trapping on high-end systems is that they usually perform trapping as a background task: after setting the trapping values, the operator is free to work on another job. Another benefit is that desktop designers don't have to worry about how the traps are built, and can focus instead on design issues.

The major limitation of trapping on high-end equipment is that PostScript graphics and page layouts must first be converted into the high-end system's proprietary format. Another potential problem is the expense: most color trade shops charge between $200 and $600 per hour for trapping services, in addition to the cost of film and proofs.

One variation of high-end trapping is the Scitex Full Auto Frame (FAF) trapping program, which is built into some Scitex Dolev imagesetters. FAF rasterizes PostScript files, converts them to Scitex format, and then performs trapping in the RIP before outputting film.

Object trapping

The third main trapping method is called "object-based trapping," and it too requires a very skilled designer and, in many cases, plenty of time. The designer, illustrator or prepress technician opens the original graphics or page layout file, analyzes its contents, and constructs additional strokes, layers, background objects, and overprinting settings. The result is a new file with traps applied as individual objects. Most object trapping is done in Adobe Illustrator, FreeHand or CorelDRAW.

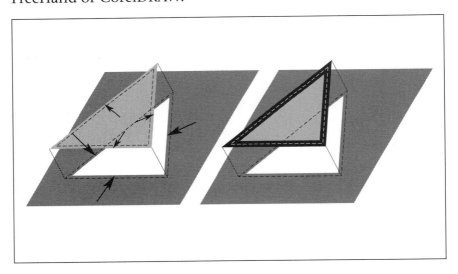

Fig. 12-25
In a conventional trap (left), additional film exposures are used to spread the foreground color and choke the background. In an object-based trap (right), the stroke line overprints.

Object-based trapping can be a very time-consuming procedure and requires a highly skilled technician. Another potential problem is that a change in printing conditions (using a different paper or press, for instance) means adjusting all trap widths to compensate, which can take a great deal of time.

The most essential skill in object trapping is adjusting the stroke (external outline) of an object precisely. In PostScript, the width of the printed stroke is centered on the path, with half the specified width printing inside the path and half printing outside it. The stroke (which can be of a different color than the object) is often specified to overprint, which means that the adjoining color will print under the outside half of the stroke, thereby creating the trap.

The graphics or page layout program must place illustration and type with absolute precision. The ability to work with graphic elements on multiple levels is an important feature, because it allows isolation of traps for easy access and manipulation. You need to be able to specify which color will overprint all others.

Note that overprinting is an important control, even when you're not trapping. For instance, black ink will normally always overprint all others, even though this can cause a color shift where it crosses colored areas. One common solution is to add 20% to 40% cyan to the black, which minimizes the effect. But overprinting must be used judiciously, because it can result in too much ink in a given area.

It is essential to understand ink mixing, because the trap must share the color characteristics of both the object and its background. Mixing the inks properly can be challenging, especially where gradient fills adjoin solid colors or other fill patterns.

A variation on object-based trapping is the "automatic trapping" feature in some desktop programs, such as QuarkXPress. However, there are a number of limitations with this approach; for example, they don't provide any way of trapping an object that abuts more than one color—and today's funky design world is full of graphics with every possible blend of colors. Another problem is that they don't trap EPS graphics placed on the page, which effectively limits their usefulness to the simplest pages.

RIP-based trapping

The migration of trapping to the desktop has forced a re-evaluation of the whole trapping process—not just the technology, but who should be responsible for it. This is one area in which the convergence between design and production has probably gone too far.

Just because a software program includes trapping features doesn't mean you will benefit from using them. Designers are paid to *design*, not to spend hours figuring out how to build chokes and spreads. Except in the case of very simple graphics, trapping should be part of the output process, not of the design process.

The new paradigm in trapping is based on the fact that virtually all graphics, images and page layouts now originate in PostScript form, rather than as mechanical artboards. A software RIP is used to analyze the original EPS file and add traps constructed from discrete PostScript objects.

TrapWise

The first program in this new category of *RIP-based* trapping software is Adobe TrapWise, which has redefined the market for electronic trapping. TrapWise automatically traps any properly constructed EPS file, including those from all major Mac and PC applications, such as Adobe PageMaker and FreeHand, Adobe Illustrator, and QuarkXPress. TrapWise analyzes the file, traps its contents, and creates a new EPS file that includes both the original graphics or pages plus any required traps.

Fig. 12-26
TrapWise includes a job queue that enables you to set the trapping values and other parameters for each job.

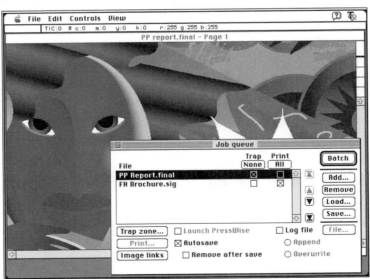

TrapWise uses a four-step process to generate traps:

- ◆ a software-based RIP translates the PostScript file into an intermediate bitmapped file format, at a resolution that matches or exceeds that at which the file will ultimately be output;
- ◆ TrapWise analyzes the bitmap to find edges between adjacent color areas, then compares the ink percentages to determine whether the colors are sufficiently similar to compensate for any misregistrations on press;
- ◆ the program calculates the size, placement, and color of any necessary traps, based on the file contents and parameters specified by the user;
- ◆ TrapWise creates tiny PostScript objects to form the required traps, then writes out a new EPS file that consists of the original EPS instructions plus the new objects.

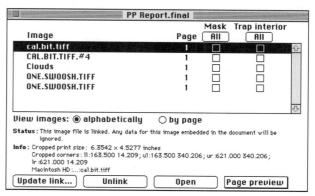

Fig. 12-27
TrapWise provides complete control over all aspects of trapping, and supports automatic linking of image files.

The first version of TrapWise ran only on Windows-based computers, but version 2 runs on the Macintosh. Actually, many prepress operators have found it just as easy (and more economical) to pass Macintosh EPS files across the network to a PC to apply trapping, then shoot the files back to the Mac for imposition, color separation, and film output.

TrapWise 2 adds several new prepress controls, including image trapping, color-separation capabilities, batch processing, and the ability to trap up to 16 colors at once. In addition to single-page EPS files, it will trap multi-page PostScript files that conform to the Adobe Document Structuring Convention.

There are a number of advantages to the approach adopted by TrapWise, especially when contrasted with traditional methods of trapping:

- ◆ TrapWise traps the entire page, including type, ruling lines, imported graphics, and bitmapped images;
- ◆ it fits into the electronic publishing workflow, by importing EPS files from all desktop applications, then exporting trapped EPS files that can continue on in the prepress production cycle, either as complete pages or as pre-trapped elements that can be placed in a PageMaker or QuarkXPress document;
- ◆ it handles complex color relationships everywhere on the page, no matter how many objects, blends, imported images or thin elements are on the page—it can even spread and choke around the same object if necessary;
- ◆ it's fast: most pages can be trapped in ten minutes or less, and even very complex pages containing small type and fine lines can be trapped in 20 minutes.

TrapWise costs $4,995, and many prepress houses have found they can more than cost-justify both the program and the hardware on which it runs, based on the time and money saved in trapping just a few complex jobs.

IslandTrapper

IslandTrapper is a Macintosh-based trapping program from Island Graphics, a subsidiary of Dainippon Screen. The program traps EPS files created in any desktop publishing package, including QuarkXPress, PageMaker, Adobe Illustrator, and FreeHand. It can trap all the elements on the page, including text, tints, images, and vignettes, even embedded EPS graphics. It is similar to Adobe TrapWise in that its workflow is also based on EPS-in, EPS-out.

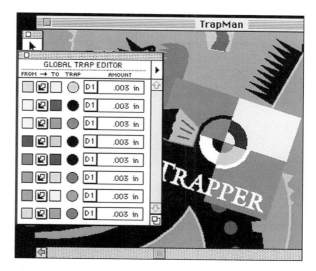

Fig. 12-28
IslandTrapper provides global trapping controls for EPS files, but
includes an expert mode that allows you to manually build custom
chokes and spreads.

IslandTrapper can trap multiple overlapping or partially overlapping objects, and you can set trapping values globally or locally. It also features an expert mode, so you can select objects and override the default values with manual chokes and spreads.

Finally, there's always one other way to handle trapping if you can't be bothered doing it yourself: pay a commercial printer to set the traps conventionally, starting with your regular graphics or page layout files. Because you will have turned knockouts off, be sure to provide the printer with a color comp, so the press operator knows what the colors are supposed to look like.

Without in any way minimizing the value of desktop publishing, it is true that—at least for the time being—trapping is one area in which it may be both cheaper and easier to contract out than do it yourself.

Color, creativity, and the future

Today we are in the early stages of a transformation that will surely sweep aside many of the old tools and techniques for color production, and replace them with new, faster, better tools. The pace of technological change in this field will be rapid throughout the 1990s.

We are now near the end of the adventure that began way back in Chapter 1 with fundamental distinctions of the RGB and CMYK color models. We have come a long way, and if you have followed closely the progression from basic concepts to advanced techniques, you have a great deal of new knowledge that will improve the efficiency and quality of all your color publishing activities. Other than my congratulations for your commitment to learning, the reward for your dedication is new-found competence in desktop color.

As van Gogh said, color, of itself, really does express something. As color production migrates to the desktop, it enriches your ability to take hold of new technology and use it to express the vibrancy and color of your unique, creative impulses—in the most satisfying sense, to color your world.

Vendors

Adobe Systems Corp.
1585 Charleston Road
P.O. Box 7900
Mountain View, CA
94039-7900
phone 415-961-4400

Agfa Division, Miles Inc.
100 Challenger Road
Ridgefield Park, NJ
07660
phone 201-440-0111
fax 201-440-8187

Agfa Matrix Division
1 Ramland Road
Orangeburg, NY
10962
phone 914-365-0190
fax 914-359-3201

Aldus Corp.
411 First Avenue South
Seattle, WA
98104-2871
phone 206-622-5500
fax 206-343-4240

Altamira Software
150 Shoreline Highway, #B-27
Mill Valley, CA
94941
phone 415-332-5801

Apple Computer Inc.
20525 Mariani Avenue
Cupertino, CA
95041
phone 408-996-1010

Ares Software Corp.
565 Pilgrim Drive, Suite A
Foster City, CA
94404
phone 415-578-9090
fax 415-378-8999

ATI Technologies
3761 Victoria Park Avenue
Scarborough, Ontario
Canada M1W 3S2
phone 416-756-0718
fax 416-756-0720

Barco Graphics Inc.
721 Crossroads Court
Vandalia, OH
45377
phone 513-454-1721
fax 513-454-1522

Calcomp Inc.
2411 West La Palma Avenue
Anaheim, CA
92801
phone 714-821-2000
fax 714-821-2832

Canon U.S.A.
1 Canon Plaza
Lake Success, NY
11042-1113
phone 516-328-5326
fax 516-328-5349

ColorAge Inc.
900 Technology Park Drive
Billerica, MA
01821
phone 508-667-8585
fax 508-667-8821

ColoRip Pre-Press Inc.
130 Bridgeland Avenue
Suite 100
Toronto, Ontario
Canada M6A 1Z4
phone 416-784-1234
fax 416-784-2865

The Color Resource
708 Montgomery Street
San Francisco, CA
94111-2104
phone 415-398-5337
fax 415-398-5339

Compumation Inc.
100 North Patterson Street
State College, PA
16801
phone 814-238-2120
fax 814-238-2246

Corel Corporation
1600 Carling Avenue
Ottawa, ON
Canada K1Z 8R7
phone 613-728-8200
fax 613-728-9790

DuPont Imaging Systems
(Crosfield)
65 Harristown Road
Glen Rock, NJ
07452
phone 201-447-5800

DK&A, Inc.
1010 Turquoise Street, Suite 301
San Diego, CA
92109
phone 619-488-8118
fax 619-488-4021

Danagraf North America
3456 Lindell Boulevard
St. Louis, MO
63103
phone 314-535-8807
800-535-7689
fax 314-535-9829

Davis Inc.
2704 Ontario Road N.W.
Washington, DC
20009
phone 202-667-6400
fax 2021-667-6512

DayStar Digital
5556 Atlanta Hwy.
Flowery Branch, GA
30542
phone 404-962-2077
fax 404-967-3018

Desktop Publishing Associates
1992 Yonge Street, Suite 301
Toronto, Ontario
Canada M4S 1Z7
phone 416-480-1376
fax 416-480-0192

DS America Incorporated
(Dainippon Screen)
5110 Tollview Drive
Rolling Meadows, IL
60008
phone 312-870-1960
fax 312-870-1063

DuPont
PO Box 80016
Wilmington, DE
19880-0016
phone 302-992-5022
fax 992-4442

ECRM
554 Clark Road
Tewksbury, MA
01876
phone 508-851-0207
fax 508-851-7016

Eastman Kodak Co.
343 State Street
Rochester, NY
14650
phone 716-724-4000
fax 716-724-9829

Electronics For Imaging
2855 Campus Drive
San Mateo, CA
94403
phone 415-286-8600
800-245-4565
fax 415-286-8686

ElseWare Corporation
3201 Fremont Avenue North
Seattle, WA
98103-8866
phone 206-632-3300
fax 206-632-7255

FITS Imaging
8 rue Remusat
75016 Paris
France
phone 33-1-4520-3304
fax 33-1-4524-6394

Focoltone Ltd.
Springwater House
Taffs Well, Cardiff
CF4 7QR
United Kingdom
phone 44-222-810940
fax 44-222-810962

Fractal Design Corporation
335 Spreckels Drive,
Suite F
Aptos, CA
95003
phone 408-688-8800
fax 408-688-8836

Frame Technology
1010 Rincon Circle
San Jose, CA
95131
phone 408-433-3311
fax 408-433-1928

General Parametrics
1250 Ninth Street
Berkeley, CA
94710
phone 510-524-3950
fax 510-524-9954

Gretag Color Control Systems
2070 Westover Road
Chicopee, MA
01022
phone 800-637-0010
fax 413-788-0940

Harlequin Incorporated
One Cambridge Center
Cambridge, MA
02142
phone 617-252-0052
fax 617-252-6505

Heidelberg USA
355 Valley Drive
Brisbane, CA
94005
phone 415-468-6040

Howtek Inc.
21 Park Avenue
Hudson, NH
03051
phone 603-882-5200
fax 603-880-3843

HSC Software
1661 Lincoln Boulevard
Suite 101
Santa Monica, CA
90404
phone 310-392-8441
fax 310-392-6015

Human Software Company
14407 Big Basin Way
Saratoga, CA
95070-0280
phone 408-741-5101
fax 408-741-5102

Hyphen Inc.
181 Ballardvale Street
Wilmington, MA
01887
phone 508-988-0880
fax 508-988-0879

Image-In Incorporated
406 East 79th Street
Minneapolis, MN
55420
phone 612-888-3633
fax 612-888-3665

Imapro Corporation
2400 St. Laurent Boulevard
Ottawa, ON
Canada K1G 5A4
phone 613-738-3000
fax 613-738-5038

Indigo Ltd.
PO Box 150
Kiryat Weizmann
Rehovot 76101
Israel
phone 972-8381-818
fax 972-8408-091

InSight Systems, Inc.
10017 Coach Road
Vienna, VA
22181
phone 703-938-0250
fax 703-938-0302

Insignia Solutions
1300 Charleston Road
Mountain View, CA
94043
phone 415-694-7600
fax 415-694-3705

Intel Corp.
3065 Bowers Avenue
PO Box 58065
Santa Clara, CA
95052-8065
phone 800-548-4725

Information Presentation
Technologies, Inc.
555 Chorro Street
San Luis Obispo, CA
93405
phone 805-541-3000
fax 805-541-3037

Intergraph
1 Madison Industrial Park
Huntsville, AL
35894-0001
phone 205-730-6392
fax 205-730-6239

IRIS Graphics, Inc.
6 Crosby Drive
Bedford, MA
01730
phone 617-275-8777
fax 617-275-8590

Island Graphics Corp.
4000 Civic Center Drive
San Rafael, CA
94903
phone 415-491-1000
fax 415-491-0402

JVC Information Products Co.
19900 Beach Boulevard, Suite I
Huntington Beach, CA
92648
phone 714-965-2610
fax 714-968-9071

KEPS, Inc.
A Kodak Company
164 Lexington Road
Billerica, MA
01821
phone 508-667-5550
fax 508-670-6552

Lasergraphics Inc.
17671 Cowan Avenue
Irvine, CA
92714
phone 714-727-2651
fax 714-727-2653

LaserMaster
7156 Shady Oak Road
Eden Prairie, MN
55344
phone 612-944-9330
fax 612-944-0522

Leaf Systems Inc.
250 Turnpike Road
Southborough, MA
01772-1742
phone 508-460-8300
fax 508-460-8304

Light Source
17 East Sir Francis Drake Boulevard
Suite 100
Larkspur, CA 94939
phone 415-461-8000
fax 461-8011

Linotype-Hell Company
425 Oser Avenue
Hauppauge, NY
11788
phone 516-434-2744
800-842-9721
fax 516-434-2706

Management Graphics Inc.
1401 East 79th Street
Minneapolis, MN
55425
phone 612-854-1220
fax 612-851-6159

Matrox Electronic Systems
1055 St. Regis Boulevard
Dorval, Quebec
Canada H9P 2T4
phone 514-685-2630

Media Cybernetics, Inc.
8484 Georgia Avenue
Silver Sprint, MD
20910
phone 301-495-3305
fax 301-495-5964

Micrografx Inc.
1303 Arapaho
Richardson, TX
75081
phone 214-234-1769
800-733-3729
fax 214-994-6334

MicroNet Technology
20 Mason
Irvine, CA
92718
phone 714-837-6033
fax 714-837-1164

Microsoft
1 Microsoft Way
Redmond, WA
98052-6399
phone 206-882-8080
fax 206-936-7329

Mirus Corporation
758 Sycamore Drive
Milpitas, CA
93035
phone 800-654-0808

NEC Technologies
1414 Massachusetts Avenue
Foxborough, MA
01719
phone 508-264-8743

Nikon Electronic Imaging
A Division of Nikon Inc.
1300 Walt Whitman Road
Melville, NY
11747
phone 516-547-4355
800-526-4566
fax 516-547-0305

North Atlantic Publishing Systems
9 Acton Road, Suite 13
Chelmsford, MA
01824
phone 508-250-8080
fax 508-250-8179

Olympus Image Systems
15271 Barranca Parkway
Irvine, CA
92718-2201
phone 714-753-5935
fax 714-453-4425

Optronics
7 Stuart Road
Chelmsford, MA
01824
phone 508-250-8711
fax 508-256-1872

Pantone, Inc.
590 Commerce Boulevard
Carlstadt, NJ
07072-3098
phone 201-935-5500
fax 201-896-0242

PhotoDisc, Inc.
2013 4th Avenue, Suite 200
Seattle, WA
98121
phone 206-441-9355
fax 206-441-9379

Pixar
1001 West Cutting Boulevard
Richmond, CA
94804
phone 510-236-4000
fax 510-236-0388

PixelCraft Inc.,
A Xerox Corp. Company
130 Doolittle Drive, Suite 19
San Leandro, CA
94577
phone 510-562-2480
fax 510-562-6451

Presstek, Inc.
8 Commercial Street
Hudson, NH
03051
phone 603-595-7000
fax 603-595-2602

QMS Inc.
1 Magnum Pass
Mobile, AL
36618
phone 205-633-4300
fax 205-633-0013

Quantel Inc.
85 Old Kings Highway North
Darien, CT
06820
phone 203-656-3100
fax 203-656-3459

Quark Inc.
1800 Grant Street
Denver, CO
80203
phone 303-894-8888
fax 303-894-3399

Radius Inc.
1710 Fortune Drive
San Jose, CA
95131
phone 408-434-1010
fax 408-434-9575

RasterOps Corp.
2500 Walsh Avenue
Santa Clara, CA
95051
phone 408-562-4200
800-729-2656
fax 408-562-4066

Ray Dream, Inc.
1804 North Shoreline Boulevard
Mountain View, CA
94043
phone 415-960-0768
fax 415-960-1198

Savitar
139 Townsend Street, Suite 203
San Francisco, CA
94107
phone 415-243-3030
fax 415-243-3080

Second Glance
25381-A Alicia Parkway, #357
Laguna Hills, CA
92653
phone 714-855-2331
fax 714-586-0930

Seiko Instruments USA
1130 Ringwood Court
San Jose, CA
95131
phone 408-922-5840
fax 408-922-5950

Sharp Electronics Corp.
Sharp Plaza
Mahwah, NJ
07430
phone 201-529-9500
fax 201-529-9637

Silicon Graphics
2011 North Shoreline Boulevard
P.O. Box 7311
Mountain View, CA
94039-7311
phone 415-390-1029
fax 415-960-1737

SuperMac Technology
485 Potero Avenue
Sunnyvale, CA
94086
phone 408-773-4403

Technical Publishing Services, Inc.
739 Bryant Street
Suite 200
San Francisco, CA
94107
phone 415-512-1230
fax 415-512-1232

Tektronix Inc.
P.O. Box 1000
Wilsonville, OR
97070
phone 503-685-3000
fax 503-685-3063

3M Printing & Publishing Systems
3M Center Bldg.
St. Paul, MN
55144-1000
phone 612-736-0801
fax 612-737-4771

Trumatch, Inc.
25 West 43rd Street
New York, NY
10036-7402
phone 212-302-9100
fax 212-302-0890

Ultimate Technographics, Inc.
800 Rene Levesque Boulevard
Suite 2660
Montreal, QU
Canada H3B 1X9
phone 514-954-9050
fax 514-954-9057

UMAX Technologies Inc.
3170 Coronado Drive
Santa Clara, CA
95054
408-982-0771
fax 408-982-0776

Varityper, Inc.
11 Mount Pleasant Avenue
East Hanover, NJ
07936
phone 201-887-8000
800-631-8134

Xerox
100 Clinton Avenue South
Rochester, NY
14644-1877
phone 716-423-5090
fax 716-423-5479

Glossary

achromatic
neutral colors, such as white, gray and black, that have no hue

additive primaries
red, green, and blue light, which produce the sensation of white light when
added together; see subtractive primaries

airbrush
small pressure gun that sprays paint with compressed air; or its electronic
equivalent, found in most imaging programs

analog
information, such as brightness levels, in non-discrete values rather than as
numeric digits

anti-aliasing
a way of averaging the brightness values of adjacent pixels in order to
eliminate jagged edges in computer images

AppleTalk
a low-cost local area network, built into every Macintosh and accessible from
some other LANs

application
a computer program written to perform a specific function, such as
illustration or page layout

art
all visual materials use in preparing a job for printing; any copy to be
reproduced

ASIC
application specific integrated circuit—a semi-customized chip made to
perform a specialized function

ASCII
American Standard Code for Information Interchange; a common file format
for plain text

auto-trace
the ability of a draw program to automatically trace imported bitmap images to create editable lines

Bézier curve
a line segment that can be interactively altered by moving not only the nodes that define the line, but also by moving control points that modify the angle at which the line approaches each node

bit
a binary digit, the fundamental unit of digital information; a zero or one

bitmap
an array of bits that defines a character or image; a raster

black
the absence of all reflected light, caused by printing an ink whose colorant gives no apparent hue; one of the four process inks

black printer
the black plate produced from the four-color separation of an image; used to increase contrast, especially of dark tones

bleed
to extend the printed image beyond the edge of the paper, so it goes right to the edge of the paper after binding and trimming

body type
the main text of a document, as distinct from the headings; also called body copy

brightness
the lightness value of a color or tone, regardless of its hue or saturation; also, the intensity of a light source

buffer
computer memory for storage of data, especially images, awaiting processing

byte
eight bits, equivalent to a single alphabetic or numeric character

calibrate
to set up a scanner, monitor, printer, or imagesetter so that it produces accurate and consistent results, especially predictable halftones

CCD array
a row of charge-coupled devices, each of which converts light into electricity

CEPS
color electronic prepress systems

chrome
a color transparency, named after brands such as Kodachrome, Ektachrome, Agfachrome and Fujichrome

CIE
an international color standard based on definitions and measurements established by the Commission Internationale de l'Eclairage

CMYK
the four-color process inks used in printing: cyan, magenta, yellow and black

color balance
a combination of cyan, magenta and yellow that produces a neutral gray

color cast
modification of a hue by the addition, often unintentional, of another hue

color correction
a photographic or electronic process used to compensate for the deficiencies of the process inks and the color separation process; also, any color change requested by the client

color gamut
the range of colors that can be formed by all possible combinations of colorants in any color reproduction system

ColorKey
an overlay color film proof method from 3M

color model
a method for representing color information as numeric data that can be stored and manipulated in a computer

color proof
a representation of the final printed piece, used for checking color accuracy

color separation
converting RGB color information into four channels, one each for cyan, magenta, yellow, and black, from which printing plates can be made

color sequence
the order in which inks are applied on a printing press

color space
a geometric representation that describes a domain of visible or producible colors in any color model

color temperature
the temperature (measured in degrees Kelvin) to which a object would have to be heated before it would radiate a given color; the higher the color temperature, the bluer the light

colorant
dyes, pigments, toners, waxes, and phosphors used to create color

colorimeter
an optical measuring device designed to respond to color in a manner similar to the human eye

comprehensive
a preliminary version of a design, often created for client input or approval; also known as a comp

continuous tone
images that are represented, not by pure black and white, but by a series of evenly graduated tones, as in a photograph; sometimes called a contone

contrast
the variation between the lightest and darkest parts of an image

Cromalin
a popular color film proof from DuPont

crop
to select part of an image, discarding the rest

cyan
a subtractive primary, and one of the four process color inks (sometimes called process blue); cyan absorbs red light, and reflects or transmits blue and green

DDES
Digital Data Exchange Specifications, a standard high-end prepress file format

densitometer
an electronic device for measuring the amount of light transmitted through or reflected from a sample, such as the gray percentage values in a halftone

density
a photographic image's degree of darkness or opacity; ranges from 0 (clear) to 4.0 (totally black)

desktop publishing
the use of microcomputers to produce typeset documents

digital
the use of discrete pulses or signals to represent data (as the digits zero and one); see analog

digitizer
device used to scan a video input and convert it into a bitmap that can be stored and manipulated in a computer

direct digital color proof
proof made directly from digital data output by a desktop or high-end color prepress system, without an intermediate film stage

dithering
alternating the values of adjacent dots or pixels to create the effect of intermediate values or colors

DOS
disk operating system; the master control program that integrates the various parts of an IBM-compatible computer

dot area
the proportion of a given area covered by halftone dots, usually expressed as a percentage

dot etching
a manual technique for chemically changing the dot size on halftone films, usually for localized or general color correction

dot gain
the change in size of a printing dot from the film to the printed sheet, expressed as a percentage; an increase in dot size from 50% to 60% is called a 10% gain

dot pitch
the distance between adjacent dots of the same color in a display monitor

dpi
dots per inch; a measure of the resolution or addressability of a display or output device

drum scanner
a color scanner in which the original is wrapped around a rotary scanning drum

dye
a soluble coloring material, such as those used as colorants in color photographs; as opposed to pigments, which are insoluble

dye transfer
a method of producing color prints by making separation negatives, then transferring cyan, magenta and yellow images from dyed matrices

EPS
Encapsulated PostScript, a file format that facilitates the exchange of PostScript graphic files between applications

emulsion
in photograph processes, the photosensitive coating on film

exposure
the time and intensity of illumination acting upon the light-sensitive emulsion on a film

file
a set of related information stored in a computer

filling in
in offset lithography, the problem caused by ink filling the areas between halftone dots or plugging up the small spaces in type

filter
a transparent material that selectively absorbs light of certain wavelengths; used to separate the red, green, and blue components of an original during the color separation process

flat
the assembled composite of film for each set of pages, ready for plate-making

font
the complete set of characters in a typeface, in a specific size, weight, and attribute

four-color process
method of reproducing full-color artwork and photographs by separating the original into its cyan, magenta, yellow and black components

frequency
the number of lines per inch in a halftone; also called screen ruling

frequency modulated
see stochastic screening

front end
the hardware on which graphics and documents are created and stored, prior to being output on the back end of the system

Gb
gigabyte, a billion bytes, a thousand megabytes

gamma
a measure of the contrast in a photographic image or display; the ratio of the density range of a negative to the density range of the original

GCR
gray component replacement, a separation technique for replacing cyan, magenta, and yellow inks with black

gradient
a blend between two colors or shades of gray

gravure
printing method in which the image area is etched below the surface of the printing plate

gray balance
the values of cyan, magenta and yellow needed to produce a neutral gray when printed at normal density

grayscale
the file created by scanning a continuous tone original and saving the information as shades of gray; also, an image containing a series of tones stepped from white to black; a step wedge

halftone
an image composed of dots that vary in size but are constant in spacing, giving the appearance of different colors or shades of gray

hardware
any tangible part of a computer system

highlights
the whitest or brightest parts of a photograph; the opposite of shadows

hints
algorithms contained in PostScript or TrueType fonts that increase type quality when printing at low resolutions or in small point sizes

hue
the color family or color name, such as green, purple, orange or red

icon
image on a computer display that graphically represents an object, function, message, or concept in the underlying program or operating system

imagesetter
a device for recording high-resolution type and graphics on photographic film or resin-coated paper; a PostScript film recorder

imposition
the arrangement of pages in a press form so they will appear in correct order when the printed sheet is folded and trimmed

intensity
another name for color saturation

jaggies
the jagged edges on type and bitmapped graphics formed on a raster device such as a display monitor or laser printer

Kelvin (K)
unit of temperature measurement starting from absolute zero (-273 Celsius)

Kb
kilobyte, a thousand bytes

keyline
thin line around a box containing a graphic or image

knockout
the absence of ink in a specified area, so that the color of an object printing on top of it is not altered

lightness
the variation of any hue along the scale from black to white

line art
artwork made of solid blacks and whites, with no tonal (gray) values

lithography
a printing process in which the image areas are separated from the non-image areas by means of chemical repulsion

local area network
computers connected together within a single building or cluster of buildings in order to share files, printers, or other peripheral devices

lpi
lines per (linear) inch, a measure of screen frequency

luminance
the amount of light emitted by any radiant source

Mb
megabyte, a million bytes

macro
a single keystroke that can play back a complex series of previously performed keystrokes; an essential software tool for automating repetitive tasks

magenta
a subtractive primary color that reflects blue and red light, and absorbs green; one of the four process colors; originally called process red

make-ready
setting and testing all the press controls just prior to a print run

mask
photographically isolating one part of an image for color correction, contrast reduction, tonal adjustment, or detail enhancement

memory
a computer's temporary storage area; RAM (random access memory)

metamers
colors that are spectrally different, but visually identical for a given observer under specified viewing conditions

micron
one millionth of a meter

microprocessor
an integrated circuit that carries out programmed instructions

modem
a device for transmitting computer files across telephone lines

moiré
unsightly patterns that appear in printed materials when the halftone screen angles of the separations are set to the wrong angles

mouse
small hand-held table-top device that you move to control the motion of the cursor on screen

multi-processing
having two or more microprocessors working on a software task at the same time

multi-tasking
running two or more jobs in a computer at the same time

negative
a reverse photographic image on paper or film; the opposite of a positive

neutral
a color that has no hue, such as white, gray or black

object-oriented graphic
a graphic made up of distinct parts that can be individually modified

offset
common term for offset lithography, in which the image is offset from the printing plate onto a rubber blanket and from there to the paper; also known as litho

opacity
a material's lack of transparency; for printing ink, the ability to hide or cover up the image or tone over which it is applied; for paper, the ability to prevent an image printed on one side of the sheet from showing through on the other side.

optical disk
a high-density mass storage medium using a laser to read and write data

overlay
transparent paper or film placed over artwork to protect it from damage; to indicate instructions to the printing; or to show the breakdown of color in mechanical color separations

overprint
an object that prints on top of other colors; the opposite of a knockout

PANTONE MATCHING SYSTEM
Pantone, Inc.'s check-standard trademark for color reproduction and color reproduction materials; a system of solid ink color mixing, matched to swatch book samples

PC
personal computer, especially an IBM-compatible

peripheral
an input or output device attached to a computer

photomultiplier
a highly sensitive electronic component, used in many color scanners, that transforms variations of light into electric currents

photon
a bundle of light energy

pica
a unit of measure, about one-sixth of an inch; composed of 12 points

pigment
an insoluble coloring material, used as a colorant in printing inks

pixel
a single picture element, the smallest unit of information in a scanner or monitor

point
a unit of measure for specifying type; about $1/72^{nd}$ of an inch, or $1/12^{th}$ of a pica

positive
a photograph reproduction on paper or film in which the tonal values correspond to the original

PostScript
the standard page description language for graphics and publishing

ppi
pixels per inch, a measure of resolution

primary colors
the set of colors that can be mixed to produce all the colors in a color space; in additive systems they are red, green and blue, while in subtractive systems they are cyan, magenta and yellow

printing plate
a surface, usually metal, rubber, or plastic, that has been treated to carry an image

process colors
the four ink colors (cyan, magenta, yellow, and black) used in full-color process printing

program
a collection of instructions that activate a computer to perform a task

progressive proofs
a set of press proofs that includes the individual process colors, plus overprints of two-, three-, and four-color combinations in their order of printing

proof
a hard-copy sample designed to approximate how an image or document will appear when printed

punch register
the use of punched holes and pins or studs to hold copy, film, masks, negatives, and plates in precise register

RAM
random access memory; the internal memory chips in a computer

rasterizing
the conversion of computerized graphics and images into tiny printer spots, which are often combined into halftone dots

reflection copy
artwork, such as photographs or paintings, viewed by reflected light; compare with transparency

registration
the precise alignment of films or plates for printing

registration marks
crosshair targets on color separations to allow precise positioning of the various pieces of film

resolution
the ability to distinguish adjacent small details, either visually, photographically or electronically

retouching
correcting imperfections in a photograph before it is reproduced

reverse type
white type against a black or colored background

RGB
the red, green, and blue color system used for scanners and color video displays

RIP
raster image processor; the component of an output device that converts the image or page layout into a bitmap and forwards it to the film recorder

ROM
read only memory; memory chips that hold information permanently in a computer, such as the chips containing its operating system; contrast with RAM

rosettes
the patterns formed when halftone color images are printed in register at the correct screen angles

rough
a very preliminary layout or design, often done on tracing paper, to give a general idea of the size and position of various type and graphic elements

saturation
the vividness or purity of a color; the less gray a color contains, the more saturated it is

scanner
device for converting analog visual information into digitized data

screen
traditionally, the glass or film device through which a photograph is converted into a halftone; now used to mean the halftone pattern itself

screen angle
the angle at which the rulings of a halftone screen (or its digital equivalent) are set when making screened images for printing halftones

screen ruling
the number of lines per inch on a halftone screen; also called screen frequency

SCSI
Small Computer System Interface, an industry standard for connecting peripherals (such as scanners, printers, and hard disks) to computers

secondary color
a color that results from mixing two primary colors; orange (yellow and red), purple (red and blue), or green (blue and yellow)

shadows
the darkest points in an image; the opposite of highlights

sheet-fed
a method of printing in which the paper is fed into the press as individual sheets rather than a continuous web

signature
a group of pages printed on a sheet of paper, which when folded and trimmed will appear in their proper sequence

software
computer programs; either applications programs or operating systems

spot color
a solid color, such as those specified by the PANTONE MATCHING SYSTEM; the opposite of a process color

spread
in page layout, a pair of facing pages; in printing, the enlargement of a color area to build traps with adjacent areas of different color

stochastic screening
a halftoning method in which identically sized microdots appear to be randomly placed, as opposed to the regular grid pattern of conventional halftones; also known as frequency-modulated screening

stock
paper or other material to be printed upon

stripping
taping together pieces of film so they can be composed into a single film, prior to making a printing plate

subtractive primaries
yellow, magenta, and cyan, the inks used (often with black) for process color printing

Tb
terabyte, a trillion bytes; a thousand gigabytes

TIFF
Tag Image File Format, used for transferring bitmapped, grayscale and full-color images between computer applications and platforms

tint
a halftone area made up of dots of equal size; a color obtained by adding white to the solid color

tone
the variation in a color or the range of grays between black and white

transparency
any artwork viewed by having light pass through it, rather than reflecting off it

trapping
creating small overlapping areas wherever two colors meet, to ensure that slight mis-registrations on press do not show up as white gaps on the printed piece

UCR
undercolor removal, a color separation technique that replaces cyan, magenta, and yellow inks in the shadow tones with black ink

wavelength
the physical property of light that determines its color

web
printing method in which paper is fed into the press in continuous rolls, rather than as individual sheets

WYSIWYG
a hypothetical condition in which what you see (on the screen) is what you get (on the printed page)

xerography
an electrophotographic copying process that uses electrostatic forces and toner to form an image

yellow
a subtractive primary, and one of the four process ink colors; yellow reflects red and green light, and absorbs blue

Bibliography

Josef Albers
Interaction of Color
Yale University Press, New Haven, 1975

Nancy Aldrich-Ruenzel, editor
Designer's Guide to Print Production
Watson-Guptill Publications, New York, 1990

Kim & Sunny Baker
Color Publishing on the Macintosh: From Desktop to Printshop
Random House, New York, 1992

Kim & Sunny Baker
Color Publishing on the PC: From Desktop to Printshop
Random House, New York, 1993

David Bann & John Gargan
How to Check and Correct Color Proofs
North Light Books, F&W Publications, Cincinnati, 1990

Mark Beach, Steve Shepro, & Ken Russon
Getting it Printed: How to Work with Printers & Other Graphic Arts Services to Assure Quality, Stay on Schedule, and Control Costs
Coast to Coast Books, Portland, OR, 1986

Stephen Beale and James Cavuoto
The Scanner Book: A Complete Guide to the Use and Applications of Desktop Scanners
MicroPublishing Press, Torrance, CA, 1989

Michael Beaumont
Type and Color
Phaidon Press, Oxford, 1987

Faber Birren
Principles of Color
Schiffer Publishing, West Chester, Penn., 1987

Faber Birren
Color and Human Response
Van Nostrand Reinhold, New York, 1978

David Blatner
Desktop Publisher's Survival Kit
Peachpit Press, Berkeley, CA, 1991

David Blatner & Keith Stimely
The QuarkXPress Book,
Peachpit Press, Berkeley, CA, 1991

Franklyn M. Branley
Color From Rainbows to Lasers
Thomas Y. Crowell Co., New York, 1978

Michael Bruno, editor
Pocket Pal: A Graphic Arts Production Handbook, 15th edition
International Paper Company, Memphis, TN, 1992

Rudolph E. Burger
Color Management Systems
The Color Resource, San Francisco, 1993

Tom Cardamone
Mechanical Color Separation Skills for the Commercial Artist
Van Nostrand Reinhold, New York, 1980

Hideaki Chijiiwa
Color Harmony: A Guide to Creative Color Combinations
Rockport Publishers, Rockport, MA, 1987

James Craig
Production for the Graphic Designer
Watson-Guptill Publications, New York, 1974

Linnea Dayton & Jack Davis
The Photoshop WOW! Book
Peachpit Press, Berkeley, CA, 1993

Luigina De Grandis
Theory and Use of Color
Harry N. Abrams, Inc., New York, 1986

Chris Dickman
Mastering CorelDraw, 4th edition
Peachpit Press, Berkeley, CA, 1993

Helene W. Eckstein
Color in the 21st Century
Watson-Guptill Publications, New York, 1991

Leatrice Eiseman & Lawrence Herbert
The PANTONE Book of Color
Harry N. Abrams, Inc., New York, 1990

David Falk et al
Seeing the Light
John Wiley & Sons, New York, 1986

John Fauvel et al
Let Newton Be!
Oxford University Press, New York, 1988

Gary Field, editor
Color and its Reproduction
Graphic Arts Technical Foundation, Pittsburgh, 1989

Gary Field
Tone and Color Correction
Graphic Arts Technical Foundation, Pittsburgh, 1991

Bruce Fraser, Rudolph Burger & Thad McIlroy
Color Management Systems
The Color Resource, San Francisco, 1993

Karl Gerstner
The Forms of Color
MIT Press, Cambridge, Mass., 1986

Vern Groff
The Power of Color in Design for Desktop Publishing
Management Information Source, Inc., Portland, OR, 1990

Tricia Guild & Elizabeth Wilhide
Tricia Guild on Color
Rizzoli, New York, 1993

Johannes Itten
The Elements of Color
Van Nostrand Reinhold, New York, 1970

Tom Douglas Jones
The Art of Light & Color
Van Nostrand Reinhold Co., New York, 1972

Michael Kieran
Desktop Publishing in Color
Bantam Electronic Books, New York, 1991

Harald Kueppers
The Basic Law of Color Theory
Barron's Educational Series, Woodbury, NY, 1982

Patricia Lambert
Controlling Color: A Practical Introduction for Designers and Artists
Design Press, New York, 1991

Brian P. Lawler
The Color Resource Complete Guide to Trapping
The Color Resource, San Francisco, 1993

Nita Leland
Exploring Color
North Light Books, Cincinnati, 1985

Lim Ching San & Gim Lee
MAC-graphics: A Designer's Visual Guide to Graphics for the Apple Macintosh, second edition
Octogram Books, Singapore, 1993

Rafiqul Molla
Electronic Color Separation
R.K. Printing and Publishing Company, Montgomery, WV, 1988

Conrad Mueller & Mae Randolph
Light and Vision
Time-Life Books, New York, 1966

John Negru
Desktop Typographics
Van Nostrand Reinhold, New York, 1991

Mattias Nyman
Four Colors / One Image
Peachpit Press, Berkeley, CA, 1993

William F. Powell
Color and How to Use It
Walter Foster Publishing, Tustin CA, 1984

Jan Rowell
Picture Perfect: Color Output for Computer Graphics
Tektronix, Inc., Beaverton, OR, 1991

Patricia Sloane, editor
Primary Sources: Selected Writings on Color from Aristotle to Albers
Design Press, New York, 1991

Patricia Sloane
The Visual Nature of Color
Design Press, New York, 1989

Donna & Miles Southworth
Color Separation on the Desktop
Graphic Arts Publishing Company, Livonia, NY, 1993

Donna & Miles Southworth
Glossary of Color Scanner, Color System and Communication Terms
Graphic Arts Publishing Company, Livonia NY, 1987

Donna & Miles Southworth
Quality and Productivity in the Graphic Arts
Graphic Arts Publishing Company, Livonia NY, 1989

Miles Southworth
Pocket Guide to Color Reproduction Communication & Control
Graphic Arts Publishing Company, Livonia, NY, 1988

Miles Southworth, Thad McIlroy & Donna Southworth
The Color Resource Complete Color Glossary
The Color Resource, San Francisco, 1992

L.G. Thorell & W.J. Smith
Color: Using Computer Color Effectively
Prentice-Hall, Englewood Cliffs, NJ, 1990

Fred Wentzzel, Ray Blair, & Tom Destree
Graphic Arts Photography: Color
Graphic Arts Technical Foundation, Pittsburgh, 1987

Jan White
Color for the Electronic Age
Watson-Guptill Publications, New York, 1990

Paul Zelanski & Mary Pat Fisher
Color for Designers and Artists
Herbert Press, London, 1989

Periodicals

Aldus Magazine
Aldus Corporation
411 First Avenue South
Seattle, WA 98104-2871
phone 206-343-3205

Bove & Rhodes Inside Report on Desktop Publishing and Multimedia
Bove & Rhodes
P.O. Box 1289
Gualala, CA 95445
phone 707-884-4413

Computer Artist
PennWell Publishing Company
1421 South Sheridan
Tulsa, OK 74112
phone 603-898-2822
fax 603-898-3393

Computer Graphics World
PennWell Publishing Company
One Technology Park Drive
Westford, MA 01886
phone 508-692-0700
fax 508-692-7806

Digital Media: A Seybold Report
Seybold Publications, Inc.
P.O. Box 976
Media, PA 19063
phone 610-565-6864
800-325-3830
fax 610-565-1858

EC&I
2240 Midland Avenue, Suite 201
Scarborough, Ontario
Canada M1P 4R8
phone 416-299-6007

Graphic Monthly
North Island Publishing
1606 Sedlescomb Drive, Unit 8
Mississauga, Ontario
Canada L4X 1M6
phone 905-625-7070
fax 905-625-4856

Graphic Arts Monthly
Cahners Publishing Company
249 West 17th Street
New York, NY 10011
phone 212-463-6834
fax 212-463-6530

Graphic Exchange
Brill Communications
65090-358 Danforth Avenue
Toronto, Ontario
Canada M4K 3Z2
phone 416-961-1325
fax 416-961-0941

How
F&W Publications, Inc.
1507 Dana Avenue
Cincinnati, OH 45207
phone 513-2222

Macworld
Macworld Communications, Inc.
501 Second Street
San Francisco, CA 94107
phone 415-243-0505

MacWEEK
Ziff-Davis Publishing Co.
301 Howard Street, 15th floor
San Francisco, CA 94105
phone 415-243-3500
fax 415-243-3651

Mastering CorelDRAW Journal
Kazak Communications
Box 123, Station Q
Toronto, Ontario
Canada M4T 2L7
phone 800-565-0815
CompuServe 70730,2265

MdN: Macintosh Designers Network, International Edition
Radio Technology Publications Incorporated
6-12-5 Shinjuku shinjuku-ku
Tokyo 160, Japan
fax 81-3-5269-7130

Multimedia Computing & Presentations
Multimedia Computing Corporation
2900 Gordon Avenue, Suite 100
Santa Clara, CA 95951
phone 408-245-4750

Pre-: The Magazine for the PrePress Industry
South Wind Publishing Company
8340 Mission Road, Suite 106
Prairie Village, KS 66206
phone 913-642-6611
fax 913-642-6676

Print: America's Graphic Design Magazine
355 Lexington Avenue
New York, NY 10017
phone 212-682-0830

Publish
Integrated Media Inc.
501 Second Street
San Francisco, CA 94107
phone 415-243-0600

Seybold Report on Desktop Publishing
Seybold Publications, Inc.
P.O. Box 644
Media, PA 19063
phone 610-565-6864
800-325-3830
fax 610-565-1858

Seybold Report on Publishing Systems
Seybold Publications, Inc.
P.O. Box 644
Media, PA 19063
phone 610-565-6864

Step by Step Electronic Design:
The How-To Newsletter for Desktop Designers
Dynamic Graphics, Inc.
6000 North Forest Park Drive
Peoria, IL 61614-3592
phone 800-255-8800

Verbum: The Journal of Personal Computer Aesthetics
Verbum Inc.
P.O. Box 15439
San Diego, CA 92115
phone 619-233-9977

Wired
Wired USA Ltd.
544 Second Street
San Francisco, CA 94107-1427
phone 415-904-0660
fax 415-904-0669
Internet subscriptions@wired.com

Groups & Associations

ADEPT—Association for Development of Electronic Publishing Technique
360 North Michigan Ave, Suite 1111
Chicago, IL 60601

Association of Desk-Top Publishers (AD-TP)
Suite 800, 4677 30th St.
San Diego, CA 92116
phone 619-428-4285
fax 619-690-5955

Association of Imaging Service Bureaus
5601 Roanne Way, Suite 605
Greensboro, NC 27409
phone 919-854-5697
fax 919-632-0200

Berkeley Macintosh Users' Group (BMUG)
1442A Walnut St., #62
Berkeley, CA 94709
phone 415-549-2684
fax 415-849-9026

Electronic Publishing Special Interest Group (EPSIG)
6565 Frantz Road
Dublin, OH
43017-0702
phone 614-764-6000
fax 614-764-6096

Graphic Arts Technical Foundation (GATF)
4615 Forbes Avenue
Pittsburgh, PA 15213
phone 412-621-6941
fax 412-621-3049

Graphic Communications Association (GCA)
Suite 604, 1730 N. Lynn Street
Arlington, VA 22209-2085
phone 703-841-8160
fax 703-841-8144

Hell Users Group, North America
P.O. Box 1665
Orlando, FL 32802

Institute for Graphic Communication (IGC)
77 Rumford Avenue
Waltham, MA 02154
phone 617-891-1550
fax 617-891-3936

IDEA: International Design by Electronics Association
1120 Connecticut Avenue N.W.
Washington, DC 20036

International Association of Laser Printers
4828 Loop Central Drive, Suite 50
Houston, TX 77081

International Prepress Association
552 West 167th Street
South Holland, IL 60473

National Association of Desktop Publishers (NADTP)
Museum Wharf
300 Congress Street
Boston, MA 02210
phone 617-426-2885
fax 617-426-2765

National Composition & Pre-Press Association
1730 N. Lynn St.
Arlington, VA 22209
phone 703-841-8165
fax 703-841-8178

National Newspaper Association
Suite 400, 1627 K St., NW
Washington, DC 20006-1790
phone 202-466-7200
fax 202-331-1403

National Printing Equipment & Supply Association (NPES)
1899 Preston White Drive
Reston, VA 22091-4326
phone 703-264-7200

Open Software Foundation (OSF)
11 Cambridge Street
Cambridge, MA 02142
phone 617-621-8700
fax 617-225-2782

Printing Industries of America
100 Daingerfield Road
Alexandria, VA 22314
phone 703-519-8146
fax 703-548-3227

PostScript Imaging Centers Association
c/o CIS Graphics
234 Broadway
Cambridge, MA 02139

Professional Prepress Alliance
739 Bryant Street
San Francisco, CA 94107

Scitex Graphic Arts Users Association
P.O. Box 290249
Nashville, TN 37229

Society for Imaging Science and Technology
7003 Kilworth Lane
Springfield, VG 22151

Typographers International Association (TIA)
2262 Hall Place NW
Washington, DC 20007
phone 202-965-3400
fax 202-965-3522

About The Author

Michael Kieran is president of Desktop Publishing Associates, a Toronto-based training and consulting company specializing in electronic publishing. He is the author of *Desktop Publishing in Color*, (Bantam Electronic Books, 1991).

Desktop Publishing Associates was formed in early 1985, and is an authorized training center for Adobe, Corel, Quark, and other leading publishing and graphics software suppliers.

Michael provides consulting on color publishing for vendors and color trade shops, and is a contributing editor on color prepress for Graphic Monthly magazine.

He has been a guest speaker at many industry associations and conferences, including Macworld Expo, Comdex, the Seybold Electronic Publishing Conference, the International PrePress Color Conference, the Electronic Desktop Publishing Association, the Association for Systems Management, and others.

Michael worked for eight years researching and writing educational television programs at TVOntario, and has won awards for his television writing in Canada, the United States, Europe and Japan. He spent three years as a technology reporter for The Globe and Mail. He lives in Richmond Hill, Ontario with his wife Jane and his sons Christopher and Andrew, and is currently working on another book on desktop color.

Colophon

This book was written in the obscure GonzoWrite word processing program, with page layouts expertly created in PageMaker 5.0 on a Macintosh Quadra by Peter Dako of Casual Casual Design in Toronto.

The drawings were created in FreeHand. Most of the photographs were digitized via Kodak Photo CD by Mike Fanning at Scarboro Colour Labs in Toronto, with the rest scanned on a variety of desktop flatbed and drum scanners.

The digital camera images are courtesy of Ted Knight of Kodak Canada. The comparison of high-end and desktop drum scanners is courtesy of Michael Paterson of Screen Canada.

Photographic effects were created with PhotoStyler and Adobe Photoshop. Some special effects were created with Aldus Gallery Effects.

Color page comps were output to Tektronix Phaser 200i and 220i thermal wax printers.

A

J

K

L

N

U

V

W

X

Y